THE ICE ROAD

THE ICE
ROAD

An Epic Journey from the Stalinist
Labour Camps to Freedom

Stefan Waydenfeld

MAINSTREAM
PUBLISHING

EDINBURGH AND LONDON

First published in Great Britain in 1999 by
MAINSTREAM PUBLISHING COMPANY (EDINBURGH) LTD
7 Albany Street
Edinburgh EH1 3UG

ISBN 1 84018 166 4

A catalogue record for this book is available from the British Library

Subsidised by THE SCOTTISH ARTS COUNCIL

Typeset in Garamond
Printed and bound in Great Britain by Butler & Tanner Ltd

For Alice, Alexander and Ian.
With infinite love and gratitude to Danuta in
the year of our Golden Wedding Anniversary

CONTENTS

✳

ACKNOWLEDGEMENTS

I wish to express gratitude to my wife, Danuta, for her great patience in reading, re-reading and correcting the manuscript, as well as for her devoted help and encouragement, without which the book would never have been completed.

I am also indebted to relatives, some of whom could have told a similar tale, and to friends for their comments, to June Evans for her assistance with some maps and her drawings and to Anthony Masters for his helpful words and his faith in me. Last but not least I wish to acknowledge with thanks the invaluable help and advice I have received from Sonia Ribeiro of the Hampstead Garden Suburb Institute and to the Polonia Aid Foundation Trust for their generous financial donation.

FOREWORD

✵

Most people in Britain and America cherish a simple view of the Second World War in Europe. They remember a struggle of Good against Evil, where the Allied powers gained a famous victory over the malign forces of Fascism. Stories of survivors and heroic adventurers are all concerned with people who pitted their wits against the Fascist enemy. Such, after all, was the western experience. Yet it is a view of the war which ignores events in the larger, eastern half of Europe. There, in the east, the scale of the fighting was much larger; and the ideological struggle more ruthless. Individuals did not count. Millions of Europeans were faced not with one totalitarian enemy, but with two. They saw their homelands invaded and destroyed by Stalin's Communists as well as by Hitler's Nazis. In the case of the Poles, they saw their country overrun first by Hitler and Stalin acting in unison, then by Hitler's legions triumphant over Stalin and finally by a resurgent Red Army victorious over the Nazis. To survive in the successive waves of that maelstrom required rather more complicated strategies than anything encountered in Western Europe.

The memoirs of Stefan Waydenfeld, therefore, grip the imagination not only as a stirring tale of human endurance, but also as an illustration of wartime conditions in very unfamiliar parts of Europe. Born near Warsaw in 1925, he witnessed the brutal German onslaught on Poland as a fourteen-year-old boy, hiding from the *Stukas* and the stormtroopers, swept along in a tide of helpless refugees. Fleeing to the Soviet-occupied East, he embarked on a dangerous and exotic odyssey which took him from Arctic Russia to Central Asia and thence to Persia and Palestine and eventually to service with the British Eighth Army in Italy. On the way, he is able to compare the Nazi and Soviet occupation, to watch the NKVD at work alongside the Gestapo, and to witness the mass deportations. Forcibly deported to the Arctic, he sees life and death in cattle wagons, in Soviet schools, camps, and collective farms. He works on an ice road, escapes by raft towards the White Sea, sails down the Volga on a luxury steamer, sees Stalingrad, crosses a high mountain chain in Kazakhstan and finally leaves Stalin's paradise by boat on the Caspian. At every stage, he is surrounded by hunger, disease, poverty and political repression.

Dr Waydenfeld has a keen sense of the everyday suffering that underlies great political events. His vivid picture of family solidarity, civilian struggles, and raw courage, often in settings of great natural grandeur, throws light on unusual aspects of the Second World War. Above all, it portrays a thrilling adventure, all the more remarkable for being true.

Norman Davies
University of London

ONE

BEFORE THE HAVOC

✳

The town of my childhood was Otwock, pronounced Otvotsk, situated some thirty kilometres south of Warsaw. We lived in the middle house of three which stood together in a large, fenced, woodland plot where pine trees kept company with chestnuts and limes, where birch trees towered over acacias.

The villa was only ten or fifteen minutes' walk from the railway station. You passed quiet, sleepy streets, cobbled or sandy, with paved footpaths planted with trees and cars were seldom seen. Even much later, in the late 1930s, when I became an expert in such matters, the town – for all its 30,000 inhabitants – could boast of only three taxis and perhaps a dozen private motor cars.

Should you not feel like walking, you could hire a *dorożka*, a horse-drawn cab, one of the many which waited at the station, the drivers eager for your custom.

You gave the driver our address: Aleja Kościuszki no. 1 and the *dorożka* deposited you by the wooden gate of the villa.

From the gate, a gravelled path with borders filled with flowers took you to the cream-painted clapboard bungalow divided into two flats. We lived in the back flat and the path passed between the bungalow on your left and the large multi-coloured flower borders on your right. On a June morning the fragrance of the tree balm mingled with the scent of the flower-beds and the sweet smell of the freshly scythed lawns.

During my childhood Otwock was a peculiar town, a health resort specialising in the treatment of diseases of the lungs, of which the main one was tuberculosis. In addition to its 30,000 permanent inhabitants and some 10,000 all-year-round patients, its population would be doubled in the summer by holiday-makers coming from the nearby capital city of Warsaw to take the famous Otwock air.

Otwock air was very refreshing. It was said to have a very high ozone content. 'Here you can breathe,' were the first words exchanged by holidaymakers getting out of the train in the smoke-filled Otwock railway station. The Otwock soil was sandy, its landscape flat and its wooden houses, villas, boarding houses known as *pensions*, sanatoria and hospitals were scattered in pine woods. It was the Otwock pine which had been credited with producing ozone in preference to 'ordinary' oxygen given off by 'ordinary' trees. This fact was discovered by Dr J.M. Geisler[*] who had become 'the father of Otwock as the health resort'. Now, as every chemistry student knows, one molecule of ozone contains three atoms of oxygen, as against two such atoms per molecule of oxygen in ordinary air. This had to be good for patients with diseased lungs who didn't get sufficient oxygen. Simplistic reasoning? Perhaps, but neverthe-less at least some of the Otwock patients got better.

Until the advent of anti-tuberculous drugs after the Second World War, TB was a veritable scourge, comparable to syphilis and leprosy in earlier years. It could affect almost every organ of the body, but in humans it had a special predilection for the lungs. The disease struck mainly young people, but no age group was exempt. It was a serious economic strain on the family and on the state. It had a high mortality rate, but usually the consumptive took a long time dying. For some reason a proportion of the patients survived, and apparently the chances of survival were better in such health resorts as Davos, in Switzerland, and Otwock, in Poland. Of the two, Otwock was much more affordable.

The mainstays of treatment of tuberculosis in Otwock were rest and diet. The Otwock cuisine had a character of its own, its main ingredient was fat: butter, cream, sour cream, eggs, fat

---

[*] *Zarys Dziejów Miasta Otwocka* (An Outline of the History of Otwock), Otwock, 1996, page 7.

poultry, rich soups, cream-laden cakes. Food was meant to be 'nutritious'; moderate obesity was 'good'; 'Sugar makes you stronger' was the slogan of the day, sanctioned by medical authorities; and 'The thin man dies before the fat man loses weight,' was the wisdom of the masses. Cholesterol levels must have been sky-high, but this was still an unrecognised problem. In tuberculosis, progress of the disease was marked by loss of weight, while improvement was heralded by weight gain. A fattening diet seemed, therefore, just the thing.

My father was a physician who specialised in the treatment of tuberculosis in children and young adults. He was a warm, compassionate man, popular with patients of all ages. Over the years he had built up a large practice. He saw patients in his office in our house from 9 a.m. to 11 a.m. and from 6 p.m. to 8 p.m., Monday to Saturday, and in the mornings only on Sunday. Between the end of the morning session and the family lunch, served at 3 p.m., he made his home visits.

My earliest memory of family life was the daily dinner. We would all sit round the table, Father, Mother, my older brother, Jurek, I and whoever else happened to be staying in our hospitable home. After dessert, Father would half-stand. 'Who is going to tuck me in today?' he would ask. Without waiting for the volunteer, he would count us out pointing to each diner in turn: eeny, meeny, miny, mo (the Polish ditty was *entliczek, pętliczek, czerwony stoliczek*, equally mysterious as its English equivalent). Somehow the 'mo' always came when his finger pointed at me. I would have been very disappointed if it hadn't, but this never happened. Affecting surprise, but up in a flash, I would follow Father to my parents' bedroom. There he would lie down on the sofa and it was my job to cover him with a woollen rug and kiss him on the cheek. An hour later, Olesia, our maid, would call me to the kitchen and hand me a cup of strong black coffee to take to Father. He used to say: 'Unless I have my coffee, the first patient wastes his money.'

In those days the majority of medical practices were private. In pre-war Poland, the poorer people had access to the centrally funded *Kasa Chorych* (a network of dispensaries for the poor), and to institutions supported by various Polish and Jewish charities to which doctors gave their time without payment. My father was one of the *Kasa Chorych* organisers after the First World War.

'Anyway,' he would say to me when I was a little older, 'forty per cent of my patients can't spare the money for doctors' fees. Often enough, God knows, I have to give them several złotys for the prescription. Remember, Stefanku, provided that sixty per cent of your patients pay your bills, you make a comfortable living.'

I loved my father. I always wanted to follow in his footsteps. In fact, it had never occurred to me to be anything but a doctor.

When I was about five or six, we moved to the ground-floor flat of another house on the same private estate. The flat was much bigger and I had a room of my own, next to my brother's. I don't remember much about the flat, except that in the winter my brother and I played football in the long corridor and that once a week, usually on Friday, a big fish – either a pike or a carp – swam in the bath, awaiting execution. Later in the day Olesia would chop its head off and the headless body would jump about on the kitchen table. I used to watch the execution with fascination. Once, my brother, who usually avoided the kitchen, saw the headless body dance on the floor and vowed never, ever to eat fish again.

In the spring of 1936, before my eleventh birthday, we moved a couple of hundred yards up the street, to our newly built house at Aleja Kościuszki no. 6a, at the corner of the *Szopena* street. My father had bought the plot of land a year or two earlier after a fire had destroyed the wooden villa; the blackened timbers still showed through the undergrowth. The plot was half a *morga* (about four-fifths of an acre) in size and, when finished, our house was the most modern and the most spacious private villa in Otwock. It had eleven rooms on two levels, including my father's surgery, the waiting-room, and Mother's bacteriological laboratory. At the back of the house there was a conservatory, its walls consisted of large glass panels which were removed for the summer and its flat roof served as the first-floor terrace.

The plot had a little history associated with it. In the earlier part of the century the original house was a *pension* and one of the holidaymakers spending the summer of 1915 there was

Józef Piłsudski. Piłsudski later became the liberator of Poland and its prime minister, then its benevolent dictator, idol and national hero. When he had bought the plot, Father offered a corner of it to the town council for a Piłsudski monument. The monument had been ceremoniously unveiled on 11 November 1938, Independence Day. It was a rough granite obelisk, over two metres high, with a bas-relief of Marshal Piłsudski's head and a carved inscription. From then on all national celebrations were supposed to take place in front of our house, but we were away when the first parade took place on 3 May 1939, and then the war started and there were no more celebrations.

There was another monument in Otwock and that was the monument of Kościuszko, an eighteenth-century Polish national hero and a general of the American Revolutionary Army. It was comprised of a cream-coloured pedestal with a bust of the great man. The two monuments had a chequered history. During the Second World War, when Poland was under German occupation, the Kościuszko statue was blown up by the Germans in retaliation for the destruction by the Resistance of some Nazi emblems in front of the local German police authority. The Piłsudski monument survived the war, but when I visited Otwock in the early-1960s – by which time Poland was a Soviet satellite – it lay on its side, overgrown and neglected. On my subsequent visits to Otwock in the 1970s and 1980s, it was nowhere to be seen; mysteriously, the obelisk had disappeared. In the early-1990s, when Poland once more regained its independence, the monument reappeared in its rightful place.

My mother had a degree in biology, or natural sciences as it used to be called, and she specialised in medical bacteriology and clinical pathology. For many years she worked in the State Institute of Hygiene in Warsaw. But in the new house she ran her own clinico-bacteriological laboratory. The room was full of wonders: there were instruments made of brass and stainless steel, glassware in all shapes and sizes and bottles labelled 'poison'. By the age of eleven, I was – at least in my own eyes – an expert operator of the microscope, the polarimeter, the centrifuge and the steriliser. I spent hours enthralled by the microscope, examining drops of water, my own blood and my mother's preparations of various cocci and bacilli, stained different colours.

In contrast, Father's X-ray equipment, which was the first in private hands in Otwock and had moved with us from the old house, remained forever taboo.

The land around the villa had rapidly become a much-cherished garden, lovingly tended by my parents and by Antoni, our gardener-cum-coachman. Antoni, his wife, who helped with the housework, and their small daughter lived in the lodge that Father had built at the back of the garden. Next to the lodge was the stable which housed our pale chestnut horse, whose job it was to take Father on his rounds all over the town and sometimes to outlying estates, villas and *pensions* in our *britzka* (an open carriage). On Sundays and during school holidays I would accompany Father, and sometimes Antoni would give me the reins. Occasionally, we would leave Antoni behind and I would take my father on his rounds.

There was one part of Otwock which was very different from the rest. This was *miasteczko*, or little town, the poor Jewish quarter on the west side of the railway line, separated from it by a large, open, market area. Narrow streets, which were sandy, or at best cobbled, led to the noisy and smelly area, with its semi-derelict houses which were terribly overcrowded, crooked walls and very little vegetation, only an occasional stunted tree. Here people talked in Yiddish, which I did not understand, or in heavily accented Polish. They were very friendly to us and held Father in high esteem. Most of his patients who could not and did not pay their bills lived here. Under the German occupation the area had become the Otwock Jewish ghetto and almost all its inhabitants had been murdered by the Nazis.

I always had a book to read while waiting for my father outside the patient's house, but when it was Antoni driving, and should he be in the mood, instead of reading I would listen entranced to Antoni's often funny and sometimes scary stories. They were crowded with saints, devils, ghosts, all kinds of supernatural creatures, and full of very vividly described facts of life.

At the time schools didn't provide sex education. Also, generally speaking, my parents' generation were either unwilling or could not bring themselves to talk to their children about matters of sex. The subject was taboo. Not among adults, of course, but *pas devant les enfants*. Consequently, I had to supplement my sex education, as provided by Antoni, by my own efforts.

I soon discovered that in the evenings when my parents and Jurek were out and Olesia was totally wrapped in a trashy novel in her kitchen alcove, I could sneak into my father's office and have the run of his library. Left on my own, I would be engrossed in *Vita Sexualis*, or some such book. The title was often in Latin but the text was in Polish and the language of the drawings was, of course, universal. The text was neither as explicit nor as colourful as Antoni's 'lessons' but, in a way, it was easier to understand; it made more sense to me.

In late 1936 the situation became a little easier when Olesia acquired a boyfriend, a local policeman, who absorbed her attention even more completely than her trashy novels had previously done.

Also by then, Jurek, my brother, had been sent to university abroad and this left me with the run of the house.

Jurek, diminutive for Jerzy, the Polish equivalent of George, was six years older than me and, apart from having the same parents, we did not have much in common. When I was little Jurek was very protective of me, but later I often felt his heavy hand when nobody was looking. I was certainly not an angel, so perhaps I deserved it.

It would probably be true to say that while I was Father's favourite, Jurek was Mother's. This fairly usual problem was magnified by our complicated family circumstances.

My father was born in 1890 in Płock, while my mother was born in 1889 in Mława. At that time Poland did not exist as an independent country and the part of Poland where they had lived was reigned over by the Tsar of Russia. Father had obtained his medical degree in Moscow in 1914, at the start of the First World War, and was almost immediately drafted into the Russian Army. Holding the rank of *shtabs-kapitan* (junior captain), he served as the medical officer for an artillery division. Mother studied natural sciences at the University of Warsaw which, because of the war, had been evacuated to Kharkov, in the Ukraine. My parents met at university and were married in 1915. In 1917, at the time of the Russian Revolution, they escaped back to Poland. The country soon regained its independence and my father joined the Polish Army. It was the time of the Polish–Bolshevik war and my father stayed in the army until 1922.

Jurek was born on 2 June 1919 and consequently, for the first three years of his life, he had known Father only as somebody who periodically invaded his home and displaced him for a day or two as the centre of Mother's attention; not surprisingly, Father's relationship with Jurek had never been good.

After my father's demobilisation, my parents settled in Łódź – a big industrial town west of Warsaw. There my father contracted – probably from a patient – tuberculosis of the larynx. There was no real prospect of a cure. On the advice of his superiors Father went to Berlin, where some bold surgeons had tried to eradicate the disease by excision or cauterisation of the diseased tissue, but the price of this experimental treatment was the loss of voice. There, while already strapped in the chair, he changed his mind and decided on a more conservative treatment.

So my parents moved to Otwock, where my father became a patient. To give his larynx a complete rest he did not speak for two years. He spent his days in a deckchair, wrapped in a rug. He was forever writing notes to Mother and he read voraciously; hence our enormous library, most of which gathered dust in the loft. In 1924, after two years of this treatment, he went to Berlin once more. The check-up revealed no trace of the disease and until the Second World War Father had no serious health problems.

Due to the need to keep Jurek away from Father because of the fear of contagion, my brother had only minimal 'paternal care'. Also, soon after Father's recovery, the situation was further complicated by my arrival in 1925, and the inevitable shift of our parents' attention. It was all very unsatisfactory from poor Jurek's point of view.

Jurek obtained his *matura*, or high-school certificate, in 1935 at the young age of sixteen, instead of the more usual eighteen. There was no doubt that the next step would be university – in our social circle a university degree was *de rigueur* – Father wanted Jurek to study medicine, but this very fact was enough to put Jurek off. He enrolled at Warsaw University, in the department of mathematics.

One day, in the winter, he returned home much earlier than usual and had a heated discussion with Father behind locked doors.

Later the same day Father called me to his study. 'Jurek is adamant that he is not going back to Warsaw University. Members of the right-wing students' association blocked the university's entrance to those of Semitic appearance. They did not stop him, but some of his friends were told to go to the left side of the lecture theatre. "Left side for the leftists, communists and Jews," they shouted. Jurek's friends refused to give in and to avoid a fight they left the lecture hall. He left in sympathy.'

Father stopped, sighed deeply, got up and turned to the window with his back to me. 'You know,' he continued, 'what is happening in Germany. I have noticed that you have become an avid newspaper reader. Good. Good. It's getting very depressing, isn't it? Not what we fought for in the war. No, not at all. It looks as if our nationalists want to follow in the footsteps of Hitler and his Brown Shirts. I am going to send Jurek abroad, maybe to England or France. I don't know where and how yet. He wants to study industrial chemistry, he also mentioned shipbuilding in Italy, but he must make up his own mind. Aunt Lola has been living in Paris for some ten years now. She has been writing about the situation to Mother and she has offered to have Jurek to stay. I don't know. I would have to find a way of sending money abroad to him and there are restrictions in place.' He stopped and returned to his chair. His usually kind face was now stern, his brows knitted tightly together in concentration, his lips – drawn to two thin lines – had almost disappeared. Then he relaxed, lit a cigarette and inhaled deeply.

'As soon as Jurek has gone,' he said, 'we will have to start thinking about you, Stefanku. It may be wise for you too to go to a boarding school abroad as soon as you get your *gimnazjum* [secondary school] certificate. Now, let me see . . . that will be in 1940, won't it? You will be only fifteen. Mother won't like it. We shall see. I hope peace will last that long. A pity that they don't teach you English at the *gimnazjum*. You must work hard on your French, but you do that anyway, don't you?'

It wasn't that I was working particularly hard, I just did well at school without too much effort.

In September 1936, soon after Jurek's departure abroad, I entered the first form of the Otwock *gimnazjum*. Father's calculation was right: four years at the *gimnazjum* would take me to 1940. Then two years at the *lyceum* (college) and in September 1942, at the age of seventeen, I should get my *matura* and be ready to enrol at a university – faculty of medicine, of course.

The next three years were as idyllic as one could wish. Or perhaps they became so in retrospect. We continued to live well. As far as I knew my parents had no financial worries; ours was a prosperous middle-class life. Except for their short trips abroad once a year, my parents were always there for me. Olesia, our maid of many years' standing, was there and Antoni and his wife were there.

For me, the highlight of those years was a cruise in May 1939. It was my first ever trip abroad. After much deliberation my parents narrowed the choice to one of the two Polish sister ships, luxury liners. *Piłsudski* was going in May to the 'southern sun', while *Batory* was scheduled to go in August to New York for the World Exhibition. As August was my father's busiest month in his practice, we went in May to the southern sun. My teachers saw no reason why I should not be given an opportunity to broaden my mind by travel and agreed to give me a month's leave from school. The fact that ours was a private school and that my father was our school doctor probably helped. It was all very exciting.

We left from Gdynia and went through the Kiel Canal into the North Sea. Then through the English Channel and the Straits of Gibraltar and into the Mediterranean. We visited Lisbon, Naples, Palermo, Tripoli and Ceuta. We returned to Gdynia towards the end of May. The trip was the greatest adventure of my childhood. It made me a seasoned traveller, at least in Otwock. Nobody I knew, even among the adults, had had a similar experience.

❋ ❋ ❋

One interesting point: should my parents have opted for the New York cruise, our lives would have taken a very different path. The liner *Batory* was still in New York when the war started. The passengers spent the war in the USA and most of them settled there permanently after the war.

❀ ❀ ❀

I am not sure where to place the end of my childhood. On 18 June 1939 I felt very grown up; it was my fourteenth birthday and instead of arranging yet another children's party, my parents took me to the theatre. I was no stranger to the theatre because although there was no permanent theatre in Otwock, the centre of Warsaw with its many excellent theatres – Wielki, Polski, Mały, Letni and Kameralny among them – was only half an hour away, and was easily reached by frequent and comfortable electric trains. About once a month I went to a matinée either with my mother, or with one of my many aunts, or with the school. Warsaw theatres had about half-a-dozen special performances for schools during the academic year. We saw all kinds of classical and modern plays by Polish and foreign playwrights.

On this particular day we were not going to any old theatre; we were going to the AliBaba, a review theatre, a kind of sophisticated music hall. Also, it was to be the evening performance. I became very impatient when, in my judgement, it was time to start on our way. Antoni was not yet ready to take us to the station. What was happening? At my most debonair, I had been ready and waiting for over an hour. I wore my white woollen trousers, a white shirt, a blue silk tie and my new navy-blue school blazer, I felt really grown up. But we were running late, very late. I could not stand the suspense any longer so I ran to the lodge and found Antoni in the stable grooming the horse. A cigarette hung unlit from his lip – Kasztan (the chestnut) did not like smoke.

'We are going to miss the train! We are late! We will be late for the theatre!'

'I ain't going nowhere,' Antoni shrugged his shoulders. 'I haven't been told nothing.' His shoulders popped up and down again.

I ran back to the house. I was making for the stairs and my parents' bedroom when an unexpected sight caught my eye – Olesia was holding the wide, heavy oak front door wide open and there, outside the gate, was a car. I knew that car; I had travelled in it before. It was the dark-green Buick limousine belonging to my parents' friends, the Skotnickis. Mr Skotnicki was at the wheel and his wife was in the passenger seat. To me a car, any car, had been an object of long-suppressed envy. Father could afford a car, but he did not want to own one. 'Jurek will break his neck on his first trip back,' he would say. And perhaps a motor-car was not a practical means of travel on the cobbled or sandy streets of Otwock.

I looked up. My parents – Father in his dinner jacket, Mother in a black evening dress – were coming down the stairs. An hour later, with the Skotnickis, we were in the theatre.

The foyer and the street outside the theatre were packed with adults. I looked around and thought how different it was from the matinée. In those days people would dress up for the evening performance. Most men sported either dinner jackets or dark lounge suits, many ladies wore long dresses. A boy standing near me was also wearing a school blazer, but the red school badge on his left sleeve and the thin red trimmings on his blazer cuffs indicated a *lyceum* (equivalent of the sixth form) pupil. He was thus at least two or three years older than me. He was also much taller than me and he was arm in arm with a slim brunette. Perhaps in two or three years that might be me.

The bell sounded and we went to our seats in the stalls. The AliBaba had only a small auditorium, but it was the most renowned of the Warsaw review theatres. The current review was called *Orzeł czy Rzeszka*. It was a mixture of satirical poems, political sketches, jokes by the famous compère, Krukowski, bits of music, risqué playlets and cabaret. I still remember the look of surprise on my mother's face when I had no problem in understanding the most risqué jokes, innuendoes and situations. Even the title of the review was a *double entendre*: the Polish meant 'Head or Tail', but the addition of one letter changed the meaning to 'Polish Eagle or The Reich'.

After the theatre we went to the Bristol Hotel restaurant for my first late-night meal out. A liveried doorman opened the door of the Buick. I remember that the night was warm, the sky studded with stars.

The light-blue dining-room was crowded. People, many in

dinner jackets, sat at tables that were covered with white starched tablecloths and they were waited upon by other men in dinner jackets, distinguishable from the diners only by the fact that they moved about very quickly. Two waiters guided us to a table and held the chairs out first for the ladies, then for the men and lastly for me. One of them took our orders, another brought the list of vodkas and wines.

I felt like an adult and was being treated as such. Having been a regular reader of daily newspapers, I was up to taking part in serious conversation. Or maybe I was allowed to have my say out of kindness to the birthday boy – but I was given only one vodka.

This was a time of rapidly increasing tension in Europe. Neither my parents nor their friends doubted that the war was just round the corner. 'But we have a non-aggression treaty with Germany,' I objected. 'Don't we?'

'Yes,' said Mr Skotnicki, 'but treaties have never yet stopped them from attacking their neighbours at the time of their choosing.'

Father was more optimistic. 'With France and now also England on our side,' he said, referring to the recent English guarantee of Polish frontiers, 'we ought to be all right, even if they do attack.'

'What about the Russians?' said Mother.

'We also have a non-aggression treaty with them,' I said. 'We were discussing it at school last week during the Latin lesson. *Pacta servanda sunt*, and all that . . . *Coniugatio periphrastica passiva*,' I added for no obvious reason. Conscious of showing off, I blushed and laughed at the same time. It must be the vodka, I thought.

'It is no laughing matter,' Mr Skotnicki sternly told me off. 'Sooner or later Hitler and Stalin will work hand in hand,' he prophesied.

Now everybody laughed. 'Incompatible ideologies. Impossible!' said Father.

Others agreed: 'Preposterous . . . Out of the question.'

'I hope that you are right, but I wouldn't bet on it,' said Mr Skotnicki.

I was puzzled by what Mr Skotnicki was saying, and by the

vehemence with which he said it. He was well connected in Warsaw, he had friends in government circles, perhaps he knew something the others didn't. But it was all so different from what the papers were saying: OUR CAVALRY SHALL REACH BERLIN . . . WE SHALL WATER OUR HORSES IN THE RIVER SPREE. I was mystified.

TWO

THE END OF MY CHILDHOOD

✳

Perhaps I only like to think that the end of my childhood was marked by the magnificent June evening of my fourteenth birthday. Perhaps a more accurate time of my metamorphosis into an adult would be 3 p.m. on Wednesday, 6 September 1939, the day I left home. I was fourteen years, two months and nineteen days old – but that was still in the future.

In the meantime the school term finished at the end of June and the long summer holiday which followed did not differ much from those of the years past. Most mornings I cycled two kilometres to the open-air swimming-pool in Celystynów and spent most of the day swimming, playing volleyball and tennis. I am not sure which was the greatest attraction, the pool, or the pupils of a particular girls' secondary school in Warsaw who were spending their summer holidays in the area. In the evenings I worked on my three-dimensional plasticine map mounted on glass. This year it was a map of Africa.

The new term was supposed to start on Monday, 4 September. Through July and August rumours of impending war intensified. The radio was constantly broadcasting them and grown-ups talked of hardly anything else. With France and England on our side we felt reasonably safe. The general opinion was that they would keep the USSR from intervening. In this atmosphere, the Ribbentrop–Molotov pact came as a cruel surprise, a bombshell. The war was now inevitable.

Ten weeks after my fourteenth birthday, on 1 September 1939, the German Army crossed our borders in the west, north and south. It was a new kind of war, the *blitzkrieg*. The Red Army, ordered by Stalin acting in collusion with Hitler – and both breaking international treaties – invaded Poland from the east on 17 September. Warsaw fell to the Germans on 27 September.

I remember particularly well one beautiful, warm, summer afternoon. To be exact it was the afternoon of Sunday, 27 August. I was watering the beds of the red begonias lining the sides of the paved path leading from the gate to the front door of our house, when a motor car stopped by the gate. The door opened and a man in the field uniform of a captain stepped out. 'Stefan?' he said hesitantly and with an audible question mark at the end.

'Yes . . . ?' I was just as hesitant. I didn't know the man. Or did I? He opened his arms to me, I did not know what to do and just stood there. He approached me, put his arms on my shoulders and kissed me on the forehead.

'I am your Uncle Adam,' he said. 'Haven't you grown?'

Of course I knew about my father's brother, but I hadn't seen him for years. A cardiologist, he lived in Warsaw, but having married into a wealthy family, he was said to prefer business to medicine. He owned forests, sawmills and timber works. I had also heard that several years ago Father had quarrelled with his brother. This happened when Adam – who thought of my Father as still his 'younger brother with no head for business' – sold a piece of forest, which they owned jointly, without my father's knowledge.

The estrangement ended when Adam came to our door on that August afternoon. As officers of the reserve in the Polish Army Medical Corps, the two brothers were due to report on the eleventh day of the general mobilisation to the Army District Hospital No. 12, in the fortress of Brześć, some two hundred kilometres south-east of Warsaw.

Rumours about mobilisation were circulating, but it was still three days to its declaration. We did not know at the time that, leaned upon by France and Great Britain, our government agreed to wait and 'to give peace a chance'. Undeterred by the facts and guessing (quite rightly) that once the war started the bombing and the resulting chaos on the roads and railways would make travel difficult, Adam decided to leave for Brześć while the going was good and he came to us to make it up with his younger brother and to offer him a place in his car.

We had tea on the verandah and the adults caught up on the events of the preceding few years. Uncle Adam seemed duly impressed by my being near adulthood. He did not even know that my brother, Jurek, had been studying abroad since 1936. He had never seen our new house.

The day of Uncle Adam's arrival still lives in my memory, perhaps because I never saw him again, or perhaps because it was the first time when financial matters were discussed in my presence and I listened with great attention. One piece of information in particular was meant for me as the youngest – and therefore the most likely to survive – member of the family present at the time. It referred to Uncle Adam's numbered bank account in Switzerland. '100,000 American dollars,' he said looking directly at me. 'By now, with interest, it must be quite a bit more. Never forget that, Stefan. It's hard-earned money, and getting it out of the country was even more difficult than earning it – blasted currency restrictions. To get the money into Switzerland, I had to waste thirty per cent of it in fees to assorted scoundrels. But it is my family's security.' Adam had a wife, two daughters, one son-in-law and two grandchildren. None of them survived the war. Nobody has so far been able to reclaim the money.

❉ ❉ ❉

After the war, I did try to reclaim the money but my uncle's account was a numbered one and I didn't know the number. I am not sure whether I was actually told it. Probably not. The data which I had been able to provide (my uncle's name and address, his date of birth, the names of his wife and daughters, etc.) proved insufficient.

❉ ❉ ❉

After tea, Mother and I saw my father and his brother off. The war was imminent, but it was not expected to last very long, perhaps a few weeks. 'Daddy will be back soon,' said Mother, perhaps more to reassure herself than me. In the event, the war lasted six years and neither of the two brothers ever returned to Poland.

Mother wiped a few tears away. Bela, my mother's friend, who was spending the summer in our house and was teaching me to play piano, Olesia and Antoni's wife cried their eyes out – but Bela, a very emotional woman, surpassed all the others.

The next three days were very peculiar and quite outside all my previous experiences. Mother took charge. The same evening she dictated to me two shopping lists for Olesia for Monday morning, one for foodstuffs: 'Flour, sugar, buckwheat, semolina, barley, dried peas, dried beans, a whole smoked ham, and any other dried sausage you can get. And at the bottom, Stefanku, add jars and tins – as many as possible.' The other list was for the hardware store: 'Candles, paraffin oil (for oil lamps which had been out of use for at least two decades) and matches.

'I will go to the pharmacy myself,' she said. 'Just make a list for me: cotton wool, bandages, soap, tincture of iodine, aspirin.'

In Central Europe, with its long history of wars and revolutions, a time of uncertainty was the time for stocking up. It was not panic buying, but a reflex, a logical move in anticipation of the inevitable breakdown of order.

Antoni and I, as the only remaining men of the household, set about making a bomb shelter. This had to be big enough to accommodate eight to ten people: seven of us and any possible strangers caught in an air raid. First we dug a trench. We started at the gravel path which bisected the garden running from the house to the caretaker's lodge. The trench was about five metres long and sloped steeply down from the path to the entrance of the garden cellar. Before refrigerators became popular, such deep, brick-lined and brick-vaulted cellars had been used for the storage of ice in the summer and potatoes in the winter. By now, however, with the regular deliveries of ice blocks for the zinc-lined ice-boxes, the garden cellar was empty. We tidied it up, put our garden seats and deckchairs inside, reinforced its door with thick boards as protection against bomb fragments and cleaned the ventilation ducts.

'How do we make it gas-proof?' I asked Antoni, but got no answer. Father would have known, I thought to myself. For weeks, he had been attending the poison-gas defence lectures for doctors in Warsaw. Chemical warfare was expected and the military were equipped with gas masks, but there were none for civilians. Warsaw radio and newspapers repeatedly advised about the gas-proofing of doors and windows in houses, but no advice was given for garden cellars with their flimsy doors and ventilation ducts. We just had to hope for the best.

In the evening we were all busy making our windows safe by criss-crossing glass panes with strips of sticky paper, this was supposed to stop shattered glass flying about during bombing. We secured the gaps between door jambs and window frames against poison gas by stuffing them with long strips of cotton wool; and we blackened the window panes in several rooms – 'in at least two rooms per family', said the regulations – with sheets of thick, black paper fixed to the frames with drawing pins. 'I'll leave my windows as they are. I won't use the lights in my room,' said Bela.

I was also naive enough to lay down a store of books to be read during the war. Little did I know what this war was going to mean for us.

The morning of Friday, 1 September, was warm and sunny. About 8 a.m., as usual, we sat down on the verandah for breakfast. There were three of us at the table: Mother, Bela and me. Olesia came out with the breakfast tray: soft-boiled eggs, coffee, fresh rolls, butter and jam. Suddenly, as if at a signal which we had been secretly waiting for, we stopped eating. Mother froze with her spoon halfway to her mouth, egg yolk dripping onto the white tablecloth. Bela sat there with her mouth, full of munched roll, half open. An odd, muffled, repeated banging was reaching us. The noise went on for a minute or two and then it stopped momentarily, only to start again. Mother turned to Bela, 'Antoni must be upstairs blacking out your bedroom windows.'

'It does not sound like somebody pacing upstairs,' said I. The noise stopped and we returned to our meal. Then a new series of loud noises startled us again. This time the sounds definitely came from outside. I ran upstairs, the first floor was empty and silent, so I went out on the terrace. The morning was beautiful, sunny, with not a single cloud spoiling the azure serenity of the sky. Once more it was very quiet.

Otwock was a sleepy town. Traffic noise at 8 a.m., in our purely residential area? Impossible. I turned to go back inside. I was halfway to the staircase when I was stopped in my tracks by a distant buzzing noise coming from somewhere to the north. I returned to the terrace. I looked and looked, I screened my eyes with my hand, but I could see nothing. Then, suddenly, several specks appeared in the sky. They grew rapidly in size. Now they were silver, now black, now they glowed with the gold of the sun. They multiplied in numbers, took shape . . . an aircraft formation!

I had never seen more than one or, at the most, two planes at a time – except at air shows – and here there were more than a dozen. Within seconds the aeroplanes were directly overhead, the black crosses plainly visible on their wings – German planes!

I was still looking up when a loud whizzing sound, a sharp 'shshshsh', followed by three explosions within seconds of each other, shook the house and frightened me out of my wits. I ran downstairs. Bela was crying hysterically and Mother was talking on the telephone. She covered the receiver with her hand. 'It's Bela's husband, Bernard,' she said. 'The war has started. The Germans crossed the border in several places . . . Warsaw has just been bombed . . .' She hesitated. 'Hallo . . . ? Hallo . . . ?' The connection was lost.

Of the three bombs dropped on Otwock, two left craters on empty ground, but the third one hit Centos, the home for Jewish orphans and disabled children; there were many dead and wounded.

In the next few days we had to get used to the distant thuds and thumps of bombs falling on Warsaw and to the occasional bomb landing nearer to home. When fires started in Otwock, the timber houses and villas scattered among pine woods burned like matchsticks. The inhabitants only just managed to scramble to safety before their houses and their possessions were reduced to heaps of ash.

The day the war started, the town council organised first-aid-cum-fire-patrols of volunteers. I joined on Saturday morning and at fourteen years old I was by no means the youngest. We patrolled our designated area for several hours at a time in shifts, both day and night. Most of the time I was terrified, but there was no way I would have admitted it. I went about the streets with two men from the neighbourhood; somehow I felt safer when one of them was Antoni.

Our job was to raise the alarm, to give people time to hide in their shelters or trenches, to aid children, the old and the disabled and to help extinguish fires. This last eventuality filled me with dread. I hated fires, I was afraid of them.

Otwock was not significant enough to be mentioned in radio warnings meant for Warsaw. '*Uwaga, Uwaga nadchodzi* (attention, attention, bandits coming).' The radio warning was followed by coded numbers and words which were meaningless to us. Usually, by the time we heard the engines and ran to knock on the doors, the bombers were overhead. Otwock had its Volunteer Fire Brigade, but often it arrived too late to do anything useful. Thankfully, the Germans wasted only a few bombs on us. Even the occasional bomb wrought enough havoc, however, especially where the wooden houses were packed densely together.

In the first week of the war, a bomb was dropped on Reymonta Street. This was a lane of small shops and workshops with private dwellings above. One of the premises, the undertakers, belonged to Mrs Rzewuska, the widowed mother of Waldek with whom I shared a desk at school. Reymonta was a busy, narrow, cobbled street with pavements and without a tree in sight to relieve the gloom. The one-storey, wooden houses practically leaned on one another.

On that hot, dry afternoon one bomb was enough to convert the long narrow street into a corridor straight from hell. My patrol was on duty in a different part of the town, but we ran to help. The bomb fell in a backyard and started a fire which spread along the whole length and to both sides of the street within minutes. To my best recollection there were no deaths and no serious injuries, but there were plenty of burns, cuts and bruises. We worked frantically trying to save anything from the conflagration, but to no avail. After an hour or so we gave up, left the ashes to the fire brigade to soak with water from their horse-drawn barrel, and went home.

I returned home late that evening, shaking, teeth chattering. Bela took one look at me and burst out crying. Mother, her eyes red, was visibly relieved and took charge. Olesia ran a bath and added pine fragrance, which came in small, yellow, soluble egg-shaped containers. I hadn't had a pine egg in my bath for years, they were for children! I wouldn't have minded being a child again, for a short while at least. My mother cleaned and dressed the superficial burns and cuts on my arms, legs and head. For days I could not get the smell of smoke out of my hair or my nostrils. Clean and relaxed I crawled into bed. I wished that I wasn't a teenager, then I could have sneaked into my mother's bed, on Father's now-empty side. But at my age, how could I?

During those first few days of the war our only source of information, apart from gossip, was our Telefunken radio set. Martial music, wistful soldiers' songs, Chopin's marches and *mazurkas* now crowded the airwaves and were sometimes interrupted by warnings of air-raids on Warsaw, by confusing news bulletins and still more confusing political commentaries; it was all very unnerving. The weather was on the side of the Germans: the sky was clear with not a cloud in sight, providing perfect conditions for the bombers. Days were hot, nights were cool but dry. Many Polish country roads were just dirt tracks and we needed rain; lots and lots of rain to change them into an impassable quagmire. On the morning of Wednesday, 6 September, our breakfast on the verandah was interrupted by: 'This is Radio Warsaw. Stand by for an announcement from Colonel Umiastowski.' We recognised the voice of the official government spokesman. The gist of his broadcast was that western Poland was as good as lost, with fierce fighting still going on in the Bzura region; that a new line of defence was being set up on the Bug–Narew rivers in the parts of the country which bordered the Soviet Union in the east and Romania in the south, and that all males capable of bearing arms were expected to go east and do their duty for their country.

The USSR was expected to remain neutral as the Polish–Soviet non-aggression pact was still in operation. With Romania we had a friendship treaty and Anglo–French help was rumoured to be on its way through the Romanian ports on the Black Sea.

All that was, of course, wishful thinking. In the event, members of the Polish Establishment who reached Romania were promptly interned, while the Anglo–French help never materialised, either in the form of supplies, or as the promised offensive in the west. The USSR invaded Poland from the east, while our Western allies were busy just sitting on the Maginot line. This phase became known as 'the phoney war'.

I took the call to arms, to defend my country, very seriously. Such was my upbringing. Patriotism was something inculcated in us at home and at school; we imbibed it from the books we read, from tales the grown-ups told in the long winter evenings by the tiled stoves, of wars and uprisings of the past.

I was only fourteen, but strong and tall for my age. In fact, I had almost reached my adult height about that time.

I spent the next hour talking to my friends on the telephone. Eventually, with my mother's very reluctant blessing, I decided to try and join the army and I left in the company of three boys: Sam Kagan was my age and my class mate, his brother, Emil, and Witek Pelc, the last two were two years older than me and Sam.

I went to my room. Mother was sitting on my bed holding my rucksack in her lap. She was cool, collected, but her eyes were red. When did she do her crying? I asked myself. In those days her eyes were often red but, by the time I saw her, they were dry. How did she do it?

'Here, Stefanku,' she said. 'I have put in a change of under-clothes and socks, pyjamas, your toilet bag, a clean shirt and a sweater. Oh yes, it's bulky because I have put in your winter coat. You may not need it, you will be back soon, won't you? But soon the nights will be cold.' Then she handed me a packet in greaseproof paper and a small cloth bag with two tapes attached. 'Here are some sandwiches, and here is all the cash I could find at home; keep it in the bag, tie the tapes around your neck and don't take it off, even at night. You must promise me one thing, before you try to enlist, or do anything else, try to find your father in the Brześć Fortress Hospital.'

'Thank you, Mother,' I said, 'but I won't need any money in the army.' I had only half-listened. Surely all the necessities would be provided. Little did I know of the plight of a vanquished army. *Vae victis*, indeed.

When I opened my money bag some time later I counted two hundred złotys, a fortune. My weekly pocket allowance was one złoty, and that was more than most of my friends got. There was also a piece of paper in the bag with Father's address.

So, on Wednesday, 6 September 1939, hugged in turn by my mother, by the tearful Bela, by Olesia, by Antoni, his wife and his daughter and, after a quick '*Do zobaczenia*', or see you soon, I was on my way to the war.

❋ ❋ ❋

I did not see my mother again until November 1939.

I did not see our house in Otwock until Christmas 1947.

I never saw Bela again – she was shot by a German officer in Warsaw in 1939 – or Olesia, or Antoni, or his wife, or his daughter whose name I cannot remember.

That was truly the end of my childhood.

THREE

FLYING THE NEST

✳

To start with there were four of us on the road: Witek, Sam, Emil and me. The streets of Otwock were quiet and peaceful. Warsaw was not being raided that night, or we would have heard the distant rumble. We crossed the end of Reymonta Street, where the smell of the recent fire still lingered, and then we breathed the clean air of the country. The Wiązowska highway, a narrow, cobbled road, wove its way through the pine woods round Otwock. We marched almost due east, our backs caressed by the warm hand of the setting sun.

Normally, we would have had a lot to say to each other, with at least two or three of us talking all at the same time, but when we had met earlier in the afternoon we just shook hands, exchanged the usual schoolboy greetings: 'Serwus,' 'Serwus,' and now we were strangely quiet. I was lost in my thoughts: a mixture of elation and apprehension, the regret at leaving the only home I had ever known and the joy of a newly found independence, the fear of an uncertain future and the exhilaration at the prospect of having to meet it on my own, filled my heart with a chaos of emotions which I could not even begin to untangle.

The road was deserted. Normally, on a late summer afternoon and early evening it would have been busy. On a Friday – market day – the Wiązowska road would be crowded with people of all ages on foot, on bicycles, in peasant carts whose metal-rimmed wheels would be making an infernal noise on the cobbles. At long intervals a car, or a motorcycle, or a bus would go past, bouncing up and down on the uneven road. Even on a non-market day the road would be busy with people going about their business, returning to their villages from work in Otwock. Here a woman with a stick in her hand would drive a cow across the road, there a girl would steer a flock of snow-white geese home for the night. Greetings would be exchanged:

'*Niech będzie pochwalony* – Praise be to the Lord.'

'*Na wieki wieków* – For ever and ever.'

Now the road was empty and silent; and we were silent too, but not for long. Soon we were discussing our plan again and again. From the Otwock railway station trains went only north to Warsaw or south to Dęblin. There was no point trying to get to Warsaw to look for a train going east, as trains had become unreliable and were frequently strafed from the air. Any day now Warsaw would be under siege; even the Warsaw residents had been urged to leave the city. Once more we succeeded in convincing ourselves that our decision to go first to Łuków, on foot if necessary, and from there to catch a train going east, was the right one. Emil, the older of the two Kagan brothers, summed it up. 'Let's be clear about it, our first objective is the Łuków railway station and then Brześć. At the Brześć fortress we shall find Stefan's father and the two of you,' he looked at me and Witek, 'will stay there. But we,' he meant Sam and himself, 'have promised our parents to go further east, to Prużany, to our uncle's house. Agreed?' He looked at me. I nodded. So did Sam. But Witek? Oh no, trust Witek to raise problems.

'His father,' he pointed to me, 'is stationed in the Brześć fortress. Fine, but how do we get in? There is a war on. At least you,' he looked Emil up and down, 'and I are in khakis. But they . . . they will be shot on sight.'

Was he trying to frighten us? Was he serious? True enough, while he and Emil sported the military-style tunics of school cadets, Sam and I wore our school outfits: navy-blue jackets and trousers with blue piping down the trousers and round the cuffs, blue shields bearing our school number (74) on the left sleeve and navy-blue peaked caps with the flame-of-learning emblems. It was not very military, but on the other hand, it was obvious that we were schoolboys. Surely, they wouldn't shoot us. We left it at that and fell silent again. The cobbles were hard on our feet. We left the road for the sandy footpath alongside it and walked in single file. Once more I was lost in thought.

I was brought out of my reverie by the increasing noise of many voices around me. By now the road was far from deserted. People were coming singly and in groups from the side roads and from paths leading to outlying houses. Before nightfall, the road was crowded. Were they, like us, driven by the patriotic duty to defend Poland, to man the new lines of defence?

'Do you think,' I asked Sam walking behind me, 'that they are all going to join the Army?'

'Some army,' he answered. 'Just look at them.'

It was already dark, but the night was clear, lit by an almost-full moon and innumerable stars. 'Let's have a rest,' said Witek. 'We have been walking for hours.' We sat down on the soft verge of the ditch by the side of the road and had a good view of the crowd streaming by, like a river close to overflowing after copious rains. Sam was right. The great number of women, old people and small children in the crowd made it a most unlikely recruiting ground for an army. People were loaded with bundles of all kinds and shapes, some were pulling or pushing carts, prams, makeshift trolleys, many full of domestic junk. Others travelled in the dubious comfort of horse-drawn carriages, carts, *droshkies* and wagons, sprawled on top of their bundles and bags. Every few minutes a packed motor-car, a van, or a crowded bus would hoot its painful way through the crowd. There were people on single motorcycles, motorcycles with sidecars and push-bikes. A lad passed us by, pushing an invalid chair with a legless man, a huge box in his lap.

We had heard radio reports of roads packed with refugees in western Poland being strafed by German planes. Television was still in the future and we had no mental picture to attach to the broadcasts, but I could just imagine the chaos. Suddenly, I was frightened.

Witek, one of the school-toilet smokers, finished his cigarette, flicked it into the ditch and got up. 'Let's go,' he said and we followed. Soon the sandy footpath veered off into the woods and we had to return to the cobbled roadway. Except for a few faces familiar from the Otwock streets, the crowd on the Wiązowska road were strangers. It was an orderly crowd, but the very numbers made it difficult to keep close to my friends. We walked and walked. The phosphorescent hands of my watch showed past midnight. I was tired and drained. With difficulty I dragged my feet one after the other: left . . . right . . . left . . . right . . . I was terrified of losing my group, of being left on my own in the crowd. My legs were moving mechanically and my eyes were fixed on Witek's uniform tunic. Everybody around seemed taller than me. But Witek was there, just in front, Emil was to my side and Sam just behind me.

All I could think of was that my father was in Brześć, nearer with every step, and that I left my mother on her own in Otwock. Was I a potential soldier or just a boy running away? Never before had I felt so very tired, so completely alone and so hopelessly lost.

Eventually, half asleep, I got hold of the smooth wooden side-beam of one of the peasant carts that was passing by and I leant on it; this helped. Sam did the same. By now I hardly knew what was happening around us any more. There was little noise, one could hear only the whimper of children and the indistinct whisper of many voices.

I must have fallen asleep holding on to the cart and I was being half-dragged along when I woke up with a start. I was being pulled up by a strong arm over the side of the cart. Once I had been deposited on top of some bundles among the cart's fast-asleep passengers, the man pulled up Sam and placed him next to me; Sam did not even wake up in the process. Some of the cart's occupants stirred momentarily, grumbled a little and moved closer together to make room for us. Fully awake by now, I took stock of the situation: Sam was asleep, Witek and Emil were now holding onto the cart's side. Our benefactor, the driver of the cart, had a cigarette in his mouth. And in its glow, helped by the light of the star-studded sky, I recognised him. The driver was Mr Sławin, the owner of the combined stationers, bookshop and lending library in Otwock, close to our school. He knew my father, of course, and he knew us all, by sight if not by name.

I thanked him profusely.

'Oh, that's all right,' he said. 'Your father would have done the same for my kids.'

'I did not know that you had a cart and horse,' I said for the sake of saying something.

'They're not mine,' he laughed – and that was the first laugh I heard that night – 'I hired this lazy beast with its slow-witted driver. I paid him to take us to Stoczek and then we will see. The yokel,' he added sarcastically, 'is snoring there in the corner, his head in my mother-in-law's lap. He is welcome to her.' He laughed again. I liked the man. But why did he call the peasant a yokel? I was puzzled. Everybody knew that both Mr Sławin and his wife were members of the banned Polish Communist Party and that every year, around 1 May, the Labour Day, they spent about a week in the Otwock prison – it was called preventative arrest. He didn't seem to be following his principles now, though.

I must have fallen asleep as I remember nothing of the next few hours. I woke up in full daylight, to shouts, cries, the roar of aircraft engines and a strange staccato noise, which only later did I get to know so well: machine-gun fire.

It was pandemonium. Terrified people ran here and there, some tried to hide under the overturned vehicles, others ran into fields, yet others were cowering in the ditches by the road. The frightened horses, still harnessed to the half-empty carts, scattered in all directions, some carts overturned into ditches with the horses half-kneeling on the edge or lying on their sides. Our cart, its passengers all gone except for me, was stationary at the edge of the ditch. Our horse, either deaf, or perhaps simply apathetic, just stood there nibbling at the grass. In the next moment I dived into the nearest ditch and curled up like a hedgehog.

The staccato noise stopped and, cautiously, I lifted my head. The eastern sky was golden red, the morning sun was just over the horizon. Not far away, low overhead, were the German planes, their black crosses clearly visible in the morning light. The machine-guns were now silent, they were flying away. The terror quickly dissipated and inquisitiveness took over. I stood up.

The ditch was full of men, women and children, crouching or prostrate, covering their heads with their hands, adults protecting children with their own bodies. A woman standing near me kept calling out again and again: 'Władek, Janek! Władek, Janek!' Many people prayed, some loudly, others silently, their action betrayed only by the movement of their lips and of the rosary in their hands. By the ditch across the road a priest was leading a group in prayer.

Suddenly, the hum of engines changed again into a roar. They were coming back. In seconds they were overhead, the clatter of machine-guns deafening again. I ducked into the ditch and, aping others, crouched and covered my head with my hands.

This was my first experience of being shot at. I have no words to describe the terror of it, but even now, after more than half a century, I still remember it in every cell of my body.

So, radio reports of German pilots strafing roads crowded with refugees were not propaganda. Now I had the sight, the sounds and the smells to add to the words of the broadcaster; now it was happening to me, to us, on the road. Not far away, it was happening to other people. I looked up. Did I see, or did I imagine seeing the laughing face of the pilot enjoying his sport? Did I shout? I don't know.

Panic reigned. Terrified people tried to hide, but there were no trees within an easy reach and the road was flanked on both sides by harvested fields with no refuge in sight. The planes passed overhead twice more, machine-gunning the hapless crowd. The raids lasted a few minutes only, but this encounter with modern warfare left many dead and wounded people and animals on the road, in the ditches and in the fields.

I had never seen a dead person before. I had seen dead birds and dead insects and, some two years before, with my father's help, I had buried my Dobermann puppy, Tommy, who died of glanders; he was six months old. Now the road was littered with human and animal shapes, some absolutely still and quiet, like Tommy.

With the drone of the planes fading, the air was thick with cries, with groans and moans, with shouts for help, with sing-song words of prayer in Polish, in Yiddish, in Hebrew. A group of women chanted the rosary.

People hit while on the road and in the fields were now

trying to crawl into the safety of the ditch, leaving trails of blood behind them. Hands stretched out to pull the wounded in. Helping mechanically, I kept searching the sky and listening for the rumble of returning planes. But the sky, so full of menace a minute ago, was now empty and serene, as if incapable of inflicting harm. But it had, indiscriminately, on man and beast, on the very young and on the very old, on man, woman and child. My friends and I were unharmed, but a relative of Mr Sławin was wounded and Mrs Sławin was bandaging her arm.

On the road next to the ditch was our horse, still in its harness with the cart behind him, its contents in place. He wasn't nibbling grass anymore, his head was hanging down, he was shivering and there was a puddle of dark blood under his belly. Then he became fidgety, his head hung lower still, he kept stepping from one hoof to the other. Then his forelegs gave way and the animal was on his knees. In the next minute he was down on his side in a puddle of blood. His owner, the yokel, scrambled out of the ditch, knelt by the animal and kept stroking its neck.

With no sign of the planes coming back, one by one we crawled out of the ditch. The rapidly rising, brilliant sun only accentuated the horror of the moment. The area seemed even more crowded than before. By the side of the road people, some crying loudly, some wailing, others quiet, dumbfounded, were digging shallow graves and tying sticks to make crosses and tending to the wounded. Emil, Witek, Sam and I tried to help for a while but then we felt that we were intruding on private grief. No extra pairs of hands were really needed. The Sławin family were getting ready to continue the journey on foot, with Mr Sławin firmly in command. Of their belongings they took only what they could easily carry.

I remember little of the rest of that Thursday, 7 September 1939. Soon we were marching east again, with people in front and people behind us. Compared with the mighty torrent of humanity this road had been in the morning, now it was only a rivulet. Somehow the refugees had dispersed. We spent the night sleeping in a small wood next to the road and on Friday we were again on the march all day. When our sandwiches ran out, we helped ourselves to fruit from the tree branches over-hanging the road. At one point we dug out some carrots, peeled them with our scout knives and ate them raw.

We passed several villages. People kept asking the same questions: were the Germans close behind us? Had Warsaw fallen? Was that the end of the war? The women, on hearing that we were about to join the army, would start fussing, calling: 'But you are only children. Your mothers should not have let you out of their sight! They should have locked you up in their cellars.' Then they would bring out thickly buttered bread, cucumbers, fruit, fresh milk. Podlasie – as this part of Poland was called – was not a rich area and we tried to pay, but they wouldn't take our money.

We kept walking. It was interminable. We kept together, the four of us. At times we exchanged greetings and gossip with other marchers; we refused to think of ourselves as refugees.

Late on Friday evening, some eighty kilometres from Otwock and just over forty-eight hours after leaving, we reached Łuków, a railway station on the Warsaw–Brześć line. Soon I'll be reunited with my father, I thought with relief, and he will take over. After all, solving problems was my father's business, not mine. Also, after two days of close proximity to my friends, I wouldn't be too sorry to say goodbye to them. We didn't quarrel. We were still friends, closer than ever before, but . . .

Witek was confident that in Brześć he would become a war correspondent. He was almost seventeen, he wanted to be a journalist and he had his camera with him. 'Didn't Colonel Umiastowski,' he kept reassuring himself, 'say on the radio that we must only reach the other side of the Bug–Narew river to join the army? The army needs war correspondents, doesn't it? Propaganda talks louder than bullets.' Brześć was just the place. Emil and Sam were still determined to proceed to Prużany.

There were not many people waiting for trains in the Łuków railway station, only about a few dozen. Earlier in the day the station had been bombed. Most of the roof and of one wall of the station building were missing; the floor was only partly cleared of debris, some fallen roof beams were still smouldering; puddles of dirty water were witness to the firemen's efforts to put out the fires. One had to watch one's step. The smell of burning hung in the air but, exhausted as we were, we paid no heed to such details. Having found out that the tracks damaged in the raid were already being repaired and that a train to Brześć was expected 'some time tomorrow', we cleared a small space by an undamaged part of the wall, munched the last of our bread and fruit, drank fresh water from a miraculously intact tap and, as the evening turned quite cool, we wrapped ourselves in our coats and lay side by side on the concrete floor.

The morning was bright when I woke up. I was very stiff and, as I tried to move, I almost shouted out with pain. The pain was in my right hip, the side on which I had slept. My first thought was that I had been wounded. Had I slept through another raid? Would I be able to walk?

My hip hurt abominably. I was sweating, panicking that I was about to be left alone in Łuków with the Germans closing in fast. I tried to move again, to sit up. This proved easier than I anticipated and, to my great surprise, the pain eased off. I loosened my belt and felt my hip. It was not really tender and the skin seemed intact, there was no trace of blood on my hand.

With the others stirring to life, I got up, I could walk without any difficulty. As it was cold I picked up my coat from the concrete floor and put it on. Then I put my hands in its pockets and laughed out loud. 'Have you gone crazy?' asked Sam suspiciously. As I kept laughing, they looked at me, then at each other. Witek outlined a little circle on his forehead, indicating madness.

'I slept on these,' I said, getting out two thick carrots from my coat pocket. 'My side hurt like hell. I thought that I was wounded. What a relief.'

In the meantime the crowd in the station hall was getting ready for another day. Somebody organised free coffee at the station buffet and a horse-drawn baker's van pulled up by the station entrance with a load of delicious-smelling freshly baked bread and rolls. The buffet staff provided unlimited butter. Life was looking rosier. When we also learned that the Brześć train was due any minute, we were positively happy.

We were still eating when a passenger train pulled into the

station; it was almost empty. 'They all fled when we were machine-gunned just out of Warsaw,' said the guard. Most of the train windows were broken and its walls were pockmarked with bullet holes, but it had a working locomotive and it provided seating for everybody who wanted it. We swept the glass fragments from the seats onto the already littered floor. It was going to Brześć and nobody bothered about tickets.

The journey was comfortable and peaceful. Some passengers got off, others boarded the train at various stations. It was all unbelievably normal. Only the conversations and the glass fragments under our feet were a reminder of what was happening.

In Biała Podlaska, just over halfway to Brześć, a policeman entered our compartment. I eavesdropped on his conversation with his neighbour. 'Nothing doing,' he was saying. 'We have no planes left. The airport was bombed on the first day of the war. All the planes were destroyed on the ground.'

His interlocutor, a cadaverous-looking man, was puffing on his pipe: 'Must have been the work of the fifth column,' he said. 'Men with German names, you know, all those Fritzs and Hermans.'

'You might be right,' said the policeman. 'They found one, he was signalling with a torch to the German planes. We hanged him.'

We reached Brześć before noon. It was Saturday, 9 September. We wasted no time in reaching the fortress. The ramparts were turf-covered and there was a grass-lined dry moat, but no portcullis, no gate, no drawbridge. The entrance was a kind of tunnel in the rampart; it was some twenty to twenty-five metres long and partly blocked with empty vehicles, small tanks, armoured personnel carriers and lorries. There were no guards to be seen, let alone to stop us or shoot at us.

We made our way between and over the vehicles. We took time over it. Climbing over a tank was a new experience. The vehicles were open and we could not resist getting in, sitting in the driver's seat and in the gunner's place, pretending to drive and to shoot. We were laughing and frolicking, the toys being the right size for us. We played at being soldiers. But German spies would have had no trouble getting either in or out of the Brześć fortress. We crossed the tunnel gate and, a little ashamed of our behaviour, found ourselves in the grounds of the fortress proper. Finding the hospital was no problem: it was a big squat brick building with red crosses painted on the sloping roof. Men and women in uniform were milling around. I accosted a woman in a sister's garb. 'I am looking for my father,' I said. '*Kapitan doktór* Wajdenfeld.' I explained my business to her.

'He didn't say anything about you coming.' She was puzzled.

'I know,' I said. 'I had no opportunity to warn him.'

Now we were talking all together.

'We want to join the army. Where do we go?'

'We are strong enough to carry rifles.'

'It was the radio broadcast about the new line of defence. So here we are.'

'You would not expect us to go anywhere else but to my father? Would you?' I concluded. I did not say that we expected him to be omnipotent. This thought did not come to me until many years later. The sister, suddenly worried, but without further argument, took us to a room with my father's name on the door.

It said '*Kapitan* Władysław Wajdenfeld.' I pointed it out with pride to my friends.

My father was not there. Another man was sitting behind the desk, a lieutenant, with the amaranth insignia of the medical corps on his collar.

'Who are you?' he asked looking surprised.

'My name is Stefan Wajdenfeld,' I said. 'I am my father's son,' I added, not very imaginatively.

The lieutenant laughed. He asked several questions and then, reasonably satisfied that I was indeed who I said I was, he introduced himself as my father's deputy. He got up, came around the desk and shook hands with us. 'I am sorry, Stefan,' he said, 'but the hospital is being evacuated, your father left early this morning.'

Suddenly I felt lost. I had a sinking feeling. 'Will he be coming back to Brześć?' I asked. 'What about my Uncle Adam?'

'No, he won't,' said the lieutenant, 'and your uncle left even earlier with the advance party.'

I was shattered. We were all struck dumb. My eyes itched

with excess moisture but, after all, we were here to join the army. The thought gave me an idea. 'Can we enrol in the army now and leave with the next evacuation party?' I asked. This seemed a logical and ideal solution.

The lieutenant did not laugh this time.

'I haven't heard of any recruiting office either in the fortress or in Brześć town,' he said. 'We did listen to Colonel Umiastowski's broadcast but, as far as I know, there had been no preparations made. I really don't know how to advise you. You can stay with us today, spend the night here in the hospital – we still have many free beds – and we can feed you, but tomorrow you will have to leave. By all means, talk to each other about it,' and he picked up some papers from the desk and returned to his chair behind it.

We had a quick 'war council'. But we had no other option; we had to proceed to Prużany. Dr Nussbaum's house seemed to be the only place in eastern Poland where we could hope to be welcomed, at least according to Emil and Sam.

Disheartened, I thanked the lieutenant for his help. We were about to leave, when, on impulse, I turned round and asked: 'May I leave a note for my father? Please. Just in case he does come back to Brześć, or if you meet him later.'

Without a word the man handed me a piece of paper and a pencil. 'What's the address of your uncle?' I asked.

'Just put Dr Nussbaum,' said Emil who was looking over my shoulder, 'it's only a small town.'

I added the name to the note and handed it to the lieutenant: 'Thank you.' He placed the note under a paper-weight on the desk. That piece of paper probably saved my father's life, and perhaps mine as well.

We retraced our way to the gateway in the ramparts and once more climbed over the barricade of military vehicles, but this time we did not play soldiers.

As soon as we were out of the gate the ear-splitting din of an air-raid siren made us scuttle into the dry moat by the rampart. German planes were overhead. The raid on Brześć fortress and town lasted only a few minutes. The roar of the low-flying aircraft, the swish and explosions of bombs, the clatter of machine-gun fire and of anti-aircraft guns was deafening.

Terrified, I flattened myself against the side of the moat, my hands over my head. I wished that I knew how to pray.

The all-clear siren sounded and we started getting up. Slowly, crouching, I looked suspiciously at the clear blue sky. Were they coming back? 'Let's wait a few minutes,' said Emil. Nobody objected. But the planes were gone for good. Or at least there was no sign of them coming back just yet. Columns of smoke were rising from inside the ramparts and over Brześć town, but we were all right. Soon we were on our way to the railway station.

❈ ❈ ❈

Some weeks later I learned that the lieutenant in the Brześć fortress hospital was misinformed. On that Saturday morning Father had not left for good as yet, but just went to Brześć town on some errands. He returned to the fortress about the same time as we were leaving it. Like us, he was caught in the morning's bombing raid. Like us, he cowered in the fortress's dry moat, but by another gateway.

❈ ❈ ❈

A train going east was expected later in the day. In the meantime we explored the station. It was almost empty. There was some bomb damage and the outer walls were pockmarked by machine-gun bullets. To our great relief, however, the station buffet was open for business. As we had had nothing to eat since our early breakfast in Łuków, we were soon tucking into huge portions of scrambled eggs with rolls and butter.

In the afternoon a very long, almost empty, goods train pulled into the station and we boarded it with no questions asked and found an empty carriage in the middle of the train. Only a few men got on the train in Brześć and after a few minutes we were on our way east. Expecting an hour's or perhaps two hours' journey we made ourselves comfortable, but after about half an hour of laborious puffing the train stopped in a place called Żabinka.

The station was empty. There was not one railwayman in

sight. Then, 'Look,' said Sam. I followed his gaze. Our engine driver and his mate were leaving the train. We watched them enter the station building. They came out with bicycles. Oblivious to our shouts they left; so did the few passengers.

Once again we had to rely on our feet as the only means of travel.

For hours we followed a footpath running along the railway line; it was sure to take us to Prużany. Then we came on a cobblestone road crossing the line. It was signposted, but the sign was broken. It showed to the right: Kobryń and Bereza, and to the left Pru– the rest was missing. Could we be sure that Pru– was for Prużany? We were in a quandary. Also we were dead-beat. 'Let's sleep on it,' said Emil. 'We're east of the new defence line. The Germans won't get across the River Bug.' We lay down on the dry grass.

A muffled conversation woke me up. A woman's voice was saying: '*Nie panoczku*, no sir. The railway line won't take you to Prużany. This is the road you want.' I sat up. A peasant woman was sitting on a tree stump with a basket full of wild mushrooms in her lap, and was talking to Witek. Sam and Emil were still asleep. 'Take the forest road,' she repeated, pointing to the cobbled road. 'It goes straight to Prużany. It's only ten kilometres. There are villages on the way, you might get a lift if you are lucky.'

We followed her advice, she was right. In the villages we were offered bread and soured milk, a staple food in Poland. We helped ourselves to apples from the trees by the road. Twice we got lifts on peasant carts. The countryside was peaceful, the sky blue and the sun very warm.

We arrived in Prużany at dusk. We were tired, but surely this was to be the end of our problems – at least for a while. But Witek – our Cassandra – specialised in dire predictions: the Nussbaum house would be locked; they would have left Prużany; being cautious people they would have escaped further east. We would have to walk on and on . . . He was wrong. Prużany was a small town of some 5,000 inhabitants and the first person we met and asked about the Nussbaum house accompanied us to the door and told us all the local gossip on the way. Here our luck changed: the Nussbaums were at home.

They received their nephews, Emil and Sam, as their own, but the reception which Witek and I, two complete strangers, got was no less cordial. We were all hugged in turn, together and separately. We were welcomed, we could stay as long as we wanted. 'Our home is your home. *Gość w dom, Bóg w dom*, A guest in the house brings God to the house.' They kept repeating these old Polish sayings and they truly meant it. The next few weeks proved it.

I cannot even begin to describe my feelings at the reception we got. In no time we were sitting down to a family meal, while the maid was putting up camp-beds, borrowing whatever was necessary from the neighbours. Like a stone thrown on the surface of a pond, our arrival must have produced ripples of excitement in the sleepy town. Within minutes the Nussbaum house was full of people, predominantly men, densely packed into the dining-room and corridor. Some kept darting in and out bringing another pillow, another blanket, an eiderdown. They were all talking at the same time, in between sips of lemon tea served in glasses from the *samovar*. They asked us dozens of questions but, in fact, they were much better informed than we were. Fearful for their own future, they commiserated with our plight. The air in the room was thick with cigarette smoke and heavy with general gloom.

Most local people, whether Polish or Jewish, especially the older ones, spoke Russian fluently. The conversation in the Nussbaum dining-room was thus conducted simultaneously in Polish, Russian and Yiddish. Neither I nor my friends knew Yiddish and, while Emil and Sam spoke fluent Russian (the Kagan family came from Russia), neither Witek nor I did. Fortunately, the home language of the Nussbaums, like that of all the assimilated Jews in Poland, was Polish.

Opinions were being thrown about like balls in a ping-pong competition.

'The war cannot last much longer . . . The Narew–Bug defence line is a pipe dream of some general in Warsaw . . . Rydz-Śmigly probably . . . They say that Piłsudski never wanted him at the top . . . Were he alive now, Piłsudski wouldn't have allowed this disaster to happen . . . Pity that the French didn't agree when he suggested marching on Berlin back in 1933

. . . Nobody listened then. The English wanted Hitler as a counterweight to Stalin . . .'Anyway, Piłsudski was just another dictator. A fascist.'

No point listening to all this, I thought to myself. Then, suddenly, I heard myself saying: 'Piłsudski was no fascist. He was a member of PPS.'*

'That was a long time ago,' said a tall bearded man who seemed to be listened to with greater respect than anybody else. 'It's true. They used to call him *żydowski tata*, Jews' Daddy, but he changed his allegiance.'

I was tired, my eyes kept closing. It was a relief when Mrs Nussbaum motioned to Witek and me to follow her. Campbeds had been placed in Dr Nussbaum's surgery for us.

After one night spent on the soft but uneven ground in the woods and another on the stone floor of the Łuków railway station, I appreciated the hot shower, my own clean pyjamas and the white sheets of a freshly made bed as never before.

In the morning we had breakfast with the family. 'You are welcome to stay with us until you can return home,' Dr Nussbaum repeated yesterday's invitation. 'The war cannot last much longer. Soon the Germans will overrun the rest of Poland.'

He wouldn't hear of taking any money from either Witek or me towards our keep and, when I boasted that I still had close to two hundred złotys in my bag, he said: 'Keep it, you may still need it. You never know. I'll discuss it with your father when he comes to Prużany to take you home,' and he smiled.

The lifestyle of the Nussbaum household did not differ much from that of my own family. I missed my parents, especially my father, and I missed having my own room, but I was adult enough to appreciate my good fortune.

Encouraged by Dr Nussbaum, who was quite certain that my father would have wanted me to do so, I enrolled in the Prużany *gimnazjum*. The term had started on 4 September and I was a week late. I recall nothing of the school, except that it was coeducational and that, inevitably, I fell in love. Lola is thus the only person I remember. We often did our homework together in her room. She had heavy long plaits wound tightly round her head.

---

* Polish Socialist Party.

I still have a snapshot of Lola and, probably, it is the photograph I remember now rather than the girl.

Life was thus back to normal. I forgot all about my reason for leaving Otwock. Without any difficulty whatsoever I gave up the idea of defending Poland. Then a bombshell. On Sunday, 17 September, Moscow radio – by then the main source of information – announced that the Red Army crossed the Polish border along its entire length of a thousand kilometres. Did they come as friends? They didn't, they invaded as allies of Hitler.

Next day, I was returning home from school when I witnessed an extraordinary scene in the market square. The square was full of people and the crowd surrounded three tanks marked with red stars. The hatches were open, the gun barrels covered. The Red Army soldiers, some standing up in the hatches or next to their vehicles, others sitting on top of the tanks, were throwing cigarettes into the outstretched hands of the delighted crowd, predominantly and recognisably Jewish. Friendly shouts, laughter and loud conversation dominated the square, the air was heavy with the pungent smell of tobacco.

One corner of the market square, the corner I had to pass on my way home, was particularly noisy. Also, the noise was different: angry shouts, swearing, sounds of blows mixed with groans. The mob there was densely packed around something that I was unable to see. Unlike the good-humoured crowd around the tanks, which included women and children, the mob in the corner consisted mainly of men and was excited, frenzied even. Frightened, I was about to run home, when a gap in the crowd let me see the prostrate and still body of a man, or what was left of a man, wearing the remains of the navy-blue uniform of a Polish policeman. I froze, unable to move. He lay there in a pool of blood, his face smashed to a pulp. The men were kicking the body, one even jumped on it. I wanted to run away but I could not; my feet took root in this Prużany market square. The soldiers in the tank turrets must have seen what was happening, but they chose to ignore it.

Perhaps the policeman had been a hard and a despicable man. Perhaps he did extort bribes, but I strongly felt that nobody deserved this kind of death. Having regained the use of my legs, I ran all the way home, but the sight in the Prużany market square stayed with me forever.

❋ ❋ ❋

To add a short, historical note, I believe it is most unlikely that any of the Nussbaum family survived the Nazi rule after the Germans attacked the USSR on 22 June 1941 and overran the area. They were almost certainly murdered with countless others in what has become known as the Holocaust. Martin Gilbert's monumental book on the Holocaust – *The Holocaust (the Jewish Tragedy)* – does not relate the fate of the Prużany Jews in particular, but it does describe in some details the extermination of Jews in other mainly Jewish towns of the area, such as Kobryń, Pińsk, Równe, Dubno, Łuck and innumerable others.

But I can still bear witness, even sixty years after the events. In all those years I have never met people so hospitable and so instinctively good, warm, spontaneous and generous as the Nussbaums of Prużany.

FOUR

INTERLUDE WITH FATHER

✳

Within days of the Red Army's advance into Poland all pretence of their coming as our friends evaporated. Yes, they intervened as friends, but friends of the German invader. With the Soviet authority established, life in Prużany returned to normal. Admittedly, a stranger, I was not the best judge of what passed for normal. The names of people arrested and of those who had mysteriously disappeared meant nothing to me. I heard rumours, but I wasn't interested. My world was the Nussbaum house, school and Lola's digs.

I was waiting for Father. I had no doubt that my note left in the Brześć fortress hospital had reached him and that he was on his way to Prużany. Surely he would not let me down now, when I needed him more then ever. He had never let me down before. It was only a question of time, days perhaps.

Days passed, then a week, another week, and another.

I began to wonder what would come first: Father's arrival in Prużany, or the end of the war, when we would make our separate ways back to Otwock. The war could go on until Christmas!

One afternoon in October, Sam and I were sitting at the table in the Nussbaums' sitting-room doing our homework when the bell rang. The maid opened the door. The newcomer's voice was familiar. The maid shouted my name.

My father was on the doorstep, I ran to him and we had a long hug. Within minutes the whole household were around us: the maid was there with her mouth still open; Dr Nussbaum left his patients; Mrs Nussbaum stood there; their son and daughter came running and so did Emil, Witek, Sam and even the patients from the waiting-room. Father looked exhausted. He had a few days' stubble on his chin and his army coat hung from him, it looked like it was a size too big and there were no stars on his epaulettes. The two remaining coat buttons were ordinary, brown, not the regulation shiny, metal buttons with the white eagle.

His whole luggage was a small rucksack. We let him have a bath and a shave, and soon we were all sitting at the table and having tea from the *samovar*, while my father was making his way through a heap of sandwiches.

❀ ❀ ❀

Having left Otwock just before the war started, Father and Uncle Adam made their way to the Brześć fortress. As senior medical men, officers of the reserve, they took charge of their respective units but, with the war still far away, had little to do. And then the order came for the Brześć fortress hospital to be evacuated to Łuck-Równe, some two hundred kilometres south-east of Brześć. The Polish Army, or what had remained of it, was meant to regroup in the south-eastern corner of the country. Uncle Adam's unit left first, while Father remained in the fortress a few more days. As I mentioned earlier, on Saturday, 9 September, in the early morning, he went to Brześć town on an errand and as he was on his way back, the fortress came under air attack. As the all-clear sounded he went to his private quarters in the fortress hospital. He did not see either his unit sister or his deputy until lunch-time. By the time he was handed my note, we were on the road to Prużany. He had missed us by about half an hour. He tried to raise Prużany on the phone, but to no avail. As his unit was on stand-by for evacuation, he could not get even a day's leave and absconding was not my father's way of doing things.

When the order came and they left for Równe, their progress was slow as in 1939 the mobility of the Polish Army still largely depended on horse power. On 17 September, together with other units, they were surrounded by a detachment of the Red Army, taken prisoner and marched under guard to Krzemieniec, some forty kilometres further south-east. In Krzemieniec, officers were separated from other ranks and marched to the market square. The square rapidly filled with captured officers of the regular army, freshly called-up reserve officers, some still in mufti, and policemen of all ranks.

The market square was surrounded by Red Army soldiers with machine-guns and rifles at the ready. The prisoners were advised through loudspeakers to pray, to make peace with their God. The exhortations caused much merriment among the guards.

There was no panic. The prisoners had good reason to take their captors seriously. Many of them had fought in the 1919–20 Polish–Bolshevik war and knew what the Bolsheviks were capable of. Most of them were religious and many had been praying in earnest even before the mocking exhortations to do so.

Father did not wait to see what would happen later in the night in the Krzemieniec market square; worried about me, he decided to escape.

We did not know it then, that tea-time on the day of Father's arrival in Prużany, but the prisoners massed that night in the Krzemieniec market square did survive – for a while – only to be murdered by the Soviet secret police, in cold blood and on the order of Stalin himself, in the spring of 1940 in the Katyn Forest and in other places in the USSR. Uncle Adam was among them.

Father did not have time to plan his escape. He tried to induce his brother and a few others to take their chance with him but all, except one, refused. Perhaps they did not believe the threat implied in the exhortations to pray. Perhaps they did not rate their chance of escape highly enough, perhaps they were not as motivated as my father was by his anxiety about me.

When darkness fell and, under the influence of vodka, their captors relaxed, my father and a Dr Becker simply walked out of the market square, unchallenged. The streets of Krzemieniec were deserted, except for gangs of tipsy Russian soldiers. Once out of town they hid in the forest. Dr Becker was a psychiatrist from Zofiówka, a big mental hospital in Otwock. A bald, short, tubby man, with a gold pince-nez always precariously balanced on a proboscis of Cyrano-like proportions. His daughter, Ninka, was one of my Otwock class mates.

The two fugitives agreed that on the first night they would put as much distance as possible between themselves and Krzemieniec, but within a few hours of leaving the town Dr Becker, ostensibly a fit man in his late forties, collapsed with pain in his chest and, in spite of Father's ministrations, died there and then, probably from a heart attack. Father buried him in the forest and continued on his own.

In the first village – before entering he made sure that the inhabitants were speaking Polish and not Ukrainian – he found the house of the *sołtys*, the village headman, he was fed and given the barn to spend the night in.

In the morning, the man's wife replaced his uniform buttons with civilian ones and removed the stars from his epaulettes. His new identity was that of a private released by the Soviets and going home and, should anybody ask, his home was Prużany. He walked most of the way, hitching an occasional lift in a peasant cart. He avoided railway stations and towns. He was careful to buy food and to stop for the night in Polish villages. No Polish soldier would have been safe among the Ukrainians. He had been on the road for almost three weeks. 'And here I am, with very sore feet,' he concluded.

Next morning Father wanted us to move to a hotel, but there wasn't a hotel in Prużany. Anyway, Dr Nussbaum would not let us go. We stayed a few more days in his house. As Polish money was still in circulation, Father tried to settle the debt I incurred with Dr Nussbaum. The latter wouldn't hear of it, but eventually, with great reluctance, he accepted a small sum, no more than a token.

Over the next few days Father tried to find out what was happening in Warsaw, in Otwock and under the German occupation in general. We didn't even know whether Mother was still in Otwock. All Father heard were just more rumours. Except for the Soviet radio, Prużany was cut off from the world, newspapers did not reach us, telephones were restricted to local calls, the post office accepted telegrams, but did not guarantee their delivery, travellers, few and far between, were mostly local people on local trips who brought just more gossip. The general situation seemed fairly clear, Warsaw had capitulated at the end of September.

After the Soviet knife-in-the-back invasion, Polish resistance collapsed and the first phase of the Second World War was all but finished.

After about a week of discussions, heart-searching, numerous failed attempts to contact Mother and friends in Otwock and Warsaw, Father decided to leave Prużany.

The new border, or the German–Soviet demarcation line, was the River Bug, while Brześć – the town Father and I had left on our separate ways several weeks before – situated on the Soviet side of the river, had become the main channel of clandestine contacts with Warsaw.

Our leave-taking in Prużany was emotional. Both Father and I were hugged in turns by all the members of the Nussbaum family, the maid, my friends Emil, Sam and Witek, as well as the friends and neighbours of the Nussbaums. We promised to keep in touch or, should that prove impossible, to get in touch as soon as the war ended, in other words, very soon. We owed the Nussbaums a great deal. Father exchanged letters with them over the next year or so, but with the German attack on the USSR the letters stopped.

Trains were running again and it was only an hour's journey to Brześć. In the six weeks since the beginning of the war Brześć had become a true frontier town. Its normal population of about 100,000 had been greatly swollen by the influx of refugees from the German-occupied part of Poland and by hordes of Soviet military personnel. In the early stages of the Soviet rule in Poland the old capitalist market economy was still in operation, so that food was plentiful and private cafés, restaurants and snack bars were doing good business. There was however, a shortage of accommodation. Dr Nussbaum had given Father a letter to a lawyer friend of his, Mr Łoziński, and we hoped to enlist his help in finding lodgings, but we didn't expect to find it in his own flat. We arrived and a woman opened the door.

'Good morning. May I see Mr Łoziński?' said Father. 'I have a letter for him.'

'My husband is not here,' said the woman and put out her

hand. Father handed her the letter. She opened it, read it and, with tears welling in her eyes, said, 'He was arrested a week ago, in the middle of the night. I still can't find out where he is.' She stopped and the tears rolled down her cheeks. 'The day after his arrest,' she continued, 'my maid left me and now I am alone in this big apartment.' She paused. She re-read Dr Nussbaum's letter. She looked up and smiled. 'The dear man talks highly of you, doctor,' she said. 'To tell you the truth, I need money. My husband's bank account has been frozen and I have to let rooms. My spare bedroom has been taken by a nice couple from Warsaw, they should be moving in tonight, but my husband's study is free. Would you like to have it? It would make me feel safer, too.'

'I can pay whatever the going rate is for two, or three weeks in advance,' said Father. 'But I really don't know how long we will be here for.'

'That's all right,' said our prospective landlady. 'We, all of us,' she corrected herself, 'don't know what's going to happen from one day to the next, from one hour to the next. People are being arrested.' She paused suddenly and put her hand to her mouth. 'I am talking too much and you must be tired. You can pay me twenty złotys a week, the same amount as the other couple. But there is only one sofa in the study and no bed. Perhaps your boy could sleep on my spare camp-bed, but you will have to put it up by yourself. I have enough bedding and bed linen.'

We followed her to the study. It was a big room with a large desk in one corner, a leather-covered sofa, an armchair and a glass-fronted bookcase occupying an entire wall.

'Of course,' said Mrs Łozińska apologetically, 'I have only one toilet and one bathroom. I expect that there will be a queue in the morning. Also, we shall have to share the kitchen.'

Thus the Łozińskis' misfortune became our good luck. We left our rucksacks in our new abode and went out to have a look round. Within minutes we found ourselves on a very busy crossing with cafés, bars and restaurants on all four corners.

Even on the short taxi trip from the station to the Łozińskis' flat, the streets of Brześć made an extraordinary impression on me. Shops were still in private hands, full of goods and crowded with customers. Compared to Prużany, Brześć was a metropolis bursting with life. The streets were chock-a-block with traffic, mostly horse-drawn. The clanging of metal-rimmed wheels on the cobblestones, the shouts of drivers and of street vendors, the incessant hooting of taxis, buses and cars produced a deafening din. It was lunch-time and all the eating places were full. We entered a big café; it was crowded but, eventually, we managed to grab a small table.

I looked around. There was something unusual about the café: all the walls of the big room were densely plastered with hand-written notes on scraps of paper of all sizes, shapes and colours. 'Are those adverts, or what?' I asked Father.

'Have a look,' he said, 'while I order soup and rolls.' It seemed that he knew what the scraps of paper were.

They were notices, mainly in Polish, but also a few in Yiddish, even in German and Russian. Some were written in a neat hand, others hastily scribbled. They were in pen and pencil, some on pieces of paper roughly torn out from larger sheets, others on pages removed from notebooks. There were proper visiting cards. All of them were messages, some were addressed to relatives, friends, others asked for information about people. Some were signed, some were not. One read: 'To Janek Kamiński. I shall wait for you here next Monday afternoon. Anna.' Another: 'Can anybody confirm that Władysław Wolski was killed in Warsaw on the first day of the war?' Another: 'Marysiu! I beg you, give a sign of life. I shall wait by this wall every day at noon. Bolek.' It was fascinating. Fascinating and infinitely sad.

I returned to our table. 'That's the only hope people have of findings their relatives and friends,' said Father. 'Or of learning anything about them. Just like in 1917 during the revolution. This went on for several years, all through the civil war. You don't know much about our story, Mother's and mine, during the revolution, do you? It's a long tale. Perhaps one day I'll tell you about it.'

Over the next few days I kept reading the ubiquitous messages. They fascinated me. They were fixed with drawing pins and ordinary pins, with gum arabic and sticking-plaster, to walls and fences, to gates of tenement houses, to trees in the streets and to advertising pillars, to lampposts and to official announcement boards, even to the backs of street and park benches.

Hundreds of thousands of people left home in the first days of the war. Some died, nobody knew when or how, others got lost, families and friends were separated, scattered all over the country. And here in the streets gusts of wind would lift scraps of paper bearing their names off the walls and off the trees and take them on similarly unexplained, unexpected journeys. From time to time café customers would witness the happiness of a reunited family, or share in the despair of bad news.

Groups of people congregated on street corners, in the gateways of apartments, around benches in the parks and city squares, to gather information, to exchange gossip, to furtively deal in foreign currency. The US dollar was the king of the market; it had become the only reliable means of exchange and its value rose from one day to the next. The penalties for currency dealing were draconian, but the Soviets were unable, or perhaps unwilling, to suppress it.

The demarcation line between the German and Soviet occupation zones was closely guarded and no passenger traffic was allowed. But it was general knowledge that people were being smuggled through the line. Arrangements for such a clandestine passage, known as 'crossing the green frontier', were also made either in the cafés or on street corners. Father searched for news from Otwock, tried to get a message to Mother, but with no luck. Otwock was rather out of the way and Warsaw was a smouldering ruin. Should we cross the green frontier ourselves? But was Mother still in Otwock, or had she caught the refugee fever and left? Where would we look for her?

In the meantime we tried to live a more-or-less normal life. A few days after our arrival Father started work in a paediatric clinic and I enrolled in the state *gimnazjum* recommended by our landlady, an ex-teacher, as the best in Brześć. Our headmaster, Mr Piekarski, had been deputy minister of education in some previous Polish government. Inexplicably, this member of the Polish political establishment, and thus an enemy of the people, escaped arrest, a fate that had befallen most local worthies. It was another new school for me and I was surprised when, within days of my starting there, the headmaster called me to his office. I didn't know what to expect as I knocked on the door. He came straight to the point: 'On Tuesday, 7 November, we will celebrate the twenty-second anniversary of the glorious Bolshevik Revolution,' said the headmaster from behind his desk and there was not a trace of irony as he said so. 'There will be official guests present. We will have to celebrate the event in the big hall and in style,' he continued. 'I need a student to read a lecture on the revolution, and the history master has recommended you. What do you say? You have just four days to prepare it, but it was only yesterday that I found out about the plans.' I was astounded. He was obviously learning quickly 'to render to Caesar what is Caesar's'. Suddenly I pitied him and the rest of the Polish staff. They had known Russian rule before and, back in 1918 when Poland regained its independence, had thought that they got rid of it for good. And now . . .

I felt flattered and after a moment's reflection I warmed to the task. 'Will I manage in so short a time?' I mused aloud. 'And where will I find the necessary books?'

'Are you asking me,' said the headmaster, 'or yourself? A few days should be enough for a bright boy like you.'

Flattery will get you everywhere, I thought to myself, I knew my weakness. But it was a challenge . . . of a kind.

Mr Piekarski continued: 'As for the books, your landlady has an excellent library, better than the school's. I know Mrs Łozińska well. Her husband is an amateur historian. I know that he was arrested. I spoke to her on the phone and she suggested that you could use her husband's library. You and your father are actually living in his study, aren't you? I am sure you will manage. It is a great honour,' he added. He got up, came round the desk and, as he shook me by the hand, I noticed that he was a good deal shorter than me. 'It's a load off my mind,' he added as an afterthought when I was about to leave. 'I had no warning. I had no idea that 7 November was the anniversary of the October revolution. It has something to do with the difference between the Gregorian and the Orthodox Church calendar which was in use in tsarist Russia at the time. A kind of holy day,' he smiled. 'Are you a Catholic?' This was an unexpected question.

'No, sir, I am an atheist,' I said. 'And so is my father.' His eyebrows shot up in surprise. 'But we are not communists,' I added hastily.

'Oh well,' he shrugged his shoulders, 'I suppose it's all right.' Then he went back to his chair.

And I did manage. But recalling the event still makes me laugh. My fifteen-minute talk had been approved by our history teacher. I was introduced to the audience by our headmaster. I read it in the presence of the entire school assembly and of the representatives of the authorities, of the Brześć communist party and of the Soviet garrison.

Our school was Polish and my talk was in Polish; it could not have been in any other language, it was the only one I was fluent in. Fortunately, our new Russian rulers sitting in the first row probably did not understand the language well enough to follow my lecture. Later, with hindsight, it seemed surprising that no arrests had followed the celebrations. At the time it did not even occur to me that we, as a school, had been engaged in counter-revolutionary activity, and that I had been the main culprit. That I had been innocent of the vagaries or absurdities of historiography in general and Soviet historiography in particular was understandable. It was also very likely that our headmaster and the history teacher had acted in good faith but, if so, they had been incredibly naive. At the time I had no notion of the Soviet habit of rewriting history and neither I, nor it would seem my teachers, had realised that what had been a glorious Polish victory for a Polish historian, could have been either a Polish defeat, or a shameful and counter-revolutionary act in the eyes of his Soviet counterpart.

The problem was that I had based my talk on the most authoritative volume on the subject that I could find in Mr Łoziński's library: *History of the Twentieth Century*, by Professor Mościcki. It was not my fault that the author, an eminent Polish historian and brother of the last President of Poland, saw the Bolshevik revolution as an abomination. And, inadvertently, in my talk, the Polish–Bolshevik war, which came soon after the revolution, had been won by the Poles, while in Soviet historiography it was a Soviet victory. It dawned on me some years later that historical 'facts' are what you want them to be. Historiography is indeed an Alice-in-Wonderland country. But, at the age of fourteen, I still trusted the written word.

Father was terrified when, innocently pleased with myself, I told him about our school celebrations and my role in them. He gave me a lecture on the five basic rules of self-preservation in a totalitarian state: don't stick your head out, don't show off, don't be clever, don't trust anybody, don't volunteer. Over the next few years the lecture stood me in good stead.

Another thing I had learned in Brześć was housekeeping. As Father worked long hours, shopping, cooking and general housework became my duties. I learned quickly. The shops were still in private hands and the market was kept well supplied by peasants bringing their produce from the surrounding villages. But buying the staple foods was one thing, their preparation was quite another. My culinary experience in Otwock was limited to being allowed by our maid to taste the things I liked. But I soon realised that to get on in the kitchen all one needed was a measure of goodwill and an ability to read. Having a prodigious appetite myself, I had ample supplies of the former, while the latter was not a problem: I found an ancient cookbook in archaic Polish in our shared kitchen and soon got the hang of it.

In this book the easiest dish to prepare was boiled chicken. But in 1939 chicken did not come 'oven-ready'. By the time I got my hands on the bird it would already have been decapitated, but it still had to be plucked, drawn and cut. There was more work, too: noodles had to be made from scratch, potatoes had to be washed and peeled, other vegetables had to be washed and cut. We didn't usually bother with desserts. Compared with chicken, steaks were easier to prepare but much more expensive. Other dishes were too complicated to cook, so we mostly had boiled chicken, but we didn't go hungry. After dinner I would do my homework, read for a while and then it was bed-time.

One Sunday, towards the end of November, Father returned from one of his gossip-seeking expeditions with news of Mother. At last! In a café, he was approached by a man from Otwock who had recognised him. The man had left Otwock the day before and crossed the River Bug in the night. Mother was well and had been left undisturbed in our house. The man was certain of it.

Since the capitulation of Warsaw, which for us marked the end of the war in Poland, refugees steadily drifted from the Soviet occupation zone back to their homes in central Poland. The living conditions under German rule were said to be reasonable. In the collective memory, the Germans were a civilised, law-abiding European nation, several grades above the Russians who were dismissed as 'Asian savages'. In 1939 nobody imagined the horrors the Germans would visit on the world in the years to come. And Mother was in Otwock, awaiting our return.

Father delayed no longer. It would thus have to be the green frontier. But crossing the River Bug at, or near, Brześć was said to be impossible. By then, the clandestine route had been well established. It led first from Brześć by rail 150 kilometres north to Białystok, then some 100 kilometres south-west to Małkinia, a town situated near the river but well downstream from Brześć. From Małkinia guides took groups of people on foot through fields and woods to the riverbank and by small boats across the river to the German side during the hours of darkness. All that had to be arranged and paid for in advance. The guides had to be paid and the middlemen had to have their cut, the Soviet and the German frontier guards had to be bribed. It was expensive and risky. Bribe or no bribe, quite frequently the guards would shoot. People were killed and maimed.

The same day Father got the news about Mother, we went to the big café in the evening and found the fixer. I expected a sort of baddie from a Hollywood thriller, or an unshaven bandit, but the man pointed out to us by one of Father's acquaintances was none of these. He was a short, fat, young man, with a black beard, a black peaked cap, in a long, black, shiny satin coat sported by the Hassidim. Was it a disguise? Perhaps. He spoke excellent Polish without a trace of the Yiddish accent. He heard Father's request, kept nodding, requested money in advance. He was not fussy and would accept roubles as Father had no dollars. In exchange, he gave Father two bits of paper, one with an address in Małkinia and a note for the guide. 'That's for the two of you. For tomorrow only, mind,' he said. 'There will be nothing more to pay,' he reassured Father and moved on to the next customer.

To avoid raising suspicion, on Monday morning we left home as usual, Father for work and I for school. On the way home I bought us steak for dinner and, as a treat, four chocolate éclairs. They were Father's favourite; and mine. I packed our belongings. By then we had acquired a suitcase, though rucksacks would be better, I thought to myself. In the evening we sat down early to our last meal in Brześć. Father was deep in thought. I was excited and not a little apprehensive of what the night had in store for us. I cleaned my plate in no time. 'I am not hungry,' said Father halfway through his. I was about to say in jest: 'You will get it for breakfast.' But I thought better of it and got up to get tea. Father got up as well: 'I'll ask Mrs Łozińska to have tea with us,' he said. 'I must tell her. And I'd better give her two weeks' rent, I suppose.'

'We must hurry,' I reminded him, 'to catch the early train.'

When I returned to the room our landlady was there, talking with Father. 'Yes, I understand perfectly,' she said. Then she continued: 'Can I ask you a favour? Will you take a letter for my sister in Warsaw? I heard from her two weeks ago. She wants me to move in with her, now her husband has been taken prisoner by the Germans.'

'Of course, with pleasure,' said Father.

'I won't be long,' she said, getting up. She was on her way out of the room when the front doorbell rang. It was unusual for this time of night.

'Militia?' Father whispered, and went pale.

This had not occurred to me and I choked on a mouthful of tea. Mrs Łozińska, frightened, looked back at Father and went into the corridor, closing our door as she went out. There was a short exchange, indistinct words and another woman's voice.

Steps approached our room, not the heavy boots of militiamen. A knock on our door.

'Come in.' Father's face had regained its colour.

The door opened . . . Mother was there, all smiles, a small suitcase in her hand. Father was up in a flash, he rushed over and lifted all the four feet ten inches of her off the floor. I was not so fast, but I still managed to grab her from the side. Mother laughed and there were tears in her eyes; my reaction was much the same. Mrs Łozińska had disappeared.

In the next moment Mother was sitting with us at the table and for the first time in my life I was fixing a meal for her – what was left of the steak and mashed potato.

Our luck was unbelievable. Mother had received none of Father's letters or cables. 'But last Friday morning,' Mother continued, 'just a couple of days ago, a woman rang the bell and told me that the night before her husband had returned from the east and that he had seen you two several times in Brześć. She assured me that there could have been no mistake.' She went on: 'He is a caretaker in TOZ, so he knows you well. Apparently, on one occasion you talked with him for a few minutes and you must have told him your address, because his wife gave it to me.' Mother paused looking at Father.

'I don't remember,' he said, 'I talked with hundreds of people. I don't remember meeting anyone from Otwock.'

I knew TOZ. It was a Jewish charity, they had a dispensary in Otwock, a cream-painted building in Kościelna Street. Father had been giving free sessions there for years.

Once she got news about us, Mother made up her mind. She signed our villa, lock, stock and barrel, over to Mrs Hirszowska, or Stasia for short, and her daughter Wanda, who later became my sister-in-law. Stasia, a widow, had been a close friend of my parents for many years. As she had just been dispossessed by the Germans who took over her residential hotel, she was glad to use our house and to run a small *pension* there.

'There and then I decided to join you,' said Mother. 'I phoned Stasia and she put me on to the right people and here I am.' Mother paused again. And then she continued, 'I am afraid I lost my handbag on the way. It had my money, not much but all I had – just as well I had paid them in advance. My jewellery was also in it, my gold watch, the rings and my gold powder compact.' Mother shrugged her shoulders. She had never been fond of jewellery and did not have much of it. She went on: 'But I still have my wedding ring. Anyway, the boat was overloaded, I sat by the side, there was a lot of pushing and shoving, even in the middle of the river. Somebody's elbow knocked the handbag off my lap and it went overboard. But still, here I am.'

❊ ❊ ❊

Several days after I left Otwock the Germans had occupied the area and laid siege to Warsaw. At first the occupation forces were well behaved. Inexplicably, in the first few days they even mounted a guard of honour at the corner of our villa by the Piłsudski monument. One morning a couple of German officers came to the house looking for billets. They went through all the rooms and made notes. They noticed a photograph of my father in uniform on Mother's bedside table. 'Is this your husband, madam?' one of them asked. Mother knew German well and answered in the affirmative. They asked no more questions. The quartermaster tore up his notes, they clicked their heels, saluted and left. And thus Mother was left in possession of the house. Bela, Mother's friend and companion, and Olesia stayed with her, while Antoni with his family stayed in the lodge.

❉ ❉ ❉

Bela's was a cruel story. She was a graduate of the famous Moscow Conservatoire and soon after the First World War she began to build a reputation as a concert pianist. However, she fell ill and a heart murmur was discovered. At the time a heart murmur was thought to mean serious heart disease. She had been advised to give up her career and was reduced to giving piano lessons. Eventually, I was her only pupil. Bela led a sheltered life, she did no housework and her mobility was limited; she was not allowed to walk further than to the chemist shop which was about two hundred metres from our house.

At the end of September 1939, as soon as Warsaw fell, Bela, who was unable to get in touch with her husband who was stranded in the capital, decided to go and look for him. With a small bag in her hand, she walked all the way to central Warsaw, some thirty kilometres or more. She arrived a bit worse for wear but alive, and it was this feat that seemed to have cured her of the supposed heart disease. She found her husband in their apartment which luckily still stood undamaged.

Several weeks later, when the behaviour of the Germans changed so tragically for the inhabitants of Poland in general and those of Warsaw in particular; Gestapo raids on apartment blocks became routine. It was during one such raid, when the inhabitants of the flats were being mustered in the yard and abused in the process, that Bela ran to the Gestapo officer in charge of the squad, grabbed the revolver from his holster and shot him, before being shot dead herself by another German. This news, which had reached Mother on the grapevine, combined with reports of mass arrests and executions, during which, to begin with, ethnic Poles suffered more than Polish Jews, made Mother think about escaping to the east.

❃ ❃ ❃

With Mother's arrival in Brześć a semblance of family life was re-established. Mother took over all shopping, cooking and housework. I had more time for homework and for exploring Mr Łoziński's library. We still lived in the one room; Mother slept on the sofa, Father moved to my camp-bed and I slept on the floor.

In the middle of December 1939 my parents were offered jobs in a polyclinic in Pińsk and, as Mother had not been able to find a suitable bacteriologist's post in Brześć, they accepted. Within a few days we packed our belongings, which by then consisted of two suitcases, we said our goodbyes and caught the train to Pińsk, a town in the middle of the Pripyat marshes.

At the time, we had no inkling that this short, voluntary train journey would be only a beginning, that we would become pawns in cynical political games, lost leaves tossed by a gale.

FIVE

THE LESSER EVIL

✳

Pińsk proved to be the last stop before a journey into the unknown. A town of some 50,000 inhabitants and the capital of the province of Polesie, Pińsk was different from any other town I had known. Except for the centre – where the roads were solid, the pavements inspired a sense of permanence and the two- or three-storey buildings were stuccoed – it was a town of wooden one- or two-storey houses, unpaved streets, virtually dirt tracks and wooden pavements whose broken planks jutted out at peculiar angles. The population of the town was a mixture of Poles and Jews, whereas the surrounding villages were largely Belorussian.

Our journey from Brześć to Pińsk was uneventful, the Polesie landscape seen through the train windows was flat and monotonous: sparse forests, fields, scattered villages, very few roads, all covered with a thick layer of snow.

'I suppose,' said Father, as the train was approaching Pińsk station, 'that we will find a taxi or *droshky* to take us to Mrs Margulis's house. Dr Weinthal had said in his last letter that it was very central, not far from the station, but also near the polyclinic and overlooking the river.'

The housing situation in Pińsk was not nearly as bad as in Brześć. Dr Weinthal, a laryngologist, and his wife, an eye surgeon, had settled in Pińsk a couple of months earlier and they also worked at the Pińsk clinic. They had one son, also called Stefan, but he was two years younger than me. His parents had become good friends with my parents when we had lived in Otwock. I tolerated Stefan in spite of the age difference. Even back in Otwock, I liked going to their house. Did I have a crush on his mother, Aniela? I think so now.

Mrs Margulis, our landlady, was a widow and lived alone in a two-storey house. She let us have the ground floor. Father was pleased: 'It is also only ten to fifteen minutes' walk from the main Pińsk secondary school. Better enrol, Stefanku, even before Christmas.'

'Christianity is out, Dad,' I pointed out. 'It's now called a "short winter break". Something to do with Grandfather Frost.'

Everything worked according to plan. The sledge deposited us outside a cream-painted, stuccoed, two-storey house in a row of houses facing the River Pina and separated from it by the width of a tree-lined street. The street, the trees, the roofs of the houses and the frozen river were all covered with a layer of virgin snow. It must have been snowing heavily just before our arrival, but now the sky was blue. The low afternoon sun created long shadows and the snow glimmered with pale gold. It was a very quiet street. On the other side of the river, which was some twenty to thirty metres wide, there were several low ramshackle structures. A big sign over one of them, partly covered with snow, said *Piń . . .ub . . .chtowy*. The Pińsk Yacht Club? A rather grandiose name for the derelict shack.

Ours was a three-room ground-floor flat. We had our own kitchen with a small range burning either wood or coal. There was no proper bathroom, but there was a washstand with the usual bowl and pitcher. A shared modern water closet was at the end of the corridor.

Soon after our arrival, I enrolled in the *gimnazjum*. It was still known by its old name: *Gimnazjum Kościuszki*. The teachers were either ethnic Poles or Polish Jews and the lessons were in Polish. Almost half the children were Jewish, a few came from the surrounding villages and some of those were Belorussians; the remainder were Polish. However, after the 'short winter break' we returned to a very different school. The pupils were the same, the teachers were the same, though a few had been arrested and failed to return, but the school had become *Pervaya Byelarusskaya Desyatiletka*, the First Belorussian Ten-

Year School. From the start of the winter term our language of instruction was supposed to be Belorussian.

But there were difficulties. Even in the old Belorussian Soviet Socialist Republic, only peasants and a few enthusiasts spoke Belorussian. In our school, except for some of the children from the country, none of the pupils and not one teacher knew the language. It was hilarious. Our teacher of Polish and Polish Literature – which had suddenly become unfashionable – was a gentlewoman of unblemished Polish ancestry who took to teaching us Belorussian as if it were a foreign language. Actually, it was foreign both to her and to us. Other teachers either stuck to Polish, or tried to conduct their lessons in, mostly atrocious, Russian. Mr Śliwiński, an elderly Polish gentleman, our maths teacher, was the only man on the staff who spoke excellent Russian. Among several teachers arrested during the winter break were the headmaster and the teacher of chemistry. The former had been replaced by a man from Mińsk, the capital of the Belorussian Republic. The trouble was that he knew neither Belorussian nor Polish. He taught us Russian and the Stalinist Constitution – yes, it was a separate subject – for an hour every week. By far the greater loss was that of the chemistry teacher. The problem was that the pupils of the tenth form had to sit final school exams, including chemistry, in the summer.

One day I was called to the headmaster's study. He came straight to the point: 'Mr Śliwiński and Mr Friesner tell me that you are good at maths and at physics. Well ahead of the form. You had been ahead also in chemistry, they tell me. Apparently the chemistry teacher had commented to them on it before his "departure". The situation is difficult, with the exams coming, I mean. Would you take the chemistry classes for the tenth form? You could use the old Polish textbooks and speak in your own language. We couldn't pay you, of course, but it would be a great help to everybody and a great honour for you.'

I couldn't believe it. My Russian was still far from fluent, had I understood him correctly? I didn't know what to say. Seeing me hesitate, he added: 'It might help when you want to join the *Komsomol* [Union of Young Communists].'

I, joining the *Komsomol*? The thought had never even occurred to me. I could just imagine the expression on the faces of my parents on learning about it. But what he wanted me to do was a challenge. And it was funny. I, an eighth-grade pupil, was to take the tenth form for chemistry. Some of the boys there were eighteen or even nineteen. I couldn't wait to tell my parents and see their amazement.

I prepared my weekly lesson with care. It was all theoretical. There was a chemical laboratory in the school, but it was permanently locked and we never got to use it. The exam was supposed to be both written and oral, but not practical. My 'pupils' were so keen to get through the exam that they gave me no headaches. I worked with the class through the appropriate Polish textbook, chapter by chapter. I would explain what I could and, when in trouble, we would either work our way out of it between us and to our own satisfaction, or I would take the problem to Mr Friesner, our teacher of physics. My prestige at school rocketed but, as we left Pińsk before the results of the exams were announced, I never learned how my 'pupils' fared.

Life in Pińsk had become difficult. All shops had been nationalised and their shelves were empty. Corruption was rampant. You had to keep shop assistants sweet, or know whom to bribe. Peasants were selling their produce in the market, but at very high prices. On the black market one could get almost anything. A middleman would even bring a ring of sausage, or a piece of salt pork hidden in an attaché case to your door – for a price, of course. Luckily, we were not short of money. Father managed to get two and a half jobs and, as each full-time doctor's post paid 400 roubles per month, his monthly pay was 1,000 roubles. With Mother's one salary of 400 roubles, we were well off. In theory, Father worked 100 hours per week, but this was, of course, a fiction. He was learning to use the system. His mentor was Dr Weinthal.

By the time we reached Pińsk, Dr Weinthal had already adjusted to life there. Among other skills, he had developed a way of dealing with the shortages. He and his wife came to see us in the evening of our first day. They brought with them bread, butter, ham, cheese, a packet of tea and sugar.

Mother went to the kitchen to make tea and I followed to help. 'How did he get all that stuff?' I asked Mother. 'Aren't the shops permanently empty?'

She answered, 'He either got it on the black market, or bribed someone. One way or another, he must be getting it under the counter.'

When we returned bringing the tea, Dr Weinthal was in the middle of explaining his methods: '. . . in my high boots, fur jacket and fur hat, I had been often taken for a high official of some kind. I decided to make use of it. In the first queue in which I tried it on, the people let me go straight in.' Dr Weinthal was tall, of imposing presence and spoke good Russian. 'I never queue now. I go straight to the head of the queue, I swear in Russian and so far I have always succeeded. I am in and out with the goods, whatever they may be, before anybody has time to think. Funny people,' he concluded and started sipping his tea.

'Your system may work for a while,' said Mother. 'But in the long term . . .?'

'Oh, I don't know,' said Dr Weinthal. 'Let me see. We have been here, three months? Yes, we got here about the same time as the Soviets marched in, just after the middle of September. They nationalised the shops in November and, as if by magic, the shelves went empty. So far, my method has worked for almost a month,' he ended on a triumphant note and laughed. And then he took up the subject again. 'When Aniela feels like it, we work together. We look for a rather disorderly queue and I start by calling for order. In Russian, of course. A few choice swearwords help. I don't mince my words. People invariably obey. Then I stand guard at the entrance to the shop and make way for a pregnant woman, for an old fellow with a limp, you know what I mean. And then I let Aniela in. She goes home with the goods and I follow five minutes later.'

In the months to come I often joined forces with Dr Weinthal and his wife. The system really did work – most of the time.

The winter of 1940 was particularly cold. Snow came down in small delicate flakes for days on end. Several events of that winter 1940 in Pińsk stand out in my memory. One was the visit of a Russian naval officer. He was a high-ranking medical man, the head of medical services of the Dnepr Navy with headquarters in Kiev. He came to Pińsk to inspect the facilities in the Pińsk river port, where my father ran the dispensary. One evening Father invited him to dinner in our flat. He accepted the invitation stipulating, however, that he would come after dark and that the curtains would be drawn all through his visit. He seemed a nice enough man, but they were talking in Russian and my Russian was not yet good enough to follow this kind of rapid conversation. Anyway, most of it was talk about work. I preferred reading in my room and went to bed. Next morning at breakfast, my parents were talking about our visitor. 'He must have felt that it would be dangerous to be seen in our company,' said Father. 'Hence the darkness, the curtains.'

I wondered: 'Is it because we are Polish, because we are refugees, or because of something else?'

Father looked at me, 'All three, I suppose.'

Mother nodded: 'They call people like us *neblagonadyozhnyye*, the unreliables, political lepers.'

'To my mind,' said Father, 'the most telling thing he said, after a few vodkas, was that in the USSR no one going to bed in the evening can be certain of still being there in the morning.'

'What did he mean?' I asked innocently. 'I can think of a few chaps even in Otwock who may have lacked this certainty. The husband might have returned home earlier than expected . . .'

Mother smiled, 'The things you pick up, Stefan.'

'Yes,' said Father, 'it's all right to be facetious but what he meant was the rounding up of people, the knock on the door in the middle of the night.'

A few days after the naval officer's visit my aunt Franka Kamzel, her husband and son joined us in Pińsk. They moved in with us and I had to give up my bedroom. With my cousin, Tadeusz or Tadek for short, I moved into our living-room. We slept on padded, collapsible camp-beds put up side by side every night. I liked my Aunt Franka and her husband. She was the younger of my father's two sisters, a teacher. Uncle Bernard was an accountant. Tadek was two years older than me and good company. We played chess and card games. He had bad eyesight and wore thick glasses, but he was always reading something, the book or the newspaper held close to his face.

Another event was Father's illness. Towards the end of January a boil appeared above his left eye. It grew rapidly in size and Father developed a high fever, he stayed in bed. Mother asked Dr Jacobson, one of the polyclinic surgeons, to call on him. 'It's a carbuncle,' he said. He took Mother by the arm and guided her into the living-room. I followed. 'It's a dangerous place for a carbuncle,' he continued, 'it's over an orifice in the skull, which lets nerves through. Bacteria may spread along the canal into the skull and cause meningitis. Sulphonamides would help, but we can't get them in Pińsk, or even in Brześć, for love or money. Up to two weeks ago they had been obtainable on the black market, but the supply has dried up. The price was horrendous, anyway.'

Mother kept nodding her head. 'I shall have a try,' she said. 'I overheard a conversation in the laboratory. Apparently the pharmacist had discovered a source.'

'What is a carbuncle?' I asked Dr Jacobson. 'I know it's a kind of boil, but what is the difference?'

He looked at me thoughtfully, 'Let's say that if a boil is a solitary Jew, a carbuncle is a congregation.' He turned back to Mother: 'Aspirin. Plenty of fluids. Local heat. Hot linseed poultice. You know the kind of thing I mean. I shall call tomorrow on my way to the clinic.' Then he left.

I hugged Mother. I felt helpless. 'We can only do our best, Mother,' I said for the sake of saying something.

'Yes,' she said, 'I'll make a fresh poultice,' and went into the kitchen.

Father remained very ill for several days, at times he was delirious. Mother and Aunt Franka nursed him in turns. Dr Jacobson called twice a day on his way to and from the clinic. Sometimes he would poke about in the carbuncle with a probe and Father would bite his lips and grab Mother's hand in pain. But Mother could not get the sulphonamides, not at any price. Eventually Father pulled through, his temperature dropped back to normal, he started eating and within a week he was on his feet again.

In early March it was my turn to be ill. My parents and the three Kamzels went to visit friends. On leaving, Father, as usual, pushed home the flap controlling the outlet of the coal-burning tiled stove in the living-room. I stayed behind doing my homework at the table near the stove; it was the warmest place.

I must have fallen asleep over my homework. I came to outside, in the snow, by the kitchen door, with my head in Mother's lap. She was sitting there right in the snow. Father was holding my hand. It was sheer luck that Mother had felt tired and they had left their friends early. They found me unconscious, slumped over the table. Father had closed the chimney flap too soon and I fell victim to carbon-monoxide poisoning. By morning I was fine again.

The thaw set in towards the end of March and the snow, which had been smothering the town uninterruptedly since November, melted rapidly, converting the unpaved streets into a morass, impassable in places. Within a couple of days the river was free of ice and only occasional ice floes drifted hurriedly down the swollen river. Widespread floods had done some damage but our street was not affected. The smell of the muddy streets and of the marshes surrounding the town, mingled with the emanations of the overflowing privies and primitive plumbing, permeated the air of Pińsk. But by the middle of April, spring was in full bloom, the sun had dried the ground and the air became sweet once again.

❈ ❈ ❈

In the spring of 1940 Pińsk was a town full of rumours. The radio and the newspapers were subject to strict censorship. From all the garbage they produced, a modicum of reliable information could be extracted only by reading between the lines. At times gossip proved more informative than official broadcasts or announcements. Everybody knew somebody who had it 'in confidence', or 'on good authority' that . . .

The first arrests took place almost immediately after the Soviet invasion in September 1939 and involved 'enemies of the people'. In other words, anybody in uniform, policemen, frontier guards, even firemen; higher-grade state and municipal employees – mainly Polish; merchants, shopkeepers and small traders – mainly Jewish; and members of political parties of the capitalist state, including PPS (Polish Socialists) and the Bund (Jewish Socialists). In the eyes of the Soviet rulers, the socialists were competitors for the soul of the proletariat. Even members of the previously illegal Polish Communist Party, some of whom knew the taste of prison bread in capitalist Poland, were now being arrested and deported to Siberia by their Soviet comrades. Large-scale deportations started in March. The first wave involved families of the previously arrested 'enemies of the people'. The deportations were an arbitrary administrative measure, without even a parody of any judicial process. The wretched families, often three or four generations living together, were rounded up in the middle of the night, taken to the nearest railway station and put in cattle wagons under lock and key. In 1939–40 a total of one and a half million people were deported from the Soviet-occupied part of Poland; only half of them survived. At the time, personally, we had no reason to feel threatened. Nobody in Pińsk knew that my father was a reserve officer of the Polish Army.

Our situation changed radically in early May 1940. Soviet authorities embarked on issuing Soviet passports* to all of the inhabitants of the annexed part of Poland. The latter had no say in the matter, but we, the refugees from central Poland, were faced with the difficult choice of either passportisation or repatriation. Which was likely to prove the lesser evil? At present? In the long term? In the perception of refugees the acceptance of Soviet citizenship was tantamount to giving up the right of returning home. Ever. The reasoning behind my parents' decision to opt to go back to Otwock was partly similar to that which led to our aborted attempt to cross the border illegally before Mother's arrival: we would be returning home and, compared with the Russians, the Germans were a civilised and law-abiding nation.

But there was another consideration in my parents' hearts. 'This country,' Mother would say repeatedly, 'is just a big prison. If we remain here we shall never see Jurek again.'

Father was equally worried about my brother. 'How does he manage without his monthly allowance?' he mused aloud. 'I sent him some extra money in the months before the war started, but he couldn't have saved much.'

The currency restrictions which had been in place in Poland at the time allowed Father to send only small amounts of

---

* Internal passports, a form of ID, also signifying the citizenship of the Soviet Union

money to Jurek. Anything extra had to go through middlemen who took exorbitant cuts for themselves.

'I am sure,' I said, 'that by now Jurek has joined the army. Polish or British. I would have done.'

It had not occurred to me that it was not the consolation that Mother expected. She got up and went to the kitchen. 'This isn't what she wants to hear,' said Father. 'But I do hope this is what he has done. But would he be safe? Where could he be now?' At the time, there had been short notes in the papers about an expedition to Norway. Rumour had it that the British force included a Polish unit. When Mother rejoined us, her eyes were red.

By then, with the improved international postal services, we had had several letters and cables from Otwock, mainly from Stasia. They all said: 'Come back home. It's not so bad. Doctors are allowed to work.' And so my parents opted for repatriation. The Kamzels would have liked to return to their own home in Płock, north-west of Warsaw, but the area had been incorporated into the German Reich and thus open only to ethnic Germans. So, they decided that they would come with us to Otwock. The Weinthals had also opted for repatriation. And so did thousands of other refugees. We talked and talked, we weighed all the options, but we had no crystal ball, no one knew which was going to be the lesser evil, no one could have guessed.

Then, in late May 1940, a German Repatriation Commission was set up at the Brześć railway station. The early-morning train to Brześć left packed with refugees. With the Kamzels and Weinthals we filled one compartment. The corridor outside was cluttered with suitcases, bundles, boxes and people. On the train our parents kept going over the well-trodden ground of the pros and cons of repatriation as against the acceptance of Soviet passports. It was an inexhaustible subject to them, except for Aniela. She joined her son Stefan, Tadek and me in a game of bridge.

The Brześć station was crowded. The German Repatriation Commission had been at work since early morning. The queue of the would-be returnees, guarded by armed militia and by NKVD* officers, extended far into the street and round the

---

* *Narodnyi Kommisaryat Vnutryennykh Del*, or the Commissariat of the Interior.

block. But it moved quickly and soon we entered the station precinct itself. It was a single-file queue paralleled by a mountain range of our belongings. Of our group the Kamzels were first in the queue: father, mother and son.

Next were the Weinthals, again in the same order. I was talking to Stefan and so I was next, followed by my mother and father.

Then disaster struck. Two German soldiers, one on each side of the queue, crossed their rifles between Stefan and me. One said something in German. I looked at Mother. She went as white as a sheet. Suddenly I was frightened. 'What did he say?' I asked in a whisper.

'It's the end,' Mother whispered back. 'They are taking no more. They have filled the quota.'

The orderly queue behind us broke up. It degenerated into a disorderly, frightened mob. A line of soldiers cut us off from the main body of the station which crawled with armed local militia and NKVD officers. The Germans were pushing us back towards the gate of the station shouting, 'Out, out,' and using their rifle butts. In minutes we were out in the street again. We stayed there for a long time, until our lucky relations and friends disappeared in the waiting train to Warsaw, with boards saying *Varshava* in the Cyrillic script and *Warshau* in German. 'Perhaps it's for the best,' said Father.

'It's okay. Don't worry!' shouted Dr Weinthal from the train window. 'The head of the Commission told me that there will be another transport in a week or two.'

At that moment a German officer emerged from the station gate and faced the crowd. He raised his arms. The shouts of disappointed and resentful people died down. He spoke excellent Polish: 'Go back to your homes. The Repatriation Commission will be back. You will be informed in good time. All those who wished to be repatriated will be repatriated.'

He did an about-turn and disappeared inside the station. The German soldiers followed and the Russians locked the gate. All we could do was to stand there and wave to our friends until the train was shunted out of sight.

Ours was a miserable return journey to Pińsk. Mother cried quietly most of the way, Father sat there by the window, not in a talking mood. The gloom spread to me. The four hours' ride seemed to stretch for ever.

But life in Pińsk had changed for the worse. Rumours became wilder than ever. But were they that wild? Were they so exaggerated? You might have thought so until a friend or an acquaintance of yours suddenly disappeared. Each night people expected that knock on the door. Even if they could not think of an earthly reason for it. Was everyone a potential counter-revolutionary? An enemy of the people? An undesirable? A heavy cloud of uncertainty, of fear, hung over the town. People were being imprisoned, deported. Even boys of my age were not safe. We had no passports, no valid documents of any kind. What's worse, I looked older than fifteen. The usually friendly streets of Pińsk became quiet and were often deserted, except for the patrols of militia and of NKVD.

School finished about 2 p.m. and, afraid of being picked up and deported on my own, I got into the habit of running all the way home. This took about two or three minutes. But even indoors I was jittery, insecure. Our landlady took to staying at her sister's.

In the meantime, with the arrival of summer, the Pińsk Yacht Club across the river had come to life. In the afternoons a dozen or more youngsters, a few from our school, would be swimming, sunbathing and canoeing. The river became my refuge. Back from school, after a quick meal, I would change, run across the street in my swimming-trunks, jump into the river and swim across to the strip of grass given the honorary title of 'beach'. I would spend most afternoons either swimming or canoeing and I made new friends there on the bank of the Pina river. I stayed on the beach until I was sure that my parents were back home. Mother would wave to me from the window: I am back, you can return now. Most days I was the last to leave the river.

Each day we waited for the promised return of the German Repatriation Commission, but in vain. The rumours in Pińsk continued unabated. Postal services broke down again. There was no news from the Kamzels. Had they reached Otwock? Had they settled in our house? We had no letters from Stasia or anyone else. Even the correspondence with Uncle Adam, a prisoner of war somewhere in the USSR, seemed to have come to an end.

Which was the lesser evil? Going or staying? The question would remain unanswered for a long time.

SIX

THE SUN IS ON
THE WRONG SIDE

✷

The bang on the door came on 29 June 1940. I had been fast asleep. The green phosphorescent hands of my watch showed 3 a.m. We had been expecting it. In a way, it was a relief when it came. As I reached the door in my pyjamas, my parents, in their dressing-gowns, were already there.

There were three of them on the doorstep. No introduction was needed. In improvised uniforms of different shapes and hues, in military-style blue peaked caps, with rifles nonchalantly slung from their shoulders and with red bands on their left sleeves, they were unmistakably the citizens' militia.

'Family Wajdenfeld,' shouted the one who seemed to be in charge; short and fat. 'Three of you. We have orders to search your flat. Wait in the kitchen. You, Yakov,' he pointed to a much younger man, tall and thin, 'keep an eye on them. No talking,' he added, and then, 'Yegor, come with me.' He turned round, noticed our landlady, Mrs Margulis, at the top of the stairs. 'Nothing to do with you!' he shouted waving her away. 'Back to bed!'

They spoke briefly among themselves. And then the fat one addressed us again: 'After the search, get dressed and I'll give you thirty minutes to pack your belongings.' From the distance of about ten feet he allowed Father a glimpse of a piece of paper. 'The search warrant,' he barked and almost immediately replaced the supposed document in his trouser pocket. But no papers were necessary. Their threatening demeanour, their official red armbands and, most of all, their rifles were incentive enough for my parents to comply.

They spoke a kind of broken Russian and pretended that they knew no Polish. As Pińsk was now part of the Belorussian Soviet Republic they ought to have been speaking Belorussian but, like most town people in this former part of Poland, they did not know this peasant dialect. The leader and Yakov both looked Jewish and spoke with a strong Yiddish accent. They were probably more used to speaking Yiddish than any other language. The third man, Yegor, short and swarthy, was, judging by his accent, a Ukrainian peasant. All three were unshaven and unwashed and, while his two companions looked menacingly more like highwaymen than militiamen, Yakov did not look particularly fierce. And so, as Yakov herded us into the kitchen and closed the kitchen door behind him, Mother engaged him in conversation. 'Where are you taking us?' she asked in her excellent Russian.

Yakov did not answer. Instead, he put his finger to his lips. Next, he motioned my parents to sit down and took the third chair himself. After a couple of minutes of silence he got up, pushed the door ajar and for a brief moment stuck his head out. Loud voices of his two companions on a rampage in my parents' bedroom drifted unintelligibly across the corridor. Reassured, he returned to his chair. Next, obviously searching for unfamiliar words, he started hesitantly in Russian: 'To the railway station. To your train.' He paused and continued in excellent Polish. 'The train to Warsaw. You have registered for repatriation, haven't you? Thousands of people will be going on the same train. It's a goods train, but it is only a short journey.'

'But why in the middle of the night?' asked Father.

'We always work at night. Didn't you know?' said Yakov with a smile. We sat there in silence. 'Are you sure that you are doing the right thing? God knows what the Germans will be . . .' He stopped in mid-sentence as the door opened and the Ukranian called for us to return to the bedroom. 'Start packing. You have thirty minutes,' he looked at the watch on his wrist. It was the same kind of watch as mine, a *Cyma*. Or was it my watch? Father saw it too. I was about to say something, but Father's raised finger shut me up.

Our rooms were in utter disarray, it was as if a whirlwind had passed through, or a band of robbers. But that's what they were, a band of robbers. They had stolen my watch!

Father and I dressed quickly. Mother did it in the privacy of the kitchen. We packed in a hurry. Originally we had arrived in Pińsk with only two suitcases, now we had additional bags of bedding, kitchen utensils, crockery, books. Hours would be required for proper packing, not thirty minutes. No matter, at last we were going home. Yakov's doubts added to my fear of the Germans, but I hoped that my parents knew what they were doing when they registered for repatriation. At least we were not being sent to Siberia. Judging from what I had heard and read, it was a place to keep away from at all cost.

The search over, the militiamen were in a hurry: '*Davay, davay, po bystreye*, move, move, hurry up,' they were all shouting over the next few minutes.

'That's to cover the traces,' Father murmured in French. 'They must have stolen a few things.' My parents had lived through the October 1917 revolution in Russia and they knew 'the standard procedure'. And indeed, much later we discovered that, in addition to my watch, a few other valuable items had found their way into the deep pockets of these guardians of the law, among them Mother's watch, Father's gold Waterman fountain pen and my Pelican fountain pen: Father's watch survived in the pocket of his pyjamas; he hid it there as soon as he heard the banging on the door.

Once we finished packing the demeanour of the militiamen changed. They stopped shouting, they helped us to load our suitcases, bags and boxes on to the horse-drawn cart waiting in the street. We had to return to the house several times to get all the stuff out. Father seemed to behave in an odd way. He went back into the house, then came out empty-handed. He went back again, still he brought nothing out. And then Mrs Margulis came down in a dressing gown clutching to her chest a parcel wrapped in newspaper: 'I have made a few sandwiches for your journey,' she stopped suddenly uncertain what to do. 'Is that all right?' she asked the nearest militiaman, the Ukrainian. He barred her way with his rifle.

'What have you got there?' asked the leader and lifted the

edge of the newspaper. 'Oh, sandwiches,' he shrugged his shoulders. 'All right, all right. Let her. Hurry up.' Father accepted the parcel and kissed Mrs Margulis on both cheeks. A very unusual thing for Father to do, I thought. Then Mother and I said our farewells to her. She was a nice old lady, at least forty. She had prepared a lot of sandwiches for the eight-hour journey to Warsaw, I thought.

'Let's sit down,' said Mrs Margulis and smiled happily. And we sat down on the stairs for a minute, as was the custom.

'Bourgeois superstition,' growled the Ukrainian, but the two Jews sat down with us. And then it was 'Hurry, hurry, move,' all over again. Father passed the parcel over to Mother. She just nodded and smiled at Mrs Margulis.

Later in the train, in the 'privacy' of our corner, Mother gave Father and me a sandwich each, then removed a packet wrapped in greaseproof paper which looked like more sandwiches and put it in her handbag. 'What . . . ,' I started, but with Mother's finger across her lips, the question remained hanging in the air.

I did not learn the story behind the packet of 'sandwiches' until later that night when, stretched next to me ready for sleep, Father whispered it in my ear.

When we had returned to Pińsk from our failed expedition to Brześć, anticipating our deportation, Father had hidden his Polish Army Officer's Book and his gold cigarette case outside the toilet window, between the leaves of the wooden window shutters. He had hoped that either he or Mother would be able to grab the packet, unseen, at the appropriate moment. Mrs Margulis was admitted to the secret, but I was not. I didn't blame my parents, I was only fifteen. Also, less than a week before our deportation, Father had exchanged a $100 bill on the black market. This was all the foreign currency he owned. In the USSR, selling and buying foreign currency, even its possession, was, at the time, a capital offence. Indeed, people were being shot for less-serious transgressions. The proceeds were also part of that hidden parcel now masquerading as sandwiches. The sum in roubles was enormous. With an exchange rate of roughly 350 roubles per dollar, he now had about 35,000 roubles.

The reason for the exorbitant exchange rate was that the Polish city of Wilno fell to the still-independent Lithuania and that via Wilno many refugees managed to escape to Scandinavia, and hence to Great Britain, America and even China. They badly needed foreign currency and the dollar rose to unprecedented heights.

Now, on that memorable night, neither of my parents had managed to get to the parcel unobserved, but our landlady did. She recognised the banging on the door for what it was and, while we were packing, she prepared the sandwiches of buttered bread. She waited for the moment when our flat was empty, removed the hidden parcel and incorporated it into the packet.

I have little doubt that the following year, along with other Jewish inhabitants of Belorussia and Ukraine, Mrs Margulis was murdered by the Nazis. Equally, I have no doubt that her action on that fateful night in Pińsk secured our survival.

❀ ❀ ❀

It was early morning when, sitting in the cart on our bags and suitcases, and escorted by Yegor alone, we started on our way. The eastern side of the sky was turning golden red. Another hot day was upon us. The town was still asleep and the streets were empty except for some stray dogs and a few early risers going about their business. Their furtive glances followed us for a few seconds and then people promptly looked the other way. It was a fifteen-minute journey to the Pińsk railway station and our undernourished chestnut horse was not in a hurry.

In contrast to the town, the station was exceedingly busy. It crawled with militiamen in their shabby improvised uniforms with the red armbands, lorded over by the regular railway police and by the NKVD men, who were instantly recognisable by their blue uniforms with the red stripes down the trousers. Our cart became the eleventh in the queue of horse-drawn vehicles and of small lorries waiting in the street at the gate in the wire-net fencing off the station. The gate was ajar and guards patrolled the long, wide, gravel path between the fence and the train.

A goods train of some forty wagons stretched motionless along the gravel path. There was no locomotive. The wide, sliding doors of the wagons were open. The train was empty. The dirty-red wagons were of the type to be seen in all railway stations. Each wagon had a notice by the door. I couldn't make out the stencilled Cyrillic letters clearly at the distance, but I knew what they said: forty men or eight horses. I had seen them before in other stations. Now they did not seem funny. Forty men, women and children in a wooden box. I wished I were a horse.

The queue was strangely quiet. The guards did not stop people talking, but we were subdued, intimidated, tired. Scanty gossip was being exchanged *sotto voce.*

We waited and waited. The queue of vehicles kept growing. Stretched out on top of our possessions, my head in Mother's lap, I must have fallen asleep. A commotion woke me up. The guards were banging shut the sliding doors of the wagons. As I sat up, a saloon car stopped at the station gate and disgorged several NKVD officers.

The place sprang to life. The guards ran down the queue of vehicles and shouts filled the air: 'Out, out. Collect your belongings. Hurry. Get moving.' Within minutes we were out of the carts and lorries and herded into a long queue to the station. The gate was now wide open. An NKVD officer counted out groups of forty. Each group was directed to a wagon and told to wait outside. But, as people found that they could not carry all their belongings in one go, all semblance of order disappeared. Men and women ran to and fro between the vehicles in the street and the train, bumping into each other, mistaking the wagons, yelling in Polish, in Yiddish, in Russian, calling their spouses, their children. While Mother stayed behind guarding the first instalment of our belongings by the assigned wagon, Father and I went back to the cart for the rest of our possessions. Surprisingly, we did not lose anything in the mêlée.

By the time we returned to the train with the remaining items, the door in the middle of the wagon wall had been slid back throwing the box open. But its floor was at least two feet higher than the gravelled path and there were no steps. People were throwing their belongings in and were helping each other up. The door in the opposite wall of the wagon was closed and the central space of the car filled up rapidly with bags and bundles. On each side of the wagon, there were two deep horizontal shelves about one metre apart, the lower one raised about half a metre above the floor. Father helped Mother up. Soon most of the women and children were inside, perching on the edge of the lower and upper shelves, like so many sparrows on telegraph wires, while the central space was littered with luggage of all shapes and sizes.

From his experience in the First World War and in the revolution, Father knew the routine and took charge. 'Listen,' he shouted. 'There are four shelves for forty people, ten per shelf. Let's do it sensibly. Stay in family groups.' In the meantime, having stepped up on some suitcases, Mother sat down on the far end of the right-hand upper shelf. 'Everything flat goes under the lower shelves,' Father continued. 'Bags of bedding and soft bundles go on your chosen places on the shelves.' Amazingly, people obeyed and order was restored. Mother had reserved three places for us and I was glad to stretch out along the wall of the wagon, with my head just below a small rectangular window in the wall which was about two hands long and one hand wide, it had no glass, only two rusty vertical bars. Here the ceiling was low and, lying down, I could touch it with my fingers. Even in early morning the metal was already warm to the touch. Unless we are on our way soon, I thought to myself, we shall be cooked in here.

My window faced the proper, raised, paved platform. All I could see was the end of the station building, an empty field to its side and houses in the distance. An armed militiaman came into view. The platform patrol presumably.

More shouting came from the other side of the train. The words were indistinguishable. And then the door was banged shut, somebody fiddled with the iron bar. We were locked in, but the train did not move.

The noise slowly died down. Hours passed. Even though the day was still young, the occupants of the car, dragged out of their beds in the middle of the night, were tired and subdued. Some were snoring already. By noon the wagon became uncomfortably hot. The only means of ventilation were the barred windows, like the one above my head, one in each corner of the car, and the summer of 1940 was exceptionally hot. But it should be no more than ten or twelve hours' travel to Warsaw. It wouldn't be too bad.

Father, stretched out next to me, breathed evenly. Mother, lying next to him, had her eyes shut. Hungry and miserable, I could not sleep. I had to pee. But we were locked in a wagon with no toilet. I sat up on the edge of the shelf, my neck bent, my head just an inch or two from the hot roof. Then I became aware of the smell rising from the floor of the wagon from somewhere near the door. I looked down. Just under my feet, there was a hole in the floor with a short wooden gutter, two planks fixed edge on, at right angles. Was this our lavatory for the day's journey to Warsaw? For forty people of both sexes? It certainly smelled like it. In towns and railway stations even the public urinals for men were totally enclosed. This contraption was in full view of everybody. The urge became unbearable, my belly hurt. Then the pain eased off and I went to sleep. But the pain woke me up again. It was early afternoon. Children were still asleep but most adults were awake, chatting. Father was awake and I told him about my predicament. By then we had been locked in for some eight hours. He got down from the shelf and banged on the door, but the negotiations with the guard outside conducted through the locked door proved fruitless. By then the 'toilet' was already in use, mainly by small children, until somebody had the bright idea of screening it off with a blanket. Instantly there was a queue for it, children and women first. For the first time in my life I was glad to be still designated a child.

I tried in vain, but I could not do it. I stood inside the blanket screen for several minutes and had to give up. My belly hurt on and off. When the queue disappeared I tried again. Nothing. My father, in both his parental and medical capacity, the provider of cures and comforts, was powerless.

Suddenly, there was a commotion outside, on the station side. Two NKVD men were running along the train shouting: 'Is there a doctor on the train? We need a doctor.'

In the next instance Father was by the window. 'I am a doctor,' he shouted. Did he do it out of habit, or had he perceived an opportunity for renewing negotiations which had failed before? In the NKVD carriage, an officer had fallen ill with a chest pain. '*Ladno*, okay,' said Father. 'I will go to see him, but not until all the doors are opened and people are allowed out.' Negotiations proceeded urgently. With power on your side, you can take a doctor to the patient, but can you make him treat him? But, perhaps you can, with a gun to his head, or to his wife's, or son's. Germans would do that, but Russians were not quite of the same mould. At least not yet. So Father had his way.

The number of armed guards on the platform doubled and the doors of all the wagons were opened. Father picked up his medical case, jumped out of the wagon and was shown to the guards' carriage. It was a proper first-class carriage, of course.

With the door open I was one of the first to jump out. We were not allowed into the station building, but there were two lavatories on the platform. Two long queues formed within minutes. I did not wait. Like an experienced dog I found a suitable lamppost at the end of the platform. It served my purpose admirably. I never suspected that the human bladder could hold so much liquid.

Before long Father was back. There was not much wrong with the patient, he had been overcome by heat. Father gave him an injection of camphor. 'He did not really need anything,' said Father, 'but I had to be seen doing something. He will come to no harm.'

While attending to the patient, Father wangled another concession: a distribution of *kipyatok*, or boiling water. This was normally available from taps at most Soviet railway stations. Ordinary tap water being unsafe, boiled water was very popular and as soon as a train stopped in a station the passengers would queue for the *kipyatok* tap. In such a huge country where people would spend days, if not weeks, in trains or in stations waiting for trains, the provision of boiled water was sensible, but it had not as yet reached the ex-Polish territories, like Pińsk, from where the vendors of soft drinks – being capitalists by definition – had disappeared.

So now the Pińsk station staff had to boil large cauldrons of water. It took a long time before the largesse reached us. But there was no hurry. We still had no locomotive. On this sweltering day the hot water was strangely refreshing and made me hungry again. Mother had five of Mrs Margulis's sandwiches left over from breakfast. She gave Father and me two each and had one herself. That was the end of our food stores.

In the evening the heat abated a little, though it was still unrelieved by even the slightest breeze. The metal roof of the car was now only hot to the touch, but no longer burning. Tired and hungry I curled up in my corner of the shelf under the window.

I woke up with a start as the train jerked suddenly. Oh, the locomotive, I thought. Soon we will be on our way to Warsaw. I looked at my watch, but it was not there and I swore under my breath, *'psia krew* (dog's blood)' – my swearing being still very genteel. Was it only this morning that it had been stolen?

But the train did not budge. The inside of the wagon was dark. I went back to sleep.

When I woke up again we were on the move, the train shaking like a peasant cart on cobblestones. I leaned on my elbow to look out. The sky was studded with stars. All I could see on the ground was a hedge of bushes and low trees and, beyond it, empty meadows dotted with patches of water, unruffled and shining in the moonlight. No houses, no lights.

Night noises filled the air of the wagon: deep breathing, moans and groans, discordant snores, short, sharp cries of bad dreams, and more 'explosive' sounds.

I must have gone back to sleep and when I woke up again the rectangle of the sky in my window had changed to greyish-blue, with a pinkish-yellow glow in the direction in which the train was going.

Sunrise. With nostalgia I remembered another sunrise. It was May 1935, I was ten, and, again, I was on a train. I was on a school trip returning from Kraków, where schools from all over the country were helping to erect a memorial burial mound for Marshal Piłsudski, *pater patriae*, who had died earlier that month. I woke up somewhere near Częstochowa, the city of the Black Madonna. I could see through the window that the bright red disc of the sun was halfway over the horizon. I was riveted to the view until the sun had fully risen and then the drama was lost. Another lifetime, another world.

I could not go back to sleep and lay there with my eyes open. Now everything was so different from that May morning: a cattle wagon, locked doors, hunger and thirst, but at least we were also going home.

The patch of sky above my head was now pale blue and the stars had disappeared. Again I leaned on my elbow, hoping to see the rising disc of the sun, but the hole was too small to lean out.

Suddenly, I was unhappy. Something was wrong. But what? And then it hit me. The sun was on the wrong side. We were going east, not west to Warsaw, but east towards the rising sun. The train veered slightly to the left and I saw the reddish gold disk just over the horizon.

I tried to think straight. There was only one railway line in Pińsk, the Brześć–Gomel line. On the map the line was perfectly straight. It went west to Brześć, Warsaw and then Berlin, or east to Gomel and then Moscow. And we were going east.

Another thought struck me. We were at least two or three hours' travelling time from Pińsk. Had we been going west, we should now be crossing the relatively prosperous areas round Brześć, whereas here the countryside was sparsely populated and desolate. We were probably by now past the old Polish–Soviet border and in Soviet territory proper. I was confused. But I was right: we were going in the direction opposite to that intended.

People were waking up. The man on the shelf opposite, who was also by the window, had also been looking out. He said something to me but I could not hear him over the clatter of the wheels. He smiled and shrugged his shoulders. He has no idea of what's happening, I thought. Is he a fool, or am I? I looked out once more. There was no doubt, we were going east. I looked to my left. My parents were still asleep. I shook Father by the shoulder. He sat up, instantly awake. 'The sun is on the wrong side,' I said in a loud whisper.

Uncomprehendingly, he looked at me. I pointed to the sun in the window. He understood instantly. He leaned over me and thought, his brows tightly knit. 'You are right,' he said. 'I was afraid that this might happen.'

There was no mistake. We had been fed lies. We were on a

journey not of our choosing. Destination unknown. And there was nothing we could do about it. Nothing whatsoever.

The news had spread. Within minutes everyone was awake. Some people burst into tears. Like yawning, crying is infectious and children echoed their mothers. The threat of deportation had always loomed large over our heads and here it came to pass. What was in store for us? The frozen north? Kolyma? Vorkuta? Kazakhstan? Siberia? The dread, the terror, the menace associated with these names were overtaken in years to come only by those of Oświecim (Auschwitz), Belsen and Mathausen, Treblinka, Chełm and Bełżec. But at the time and for us, they were full of horror.

We were helpless. Escape from the train, even if possible, would not get anybody very far. This was the USSR. The country was one great prison swarming with militia, railway police, NKVD units, informers and spies.

In the meantime, we were getting thirsty and hungry. Another hot day had dawned. Every so often our train would stop on a siding to give way to other goods and passenger trains. The siding was always in an empty field, with not a soul to be seen. The names of small stations seen on the way meant nothing to me, while bigger towns were invariably skirted around, so that we could not even guess our itinerary. The wagons remained locked and during the stops only the guards could stretch their legs outside the train. They answered no questions and ignored our demands for food and water. Our journey lasted over seven days. Occasionally the train would stop near a village and curiosity would get a few inhabitants out. They were quite obviously used to seeing transports of prisoners or deportees in cattle wagons. Some commiserated loudly with us: 'Poor, poor people. Where can they be taking them?' Women often wailed loudly: 'Look, they are deporting even babies and children. Will it never end?' A brave soul or two would bring a loaf of bread, a bottle of water, an apple. Some of the offerings could have been passed between the bars. But the brutal guards would not let the locals get anywhere near the train. Swearing, shouting obscenities, they pushed them back with their rifle butts, knocking the modest gifts from their outstretched hands. With their heavy boots they trod on bread, fruit and broken glass. Thirstily we watched the gifts of water sink into the ground. They were much rougher with their own people than they had been with us.

At every stop we all threw balls of squashed paper with our own names and with names and addresses of relatives out of the windows, we begged the finder to mail the note to the nearest and dearest. My parents were busy helping those who did not know Russian. The messages were easily thrown over the heads of the guards, and the peasants, children in particular, picked them up and ran away. We learned later that many of the notes did in fact reach their destinations. Though, as far as I know, none of ours did.

I had lost count of the days, but it was either on the third or on the fourth day of our journey that we skirted a large city, perhaps Moscow? The tracks multiplied and trains rushed past us every few minutes. Our train accelerated and suburban stations flashed by. The area was densely populated, but it seemed drab and desolate by our Polish standards. The villages were poor, reminiscent of the impoverished eastern provinces of Poland.

Empty stomach and a dry, parched mouth, hunger and thirst, were our constant companions. The heat outside continued unabated. Since leaving Pińsk we had been kept locked in our wagons and only once a day were two people allowed out of each carriage to fill our containers with water. But we did not have enough containers and water had to be strictly rationed, so there was none left for washing. Complaints to our guards during stops fell on deaf ears. Our toilet was disgustingly smelly and its emanations invariably drifted to my perch on the shelf above it. Everybody was bad tempered and sharp with each other – even Father. 'It's the lack of food,' Mother tried to explain. People were prickly, but had no stomach for loud quarrels, bitter arguments. They were too apathetic.

As from the end of the first day there was no food in the wagon. Nobody had any left. No one had expected a long journey. I do not remember individual days, they were all much the same. But I do recall the second day with clarity. It was the first whole day in my life when I had nothing to eat; not a peanut; not a crumb. Younger children, unable to understand why there was no meal coming, kept crying and asking for it, but at my age I knew better. The morning was the worst. My stomach was all in a knot. Later the pangs of hunger eased somewhat. I read for most of the day: *Tikhii Don* (*Quiet Flows the Don*), by Sholokhov, kept me occupied. By now I could read Russian without difficulty and only occasionally had to ask Father or Mother the meaning of an unfamiliar word. On the third day, the second day of our fast, I had slept most of the time. I had no hunger pangs. My stomach seemed satisfied with the scanty sips of warm water. Suddenly, in the middle of the third night, the train stopped on a siding. I heard engines rumbling. Then the door of the wagon opened a fraction and loaves of bread were thrown in by unseen hands. Before we managed to spread a blanket, the first few loaves fell on the far-from-clean floor. But nobody cared. It was food. The amount was adequate and the bread was white, fresh and delicious. '*Hunger ist der beste Koch,*' my mother used to say. Perhaps any bread would have passed the test under the circumstances.

Subsequently bread distribution was repeated every night during the journey, and on two occasions it was accompanied by soup, a bucket per wagon. It was cabbage soup with bits of meat and potato, the best soup I had ever eaten; though perhaps the same proverb applied.

The train was making slow progress, with long and frequent stops in the middle of nowhere. There was little change of scenery, the country was flat. We saw fields, meadows, forests, few roads, little motorised traffic. Tractors, so beloved of Soviet propaganda as a sign of progress, were few and far between, with horses still the ubiquitous means of transport and the main prop of agriculture. Towns and villages were quiet, sleepy.

The days and nights merged into one another almost imperceptibly and uneventfully. The dominant mood was one of apathy. The majority of passengers slept most of the time. Some played cards, a few read books or discussed politics. These discussions were uninformed; there was not a single radio set on board.

Other than their shared misery, the wagon population had little in common. Misunderstandings or incipient quarrels were quickly settled by my father, who, through no effort of his own, was thrust into the role of judge and arbiter.

Except for Mr Wasserman and Mietek, his son, I cannot recall a single face or name of our co-passengers. Mietek was two years older than me and we talked a lot. He became a good friend. Later we shared a room with the Wassermans for over a year.

Life in our prison on wheels was orderly. Water, bread and soup were distributed equitably as soon as they arrived. Cleaning of the central floor area, which we called the parlour, and of the toilet was done by everyone in turns. Many wanted to exclude my father from this chore, asserting that it was 'not a job for the doctor' but he insisted on doing his share.

During our week-long journey several people died on the train and the bodies were removed at night. My father was escorted by the guards several times to see patients in other wagons but, in the absence of any drugs, his ministrations were restricted to the medical equivalent of laying on of hands. Luckily in our wagon nobody died and nobody became seriously ill.

The weather continued to be hot and sunny and, as the train puffed its way north-east under its canopy of smoke and steam, the days grew longer. The final two nights of our journey were very short indeed, each lasting not more than a couple of hours. The sunset left the western sky in hues of grey and yellow, while the golden promise of another hot day was already spreading from the east.

My perch under the south-east facing window gave me a good view of the sunrise morning after morning, but here, in the white-night country, the sunrise was far less dramatic than it had been on the more southern leg of our journey.

Well into the morning of the eighth day the train stopped on a slightly raised riverbank just short of a bridge. With a lot of shouting, swearing and clanging of keys the wagons were unlocked, the doors slid back and we were ordered out. The area was surrounded by armed guards. We did not need a special invitation to get out of the hot, stinking wagon. It was a delight to draw in a chestful of fresh air. Like animals long accustomed to their cage and suddenly allowed out, we stayed close to ours, the train. Apart from the guards the place was deserted; not a soul to be seen; not a roof, not a tell-tale wisp of smoke in the vicinity; meadows and barren fields stretched along both sides of the wide river and, except for the distant outline of a town in the direction from which we came, the horizon all around us was a dark wall of forest.

With all the deportees out of the train, the guards stopped shouting and swearing; one of them even smiled and joked with the children. Suddenly the joker stood to attention. A major of the NKVD approached our wagon: 'Which one of you is the doctor?'

'I am,' volunteered Father.

'Thank you for your help during the journey,' said the man.

He stopped for a moment and was about to move on when Father raised his arm and asked, 'Could you please tell us what is happening? Obviously, we had been misinformed that we were going to Warsaw. Where are we now? What will we be doing here?' My father's Russian was excellent.

The major stopped in his tracks and tried to smile. This did not come easily to him, the poor man was obviously out of practice. The contortions of his face were painful to watch, the angles of his mouth moved up but his steely eyes did not take part in the effort. 'The German government had refused to have you back,' he said. He hesitated for a moment. 'And,' he almost shouted, 'you refused the offer of Soviet passports. You are an unreliable element. We had to remove you from the border area.' He stopped again. His facial expression returned to inscrutable when he continued: 'The river here is the Northern Dvina and the town over there,' he pointed to the distant break in the forest wall in the west, 'is Kotlas. You will be resettled in various forest stations in the area.' His right arm described an arc to the north and east. '*Na perevospitannye*, for re-education,' he added. He started on his way and then turned round again. '*Zdes zhit budete*, here you shall live,' he added as an afterthought.

We had heard the expression before. The rumours circulating in Pińsk had it that deportees to Siberia were often taken under guard to a small clearing in an uninhabited part of the forest and left there to their own devices with just these words, '*Zdes zhit budete*'.

Another NKVD officer joined the major and they moved on. People from several wagons surrounded Father. They talked all at once, they asked questions. I moved out of the way. I had heard of Kotlas as the gateway to the northern exile territories of European Russia, stretching from the Ural Mountains in the east, to beyond the Northern Dvina river in the west and to the White Sea in the north. At that time the railway line ended in Kotlas and only later was it extended further north into Komi, an area notorious for its labour camps. I did not listen to the discussion in the group surrounding my father. I had my own gloomy thoughts to digest. The exhilaration of being let out of the stinking wagon soon dissipated. It was still very hot, even this far north the midday sun was burning.

I looked at the river again. It was very wide and even here, not far from its source, it seemed wider than the Vistula in Warsaw.

'Fancy a swim?' said a voice. It was Mietek.

My brain cleared in a flash. 'Yes . . . but will they let us?'

Mietek asked the nearest guard. He did not seem to object, but just laughed. I wondered why. It was a mischievous kind of laugh. We stripped to our dirty underpants, ran on to the bridge and dived in.

In the next instant I knew the reason for the guard's amusement. The water was ice cold. The shock was devastating. Carried by the momentum of the dive, I went down and down. My heart, squeezed in some frosty fist, seemed to have stopped. Frantically I worked my way back to the surface. Terrified out of my wits I opened my mouth to shout for help, but could produce no sound. I could not breathe. I was overwhelmed by the thought that I would never get out of this river alive. A few moments later my muscles came back to life, I swam towards the shore and just about managed to crawl out of the water, shivering, my teeth chattering. I collapsed on the wet grass, not at all invigorated. I was the first on the shore. Mietek and several other boys who followed my example scrambled out looking half-dead. Nobody paid any attention to our plight, but no one actually went missing. After a few minutes in the hot sun we recovered, dressed and joined the multitude milling around the train. The guard who had condoned our escapade smiled broadly.

Kotlas was the end of our first cattle-train journey in the USSR. We unloaded, and the train, all forty wagons of it, departed, leaving the bank of the river crammed with people. At the rate of forty passengers per wagon – minus the few who had died during the journey – we totalled well over 1,500 people. Guards patrolled the riverbank. The hot noon merged into a warm afternoon, into a chilly evening and then into a cold night. Family groups and groups of friends huddled together round their belongings. I was again hungry when in the evening a couple of trucks arrived bearing cauldrons of soup and sacks of bread. The news then spread that we were spending the night on the riverbank. Bundles of bedding were undone and blankets, coverlets and eiderdowns came out. Soon the children stopped crying, but sleep did not come to the adults. Speculations, discussions, musings went on through most of the night. The absence of real darkness in this white-night country was also not conducive to sleep. Somebody obtained a newspaper from one of the guards by bartering it for a cake of soap. It was brought to my father to read and translate. A group surrounded our bivouac and the war situation and matters political and general were discussed at length. 'The French had not done any better than our Army . . . Mussolini is a hyena . . . to fall like that on a carcass . . . shame . . . disgrace . . . at least they did not sacrifice Paris . . . like Warsaw . . . The Americans will have to come in . . .' I listened intently at first, then with only half an ear, until, eventually, I must have gone to sleep.

When I woke up in the morning a low, dense, cotton-wool-like mist sat on the river and spread up the bank. The far bank was totally invisible. The factory chimneys and the high-rise blocks which yesterday formed the distant skyline of Kotlas in the west had also disappeared in the fog.

The day was in full swing. For breakfast we had the remains of last night's bread washed down with Dvina water. People were packing their bags and boxes, making their ablutions in the river. The sun rose, the fog was lifting slowly. Suddenly several open lorries arrived and one stopped near us. Both the driver and the driver's mate were women. One of them let the tailgate down. 'Collect your belongings!' shouted the nearest guard, the same joker who had sent us into the freezing river. Loading didn't take long. Mietek was the first to climb on board and soon the platform of the lorry was full of luggage, all the seats along its two sides were occupied, the tailgate was banged closed and we were off. We were in the first truck to leave, with the Wassermans, with another couple from our wagon and several other families I did not know. We were lucky: we learned later it was several days before the riverbank was cleared.

The lorries were big and heavy, designed for rough, unpaved dirt tracks cut through forests and for crossing clearings, meadows and swamps, where the track was recognisable only by ruts in the ground. Our journey was a good imitation of an obstacle course, with roots and upright stumps of felled trees littering the surface, while rotting fallen tree-trunks forced the driver to make detours.

Just behind the driver's cabin, I noticed two big metal drums, one on each side, with pipes attached top and bottom. Seeing my puzzled look, Mr Wasserman, an expert on all things mechanical, explained: 'This truck runs on wood gas made in those two cylinders. When it runs out of fuel, the driver just feeds it more wood. No shortage of that around here.' And sure enough, several times during the afternoon journey we stopped in a forest clearing, the two women got out, felled a tree, cut it up with saws and axes and chucked the bits of wood into the drums. It was the first time I witnessed tree felling, which was to become, so to speak, my daily bread. But was it really a job for a woman, I wondered.

It was also the first time that I saw cigarettes rolled in newspaper. At every stop, having replenished the cylinders, the two women sat down either on tree stumps or on the step of the driver's cabin, took out pouches of *makhorka*, an inferior kind of tobacco, in fact tobacco stalks and dregs, and deftly rolled their cigarettes in squares torn out of a newspaper. These cigarettes stank abominably and as I bent over the side of the truck to see better, the smoke stung my eyes. A punishment for being nosey.

We had little contact with our drivers. They were civil, even friendly, threw about just a few obscenities which, as we had already learned, were part of the daily conversation, not really meant to be offensive. Sayings like 'Fuck your mother' came naturally to most ordinary Russians and served to stress a point. Nothing personal, you understand.

After about six hours of the cross-country drive during which we had seen no human habitation, the lorry stopped just short of a small town or large village. Once more we were left with our belongings by a small wooden jetty on the bank of a river, this time with only one local militiaman on guard. An ancient rifle hung on a piece of string from his shoulder. A friendly soul, he told us that the river was called Uftyuga and the town's name was Petrakovo, that Petrakovo was the seat of the *Selsoviet*, or the rural council, and thus the administrative centre of the area. 'Tomorrow,' he concluded, 'you will go up the river, to *lesopunkt*, the forest station, Sloboda, and there you are going to live.' This expression, *zdes zhit budete*, was pursuing us and was getting on my nerves.

More trucks arrived in the course of the afternoon and deposited their human cargo in Petrakovo. By the evening two or three hundred people were camping on the riverside. We found ourselves in a group with the Wassermans, father and son, and several other couples and families: Mr and Mrs Żółtyński, Mrs Żółtyński's brother, Henryk, who was about my age, Mr and Mrs Brzeziński, Mr and Mrs Gruszyński and the Romer family.

As the crowd on the riverbank grew larger, the number of guards increased but never exceeded more than three or four, and they were local militiamen, not the NKVD. This and the absence of any guard during the truck journey was surprising. Also, puzzlingly, the village seemed dead. Occasionally a human form showed in the distance between the houses, but nobody came anywhere near us.

'This is a creepy place,' I said to Father. 'Deserted. And where are the NKVD guards?' I wondered aloud.

'We are now in NKVD country,'[*] he said. 'No guards are needed here. Escape is almost impossible. There are no roads, no footpaths, no public transport and no human habitation for hundreds of miles. Every village and town has its NKVD informers. Local people either act as informers or are so intimidated that they would be afraid to shelter you, give or sell you food or water, or help you in any way.'

Late in the evening two horse-drawn carts came to the riverbank, with *shchi*, or cabbage soup, *kipyatok* and bread. The bread was black, moist and heavy. But it was bread and, after a day without food, it was more than edible.

I must have slept like a log and did not even hear more lorries arriving during the night. By morning the crowd on the river-

---

[*] Later called *gulag* by Solzhenitsyn.

bank increased to about six hundred. In the early hours, as we were washing down the remains of last night's bread with fresh *kipyatok*, a dozen or so long narrow-boats arrived. Each boat was propelled by one man standing at the stern, wielding a long pole and driving it into the river-bed. Two more men materialised by the jetty. They were not in uniform, but the taller one in particular exuded an air of authority. He counted out several dozen people, which included our group. 'We shall walk with this first group,' he said. 'Put your belongings on the boats.'

The footpath ran along the river. 'We'll take it easy,' said the tall guide. 'It's forty-two kilometres to Sloboda,' he said. 'We should get there by tonight. White nights are good for walking,' he smiled. He looked at me. Did I imagine it, or did he wink?

But it was heavy going: the footpath was uneven and full of potholes, while projecting roots, rotting tree-trunks and stumps barred the path every few yards. We were a group of townies and not very good walkers. Mr Gruszyński had an enormous belly. He ought to have a wheelbarrow to carry it on, I thought unkindly. His puny wife was no support, so he had to be helped by others every few minutes. My mother was also on the heavy side and tired easily. In the following months, on the Siberian diet, all the fat people rapidly lost weight and, eventually, even Mr Gruszyński began to look respectable.

Again we were not guarded. The footpath was narrow and our long crocodile, at times in single file and at most two abreast, was headed by the taller of the two Russians and closed in the rear by the other. But they were not talkative. The friendliness the two men displayed at the start of our march evaporated. At some point Mr Romer managed to engage the leader in conversation. But all he learned was that his name was Volkov, that he and his companion were on the administrative staff of Sloboda, the forest settlement which was our destination, and that Sloboda consisted of two sections, Kvasha and Vasilyevo. It was also during that walk that we first heard the phrase, which we were to hear again and again over the subsequent two years and which, in my memory, will always be associated with life in the USSR. It was short, simple and to the point and in Russian it even sounds melodious: *Privýknete, a kak ne privýknete to podókhnete.* Roughly translated it means: You will get used to it or, if you won't, you will bite the dust.

The walk was uneventful. We continued along the river, usually just by the water's edge, holding onto overhanging branches here, crossing bogs and little streams over the slippery logs thrown across them there. Our feet in city shoes were saturated almost from the start. In spite of the hot summer the water was freezing cold. People generally helped each other. Father and I tried to keep near Mother who, at times, needed two pairs of helping hands. Our Russian guides did not hurry us and we rested every hour or so. What bothered us more than anything since leaving the train in Kotlas were the veritable clouds of insects. The long northern winter restricts the activity of insects to a brief period in the middle of the summer when they feed intensely, and now we were providing them with an easy meal. There were clouds of mosquitoes, hordes of ordinary flies and countless black midges which crowded into our eyes, noses and ears. The painful bites of some voracious black insects, each about an inch long, left rivulets of blood trickling down our legs, while the equally big but slimmer horseflies were also not averse to human flesh. Keeping the insects away was a full-time job, especially during rests. It required both hands and was so tiresome that after a few minutes we were eager to be up and moving, even without prompting from our two Russian leaders. There seemed to be no end to this interminable trek.

Then, after about ten hours, we stopped at the edge of a large forest clearing. From here the path went slightly downhill and deviated from the riverbank, to merge into a dirt-track, and then into a street passing between some twenty one-storey timber buildings of roughly the same shape but of various sizes.

'This is Kvasha,' said Volkov, adding the inevitable, '*Zdes zhit budete.*'

We stood there in silence contemplating the future. The prospect did not seem inviting. By no stretch of imagination could the place be described as picturesque, interesting, or pleasant. In fact, it was grey, drab and desolate. The clearing occupied by the settlement extended for about two hundred metres along the riverbank and was about a hundred metres wide. It was totally surrounded on three sides by the dark green wall of the forest from which it had been obviously wrenched by hard work. A similarly impenetrable dark line of forest blocked the view on the other side of the river. There was a column of smoke rising from a chimney of one of the buildings. The canteen? There was not a soul in view.

We had arrived.

Zdes zhit budete, here you shall live. Now, fifty-six years later, I can still hear Volkov's words, and their tacit implication: here you shall meet the end of your life.

SEVEN

SIBERIA – YOU WILL GET USED TO IT, OR ELSE . . .

✳

As we stood there on the higher ground at the edge of the forest Volkov repeated once more, '*Zdes zhit budete.*'

He stood silently, thoughtful for a while, and then continued, 'You don't know how lucky you are. When we were brought here twelve years ago this was virgin forest. We cleared it, pulled the roots out with our bare hands and built Kvasha where nothing stood before. Not many lived to see it finished.'

Kvasha – it was a peculiar name. I counted six long barracks and a dozen smaller huts huddled together in the clearing along the bank of the river. Not much of a place to spend the rest of my life in. But there was no barbed wire, no guard towers, no armed guards; perhaps we were lucky, at least we would have roofs over our heads. I had heard stories, and Volkov had confirmed them, of prisoners and of exiles like us, also euphemistically called 'free settlers', being brought, on foot and under guard, with their belongings strapped to their backs, to a place in the forest and left there to their own devices. They had to start by making the first small clearing, lighting the first fire, erecting a primitive shelter. Should the winter catch them unprepared, and Siberian winters are long and cold, few would survive to tell the tale.

A small group of people appeared on the path from the settlement. A reception committee? Apart from them the place seemed deserted. Did anybody live here? Surely they must, judging by the smoke coming from one of the chimneys.

Was it a canteen? Perhaps soup and bread were waiting for us? My mouth watered. I had learned to hope for at least one meal a day and the prospect kept me going.

In the next instance the 'reception committee' in the shape of several uniformed officers and civilians was upon us, giving me no more time to contemplate the view. One minute we stood there on the riverbank, at the edge of the forest, silent, tired, dispirited, and the next minute we parted like the Red Sea allowing a way through for the newcomers. Without shouting or pushing they divided us quickly and efficiently into two groups. Families and friends were allowed to stay together.

We found ourselves in the larger group with several of 'them' in the middle. One of the officers raised his arm. He said: 'Your friends in the other group will have to go further, to Vasilyevo, but you are lucky, you shall live here in Kvasha.'

First Volkov and now this man called us lucky. What had 'luck' got to do with our situation? I was about to share this thought with Father as the new Vasilyevians were already filing back into the forest with a couple of Russian civilians, but after a brief pause the officer continued: 'Here you shall live for the rest of your lives. Leave your luggage in the barracks and come to the meeting in front of the canteen. I shall then tell you about your work here.'

He paused again for a minute and stood still with his right arm raised as if waiting for the full weight of his words to sink in, and then he was off again: 'Single men and women and childless couples will live there, behind the canteen and the office.' The finger of his outstretched left hand pointed to a long barrack on the left side of the settlement's street. He waited a while until roughly half the group, headed by one of the civilians, moved off.

With a few gestures and not many words he separated another portion of the rapidly diminishing group, including us. 'You will live there,' he said pointing to another long barrack on the right side of the street, almost opposite the canteen. Shepherded by two men, we started on our way. I looked back. I could still hear him. He was now spreading his arms as if to embrace the remainder of the group. 'And you will live over there.' He pointed to another barrack on the right, next to ours. It took us just a few minutes to reach our new home. We dropped our bundles just inside the door and joined the crowd gathered around several officers outside the canteen.

The officers wore the usual bluish-grey Soviet uniforms and caps, but they had red stripes down their trouser legs and blue bands round their caps, NKVD men, I thought. This well-known acronym inspired fear. It stood for the National Committee of Internal Affairs, later changed to KGB, Committee of State Security. The hated 'bluecaps'.

The crowd was noisy. By now all the new arrivals were here, from grandfathers down to the youngest child still in its mother's arms.

Another bluecap emerged from the office accompanied by a couple of civilians. Most adults in the group were taller than me and I had to stand on my tiptoes and stretch my neck to see what was going on. One of the officers had three rectangles on his collar: a colonel. He raised his right arm, silence fell. He spoke calmly, in the polished Russian of an educated man. Even though my Russian was still limited, the gist of his speech was easy to follow: the settlement was called Kvasha and we would spend the rest of our lives here. We were brought to Kvasha to be re-educated into earning our living by honest toil.

These words were greeted with derision, shouts of 'Nonsense!' and a few laughs, as most of the deportees were artisans, factory workers, clerks, teachers, professional people, very few being 'exploiters of the working classes' such as businessmen or shopkeepers.

But, undismayed, he continued: 'The settlement staff will be your instructors. You will live by the basic tenet of socialism: he who does not work, does not eat.'

Then he spoke at length about the generosity of the Soviet government which took care not only of its citizens but also of foreigners, even if they were such enemies of the people as ourselves.

'You should be grateful,' he continued very loudly and with great emphasis, 'that the benevolent Soviet Government decided to ignore your foreign status and to extend to you the benefits of the great Stalinist Constitution and thus all the rights of Soviet citizens. Tomorrow you will have a free day to settle in your new dwellings and the following morning you will start work. You will be assigned your jobs by the Forest Station headman, Comrade Orlov, and his officials. You will be paid for your work and you will be able to buy your food in the settlement shop and in the canteen.'

Most of his speech had to be translated into Polish and this was done mainly by my parents and by several others who knew the language. At the end of his address the colonel asked for questions, and most of them concerned living and working conditions, wages and prices.

My father had only two questions to ask: 'I know,' he said, 'that the constitution guarantees every child the right to ten years of schooling. Will my son, who is fifteen, be able to attend school at the start of the term? And, as the constitution also guarantees everyone the right to work in one's speciality, will I be given work as a doctor?'

The colonel had no problem answering the questions: 'As to your first question, the answer is yes. As you rightly say, in the USSR everybody is entitled to ten years of schooling, but we have no school in Kvasha. The nearest school is in Petrakovo and your son would have to walk forty-two kilometres each way. Can we let him do that?' A dramatic pause followed. 'As to your second question,' he continued, 'as an intelligent man, you must realise that in every country, whether socialist or capitalist, a medical degree obtained abroad has to be validated, examinations have to be passed. As you well know it is a long process called *nostrifikatsya*.' He said the word slowly, almost letter by letter, with a vicious smile on his face.

'But that should be no problem,' countered my father. 'I graduated from Moscow University in 1914, when Poland was still part of Russia, and I have with me documents to prove it.'

The colonel's smile dissolved in a grimace. He was puzzled and, for once, at a loss for words. He thought for a moment, frowned and said 'I will have to think about that.' He walked back to the office, the meeting ended.

But his thinking process was exceedingly slow. Father was

given different types of manual work and was not appointed to the medical post until almost a year after our arrival in Kvasha.

❀ ❀ ❀

I would like to be able to describe our life in the settlement in a coherent way, day by day, but, as I kept no diary, this is impossible. Also, as is the privilege of youth, I lived my own life and only many years later, when I thought of our times in Siberia, did it strike me how ignorant I had been at the time of the sufferings of others and of the enormous difficulties of everyday life.

Couples, including newly married ones, lived in communal quarters. The old – and in those days people over fifty were 'old' – the disabled, even those simply not used to heavy physical work, must have found life very hard indeed. It was all piecework. There were no sickness benefits, no pensions, no social provisions of any kind. My father suffered ill-health in the USSR and was never to regain his strength; he died at the end of the war aged fifty-seven. My mother rapidly became an old woman, though after leaving the USSR she regained some of her previous vigour for a while; she died in London aged seventy-three.

As for me, I lost two years of formal schooling in Siberia, but I learned much which stood me in good stead in later life – hard manual work was not a bad introduction to adulthood. In the forest I managed to earn far more than my father and my earnings became an important element in our family budget. This gave me confidence and a feeling of self-worth.

I also fell in love in Kvasha for the first time. I am almost ashamed to admit it, but at times I enjoyed my time in Siberia.

❀ ❀ ❀

As the NKVD colonel disappeared into the office and the rest of the reception committee filed through the door after him, the meeting broke up into small groups. Exhausted after the long day, the ten-hour walk from Petrakovo, I only half-listened to the adults' discussion.

I may only have listened with half an ear, but both my eyes were firmly fixed on Helena Romer, who wandered sleepily and aimlessly nearby in the street. I had had my eye on Helena since the day before, when she jumped out of her wagon next to ours, after the train stopped by the Northern Dvina river. She was about my age and my height, she had dark brown hair, black dreamy eyes – with a very slight squint – a dark complexion, a small nose, full lips and a rather husky voice, not unlike Marlena Dietrich's.

My reverie was rudely interrupted by Mietek standing next to me. He nudged me in the ribs and whispered, 'Should we explore the barrack?'

'Okay,' I nodded, walked over to Helena and got hold of her arm. 'Let's explore our new home,' I said.

The long, rectangular barrack stood between the street and the river. Like all buildings in Kvasha it was a one-storey hut, built of rough logs stripped of bark and placed on top of one another, overlapping at corners. We walked all around it. It stood some fifteen paces from the riverbank, parallel to it, surrounded by rough grassy ground with a few bushes here and there. There was no other entrance to the barrack, so we returned to its only door.

The door was heavy and the hinges squeaked. We entered the hall which was littered with our hand luggage. Two corridors led out of the hall, one to the right and one to the left. We turned right first. We had been told we were lucky to have been assigned a barrack with family rooms; but had we been misled? The corridor was so narrow that, regretfully, I had to let go of Helena's arm. There were several doors on each side of the corridor. Each door led into a narrow room, much narrower than an old-fashioned third-class train compartment. Much of the room was taken up by an iron bedstead standing along one wall and leaving very little space between it and the other wall. The window opposite the door and above the end of the bed was about half-a-metre wide and a metre high.

We turned back to explore the other half of the barrack. Here the windowless corridor was wide enough for all three of us to walk abreast. It was about ten paces long and ended in a log wall. The wall on the left was also of bare logs, while the one on the right was made of whitewashed planks and had two doors. The first led into a good-sized room and the walls of the room were whitewashed. Opposite the door was a window which was about one-metre square, which looked over the river. The room was furnished with a small table, two wooden chairs and four iron bedsteads.

'Much more acceptable,' said Mietek.

Helena quickly claimed the room. 'Just right for us, but we will need at least one more bed.' The Romer family consisted of parents with four children, three girls and one boy. But there were no more beds available and eventually the family had to make do with four single beds.

The second door led into an almost identical whitewashed room, with a table, one chair and three bedsteads. A massive clay stove projected from the corridor in between the two rooms thus forming part of the wall between them. It was fed from the corridor and in the winter Helena and I would spend long evenings sitting on a log in the corridor, watching the flames, holding hands and talking, talking . . . But that was still to come.

A small family such as ours, or Mietek and his father, could not expect a room of their own. Mietek looked at me and I looked at Mietek. 'Should we share it?' I suggested.

'We shall not do any better . . .' he started saying, but steps in the hall and then voices at the door stopped him in mid-sentence. The meeting was breaking up and the future inhabitants of our barrack were joining us.

Helena's parents approved of her choice, while my parents and Mietek's father agreed to share the other room. But three single beds for five people was too much of a luxury. Another couple, Mr Brzeziński and his wife, were assigned to the room. My parents shared one bed, the Wassermans shared another and the third bed was taken by Mr Brzeziński and his wife. That left me not only without a bed, but also deprived of sufficient space for one. Here my upholstered narrow folding camp-bed, which we dragged along with us from Pińsk, came in useful. I thus became the only person in Kvasha who had a comfortable, soft bed of his own – even if it did have to be put up every night between the table and my parents' bed, under which it was stored for the day.

I was starving after the long day. As soon as we arrived in Kvasha, even before the meeting, I tried the door of the canteen. It was locked, but there was hope. A notice on the door said: bread and soup at 8 p.m. I often wondered how the grown-ups managed for hours and hours without food; I found it very difficult. Since we were snatched from our flat in Pińsk – was it only just over a week ago? – I was constantly hungry. I never got used to the feeling, but I learned to keep my mouth shut – even Father could not help. So, it would have to be 8 p.m. A long wait.

In the meantime there was still a lot to do. Our heavy bags, bundles and suitcases, including my camp-bed, had been brought by a flotilla of boats and had to be collected from the riverbank. In a shed by the office we found clean palliasse covers and straw to fill them. We unpacked our bedding and, with the beds made and covered, our room began to look habitable. Then Helena and her sister Magda came bringing two bunches of wild flowers gathered at the riverbank, one for their room and one for ours. Among our belongings Mother found a table-cloth, and with the flowers in a jar on a cloth-covered table, the overcrowded room turned into a home.

The remainder of that first evening in Kvasha was uneventful, except for our first meal in the canteen. We had soup and bread and tea; it was also the first meal since Pińsk for which we had to pay. As soon as we were back in our crowded room I dropped into bed and that was the end of the day for me. The white night did not keep me awake.

The next day started early. A meeting was called for 6 a.m. in *Krasnyi Ugolok*, or the Community Hall. As I was too young to work I did not have to attend. Afraid of missing breakfast, however, I was up early just the same.

With the last vestiges of modesty lost somewhere between Pińsk and Siberia, dressing and undressing in the presence of others of either sex came naturally. Modesty was restricted to hiding one's full frontal view from the public. My first job of the day was to fetch two buckets of water from the river. Our ablutions – we travelled with our own enamel bowl for the purpose – were rudimentary, but we still had soap and toothpaste left.

Breakfast was next. We joined the queue at the entrance of the canteen. Once inside, I had a good look round. The canteen was a large oblong hall with room for some two hundred people and it was crowded, there was hardly any room left on the wooden benches which flanked the long heavy tables, their planks polished by long use.

We joined another queue, this time at the end of the counter by the serving hatch. Chipped, heavy, white crockery plates were stacked on the counter next to a box with tin soup spoons. White enamelled mugs with blue handles and edges, also chipped, stood next to them. The 'menu' was chalked roughly on the blackboard by the hatch :

1. *Ovsyannaya kasha*, oat porridge – 30 kopecks
2. *Pshennaya kasha*, millet porridge – 1 rouble.

By the time we reached the counter the better *kasha* had been finished. I ordered a plateful of very thick oatmeal porridge and a mugful of tea. It was really a parody of porridge, a mess of badly husked boiled oat grains with a spoonful of oil in a crater on top. The only way to get rid of the husks was to spit them out, and a lot of spitting was going on – the floor was almost covered with the husks. But nothing could put me off food and, if spitting was the order of the day, I could spit as well as the next man. Actually, with the oil and some salt, the oat *kasha* was not too bad and very filling. It better be, I thought, though I did not yet know that it was to be our staple food for the next fifteen months.

We rounded off our meal with tea accompanied by our own bread. Mother had queued for our bread ration at the settlement shop before I woke up. The bread was heavy, clay-like in colour and consistency, and the daily ration for the three of us was a kilogram loaf or, as I soon worked out, twelve slices two and a half centimetres thick. At breakfast Father and I had a slice each to go with our tea. The 'tea' was brownish hot water with a remotely fruity taste and some unidentifiable, hard fragments floating in it. They also had to be spat out. Oh, well, if that is the custom . . .

As usual, Mr Wasserman was a mine of information: 'This tea substitute comes in half-kilogram packets and consists of crushed and compressed pips, stones and dried peel of various fruit. Real tea is always in short supply!' We knew that well enough by now. There was no sugar. In short supply too, no doubt.

Before long people started leaving the canteen in small groups to attend the meeting. My parents joined them and, soon after, I decided to explore the settlement on my own.

First, I discovered a small cabin with a big chimney out of proportion to the size of the building. I pushed the door but it was locked. Enigma number one.

Next to it was *kontora*, the office. Like all the buildings in Kvasha it was a one-storey hut, but unlike the others it had a small roofed-over porch with several steps leading up to it. Outside, a thermometer hung on the wall. It showed 20°C, but the scale ranged from +40°C to -40°C. Involuntarily, I shivered.

Then I came on to a round, shallow hole in the ground, some three or four metres in diameter, with two tall trestles inside it; enigma number two. Across the street from the hole was a barrack similar to ours. Further down the street and on the same side as the mysterious hole was a very long and wide barrack which resounded with neighing and stamping of horses, the stables. A man was stretched out on the sparse grass outside. Asleep? Gingerly, I opened the door, just a tiny bit.

'*Ty kuda?* Where do you think you are going?' The question was followed by loud swearing and stopped me in my tracks. By now I was used to the swearing, it was merely a way of stressing a point. The man sat up and angrily waved me away, I did not tarry.

Past the stables the settlement street petered out among several log cabins and smaller barracks, with a larger structure on the right. Loud voices were coming from it. The sign over the door read: *Krasnyi Ugolok*, the Community Hall. I turned back.

With the meeting still on, the Kvasha street was almost empty. I retraced my steps and passed between the canteen and our barrack. The next building was the shop-cum-bakery. Outside there was a queue of Russian women with coloured headscarves, the floral designs on them making the line look like a flower border. They smiled and waved to me. 'What's your name?' called a young woman.

'Stefan,' I said.

'Come here, Stefanooshka. Talk to us,' she smiled.

I smiled back, waved and said, 'Good morning.' They laughed and I blushed. I did not stop.

I came to the end of the street where it merged into a footpath rising up a low hill, the same hill from where, on our arrival, we had had our first view of Kvasha. Another path took me to a log cabin which I had not noticed the day before. The door was open and I looked in. There were benches and wide shelves all round the inside and a heap of large stones in a corner. Was it a *banya* or sauna, Russian style? I had never seen one.

I followed the path a little further. It came back to the main footpath on the bank of the river. Here the path to Petrakovo disappeared in the forest, but another one branched off to the right along the forest's edge. I followed it for a while, but turned back when it also disappeared among the trees, I had no intention of getting lost. This had to be the path to Vasilyevo taken by part of our crowd yesterday. I walked back to our barrack and found it was empty except for Helena and Magda, who were sitting in their room. Helena waved me in and I learned a little about the Romer family. They came from Piotrków Trybunalski, a town in central Poland, the seat of important law courts since medieval times. Mr Romer was a lawyer. There were four siblings: the oldest was Lala and the next was Olek (short for Alexander), they were both old, at least twenty, and university students. Helena and Magda were still 'children' and therefore, like me, not required to attend the meeting. Helena's fifteenth birthday was at the end of July while Magda was nearly fourteen. Helena was serious, rather melancholy and dreamy, while Magda was vivacious, giggly and had a twinkle in her eyes. They did not look like sisters at all. Helena was brunette and Magda was blonde. Magda, though younger, was taller than Helena; she was also taller than me. I preferred Helena.

We were talking about nothing in particular when my parents returned from the meeting, accompanied by Mr and Mrs Romer, Mietek and his father and the Brzezińskis. For no obvious reason I took an instant dislike to the Brzezińskis. In time my instincts proved right, but more about that later.

It was almost lunch-time and because my behaviour was still

controlled by my stomach rather than by my heart, I left the
company of the two girls to explore the situation in the canteen.
There was a long queue at the door. Mother decided that, as
most of our bread ration for the day was still intact and as we
still had some real tea left, we would have a meal in our room.
Others joined us and I was sent out to put the kettle on.

But the operation was not at all as simple as it sounded. We
had a primus stove, a treasured possession, but it was not much
use without kerosene. The kitchen stove in the hall was cold,
empty and dark. I needed matches, kindling and firewood.
Matches were scarce and our last box was only half full, there
was no spare paper to get the fire going.

But there was an axe leaning against the stove. And outside
the barrack door there was a stack of logs for firewood. I stood
a small log on top of a bigger one and chopped it up, it was easy.
The wood was birch, with silvery-white bark. Here and there
the bark was peeling and paper thin and dry. Large strips came
off easily and burned beautifully. I only had to use one match
and in minutes I had the fire going and the water boiling. Later,
I learned that birch bark had been used by the Siberians for
years as kindling, as writing material, for making sandals and
for many other purposes.

With the kettleful of boiling water in my hand, very proud of
myself, I returned to our room, where everybody else was busy
eating and taking part in a lively conversation. Sitting as and
where they could, my mother on our only chair and the rest on
beds, munching dry bread, the room-mates and neighbours
were speculating about the next day, their first working day in
Kvasha. Mietek and his father were assigned to one of the forest
brigades. My father, because of his age – he was fifty – was
assigned to *konopatka* and *obmazka* in a newly erected, but not
quite finished, barrack in Kvasha itself. The words meant
'caulking' and 'coating' respectively, but nobody in the room
had the faintest idea what the job entailed. Even our engineering
expert, Mr Wasserman, could throw no light on the subject.

And then Father turned to me: 'Mother was assigned to a
forest brigade. I could not allow it. I am sorry, but it means that
you will have to go to work in her place. On this condition they
agreed to leave Mother alone. One of the senior bosses still has

to agree, but this is a formality. Because of your age you will work only a six-hour day. I am sorry . . . I am sorry . . .' Father kept repeating, visibly upset.

'Never mind,' I said. 'Honestly, Father, I am glad that you did it. I was wondering what I would do here all day long. Really, I don't mind the slightest bit.' Mother had tears in her eyes. She hugged me and I was embarrassed, but not too much. I felt grown up and, suddenly, it was all right to be hugged by my mother, even in public.

'I hoped that you would take it that way,' continued Father. 'I don't know about other youngsters, but Mr Romer made the same kind of bargain. Helena will also start work tomorrow in place of her mother. Orlov, the headman, promised us,' he looked at Helena's father, 'that both of you will be given easy jobs.'

I was glad when Mother changed the subject. 'There is something peculiar about this man, Orlov. With his looks and bearing I would take him for a scion of an aristocratic family, or a tsarist army officer. He neither looks nor behaves like a peasant or a Bolshevik.'

'Catherine the Great had a Count Orlov for a lover,' I said, showing off.

'Common enough name,' continued Mother. 'But there is something about him. Perhaps he was spared one way or another in the Revolution and was then exiled? I knew a student, Sasha Orlov, in Kharkov, at the university,' she reminisced.

The possible antecedents of the headman of Kvasha remained a subject of speculation throughout our stay in Siberia. His poise and his relatively good manners, his calm and cultured voice, his most extraordinary abstinence from the use of swear-words, placed him head and shoulders above most Russians of our acquaintance.

As we were all talking about our unknown tomorrows, Mr Brzeziński and his wife remained very reticent about their work assignments. They volunteered nothing. But Mr Wasserman could not restrain his curiosity: 'Which work brigade are you joining tomorrow?'

'Oh no, I am not going into the forest,' said Mr Brzeziński.

We all looked at him. He was in his thirties, not lame, not blind, nor in any other obvious way disabled. Why should he not work in the forest like other able-bodied men of his age group?

'He who does not work does not eat,' Mr Wasserman repeated the tenet of socialism. 'I suppose you got a better job?' he added.

Mr Brzeziński could not keep quiet any longer. 'I got an office job,' he said. 'They need a book-keeper.'

'And what about you?' Mr Wasserman continued the interrogation by turning to Mrs Brzeziński. She said nothing and looked askance at her husband, who immediately came to her rescue.

'I also made a bargain with Orlov,' he said. 'I consented to work in the office, providing my wife would be left alone.'

Was he doing them a favour by *agreeing* to work in the office? Puzzling. For a while nobody said a word, then Father touched my shoulder. 'Let's go for a walk,' he said.

When we reached the bank of the river and put some distance between us and the barrack, Father looked back and said: 'Brzeziński must have agreed to become an informer. We have to be careful in his or his wife's presence. In Siberia you do not get a cushy office job without reason and the usual reason is that you agree to inform on others.'

It was exciting stuff. An informer? Almost a spy! I have never known a real spy.

We walked for a few minutes in silence. The path continued along the river. The forest was deadly quiet. I looked back. We could be alone in the world, Father and I, as the settlement disappeared behind the solid dark green wall of the forest.

I was still puzzled: 'What is he going to inform about? Should one of us say that Stalin is up to no good, or that this whole country is one big prison, for instance, what can they do? They can't send us to Siberia. We are here already.'

'They could send one to a strict-régime labour camp, or to prison. Not many survive either. Anyway, I am sure that they want to know what people think, on principle. We might conspire, form groups, plan an escape. Control of people's minds is the nature of the totalitarian state and the basis of its existence.'

Father stopped to light a cigarette and continued: 'We call this

Siberia.' His left hand made a semi-circle in front of us. 'Perhaps strictly speaking this is not quite true, but in a way it is. Siberia is not just a term out of a geography book applied to northern Asia, it also means a place of internal exile. Here we are still in Europe, not in geographical Siberia, but it is certainly a place of exile, it is the political Siberia.' He grew silent again. 'Do you know that your great-grandfather just missed being sent here some eighty years ago?'

That was news to me. My maternal great-grandfather died in the mid-1930s and I remembered him well.

'He took part in the failed January 1863 rising against the Russians. His unit was ambushed, some of them died fighting and most of the survivors were exiled to Siberia. Several youngsters, he was among them, were allowed to buy their freedom, the families paying with their country estates. Feeling responsible for the impoverishment of his family, he took to the bottle. Somehow his health did not suffer and he lived to see his ninety-sixth birthday. Do you remember, he had the red nose of an alcoholic. But he was a nice old boy really.'

It was an interesting piece of family history. I had liked him. I remembered his last birthday. He lived in Warsaw, but some summers spent several weeks in our house in Otwock. He had taught me to play chess, he would even play cards with me when nobody else would. I was always intrigued by his red nose, enlarged by a growth on its side. As a little boy I thought that he had two noses.

Father inhaled deeply the fragrant smoke of one of his last Kazbek cigarettes. I was not a little confused. A thousand questions came to my mind. How long would we be here for? What about school? What about trying to escape? Did Father like Helena?

But there was no point asking. There were no answers. And it was still too soon for the last question.

We sat on a fallen tree-trunk in silence until Father finished his cigarette and we retraced our steps to the barrack.

The rest of our last free afternoon was taken up by settling in and making the best of our living conditions. Suitcases and boxes were placed under the beds, in the corners of the room, or heaped in the corridor. The evening was warm and still bright well into the white night. Once more we joined the canteen queue. The menu offered a much greater choice than the night before.

Encouraged by Father, I had the most expensive item on the menu: *Myasnoi soop*, meat soup. It was really good, there were large chunks of fatty meat, cubes of potato and pieces of vegetables. We brought the remainder of our bread ration with us and I used the crust to wipe off the yellowish fat from the rim of the plate right down to the last droplet. Next I had a plateful of the wheat cereal with oil on top. Well salted, it was eminently edible.

That finished, I had no more bread left to clean the plate with. But my mother was watching me and gave me a crust of her bread which she had probably saved for me.

I resolved to be more careful in the future and always leave a crust to the end of the meal to polish the plate with. I never wasted food again in my life. I did not see anybody actually licking the plate. Some people wiped it with their fingers and then licked them. But licking the plate was: *Ne kulturno*, not done. Vestiges of proper behaviour had to be observed.

EIGHT

HE WHO DOES NOT WORK
DOES NOT EAT

✳

I couldn't sleep that second night in Kvasha. Was the prospect of starting my working life next morning keeping me awake? The absence of darkness in the land of white nights did not help.

At last I went to sleep, only to wake up almost immediately to the sound of banging doors and shouts of, '*Davay podvigaysya* – Get a move on!' Half awake, I looked up. Volkov, the man who had led us here from Petrakovo, was standing at the door. 'Get a move on, get moving!' he kept shouting. And then he pointed at me: 'Report to me in the forest. You will do the marking.' It was 5 a.m. Work was to start at 7 a.m., but our working site was an hour's march from the settlement. '*Markirovka*, marking,' was what he said, but in the context of the forest the word meant nothing to me.

In the canteen, over breakfast of oats and the so-called tea with dry bread, my job was discussed at length, but nobody knew what it actually entailed. 'You will be marking time, no doubt,' joked Mietek, my supposed friend. 'They've got the measure of you right away,' he laughed. I sulked for a while.

Soon we were off. It was a cloudless sunny morning, the air was cool and crisp and, once my sulking mood evaporated, I started to enjoy the walk. In small groups we followed a well-trodden path. There were a few Russians among us, but there was little mixing on that first day. The Russians were curious about the outside world of which they knew nothing, but they were also mistrustful, and not without reason. Leg pulling was a favourite occupation of our smart alecks. On this particular morning Mietek was in a teasing mood. He spoke reasonable Russian and engaged in conversation one of the locals walking in a separate group next to ours. I didn't listen until I heard Mietek asking a supposedly innocent question: 'Can you get oranges in the Soviet Union?'

'Not yet,' answered the man. And then, convinced of the omnipotence of the Party, he added: 'But they are building an orange factory in Arkhangelsk and soon we will be able to get them.' Mietek roared with laughter and we all joined in. The Russians ignored us the rest of the way, quite rightly, I thought.

I walked with Mietek. He had been given the job of team leader. Helena was not with us. She walked with her family group; there were four Romers going to work. At the working site Helena and I reported to Volkov and were told to wait while he took the forest teams, with their Russian instructors, one by one, each to their working strip or *poloska*. Then Helena was called to join one of the teams. For a long time I sat on a tree stump waiting, bored stiff. At last Volkov came back: '*Poidyom*, Let's go.'

We crossed the forest working sites and then followed a rough track with deep irregular ruts. After a ten-minute brisk walk we came to a riverside clearing. Here, heaps of timber were scattered helter-skelter along the riverbank. Several Russians were busy building them into stacks, each stack stretched down from the raised bank of the river to a little way beyond the water's edge. They worked in pairs, one pair per stack. Using sturdy sticks, about a metre long, as levers, they pushed the logs one by one from the trackside on to the stacks. One of them leaned on his stick. 'What's your name?' he asked. I told him. 'Ah, *Stepanooshka. Noo, ladno* – okay then.'

All this time Volkov did not say a word. We went to the end of the entire row of at least twenty timber stacks and stopped by the last one. Here Volkov broke the silence: 'These stacks are complete. You will measure accurately the diameter at the thin end of each log and mark it accordingly. Let's get your tools.' He searched for a while among the timbers and gave me a wooden ruler eighty centimetres long and three heavy metal hammers with the digits zero to nine prominently embossed on the sides of their square heads. 'You hit the log's end with whatever side of the hammer is required to mark it,' he said.

And that was that. 'I will return later,' said Volkov and left. It took me several minutes to figure out what I was supposed to do. But soon I got the knack of it. At their thin ends most logs had a diameter of twenty to forty centimetres and thus I marked the end of a 25-centimetre log with digits 2 and 5, for instance, or a 32-centimetre one with digits 3 and 2. Each stack consisted of some twenty layers of parallel logs laid on top of one another with two thin, long timbers separating the individual layers. Sitting on top of the stack, I measured and marked the top layer and the one below it without any difficulty. To deal with the third layer, however, I had to lie flat on my belly on top of the stack.

Then the problems started. Some of the logs protruded from the stack, so that sitting on the ends I was able to mark a few surrounding ones. But when all the ends were flush the job was difficult. The Russian workers were too far away to be asked for advice. Anyway, I had to do it myself, I had to think.

I needed a piece of wood to push between any two adjacent layers of the stack. I got down from the stack. I did not have to search for long. A piece which looked like a lever that had been left behind by the stack builders served my purpose admirably. Wedged securely between the logs of the stack it gave me a perch to sit on and I was able to mark the log ends within reach. But then I had to move the perch; this involved some acrobatics. I secured my tools between the timbers and holding on to a log with my left hand, with my toes wedged between the ends of the timbers, I moved the perch to another location with my right hand. I had to repeat this manoeuvre every few minutes.

There were moments of excitement. As part of the base of the stack extended into the water, at times my perch was a good three or four metres above the cold Siberian river; I did not fancy another plunge like the one in Kotlas. My acrobatics must have been something to behold, but I had no audience to applaud me. Other hazards, even more difficult to avoid, were hitting my fingers with the hammer and getting splinters in my hands and, even more awkward, in my behind. With my hands busy, swarms of insects, big and small, all greedy for a meal, were difficult to ward off.

About noon one of the Russians working on the stacks called me: 'Stepanooshka, Stepanooshka, lunch-time.' Like other Slavonic peoples Russians tend to use diminutives for first names, thus in Kvasha I got used to being called either Stepanooshka or Stefanooshka. It sounded friendly and I liked it.

The break was welcome. We walked together back to the forest working site. My new mates wanted to know all about me, about my family, about the place I came from. But their ignorance of the outside world was abysmal. They asked: 'Is Warsaw as big as Petrakovo?' It was not easy for them to grasp that the capital of Poland with a population of one and a quarter million was immensely bigger than their nearest administrative centre with its two miserable streets and possibly 1,000 or 2,000 inhabitants. I did not laugh. I tried to describe the streets and houses of a big town. Before the war Warsaw boasted of its first 'skyscraper', all of sixteen storeys high. They were too polite to call me a liar, but quite obviously they did not believe me.

At last we reached the clearing where the forest teams and their Russian instructors were sitting in groups having their lunch.

Lunch in the forest consisted of hot soup and *kipyatok*. The soup was brought in a big cauldron mounted on a sledge drawn by an old and very phlegmatic chestnut horse. On the same sledge, next to the cauldron, sat a big urn with *kipyatok* from which we could help ourselves to our heart's content. The soup was ladled out by one of the canteen staff into whatever container one had. Lunch at work was free, a second helping was even on offer, but on this hot midday very few people wanted it, though I certainly did.

At first the place was quiet, except for the slurping and champing. Good table manners had long been forgotten. With the first hunger gone, we became more sociable. Meanwhile there were other noises coming from the group of our Russian instructors. The giant eructations were, for a working-class Russian, a sign of satiety, an appreciation of the meal.

Having finished their lunch, smokers brought out their

makhorka pouches and rolled cigarettes in squares of newspaper. By then I was used to the reek of the tobacco dregs, but anyway we did not linger. Even before the lunch break was over people, keen to earn more money, started drifting back to work. So did I, without waiting for my neighbours, the Russian stack builders. I did not feel like facing more questions.

The track leading to the stacking area was deserted. The forest was silent; you could just hear the distant noise of axes driven into tree-trunks, of saws singing, of horses neighing and snorting. The trees on either side of the track cast a pleasant shade and in the cool semi-darkness the insects were less greedy.

I recovered my tools, steadied my perch and started on the next layer of logs. I was halfway down my second stack. The rest of my first working day passed quickly and without mishap. In the early afternoon Volkov came by and, satisfied with my output, recorded a day's pay next to my name. I was to be paid by the day, provided I had fulfilled the norm. On this first day I earned over three roubles, enough for three helpings of the best kind of *kasha* in our canteen, or for one helping of the meat soup and my daily ration of bread. My pay-packet was to come at the end of the week.

As Helena was not in evidence, I set out to walk home alone. And then a thought struck me. Home, had Kvasha become 'home'? It was a disturbing thought.

I did not mind walking through the forest on my own. The months in overcrowded flats, rooms and cattle-wagons had taught me to enjoy solitude. The path was easy to follow. In this very sparsely populated land there were no crossroads, so there was little chance, at least in the summer, of getting lost.

The forest was not dangerous. There were bears and wolves in the depth of it, but they did not venture near human habitations. It was also very peaceful. Occasionally something moved in the forest. A small animal? A distinct flutter of wings. A bird? Some of these birds were very large and noisy. I could only glimpse them here and there between the trees. I knew neither their Polish nor their Russian names. No, in the summer the forest was not frightening at all.

As a matter of fact, after the first few days, I was never quite alone on my way home. There were about a dozen stray dogs in

Kvasha. They were not used to kind treatment and after I befriended them, they reciprocated. From the time of my arrival in the settlement I took to saving scraps of food: bones, bits of pork rind too hard to chew, chunks of stale or mouldy bread, heads of dried fish, and I fed them to my friends. A Russian peasant has little sentiment for animals and a careless dog is more likely to get kicked than fed. The stray dogs were left to fend for themselves. They often held vigil by the rubbish bins at the back of the canteen. Soon they began to follow me all the way to work and back, some stayed with me by the timber stacks. I became known as the *Psi tata*, or dogs' dad in Polish. One could have a worse nickname, I suppose.

I worked with my measuring rod and hammers for several weeks. Fulfilling the norm was easy. With little effort I could have done it in four, instead of the officially allotted six, hours. As, unlike the forest workers who were on piecework, I was paid a daily rate, there was no reason why I should try to exceed the norm, so I did not hurry. I was not brazen enough to bring a book to read and I was careful not to appear idle. Out of sight of the others, stretched on my back in the sun, I would swing my hammer against the logs from time to time thus broadcasting how busy I was.

The short summer was beautiful. The air was warm, even hot, for the few hours in the middle of the day, the sky a cloudless blue. What spoiled my honeymoon with the Siberian forest were the millions of small flies which piled into my eyes, my ears, my nose and mouth.

One morning I had a surprise. As I was setting out for work, Mother handed me a big wide-brimmed hat with a long veil hanging all round the brim. It was made from an old pillowcase, the veil was a length of old net curtain stitched around the rim. Where my mother had procured the wire for the frame to give it shape, I could not guess. People turned green with envy. My hat kept even the smallest flies away but it did not obstruct my vision. In the next few days similar hats were paraded by others in the forest, but mine remained the perfect prototype. Anyway, the season lasted only several weeks and suddenly the insects were no more.

Soon I had another surprise. One evening in the canteen I

The house in Otwock
ABOVE: the view from the street
BELOW: the view from the garden

The author with his parents and
friends in Otwock, 1939
LEFT: the author's brother, 1939

<u>С П Р А В К А</u>

На основании указания НКВД СССР и директивы

Наркома Внутренних Дел БССР от 6/1У- а № 1/1767

<u>Вайденфельд Вольф-Владислав Мойшев 1890</u> года рождения,

проживавший/ая/ <u>гор. Пинск</u> Пинск.обл.

бы ла выселена Управлением НКВД по Пинской области, как

беженка б.Польши, непринятая Г нией

ЗАМ.НАЧАЛЬНИКА УНКВД ПИ ..АСТИ
Капитан Государствен.Безо. .-
/ФУКИН/

Протокол обыска

1940 года 29 июня г. Пинск.

Я инспектор Ало УРКМ НКВД по Пинской обл. Жидко П.В. произвел обыск в присутствии работника Р.К.М. т. Козак Г.Н. и хозяйки дома гр-ки Маргоши Броха Файвелевна произвел обыск у квартире гр-нина Вайденфельда Вольф-Влодислова Мойсеевич проживающего по ул. Некрасова № 2 При обыске обнаружено 40 (сорок) злотых польского серебра в монетах три по десять злотых и две монеты по пять зла. В чем и составлен настоящий протокол обыска.—

инспектор Ало УРКМ Жидук /Жидко/

свидетели { участ.упол. 2го отд. РК
Б.Маргош .ш/.

ABOVE: the deportation order based on the orders of the NKVD and dated 6 April 1940
LEFT: the report of the search of our flat at 2 Nekrasov Street, PiÒsk, 29 June 1940

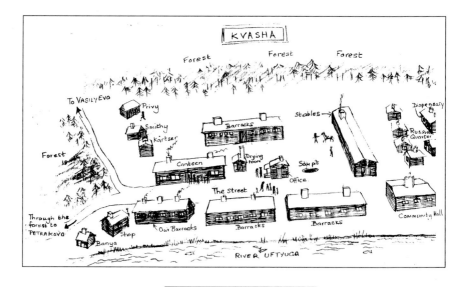

ABOVE AND OPPOSITE: drawings of the settlement at Kvasha

LEFT: the plan of our barrack

A Our room
1 My parents' bed
2 Brzezińskis' bed
3 Wassermans' bed
4 My camp-bed
5 Table
6 Chair
B Romers' room
C Entrance hall
D Cubicles for single people and some couples

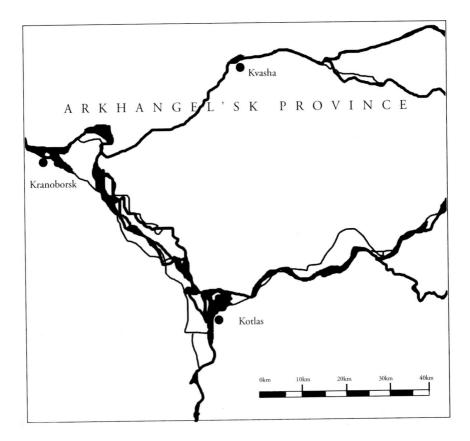

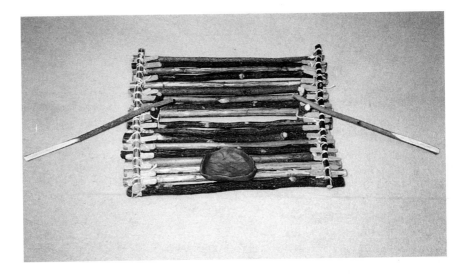

ABOVE: the River Uftyuga from Kvasha to Krasnoborsk
BELOW: a model of the raft that we built to leave Kvasha

A drawing of the log sledge

OPPOSITE: Helena, 1947

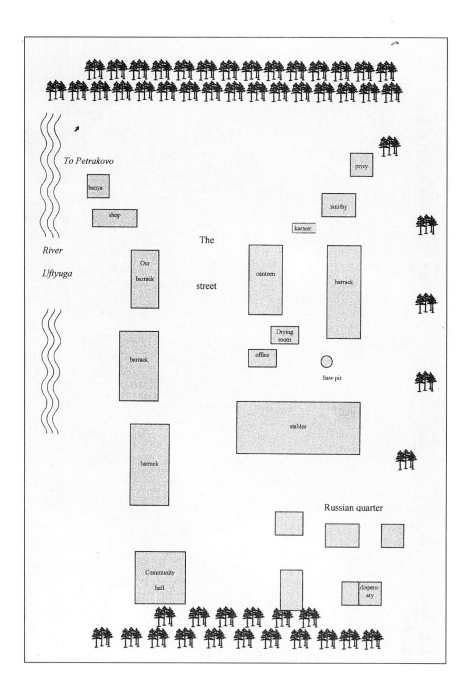

happened to sit next to Mr Rosen who lived with his wife in one of the cubicles in the other half of our barrack.

With his mouth full Mr Rosen mumbled something in Polish or in Russian. Did he speak to me? With all the slurping and smacking noises coming from his direction I could not quite get his meaning. And then I pricked up my ears. Did I hear the word *horse*?

Mr Rosen stopped eating, turned his head to me and said clearly and unmistakably in Polish: 'Would you like to take my horse to the forest for me?'

This was a very interesting proposition. I didn't even have to think, I jumped at the chance. 'I would, indeed.' I had never ridden a horse before, except a fairground pony, but in Otwock I had been quite familiar with our horse, I helped to look after the animal and we had liked each other.

Father, sitting on my other side, intervened. 'Why do you want Stefan to ride your horse?' he asked. Mr Rosen went into a long-winded explanation. As at the same time he was stuffing his mouth with *kasha*, it was difficult to make out what he was saying, but the gist of it was that he had registered his occupation as wagoner. Consequently he had been assigned to this job in the forest and wasn't happy with it.

'I was a horse-dealer,' said Mr Rosen, 'but that would have made me a capitalist, so I told them that I was a wagoner. A good proletarian occupation. Bloody hell . . .' He was very upset. Gossip had it that Mr Rosen had been a horse-thief, not a horse-dealer, but perhaps this was malicious gossip.

'All my life I had been afraid of the bloody beasts,' he continued, 'and I had never ridden one until they got us to this godforsaken place. I shake like a leaf every morning when I am to mount that damned mare. She is still feeding her foal and I have a job to get her going at all. Anyway, I am too heavy for her. She never tires of trying to get rid of me and last night, on the way back, she succeeded. Luckily I did not break my neck, although my bum and leg hurt like hell. But once I get her between the shafts of the sledge in the forest, I am all right.' He went back to his *kasha*. 'Bloody nag,' he mumbled. 'She is also supposed to be back in the stables early to feed her foal and I miss a full-day's pay.'

Mr Rosen was tall and still very fat and far too heavy for a small Siberian mare. There was little love lost between him and his mount. Father smiled. I looked at him hoping that he would agree, he liked horses and had done a lot of riding in the army during the First World War. He turned to me. 'Do you want to try it?' he asked.

'Oh yes, please!'

'All right,' said Father.

Mr Rosen's workmate was a beautiful mare. She was coal-black and her name was *Zhemchuzhina* – Pearl. All the Kvasha horses had proper names.

Some two weeks previously Zhemchuzhina had given birth to a black colt, but the Kvasha horses had a hard life and she was already back at work in the forest. However, in the afternoon she had to feed her foal. Volkov had no objection to my riding Zhemchuzhina home while Mr Rosen stayed in the forest to do other work to boost his day's pay.

Now, bareback riding through the Siberian forest was a very special experience. Mine was magnified by the fact that my mount was a young, energetic mare, eager to get back to her offspring. No wonder, she was dripping milk all the way to the stables.

My first morning's ride to work was not particularly memorable. The mare needed encouragement to leave the stables but presented no problems afterwards. At the working site I passed her on to Mr Rosen. In contrast, my first journey back to Kvasha was a hair-raising experience and I almost paid dearly for the presumption with which I mounted the horse. My presumption was that Zhemchuzhina was just a mindless conveyance. But she did have a mind of her own, at present totally driven by her maternal preoccupation.

Siberian horses are small and, with Mr Rosen holding the bridle of the impatient mare, I got on a tree stump and from it on to Zhemchuzhina's back with no difficulty. But, as soon as he let go, the mare was off. She went like a whirlwind. She obviously knew her way to the stables. She also knew shortcuts through the forest and she did not care about me. I held on to the reins as if they were a life-belt and not something I was supposed to control her with. There was no doubt whatsoever who was in charge. I hung on to Zhemchuzhina's mane for dear life, lying practically flat on her back and neck to save myself from hitting the ground below and from being hit by the branches above. She was totally unmoved by my precarious position and, had I not taken my precious hat off, I would have lost it, possibly my scalp with it, in the first few seconds. She covered the six kilometres back to the stables with the speed of a racehorse.

The stable was a long log barrack. Its low outside door opened into the central passage with boxes on either side. The routine was for the rider to dismount outside and to pass the reins to the stable man. But Zhemchuzhina chose to ignore the procedure; she did not even slow down before bolting through the door. I dropped the reins and my hat at the last moment and just managed to grab the ledge above the entrance. I remained hanging by my hands for a moment and then dropped to my feet. What saved me, however, was the manner of riding in Kvasha; with no saddle and no stirrups to hold me, I just slid off the horse's back and avoided decapitation by the door frame. The whole episode was over in a few seconds, nobody had seen the mishap and I said nothing to my parents. Frightened, but at the same time exhilarated by it all, I was certainly not giving up riding.

Next day, nervous but hiding it well, I rode Zhemchuzhina to work and back again. This time, knowing what to expect, I was better able to protect my head and hat, and I enjoyed the wild gallop home. Approaching the stable, I managed to jump off the mare's back just in time.

From then on rarely did I have to walk to work in our early weeks in Kvasha. I was in demand as a substitute rider and was only too keen to oblige. In the early afternoon I was often requested to take home either a pregnant or a recently foaled mare, a horse partly disabled or too young to work all day, while the driver stayed in the forest for the rest of the working day. I became an addict of this wild riding.

One of my mounts was called Misha. He was squat, short in the leg, but long in the tooth, a wise and wily old beast. And just as well, as, at the time, our way to work led through a swamp, a truly treacherous bog. Its grass-covered surface was deceptive.

Stretches of solid land were indistinguishable from patches of 'man-eating' swamp. Our Russian friends delighted in telling us stories about people sucked in by the mud. It was scary.

I quickly learned to give Misha free rein. He was sure-footed, cunning and knew exactly where to place his feet. Here he walked with all his four legs on a half-rotten log almost hidden in the grass and mud, there he stepped from one low stump to another. After several trips I got used to the swamp and learned to rely fully on Misha's good sense, but I was very glad, and so perhaps was Misha, when we were transferred to another part of the forest which was reached by a dry path.

Misha was also a crafty and stubborn animal and he refused to hurry under any circumstances. His driver at the time was my old friend Mr Rosen, and I often observed the pair at work, either on my way to or from lunch. With his sledge loaded, nudged by his driver to move off, Misha would first look back and examine the load. Should the result of the scrutiny not be to his liking, he would just refuse to move and no amount of swearing or cajoling would change his mind. Mr Rosen was a big strong man but, like many such men, he was rather faint-hearted. Whenever, in desperation, Mr Rosen dared to pick up a branch or a stick to hit the horse with – there were no whips in the settlement – watchful Misha would give him such a look that his raised arm would drop. He had to lighten the load and then off went Misha without further delay.

Later, when our people got used to working with horses, my 'transport' became scarce. In addition, after several weeks on the log-marking job on the stacks, I was moved to lumbering proper. My riding career was short, but it was fun while it lasted.

Now, I can just see myself cantering to work in the morning, well ahead of the others, or galloping all by myself with my veil flapping in the wind. My headgear was a far cry from a cowboy hat, but it was easy to imagine myself as *Old Shatterhand, Winetoo the Redskin Gentleman, Hawkeye, the Last of the Mohicans*, or some other hero from the pages of Fenimore Cooper, Karl May or Mayne Reid. I was usually followed by my pack of stray dogs. Out of the hearing of my compatriots, I sang, not quite in tune but very loudly, Polish or Russian popular hits, folk tunes and soldiers' songs. I also loved to recite Polish poems, of which I had a good store, or newly learned Russian ones, or the Latin and French verses learned at Otwock school.

In spite of my 'go-slow' tactics at my marking job, after several weeks I ran out of work. I finished the last complete stack and was lazing in the afternoon sun when Volkov appeared. 'Tomorrow, Stefan, you will go to the forest.' To do what? Questions crowded to the tip of my tongue, but it was no use, Volkov was a man of few words.

Next morning I walked to work with Mietek. He was a tree feller and the team leader. Yesterday his cutter left for another work brigade and I offered myself as the replacement. Volkov had no objections, but my six-hour working day was a problem. However, I could be quick when I chose to and the brigade agreed to take me on probation.

A forest area destined for felling was divided into long and narrow strips. Each team had its own strip, or *poloska*. A team usually consisted of four men and two women. The feller, who doubled as team leader, selected and cut down the trees one by one. The felled tree was then set upon by the two axe-wielding females who cleared off its branches and stacked them into heaps to be burned in the winter. The cutter's job was to cut the branchless tree-trunk into standard-length logs. The logs had to be pushed to the sides of the *poloska*, leaving the central passage clear for the sledge, or *volokooshe*. This was done by the orderly who also helped the driver, the sixth team member, to load the logs by their thick ends onto the sledge, to be dragged to the riverside for stacking.

Our team leader was Mietek, the orderly was Daniel Żółtyński, our two branch cutters were Daniel's wife, Rita, and Lala Romer, Helena's sister. Our driver was Mr Rosen. Mietek was, of course, my room-mate and all the other members of the team also lived in our barrack. I became a cutter. My new tools were a string-saw, an axe, an indelible blue pencil, a two-metre long wooden ruler and two sturdy sticks, or *styagi*, to be used as levers. I had to plan the cuts with care, so as to minimise waste. Mietek quickly showed me how. The required length of the log depended on the kind of tree, its thickness and total length and its likely use: pulping for paper, as building material, for furniture-making, or for ship and aircraft building. We were paid by the cubic metre of usable timber produced and accepted by the master forester at the end of the working day; any waste meant less pay for the team.

I soon learned to plan my cuts and to place the tree-trunk in the right position for sawing, so that the saw would not get jammed. This meant a lot of dragging and lifting of timbers with the axe driven into their ends, and manoeuvring with the levers. Often it was simpler to lift one end of the trunk with both hands and place it over a suitable support. I never knew before how strong I was!

As I still had to return home in the early afternoon – my parents would not hear of my working a full day – at the end of the first working day our strip was littered with uncut, bare tree-trunks, not enterable in the pay sheet. However, the next morning I found a horse to ride and reached our working site well before the others. That gave me time to deal with the backlog before the new day's production started piling up. One way or another, by lunch-time I usually caught up with the team's output and, except for the first day, our pay did not suffer.

In 1940 the winter was late in coming. In the middle of October the days were getting perceptibly shorter, but the afternoons were still sunny and warm. Also, with cool mornings and evenings the insects were gone, wherever insects go to at that time of year, and I did not need my hat any more. This was just as well as by that time it was falling to pieces. Worried about a hat for the next summer, one evening I mentioned it to my mother and was very surprised when tears welled up in her eyes. Only later it dawned on me that the thought of another year in Siberia meant something quite different to her than it did to me.

A daily routine became established and the days went quickly by. The concept of a free weekend did not exist in the USSR and Saturday was an ordinary working day. We also had to 'volunteer' for work most Sundays. I became quite good at my job and my team was always high on the earnings list. My weekly pay-packet was much bigger than my father's.

One early afternoon I had a particularly tall and thick tree to

cut. I marked the cuts and started with the thin end. I cut the
first two logs with the string-saw, but the lower part of the
trunk was too thick for the string-saw and I needed help. Mr
Żółtyński, our orderly, was working nearby. He was only about
twenty-five, but an adult and a married man. He could call me
Stefan, but I had to call him Mr Żółtyński. Our world was still
very formal.

'Mr Żółtyński, would you please help me with the broadsaw?' I picked up the heavy two-handled saw.

'Very well,' said Mr Żółtyński as he knelt down on the other
side of the tree-trunk. 'Quite a change from dragging logs all
over the place. A good way to rest.'

I could not kneel comfortably. My long-handled axe, which I
carried on my back under the belt, was in the way. I took it out,
lifted it and let it sink, blade first, into the nearest tree stump, or
so I thought. This was the usual practice, just thrown anywhere
on the ground the axe was easily lost in the undergrowth,
embedded in a stump it remained visible. But I chose badly. The
moss-covered stump was completely rotten. The blade went
clean through it and into my right shin. At first I felt no pain and
there was little blood. I sat down on the ground with the corner
of the blade still stuck in my leg. In the bone? I wondered. I
pulled hard, it came out. My leg was numb. In the wound there
was a reddish piece of rotten wood. I fished it out with a stick.

I heard the saw clattering from the tree-trunk onto the grass.
Was Mr Żółtyński getting impatient? 'I won't be a minute,' I
said. But there was no reply. I turned my head to look at my
partner. There he was flat out on the ground, in a dead faint. I
started to get up to help him, when his eyelids fluttered and he
came round. He was shaking his head like a man waking from a
deep sleep.

'Did I faint?' he asked. 'I hate the sight of blood. It was your
fiddling in the wound which was the worst.' I looked at this big
man, all six foot of him, and felt like laughing. But my leg was
hurting now. The only dressing I could think of was my
handkerchief. It was reasonably clean, so I tied it around my leg
and we returned to work. But it was not that easy, blood was
seeping through my dressing.

By then I was frightened and my partner called for help. The whole team came running. Lala made me lie down flat on my back, lifted my foot, rested it on the remains of the rotten stump and tied her headscarf tightly over my dressing. The bleeding stopped, but the pain was getting worse. Mietek set out in search of Volkov. The two of them came back in a few minutes with a horse for me to ride home.

It was an old, placid, patient horse and I got home without mishap. Father would make it better. Father was at work, putting finishing touches to the walls of a newly erected barrack, but Mother called him in. The nurse brought iodine and a bandage frayed at the edges from repeated washing. That was all she could offer; there were no needles, sutures, or sticking-plaster, nor indeed anything which could be of further use. 'Tetanus antitoxin?' asked Father. The nurse had never even heard of it. Father had only his hands and his bedside manner to rely on, but his magic worked. After a few hours' rest with the leg raised, the pain went.

A week later the wound had healed and I was fit for work. I only felt some pain on walking. This was my only 'war wound'. I got off pretty lightly.

To start my rehabilitation I was assigned to light work in the settlement. I was to help Sasha. Sasha was an old man who lived in the Kvasha *kolkhoz* (collective farm) and from time to time did special jobs for the forest station. He was an expert saw-setter and board-maker. My new job was to help him make boards. At last I discovered the purpose of the circular hole in the ground, which had puzzled me on my first exploration of the settlement. It was the saw-pit for board-making. Heavy logs lying in a heap by the saw-pit were to be sawn into thick boards for floors and ceilings. Some light work.

First, we had to manoeuvre several of the logs on to the two tall trestles placed some three metres apart. Just the sort of job for an old man and a 'child', and a convalescent one at that. But we managed, we had to.

The next step was to saw the logs lengthwise. Sasha would stand on top and I would stand in the pit. Our main tool was a big, heavy broadsaw with wooden handles set at right angles to the blade. The blade, tapered from above down, had monstrously long teeth. The saw would frequently get jammed and Sasha would free it by knocking a steel wedge into the track, just behind the blade.

To get the saw down I pulled and he steadied it from above. To get it up he pulled and I steadied it below.

Up and down, up and down went the saw, several times a minute, monotonously, for six hours. With only a few short breaks and a longer one for lunch, each hour seemed to last at least a thousand minutes and each five-minute break seemed to be over in a couple of seconds. It was a truly back-breaking job.

The saw-pit was not far from the canteen and I was forever waiting for the smell of soup to make Sasha stop. I was grateful for any distraction. People who were passing by called to us or stopped to gossip. One day we were joined by a woman, Andropova. She had been sent to dig a hole within speaking distance of our saw-pit. I never discovered what the purpose of the hole was.

Andropova kept us amused with funny stories during our breaks, but there was more to her than funny stories. She was the wife of a master forester, one of our instructors, and a local celebrity – not only in Kvasha. According to my partner, her fame reached as far as Petrakovo. She was in her early thirties, very friendly, and she had blue, smiling eyes in a round and open face. I had heard about Andropova before. There were two reasons for her notoriety.

First, against all the laws and regulations, Andropova worked only when she felt like it, and that happened rarely. She had spent days on bread and water in the Kvasha *kartser*, or punishment cell. As *progoolshchitsa*, or a recidivist shirker, she had also done time in prison and in labour camps. The second reason was her widely renowned swearing repertoire. Her swearing was quoted in awe by other Russians, who were all good but rather repetitive swearers. Hers was said to be most vivid, imaginative, exquisitely explicit and colourful. Naive as I was, I could not begin to understand what all those Russian adjectives and nouns actually meant. It was also said that no member of the extended family of her opposition was ever spared.

But this morning Andropova simply entertained us with friendly teasing, with Kvasha gossip and with funny stories of which she had a great store, not to mention a few personal remarks.

'Stepanooshka,' she would call roaring with laughter, 'your arse is sticking out so far that it reminds me of that big watermelon I saw years ago in the south.' Or again, 'Stepanooshka don't bend down too far or you will break your prick ... Better see your father about it, or else, it will take root and sprout leaves.' She was convulsed with laughter. And next minute, 'Take care, Sasha, or you will saw off your balls and the cook will put them in the soup tomorrow.' Or, 'Sasha, *ryadi boha*, good God, how do you manage to fart like a pregnant sow every time you yawn?'

There was no way of stopping Andropova . . . but then suddenly she did stop abruptly, in mid-sentence. A door banged somewhere behind me. Moving the saw up I looked back. A man in uniform was approaching us from the office; Borisov, the Kvasha militiaman, followed him, but not too closely.

I forgot about our work. The man was an NKVD colonel, no less. Almost certainly the same man who headed the Kvasha 'reception committee' on our arrival. The saw came to rest. 'Now,' Sasha whispered, 'keep your ears wide open, Stepan.' Andropova scrambled out of the half-dug hole and leant on her spade.

The colonel passed our saw-pit without giving us a glance and stopped several paces short of Andropova. With his right arm stretched out threateningly towards her, he began: '*Tovarishch* Andropova . . .' I was puzzled. Only Party members were addressed this way, everybody else was a plain *grazhdanin* or citizen. '*Tovarishch* Andropova,' he repeated. He talked rather softly and I missed some of it, but he seemed to be giving her the usual spiel on the nobility of manual labour, on the importance of the five-year plan for the economy of 'Our Fatherland', on the dignity of labour in general and on the exalted, privileged status of the Soviet working man and woman in particular, as compared with the exploited toiling masses in the West; on the special interest *tovarishch* Stalin had in the well-being of *tovarishch* Andropova.

He went on lecturing like that for a few minutes and then came to the point. He stuck out the index finger of his right hand and waggled it threateningly. 'I hear that again you refused to work in the forest and that even here in the settlement you will do only casual jobs.' He raised his voice. 'We have means of making you do your duty. Think of your family, your children.' The threat hung in the air.

Andropova stayed silent. The colonel came to the end of his peroration. Then she let rip. She went on non-stop and without mercy for several minutes. It was a virtuoso performance, but she lost me in incomprehensible details.

First she told the colonel what she thought about him in general and about the intimate parts of his anatomy in particular. My knowledge of Russian proved inadequate to comprehend it all. Then, she invoked his parents, his grandparents and the generations preceding them, their anatomy and their physiology, with special attention to their body prominences and orifices, not to mention their involvement with other zoological species. In my innocence I could not absorb the imagery nor even conjure up in my mind the bizarre acrobatics involved – though not for the want of trying.

As she went on, Andropova's voice grew louder, bound to be heard from one end of the settlement to the other. People started to congregate: pen-pushers from the office, Vasya the smith, the canteen staff, women and children. A small crowd gathered. Sasha, sitting on the log above, and I, in the saw-pit below, were well placed; circle and stalls, so to speak.

But the dramatic monologue finished as abruptly as it had started. The colonel was slowly backing out of the unequal engagement, his right hand still outstretched, but now in a rather self-protective gesture with his palm facing the opposition. Then he turned round and almost ran back to the office, preceded by Borisov, the militiaman, who pushed the crowd out of his way. Andropova dropped her spade and marched off to the canteen; as she passed the saw-pit she winked.

By that time the smell of the soup had at last reached us and we also downed tools for the lunch break. During the meal Andropova's 'duel' with the NKVD colonel was discussed in every detail and with a great deal of laughter. I realised once more how inadequate my Russian was and how much of the entertainment I had missed.

The rest of the day passed uneventfully. Andropova did not return to work by the saw-pit. The hole in the ground remained shallow, its destiny unknown. Andropova continued to work only on her own terms and the authorities let her be.

Sasha and I continued making boards. Oh, how I hated that job. I wanted to go back to the forest, to ride a horse, to do anything different. But I could not convince my father that standing six hours a day in the saw-pit was far worse than the work in the forest, including the long walk to and from work.

We had to slave in the wretched saw-pit for another week before relief came: the man in charge of building work decided that he now had enough boards for the barrack under construction and the saw-pit was abandoned. But even then I was not sent back to the forest. 'Tomorrow, Stepanooshka,' said the foreman in charge of Kvasha workers, 'in the morning, you will help Vasya.'

Vasya was the Kvasha blacksmith. And so next morning I became a hammer boy in the smithy, where Vasya was making horseshoes, horseshoe nails, hinges, bolts, hooks and other items as requested by the office. Iron was scarce and most building work in Kvasha was done without the use of nails. Barrack walls were constructed by placing de-barked logs on top of one another. Corners were made by the overlapping ends of alternate logs of the two walls, placed in depressions skilfully fashioned with an axe. They were secured with wooden dowels. An axe, a saw and a hand-drill to make holes for the dowels were thus the only implements required and available. Once the barrack walls and roof were finished, my father would take over as a kind of interior decorator. His job was to plug the gaps between the individual logs on the inside with dry moss and to cover the moss with a layer of clay. Once the clay had dried, he would add the finishing touch by whitewashing the walls.

My hammer boy career lasted two weeks. Winter was by now in full stride and, with a charcoal fire going all day, the smithy was the warmest place in Kvasha.

Wielding the heavy hammer also kept me warm. Sweat was

pouring down my forehead as I stood opposite Vasya, the black-smith, with the anvil between us.

With long-handled tongs in his left hand Vasya would pick up a white-hot piece of metal out of the fire and place it on the anvil. Holding it all the time in his tongs, he would turn it expertly this way and that, hitting it rhythmically with a light hammer held in his right hand. My job was to hit the same piece of metal between Vasya's blows. But my hammer was very heavy, I had to lift it with both hands high above my head and let it fall. We would go on like that bang-bong, bang-bong for several minutes until the metal cooled to red and then stopped glowing. Then back in the hot coals it went, while I operated the bellows to bring it to a white heat again.

It was heavy work, but much better than board-making. At times, when there was nothing utilitarian to make, Vasya would get out his squirreled away scraps of old iron and make fancy ornaments. Our Kvasha blacksmith was quite an artist. We became good friends, but the work bored me. I wanted to go back to the forest.

One day promised to be even more boring than usual. I was not looking forward to it when the morning came. It was still pitch-dark at 6 a.m. It was to be another day of making horseshoe nails: take a long, narrow ribbon of iron, heat it, cut it into short strips, heat each one in turn, flatten the head, sharpen the tip, dip in cold water, take another long piece of iron . . . Very boring.

We were supposed to start work well before dawn. With the forest teams long gone, the Kvasha street was empty. It was only two minutes' walk to the smithy and I liked those short moments under the sky paling slightly in the east but still full of stars.

Halfway up the little hill, there was my boss. Vasya was standing with his back to the door of the *kartser*. Several days earlier we had made a long iron bar: 'For the *kartser* window,' said Vasya.

'Good morning, Vasya. Are you coming to work?' I asked.

'Good morning, Stepanooshka. You go. Go on making horseshoe nails. I am on guard duty, Kirsh is inside and he is at it again.' The inside of the heavy *kartser* door was being savagely beaten and kicked. It was solid wood strengthened with metal bars. 'He has been at it on and off since Borisov locked him in earlier this morning. He has refused to go to the forest again.'

As Andropova was the Russian celebrity, Mr Kirschenbaum, or Kirsh for short, was ours. Kirsh was a single man, straight, thin and as tall as a beanpole. He was a professional burglar from Warsaw, familiar with the inside of many a Polish prison. We had learned all that from Mr Apfelbaum. Mr Apfelbaum, now an inhabitant of Kvasha, had been one of the owners of a fashionable fur store in Warsaw and he recognised Kirsh as the thief whom he himself had caught red-handed in his store several years before the war. Here, in Kvasha, though not exactly good friends, they seemed to have let bygones be bygones. But, while Mr Apfelbaum was just another forest worker, Kirsh became a celebrity.

Kirsh's notoriety was based on the fact that he, like Andropova, objected to work. 'I am a conscientious objector,' he would say, 'to work in general and to the work of a capitalist employer in particular. To my mind the Soviet State is a capitalist employer. I am a better communist than they are. I do not respect property. My principle is to share and share alike. I do share and help others to share with me, whether they like it or not.'

I heard him repeat this credo of his on many an occasion in the canteen. But his behaviour infuriated our Russian masters. They tried to order him and to threaten him. Neither persuasion nor cajoling proved effective. Nothing worked with Kirsh and Kirsh would not work. But somehow he kept his body and soul together. His personality helped. He was funny, friendly, obliging and he knew how to endear himself to other exiles. They paid for his bread, for his soup and *kasha*. And Kirsh survived. A sort of court jester.

But on this particular morning he had again been arrested and locked up in the punishment cell, with Vasya, my boss, on guard at the door.

I was left on my own in the smithy. Making horseshoe nails was not difficult. Hours passed by, I continued the job mechanically and my thoughts moved on to other levels; as usual, Helena was on one of them and now, at noon, meat soup was on another.

And then a desperate cry for help, '*Spasaytes!*', brought me down to earth. In one leap I was out of the door, witness to a most amazing spectacle. Kirsh was emerging from the punishment cell . . . through the chimney. Vasya, reputedly the strongest man in Kvasha, left his post at the cell door and was running at full speed down the hill shouting: '*Spasaytes! . . . Spasaytes!* Take cover! . . .'

As I watched, Kirsh jumped off the *kartser*'s roof. 'Time for lunch!' he shouted and, whistling loudly, marched to the canteen. He had his lunch, I do not know who paid for it. But after lunch Borisov, with his rifle at the ready, escorted him to a boat, with two more men aboard. Kirsch came back to Kvasha three months later, having been to prison, but he persisted in his refusal to work and continued to live on his wits.

In the meantime the Siberian winter was closing rapidly upon us. The temperature was dropping from one day to the next. From mid-October, mornings were frosty and the blue column of methylated spirit in the thermometer on the office wall refused to rise above freezing, except for a short while around midday, and only to drop again in the afternoon. As from late October, it remained permanently below freezing and through the winter it stayed between -20 and -30°C.

Days were getting shorter. By mid-October forest workers were leaving Kvasha in the dark and were not back until after the next night took over. Even my six-hour working day in the smithy started before dawn and finished after dusk. The sun came out for only several hours in the middle of the day, usually as a faintly luminous silvery patch seen through the grey canopy of clouds, rarely as a cold yellow disc, always low over the horizon.

Then the man who took over my job as cutter in Mietek's team was off work with a crushed right hand. I begged my way back into the forest. I should not have bothered. We had to leave hours before dawn, under the sky leaden with heavy clouds. From one day to the next our walk to work was made increasingly difficult by fresh overnight snowfalls. Snow fell both powdery or in big fat flakes, every day, with only a few intervals, until Christmas. By then the snow was some six-feet deep, with much higher drifts in exposed places.

One November morning snow was falling heavily when we left Kvasha, nothing unusual in that. Then, without warning, a *booran*, or snow-storm, was upon us. A ferocious wind was blowing, driving the snow almost horizontally into our eyes. We had to hold onto one another. The wind was howling like a flypast of Baba Yagas on their broomsticks. I was surprised when the icy snowflakes hitting my face like sharp needles suddenly stopped hurting. I looked at Mietek next to me, his face was covered with ice. We were crossing an open space, the wind was growing even stronger. Small whirlwinds were twisting about us, only to be swept away in sheets of snow driven by even stronger gusts. Exhausted, we reached our working site, but no work could be done until lunch-time when the wind died down.

In those early winter days I did not look forward to my lonely return home, as I was worried of losing my way. It was not too bad when I could get a horse; the animal unerringly found its way back to the stable and the warmth of the horse's back was a comfort. But when no horse was available in the afternoon, walking home on my own was quite a different matter. In late November it was dark at 3 p.m. and I had to make my way home in the night. I would not have minded the walk quite so much were the moon full and the sky bright with stars, but under heavy clouds the forest was a frightening place.

One dark afternoon I was caught by a snow-storm on my lonely trek home. Again it blew in suddenly, but, luckily, I was in a familiar area when it started – a few minutes' walk from Kvasha – or so I thought. It was a slow slog against the wind. In the next minute I lost my sense of direction. Do I now go left? Right? Straight on? The wind was pushing me and to stop myself falling I had to grab hold of trees.

I was frightened. I had never learned to pray, but now I wished I knew how. I tried to bargain: 'I shall try, I shall really try to believe in you, if only you will get me home.'

My foot got caught and I fell flat on my face. Oh, how tired I was. I decided to rest for a few minutes. I knew it was fatal to fall asleep. 'Get up. Get up,' I kept repeating to myself. Oh, how I wanted my mother. I was about to give up, and then a phrase flashed through my mind: *a chink of light . . . a door is ajar . . . somewhere . . . always . . .*

I had no idea where it came from. But it made me lift my head and then to crawl on all fours. I looked round, hoping against hope to see Kvasha lights, flames crowning a barrack chimney. But the blackness was absolute. Then I caught a sniff of smoke. With great effort I crawled out of my hole in the snow and let the smoke carried on the wind guide me back to Kvasha.

I was only paces away from the first building. I got home frightened and utterly exhausted. I found Mother alone in our room sitting by the window and watching the storm, in tears.

She got up: 'Thank God you are back.' She put her arms round me and, suddenly limp, she sat down heavily on the bed.

I knelt by her. I could only whisper, 'I almost gave up.' Unable to hold back tears, my face buried in my mother's lap; once more a little boy, I sobbed and sobbed and sobbed.

I must have fallen asleep. I woke up in my parents' bed, partly undressed, tucked in and warm. Mother was sitting on the edge of the bed with a mug of tea for me. Father, back from work, stood by the bed. And then, Father's face reminded me of the phrase: *a chink of light . . . a door is ajar . . . somewhere . . . always . . .* The phrase came from one of his wartime stories heard years ago. A variation on the theme: *Knock and it shall be opened.* Oh yes, yes, I shall go on knocking. Always.

I looked at the faces of my parents. All I could think was: I am not going to walk from the forest on my own any more. I'd rather be a live adult working full time than a dead child. So I said that, and this time it was accepted.

That evening the forest teams did not begin to trickle back to Kvasha until several hours past their usual time. Eventually all came back, though some did not straggle in until near midnight.

Next morning I was back in the forest and I was determined to work full time. But in the meantime the situation changed; the man I had replaced in Mietek's team was back.

I reported to Volkov, who smiled his foxy smile. 'I have just the job for you,' he said. 'You will be an important man now.' I took his unexpected bonhomie at its face value and smiled back. 'You will be a team leader,' said Volkov.

I was flattered and puzzled at the same time. Was he joking? What kind of team did he have in mind for me? As far as I knew forest teams were led by their tree fellers. As yet I had not felled a single tree, other than some saplings for firewood. I followed him. He stopped in a *poloska* only two minutes' walk away from Mietek's team. Four people, two men with fur caps and two women with headscarves, were sitting by a huge heap of burning branches, with their backs to us, talking and smoking. 'This is your new feller,' said Volkov to nobody in particular. Again he smiled and vanished into the forest. Volkov was not inclined to smiles. I wondered what he was up to.

Of the two men sitting by the fire one was Mr Romer, Helena's father, and the other was Mietek's father, Mr Wasserman. They were both old, pushing fifty. Of the two women one was Mrs Rosen, wife of Zhemchuzhina's and later Misha's driver, and the other was a young woman, Anna, whom I hardly knew. The team's problem, and the reason for their tree feller and leader leaving them the day before, became clear instantly. Mr Wasserman was short, thick-set, energetic and as strong as a horse. He was the team's orderly and was keen to get on with the job. Mr Romer was slim, nervous and, as long as he had *makhorka* in his pouch, a chain smoker; work was the last thing on his mind. A lawyer, a great talker, he was forever in search of an audience. Mr Romer was the cutter and his job was to cut the standard-size logs which Mr Wasserman, the orderly, was then supposed to place for removal. When the former shirked work, the latter had none to do. The two men argued constantly.

The two women were also a pain in the neck. Mrs Rosen was fat, lazy and had the vocabulary and mentality of a fishwife. She was averse to work and kept boasting how her devoted husband earned more than enough for their needs. The other woman was always unwell; she was pregnant, but we didn't learn that until much later.

And I, as their leader, was expected to make them work as a team; no wonder Volkov smiled. To all the team members, except perhaps Anna, who, to my embarrassment, called me Mr Stefan, I was just a boy with no authority whatsoever. I never managed to make them pull their weight and my team was forever at the bottom of the earnings league.

Tree felling was hard work, and dangerous at times. I had observed fellers at work and knew more or less what to do, but I had no practice. Mr Wasserman became my mentor. As my room-mate, he may have felt responsible for me, or perhaps he promised my parents to look after me. His experience, however, was limited too, but between us we managed. I did the work and Mr Wasserman was full of good advice.

With each new tree the routine was the same. First, to gain access to the trunk, I shovelled away the snow around it – several feet deep by then – next, with an axe, I took out a horizontal wedge from one side of the tree in order to determine in which direction it would fall. Then, with my back bent and with my thighs straddling the tree-trunk, I finished the job with a string-saw. At the first crunching noise, with the saw-made slit widening slightly, I had to get the saw out fast, and move back, very fast. The danger was that the falling tree would jump off the stump in an unforeseen direction and one had better not be in the way. At the same time I was supposed to shout, in sing-song, the routine warning: '*Zelenaya sama poshla ... idet ... Beregis!*' which roughly translated means: 'The green one is coming down. Take care!' To avoid accumulation of uncut tree-trunks, I could only work as fast as our cutter's efforts allowed. The first day passed without mishap.

But on the second day we met a near disaster. I didn't do anything wrong, except that perhaps I forgot to cross my fingers. This was an important precaution. You could exercise your skill to direct the tree one way or another, but it still had a mind of its own, you had to hope for the best and will it to obey the rules. This one, a tall, green, straight and very handsome spruce did not. The spruce, or *yolka*, is feminine in Russian, and thus very capricious. She crunched loudly in anger and then creaked plaintively as she slowly fell through the branches of her neighbours. And then, suddenly, halfway down, she leapt off the stump, twisted to one side and finished leaning against another tall, straight and magnificent spruce.

The entire team came to help. We heaved and we pushed the felled tree to no avail. There was no other way; I had to fell the other spruce, the one on which the first one was resting, to get them both down together. But, under the circumstances, there was no way of telling which way they would fall. I started with my axe in my hands and my heart somewhere near my boots. The first few blows of my axe were followed by crunching, ripping and tearing noises, something was breaking up there over my head – only branches, I hoped. I started sawing, there was no movement. And then my saw jammed. I got a steel wedge out of my pocket and started hitting it hard with the axe to drive it into the slit behind the blade of the saw to free it. After a few blows there was more crunching and ripping overhead, I dropped the axe and jumped to the side. But yet again nothing happened. Drenched in cold sweat, I went back to the tree, the saw moved easily now. I went back to sawing, waiting for the ominous sound of the still-intact part of the trunk breaking.

Nothing happened for a very, very long time. And then, one mighty crunch, a lot of branches broke and both trees came down together. In the instant I heard it I did an Olympic-sized long jump with the saw in my hand. Breathing deeply, I forgot about my warning cry – the green one is coming down. But my team had all kept well away; it all ended well, this time. But I began to dread mishaps. Mishaps were inevitable, however good you were and, except for Mr Wasserman, my team were anything but good.

❄ ❄ ❄

In time I learned not to be frightened, or perhaps to control my fear, but I was very glad, when after two weeks of tree felling, my dismal team was disbanded.

My next job was on the ice road. In months to come, I often wished that I had stayed in the forest. From the perspective of the ice road, tree felling was easy, and it kept one warm.

NINE

THE ICE ROAD

✳

The Kvasha ice road has remained forever my idea of purgatory; it was far too cold for hell.

On a more practical level it was a primitive method of timber transportation. Was it employed only in Kvasha? I do not know, but now, many years later, I have yet to meet another person who has heard of a road made of ice.

Timber, the main product of the area, is heavy, unwieldy, bulky. Also it had to be transported over long distances. It was usually conveyed by water, but first it had to be moved from the depth of the forest to the nearest navigable river. In a land of poor roads and scanty railway networks this was a problem.

When I had worked on the stacks in the summer, I had watched Mr Rosen and the other drivers bring the timber to the riverside. Their equipment looked antediluvian to me. The logs were simply chained by their thick ends to the beam of a primitive sledge, called a *volokooshe*, their thin ends bumping behind marking the ground heavily. A tree stump, a protruding root, a thick, loose branch, a rotting old trunk, each presented a serious hindrance. Not infrequently the contraption had to be lifted over the obstacle, or occasionally unloaded, mobilised and reloaded. It seemed like very hard work for both man and beast.

The thick layer of snow in the winter was bound to make a difference. Mietek and I had talked about it on several occasions and one evening – the time my forest team was disbanded – on our way back from the canteen Mietek told me about the ice road. It was the first time that I had heard the expression.

'Volkov was in a chatty mood at lunch-time,' said Mietek. 'He told me that in the winter all forest teams will be moved much deeper into the forest and the ice road will be used to bring the timber to the riverside.' Several other people over-heard him and came over to listen. With the audience around us he went into more detail. Apparently, well before the first snow a Russian team had been sent out to prepare the track from the forest to the riverside. Now the ice road was almost ready, Volkov said, and soon we would be using it.

He then went into a long explanation of how the ice road was made; the gist of it was that, when the snow layer reached about a metre high a horse-drawn wooden roller was dragged up and down the track to compact the snow. When the surface was hard enough, they used a sledge with miniature ploughshares at the ends of its runners to cut two parallel furrows. Then they poured water into them and the road was ready for use. What they used on the ice road was a special double sledge. Apparently, with it, one horse could pull a load of five or even six cubic metres of timber.

'The ice road needs maintenance,' Mietek continued. 'It has to be repeatedly watered to keep the ice rails in good condition.'

'I wonder where they get the water in winter,' I mused aloud.

The next day, as I was trying to guess what kind of work I might be sent to, my thoughts were interrupted by the noise of doors banging and shouts of 'Get moving!' As Father's job on the new barrack had also come to an end he too had no idea what his next assignment was going to be.

On this particular morning it was Volkov who appeared on our doorstep. He pointed to my father. '*Ty stareek*, You, old man, will now work with your son. Both of you report to me on the other side of the river,' he said and then left.

'Light work for both of us, I hope,' said Father.

At breakfast we met the Romers. Helena was also being sent to work across the river. In Kvasha the River Uftyuga was some forty to fifty metres wide. We crossed its frozen surface following a well-trodden path and the steep snow banks on either side of the path came up to my shoulders. We were following a group of several Russians leading a horse. The riverside clearing on the shore facing Kvasha stretched along the river for several hundred metres providing enough space for a great deal of timber. Several Russians were preparing foundations for new stacks. Volkov was not there, but the Russian leading the horse motioned to us to follow him.

At the end of the clearing which was covered with snow stamped flat by hundreds of feet and hooves, we stopped near a sledge, the like of which I had never seen before. It looked like a big, lidless box on runners. It was over two metres long, over a metre wide and reached to just above my shoulders.

'It's something to do with the ice road,' I said to Helena.

'What are you talking about?' she asked, but I had no time to show off my newly acquired knowledge, as our Russian guide tied the horse to a tree and said, 'Let's clear the snow. Careful at the back, don't leave the tools behind.' The snow was light, powdery, and we swept it off the box quickly and without difficulty, using only our gloved hands. In the meantime our Russian climbed into the box itself and shovelled the snow out of it. He climbed out again and, as he went to harness the horse between the shafts of the box, I had a good look at the latter. It was indeed a box on runners. It was made of thick wooden planks reinforced with metal hoops. In the back wall of the box, low down, there were two holes, each the size of a thumb, one above each runner. A wooden peg of similar size hung on a piece of string next to each hole. Below each hole a piece of sheet metal fixed to the box wall fanned out at an angle towards the ground. High on the back wall, hanging on hooks, were buckets, a pickaxe, a crowbar, a couple of axes, a couple of shovels and a small cauldron with a long handle.

'Let's go,' said the Russian. From the riverside a track opened into the forest. It was almost a proper, straight road, some two metres wide. Along its middle ran two parallel grooves about a metre apart, just as Mietek had described it. Each groove was a hand-breadth deep and just as wide, its edges smooth as if cut out with a sharp knife. With a shove our Russian companion guided the runners of the box into the ruts. They fitted in snugly. Father joined him as he led the horse, and engaged him in conversation. Helena and I followed behind the box. Under our feet the hard compacted snow felt like a layer of asphalt, a strange white asphalt.

'*Skoréye*, faster, faster,' our Russian urged the horse; the animal quickened its pace.

After several minutes Father joined Helena and me behind the box. 'His name is Alyosha,' he informed us, 'he is our team leader. This is the ice road. It runs for eleven kilometres along a stream, and this contraption is a water cistern.' He frowned in thought.

After a pause he added, 'Our Alyosha is not too talkative.'

By this time we were half-walking and half-running behind the box. I was trying to work out what the maintenance work implied, but did not share my thoughts with the others. Soon we were all short of breath and conversation became difficult. It was very cold. Each exhalation came out as a thick cloud of steam; another cloud, much bigger, surrounded Alyosha's and the horse's heads.

We reached the other end of the track, deep in the forest, having covered the eleven kilometres in about two hours. Volkov was waiting for us there. He was sitting on a log by a bonfire with several other Russians. They made room for us. I took off my gloves to warm my hands at the fire but, almost immediately, had to replace them in a hurry; my palms, which faced the flames became uncomfortably hot, the backs of my hands went white and painfully cold. The first lesson of the ice road: out of doors in the Siberian winter never, ever take off your gloves.

We had been sitting in silence for a few minutes when Volkov said to nobody in particular: '*Davay nachinat*, let's start.' Alyosha got up, grabbed the reins close to the horse's mouth and motioned to us to follow. Volkov and the other Russians stayed cosy by the fire.

The ice road went up a slight incline for about fifty metres and came close to the edge of a narrow irregular ditch in the snow. The stream? Alyosha tugged the reins: '*Stooooy*, hoooold.' He dropped the reins and as the horse, its mouth now free but for the bit, started muzzling the virgin snow, the Russian went to the back of the cistern and stoppered the two holes with their pegs. Next, he picked up the shovel and the crowbar and motioned to me: 'Stepan, get the other shovel, two buckets, the pickaxe and come with me. Both of you wait here,' he said to Father and Helena.

I grabbed the implements and followed Alyosha down the sloping bank to the snow-covered stream, several strides away from the cistern.

'First we make a hole in the ice. Just watch. Later you will do it on your own,' said Alyosha. We started shovelling the snow away. Here, in the shelter of trees overhanging the stream, it was less deep, not even a metre. As we got through to the ice Alyosha pitched the pickaxe into it. He kept hacking at the hard surface, levering out chunks of ice, crushing some with the blunt end of the axe, then returning to the sharp end of the pickaxe and to the crowbar. I watched him. It did not look difficult. In a couple of minutes Alyosha reached water. A few further blows enlarged the hole to about half a metre across. The ice was only about two to three hand-breadths thick.

This is child's play, I thought. But I was to change my mind very soon. 'The ice is thin. It is only November,' warned Alyosha.

Later in the winter we had to cut through almost half a metre or more of new ice formed between one shift and the next. It was adult work after all. There were some twelve holes to be cut along the ice road, roughly a kilometre apart.

The water hole was ready. Alyosha mustered my father and Helena into position and soon had us forming a human chain. Alyosha remained at the ice hole filling the buckets, one at a time. He passed the bucket to Father, Father handed it to Helena and Helena handed it to me. Our team leader was fair, he took one of the two difficult jobs himself and assigned me to the other. I had to lift the bucket, lean it against the edge of the box and empty its contents into the cistern. I got the hang of it quickly. But it took about two hundred buckets to fill the cistern.

At first the wooden box leaked like a sieve, until ice sealed the gaps in its walls. Within minutes the snow under my feet also turned into a sheet of ice and I kept slipping like a duck on a frozen pond. Soon emptying the buckets into the cistern became automatic. Just as well; keeping upright required all my attention.

At last the cistern was full and, with the tools replaced on its back wall, we were ready to move off. My education continued. As he came up the bank, Alyosha positioned himself behind the cistern, by one of the two holes. 'Take care of the other,' he said to me.

'Do as I do,' he said next. '*Poshól*, move.' The horse started off. It was slow, heavy going. 'Stopper out,' said Alyosha and pulled the peg out of the hole with one sharp movement. Mine would not budge, it was frozen. I dealt it a hard blow with my ice-covered gloved hand on one side and the other. I gave it another tug, it came out.

'Good lad,' muttered Alyosha and smiled. I nodded and smiled back.

Water flowed steadily from my water hole on to the metal spreader and then into the groove in the snow and on to its lips. The spreader was shaped so that more water was directed on the outer, compared with the inner, lip. You could almost see it freezing instantly into solid sheets of ice. I glanced to the other side. Alyosha's spreader was working in exactly the same way. About fifteen minutes later we stopped again at the side of the stream. There was another hole to be made in the ice, the cistern to be filled, then we were off again. We moved to another hole . . . and another . . .

About noon we stopped for lunch. There was no lack of firewood and birch bark for kindling was plentiful. In no time we had the fire crackling merrily at the side of the ice road. Alyosha cut three straight branches for a tripod and hung our cauldron from it. We filled it with snow which soon turned into *kipyatok*. It felt good to wash down our clay-like bread with hot liquid and feel the warmth spread down the gullet.

We worked hard all day watering the road all the way to the riverside, then watering it again in the opposite direction. At the end of the shift, in darkness, we walked back to Kvasha. That day we had covered well over forty kilometres.

The second day was much the same. Each ice hole had to be cut anew. We filled the cistern and we moved off. By lunch-time Alyosha became much more friendly and, as Father started talking to him again, his tongue loosened.

'This road,' he said, 'makes all the difference to the five-year plan. Now we can use the double sledges. One horse can pull a much heavier load than on the drag sledge in the summer. Did you see them this morning when we crossed the river?'

I did indeed notice these contraptions being readied at the Kvasha end of the ice road. Each consisted of two sturdy sledges with side supports, one behind the other, held together with a couple of iron chains.

'One horse,' Alyosha continued, 'can draw loads of ten to fifteen logs at a time; supported at both their ends they don't drag behind.'

'Does that mean,' asked Father, 'that the ice road is a one-way track and has to be watered outside working hours?'

'Yes,' said Alyosha. 'Exactly. It has to be done at night. It's hard work and cold.'

Our short lunchbreak was coming to an end. Alyosha was already up. 'Come, Stepan,' he said. 'Let's harness the horse.'

I looked up. The sky was cloudless and as the cold, dim yellow disc of the sun, a slice of lemon rather than of orange, reached the peak of its arc low over the horizon, there was some hazy sunshine. The Siberian winter sun did not even look hot, it was difficult to believe that its temperature reached thousands or millions of degrees. I could touch it, I thought, and the ice on my gloves would not melt. According to the natives we could expect the daytime temperature to drop soon too, it would go as low as -30 to -40°C. How cold would it be at night?

I removed the empty nosebag from the horse's head and got the animal ready. We went to the nearest water hole. We spent the rest of the day getting used to the routine. We were given the following day off.

On the way to our first night shift, after the evening meal, I looked at the thermometer hanging on the wall of the office. It showed -15°C.

At the first ice hole the front of my warm winter coat, part of my old school uniform, became stiff with ice. My feet which, in spite of all the walking, had remained painfully cold, suddenly started feeling warm. Warm but very heavy, I could hardly lift them off the ground. Worried, I looked down. My canvas boots were covered with a thick layer of ice.

Oh, well. I had learned another lesson of the ice road: ice keeps you warm. The igloo effect, I called it in my mind. I looked at Father and at Helena. Their coats and boots were in a similar state. We were all wearing ice armour.

I kept emptying the buckets into the cistern, but strangely they were increasingly heavy. Much heavier than they had been during the day. Was I getting tired? At least the cistern stopped leaking. Sealed with ice. Now it ought to fill up quickly. But it didn't. I soon found out why.

As the next pail reached Alyosha at the water hole, he knocked off the ice covering it on the outside with his pickaxe. He then tipped it upside down, giving it several more knocks. When he lifted it, the bucket left a hillock of crushed ice in the snow. No wonder the buckets were heavy and the cistern was taking a long time to fill. As I emptied the other bucket I gave it the same treatment. 'Good lad,' said Alyosha.

Soon we were on our way, once more walking behind the cistern. But the flow had now visibly weakened. Ice in the hole? I looked at Alyosha. The hole on his side of the cistern was getting obstructed too. He had a sharpened stick in his hand and pushed it into the hole. He moved it in and out. The flow increased. I had no stick. But there was the peg hanging by the hole. To grab it, I had to bend down, not easy with the ice armour on. But I got it and twirled it in the hole. I slipped and fell. I must get a stick, I decided, as I got up and caught up with the box.

Alyosha laughed. 'Good lad,' he repeated. I liked being praised.

As I was getting up I glanced back. Father and Helena were following us, walking in the middle of the track, between the grooves shining with new solid ice.

We went on at a slow walking pace. The land was flat with only slight undulations. '*Tishe . . . tishe . . .* easy . . . easy . . . ' or '*Davay . . . bistréye*. Move . . . move.' The horse responded to Alyosha's commands and kept at a more-or-less uniform pace whether up or down the inclines. 'Water must be spread evenly,' said Alyosha.

After about ten minutes the cistern was almost empty. '*Bistréye . . . bistréye . . .* move . . . move . . . ,' shouted Alyosha, adding the customary swearword for good measure. The cistern was now light and the horse went at a trot. So did we, leaving behind thick clouds of steamy breaths. '*Stooooy*,' Alyosha stopped the horse.

This was the next water hole. This time Aloysha left it to me. Making a hole in the ice proved much more difficult than watching Alyosha doing the job. The crowbar, the axe and the pickaxe kept slipping out of my gloved hands stiff with ice. I looked at my hands. They were bent into two icy hooks shaped by the hoops of the buckets. But the handles of the heavy tools I was using were thicker and did not fit them. I kept trying. The crowbar slipped out of my hands again and on to my right foot. Surprisingly, I felt no pain, the thick carapace of ice on my canvas boot did not even crack.

I kept hacking at the ice and the energetic movement warmed me up. After a few minutes I was hot. The gloves must have changed their shape as the tool handles now stayed put in my hands. Another blow with the crowbar, one more, and I was through the ice. 'Now let me shape it,' said Alyosha and gratefully I passed the tools to him.

This hole was nearer the road than the last one and it was enough to have only one person between Alyosha and myself. Alyosha was filling the buckets very quickly and passing them alternately, one to Helena and one to Father, as they both stood between us.

At first I could not cope with the speed at which the buckets were reaching me. Alyosha had to slow down and looked at me disapprovingly, then I realised what he was doing: he was using both arms alternately.

I had to change my tactics. I stood with my back to the cistern and by picking up alternately one bucket from Father with one hand and the other from Helena with the other, I was able to empty them very quickly behind me. I was keeping up with our boss. 'Good lad, Stepan!' shouted Alyosha.

As the buckets once more became too heavy, we stopped to knock the ice off them, but on the whole we had spent less time at this hole than at the previous one. And once more we were on our way to the next hole. Then the cistern was empty and we were nowhere near the stream. Alyosha stoppered the hole on his side. I did the same on mine.

'What happens now?' I asked.

'We have watered only half the distance between the two holes and we will do the other half on the way back,' said Alyosha. Then he lifted one earflap, scratched his ear and added: 'Next time we shall cover this section at a trot, so that one cistern will do. But everybody keep shtoom, mind.'

As I digested this information a thought struck me. Perhaps

... perhaps ... working on our own we could go at a trot all the time and then one cistern would cover much more of the ice road than the distance between any two holes. I did not say anything aloud, but it was an interesting thought. It would, of course, be cheating. So what?

The rest of the night passed quickly as we worked our way from one water hole to the next. At some holes we needed two people between Alyosha and myself, at others Helena and Father doubled up between us, at others, where the greater distance between the stream and the road required it, they had to circulate at a trot to hand the full buckets to me and to return empties to Alyosha.

Alyosha was fair. The two of us had the heaviest jobs at the hole and by the cistern and he kept changing places with me. He did not even swear much while working and the only butt of his obscenities was the horse. An unusual Siberian, I thought.

Most of the night we had worked by the silvery-bluish light of the moon, but by the time we got back to Kvasha, the moon had disappeared behind heavy clouds and it was snowing. Exhausted, weighed down with the icy armour, we grew quiet and slow. It was early morning, but there were some hours left till sunrise. The canteen windows shone with the light of paraffin lamps. People were milling around, getting ready for work. I could smell food and I was starving.

But first we had to go to the drying chamber. This was a small building next to the canteen. It was really one big room, the centre of which was occupied by a large, low clay stove. The iron flue was red hot above it. Except for a pile of firewood in a corner and garments hanging from pegs all round the walls, the room was empty.

To start with, I couldn't even take my gloves off. I watched Alyosha. Hitting one's hands against the wall soon got rid of the ice on them. With my bare hands I tried to undo the buttons of my coat, but they were inaccessible, buried in ice. The ice, however, was melting rapidly in the heat of the stove. 'Keep trying,' said Alyosha. 'Take your coats off as soon as you can undo the buttons. If you wait too long you will get all wet inside.' This was an important piece of advice and we followed it routinely. Fortunately, our barrack was just across the road and, once the coat was off and hung on a peg, we ran for it. Thus ended our first night on the ice road.

One morning we returned to Kvasha exhausted and, rigid in our icy armour, we were waiting in the drying room for our outer garments to become removable when Orlov, the settlement headman, walked in. He stood there, by the door, with his right arm raised, immobile except for his steely blue eyes wandering slowly from Father's face to Helena's, to mine and then back to Father's again.

'You are doing very important work,' he said. 'Tomorrow you will have a day off.' He stopped and his arm dropped to his side. Did he expect applause? I wondered.

Actually I knew what was coming. Alyosha had told us on our first night shift. For some reason we had taken it for granted that there would be two teams maintaining the ice road and we had been speculating as to who would be in the other one, when Alyosha interrupted: 'Forget it,' he said. 'You will be doing the work every night, all through the winter,' and, unusually, he swore. Now, Orlov raised his right arm again. Did they all have to ape Lenin? I thought bitterly.

'The ice road is the lifeline of Kvasha,' he said, 'and we cannot allow it to be idle even for one day.' Again he paused for effect. 'It is our duty to the Fatherland and to the Party. The five-year plan must be fulfilled. You will continue on the night work right through the winter.' Had Alyosha reported on our talk? I wondered. That was that then, our sentence had been pronounced. Orlov turned back and left, with Alyosha on his heels.

All I wanted now was a hot drink and my bed. We had overstayed our time in the drying-room. My icy armour, my private little igloo, had melted and the cold dampness had penetrated through to my skin. We took our coats off, hung them on pegs and ran across the icy street to the barrack. But my boots were already wet through and, in spite of the two pairs of woollen socks with several layers of newspaper and flannel foot wraps in between, by the time I reached the barrack my feet were ice cold again.

Our long and lonely working nights were monotonously miserable. The main cause of the misery was the unrelenting frost. Provided we remained active, the layer of ice on our gloves, boots and coats kept us reasonably warm, but our buckets and the cistern were constantly getting incredibly heavy. Getting rid of the ice which covered them inside and outside doubled or tripled our work.

On a number of occasions we returned to Kvasha towards the end of the night, only to find that the temperature had dropped to under 40°C below zero. This allowed the day workers to stay indoors, but it was too late for us to get the reprieve.

And thus every night, after our evening meal, eaten early in an almost empty canteen, we returned to the barrack to pile on extra layers of clothing, interlined with newspapers, and in total darkness walked across the river to the timber terminus. On our way we usually met the forest teams returning home.

We would start the shift with one of us harnessing the horse and the others clearing the ice from the cistern and the buckets. The first ice hole was next to the terminus. Hacking at the ice to reach water, filling the cistern, keeping the cistern holes open on the way to the next water hole and repeating the performance – it all became a routine. Night after night.

One night the sky, silent and studded with millions of stars, suddenly caught fire. Silver, flame-shaped patches of light, now spreading, now contracting, shimmering, constantly changing places against the rapidly moving cloudlets.

'The polar lights,' said Alyosha. 'Beautiful, aren't they?'

The amazing picture lasted about ten minutes and then slowly faded and disappeared. We returned to work.

Days off in Kvasha were few and far between. At compulsory meetings in the Communal Hall the workers 'unanimously volunteered to work the next four Sundays for the good of the Fatherland', and then the next four Sundays again and again.

Who would have dared to vote against an official motion? And the slogan which accompanied the motion, 'The five-year plan must be fulfilled', had acquired the significance of an eleventh commandment.

We had a day off on 7 November, the anniversary of the October Revolution. And then again we had a free New Year's Day, January 1941, and then one free Sunday in March.

Towards the end of one of the night shifts in our second week on the ice road it started snowing. At first it was not more than the usual, almost daily, dose of snow, but towards the end of the night it was snowing heavily. We thought nothing of it. We finished our shift. It was not our problem, or was it? I had a nasty feeling that it might be, but kept it to myself. We finished the night's work and walked back to Kvasha, in our usual armour, now burdened by the extra layer of snow, like so many walking snowmen.

The customary routine followed: the wait in the drying room, the quick run across the Kvasha street to the barrack. A quick bite of bread followed by hot tea. I could hardly wait to get into bed.

As usual, almost instantly, I was fast asleep, and then I was rudely awakened by heavy banging. Volkov was at the door: 'Vladislav Mikhailovich,' he addressed my father, 'Stepanooshka, get up. The ice road needs sweeping.'

Mother tried to argue, 'They just came back from the night shift, they are exhausted.' No use. The five-year plan must be fulfilled.

Sweeping the ice road clear of snow was an easier job than watering it. But a day's sweeping after the night's watering was too much. By the time we finished we had been on our feet for more than sixteen hours, with some two hours' sleep in the morning.

The previous night we had walked eleven kilometres with the full cistern and eleven kilometres back to Kvasha. Now we had to repeat the whole length of the ice road there and back again, part of it walking backward sweeping . . . sweeping . . .

First, the thick layer of snow had to be pushed off the ice road to the sides. This was done by two of us in turns, using wide wooden shovels. We walked one a little behind the other, pushing the snow from the middle and over the ice grooves, one to one side and the partner to the other side. The other two team members followed with brooms and swept the ice grooves free of snow.

Shovelling masses of snow off the road was a heavy but not a challenging job. Sweeping the snow out of the depth of the groove and from its outer lip to the side in one movement required skill. Alyosha was an expert. He did it walking backwards and watching him I soon developed the knack of doing it with reasonable speed. Helena too became very good at it, but Father was slow. He found walking backwards rather difficult. I had to help him from time to time so that he did not lag too far behind. I had become very protective of my father.

After a night's watering and a day's sweeping we were allowed the night in bed and we would get the next day off – unless another heavy snowfall brought Volkov banging at our door in early morning: 'Vladislav Mikhailovich, Stepanooshka, get up.' Fortunately a heavy snowfall which would rob us of our day's rest did not come more often than three or four times every month and sweeping the ice road became just another routine.

Even now, more than half a century later, one pathetic night on the ice road is still vivid in my memory.

My father was a very gentle man: kind, courteous and com-passionate. He never swore. Or at least I had never heard him use even such mild Polish expletives as *'psia krew'* (dog's blood), or *'cholera'* (the Polish equivalent of 'damn').

One February night the temperature was particularly low. Towards the end of the shift Father was overcome by the cold, he was not able to walk. We got him to stand on the curved, projecting runner of the cistern, just behind the warm rump of the horse. He held onto the edge of the cistern and I supported him on one side. Helena took over my stick and, with Alyosha's help, controlled the flow of water from one hole.

Then I heard Father whispering something softly, to himself. To hear better, I pushed my earflap to the side. Father was softly swearing: *'psia krew . . . cholera jasna . . . psia krew . . .'*

By the morning, when we had drifted back to Kvasha, the blue thread of the thermometer on the office wall had dropped below its lowest mark of -40°C.

With very few breaks, we thus worked on the ice road through the winter and well into the spring of 1941. At first, mostly with Alyosha, but later, often I was in charge of the team and another deportee was sent to provide the fourth pair of hands. Nights without the Russian offered us a chance to cheat, but we did it in moderation. Sometimes, having filled the cistern, we dared to get the horse to trot all the way past the next ice hole. But leaving an ice hole untouched was risky, a sledge driver passing by might notice and report us. The threat of being accused of sabotage and sent to a real prison camp hung permanently over our heads. We were also afraid of returning to Kvasha too early; it would be noticed. Staying in the cold, inactive, just resting, was asking for trouble, while lighting a fire was risky. In darkness the flames could be seen at a great distance.

By late May the temperature was rising perceptibly. The overnight growth of new ice in the holes was easier to hack through, thinner, and the ice grooves, the dual backbone of the ice road, started cracking.

On one such late May night during *zakoorka*, or the customary five-minute smoking break, we were sitting on fallen tree-trunks as usual. Helena and me on one, Father and Alyosha on another.

I took a deep breath. 'The air smells of spring,' I said.

Father and Helena agreed. Alyosha expressed no opinion.

The brief rest was pleasant. Unusually, my overcoat was damp rather than icy and, to my surprise, I was conscious of being warm, pleasantly warm. Until now the cold would not let us rest for more than a minute or two. I kept breathing deeply. Our breath was still coming out as clouds of steam but the air smelt differently: it was fresher, sweeter, it was even aromatic.

And then I realised that the aroma was coming from Father's cigarette. Several days ago we had received a food parcel in the mail from my mother's sister Rose, who lived in Zaporozhe, a big industrial town in the Ukraine. Among such luxuries as rice and flour, a jar of honey and another of rendered butter, a piece of salt bacon and a packet of boiled sweets, there was a carton of Kazbek cigarettes. Father was drawing on one and proffered the packet to Alyosha.

'*Bolshoye spasibo*, thank you very much,' said Alyosha. 'I have not had one in years.' He inhaled deeply with a blissful expression, which all of a sudden transformed his face into that of a pleasant and friendly man.

Real cigarettes were a luxury in Siberia. The only tobacco available in the settlement shop was *makhorka* in brown paper packets. Rolled into squares of newspaper, the tobacco dregs were the staple Siberian cigarette. As a great majority of adult men and quite a few women in Kvasha were smokers, one just had to get used to the abominable reek of *makhorka*.

Instead of that, our two smokers were now surrounded by the aroma of *Kazbeks*, one of the best brands of cigarettes in the USSR.

In appreciation, Alyosha became more approachable and talkative than usual.

'This is our last night on the ice road,' he volunteered. 'Tomorrow the forest teams will start moving back to the Kvasha side of the river, to the summer working sites. I am going to Petrakovo, to attend the summer course for master foresters. I enjoyed working with you,' he added.

'What about us?' asked Helena.

'That I don't know.' He became silent again. Does he really not know, I wondered, or is he, as many other Russians, afraid of talking to us, enemies of the people? And then our taciturn Alyosha, softened perhaps by the gift of the luxurious cigarette, was actually trying to answer Helena's question, hesitantly at first, starting with the usual formula: 'The five-year plan has to be fulfilled . . . All the timber has to get to the port . . . The whole workforce will be busy on floating the timber . . . One stands on top of the stack and pushes the logs into the river, one after another. The Uftyuga takes them up and carries them to the Northern Dvina river. Hence, they float all the way to Arkhangelsk . . .'

He stopped and his face, hitherto frozen into its usual expression of purposeful concentration, took on a dreamy look: 'Our timber goes all over the world . . . on ships,' he added wistfully.

And suddenly Alyosha burst out laughing: 'Mind you, you must be careful not to fall into the river yourself. It's easily done. The stacks are slippery. Once you are in, the cold kills you instantly, nobody would even bother to fish you out. If you are not careful, you've had it.'

'I am not a good swimmer,' interrupted Helena irrelevantly.

But Alyosha ignored her: 'We have enough timber to float on the river to fulfil the plan for this year and that is what matters, that is what they measure. What happens to the timber after it's floated? Oh, that's another matter.'

And then, forgetting that he was talking to us, strangers, Alyosha went on: 'Only less than half the production ever gets to Arkhangelsk, but nobody bothers. Figures look good on paper. Paper is patient, it forgives. Only people don't.' He stopped, got up and started on his way down to the ice hole. And then he looked at Father and continued: 'The floating has to be done fast, we only have a few days, while the river keeps within its banks. Otherwise, as the snow melts, the river rises and rises, and then it spreads for many miles around, taking our timber with her. A few weeks later it settles all over the place and *kolkhozniki*, collective farm workers, are left with the best pieces. And they use them for their pigsties, chicken coops and fences. They even burn pieces earmarked for ship and aircraft construction.'

He got up and with furious energy he set about enlarging the ice hole.

'Let's go back to work,' said Father. And back we went. But on its last night the ice road did not seem to deserve another watering. I did not feel like working particularly hard, neither did the others. Even Alyosha slowed down after a while.

We half-filled the cistern and went at a trot, missing out the next ice hole and later we passed idly by several more. We got back home earlier than usual. The settlement was quiet. And while spring dealt with the ice road in its own inimitable way, we, the ice-road maintenance team, were given a day off.

❊ ❊ ❊

When some two weeks later I was sent, in the company of Alyosha and another man, to take the Kvasha horses to their 'holiday' destination, on the way we crossed the old ice road several times. It was by then unrecognisable; the track in the forest was being invaded by the already abundant undergrowth.

❊ ❊ ❊

The work on the ice road was as difficult as it was boring and there was no getting out of it. The only consolation was being with Father . . . and with Helena.

One morning, as we were waiting in the drying-room for our individual igloos to melt, Volkov walked in. 'Stepan,' he said, 'I have another job for you for the next few days. You will have a replacement,' he said to Alyosha and then turned back to me. 'Tomorrow morning come to the office at six sharp,' and he left.

I was too tired and too sleepy to think straight. But Father was worried. 'What kind of job have they found for you now?' he wondered aloud as we were running across the street to the barrack. He began telling Mother, but I went straight to bed. We woke up as usual in the early evening, had our meal and Father left for work with Helena. I read late into the evening and in the morning I went to see Volkov.

It was my first sight of the inside of the Kvasha office. From a small gangway, several steps up from the street, I walked into a narrow corridor with four doors, two on each side. I knocked on the one marked *Mastera*, Master foresters. Several men I knew by sight were sitting on a bench behind a simple wooden table scattered with papers. Volkov motioned me to sit by his side. 'You are a clever lad,' said Volkov pushing a detailed map towards me. 'I told *tovarishch* Orlov that you would be able tell a *sudostroy* [timber for ship building] and an *avyastroy* [timber for aircraft construction] from the others, am I right?' I wasn't sure, but I nodded agreement anyway. After all, after several weeks of marking the stacks, which had been my first work assignment, only a fool would not recognise the straight, big, smooth, knot-free timbers destined for the ship-building and aviation industries. It was Volkov's turn to nod. 'Good,' he said. 'I have a special job for you in this section here,' he pointed to the area of the map circled in red and then his black fingernail traced an interrupted line. 'It's just off the path to Petrakovo. We must have all the suitable trees marked before we take the forest teams there when the time comes.' He got up. 'Come with me,' he said.

I had second thoughts. It was not processed logs he was talking about. He wanted me to mark live trees to yield *sudostroy* and *avyastroy* logs, that was quite a different matter. Could I do it? I wasn't at all sure. But the job sounded certainly more interesting than the ice road. I wouldn't mind joining another team for a spell.

'Come,' he repeated. I followed Volkov to the room marked 'Store'. Its shelves were laden with skis, axes, saws, hammers, drills and piles of papers, mostly maps. He picked a pair of short broad skis and a hammer with the embossed letters S at one end and A on the other.

Suddenly I realised that I was being sent into an unknown section of the forest on my own. I was frightened, my heart missed a beat. But then, I could not believe my eyes. Volkov unlocked a cupboard and handed me a pair of *valenki*, or felt boots. These were the common winter footwear for the Russians, but for us they were an unobtainable object of desire.

'The job will only take a few days,' said Volkov, 'and then you'll return all the gear back to the store. Sign for it.' He gave me a piece of paper and an indelible pencil.

Real *valenki*! I would sign anything. They were made of one piece of off-white thick stiff felt. I could already imagine how warm my feet would feel in them. No need for newspapers; woollen socks would suffice.

Carrying my equipment I followed Volkov back to the now-empty office. Again we sat down at the table. He passed me the map, a leaflet and explained the new job in greater detail. I was to leave Kvasha by the Petrakovo path along the river, up to where several colour-marked tracks dipped at various angles into the forest. I was to follow a different colour track every day, all marked on the map and each leading to a different part of the designated forest area of about four square kilometres. My job was to select trees with long, straight, branch-free sections of the trunk. He pointed to the leaflet: 'It's all here. Read it, Stepan.' I began to like Volkov.

Laden with the gear, I went back to the barrack. I told Mother about my new job. She went pale, her lips turned bluish grey, but she only said: 'Be careful, Stefanku. Don't play the hero.' She knew that there was nothing we could do about it. I put on the *valenki* and left.

I started about 9 a.m. It was still dark, but the sky was clear. Volkov had warned me not to start too early, though I didn't see why. Now I knew: not light enough to read the map. Oh, well, I knew my way without the map. And I wanted to try out the *valenki* and the skis. I followed the Petrakovo path between the snow-covered river on my left and the edge of the forest under its eiderdown of snow on the right. In the *valenki* my feet felt pleasantly warm; warm and light. On the ice road each foot with its carapace of ice weighed a ton.

I got the map out again to check, but it was still too dark. I looked back, there was no sign of Kvasha. Even the chimneys, usually visible at a great distance because of the flames dancing above them, had disappeared. Like so many beacons, the fiery chimneys were the first sign of Kvasha on our way back from the ice road. I must have rounded a bend in the river and Kvasha was now hidden behind an elevation. The colour-marked tracks should be starting about here, I thought. I looked carefully at the tree-trunks along the path. Yes! Here it was. A tree-trunk with a barkless patch marked with a cross. Trunks with bits of bark shaved off and marked with crosses were scattered over a distance of some twenty paces. But I couldn't be certain, as yet, of the colours of the marks. The edge of the forest was a dark wall, silent and forbidding. The tracks starting from the marked trees were lost in darkness.

It was a bit scary. Perhaps I didn't like Volkov all that much.

I became acutely aware of the fact that wolves didn't hibernate. The only weapons I had were my ski sticks with sharp, pointed ends, the axe and the marking hammer.

I decided to wait for daylight. I sat down on a fallen log and tried on the skis. They were snowshoes really. The *valenki* fitted snugly into the leather attachments. I secured the straps. Fish-like in shape, the skis were some three quarters of a metre long and about half that across the middle, with rounded, slightly curled up ends in front. They were made of rabbit skins, the pile facing back, stretched over a cane frame. Ideal for walking on dry snow which had drifted, as the direction of the pile prevented you slipping back. I had never seen snowshoes before, let alone used them, but, after several painless falls in the drifts at the edge of the forest, I got the knack of moving on them quickly and easily.

In the meantime the long night came to an end and the blue sky promised a sunny day – all four hours of it. If I was going to do any work at all, it was time to start. With the coming of daylight my fear evaporated. I forgot about wolves. The job was easy. Piece of cake. Once I identified a suitable tree, I sliced off a flap of bark and, with one blow of the hammer, marked the naked wood either 'S' or 'A'. In truth, I was not at all sure what was supposed to be the difference between these two types of timber. Volkov said nothing about it and the leaflet was not helpful. I simply marked alternate trees with either one or the other end of the hammer. More or less accurately. Anyway, I was not bothered by any likely mistake. 'They are not going to get me for sabotage. Soon we will be out of here,' I promised myself. The war could not last much longer.

About noon I sat down on a log to have my lunch. I polished off a hunk of bread with a thick slice of salt pork from Aunt Rose's food parcel, washing it down with fistfuls of snow. The rest of the short day passed quickly. I enjoyed having the forest to myself. It was silent, motionless and glaringly white with deep long shadows. With the low winter sun, the shadows in Kvasha were always long now. Here and there in the clearings, the smooth sheets of snow glimmered golden against the cloudless blue sky. When the shadows lengthened even further I called it a day. I reached Kvasha before night fell. I decided that I liked working on my own.

But the pleasant, though lonely, job did not last long. After several days I was back on the ice road. I was with Father and with Helena, but I liked the ice road even less than before. My warm felt boots had to go back to the store.

I had several other assignments which would take me away from the ice road for a day or two at a time. Apart from one, none was memorable. One evening, as we were getting ready for the night shift, there was a discreet knock on the door. This kind of civilised knock usually meant it was one of the deportees. Natives, however highly placed in the Kvasha hierarchy, either banged on the door with the fist, or unceremoniously threw it open, without such a bourgeois nicety as a knock. I opened the door. One of the office pen-pushers was there on our doorstep. I knew him by sight, he was short, fat and bald. Put a cigar in his mouth and you have a capitalist shark straight from the pages of the *Krokodil.*[*] 'Stefan Vladislavovich,' he said. 'No ice road for you tonight.' He handed me a thick brown envelope. 'Take this packet to the Petrakovo NKVD office. No, not tomorrow, now. Get a horse and be on your way.' The funny man did an about-turn and left. I was flabbergasted. I could not believe my ears. He did not use the diminutive Stepanooshka, nor Stepan. The man used my real name and patronymic. I felt grown up.

---

[*] A Soviet satirical periodical

Mother was upset. 'I am going to see Orlov,' said Father. 'Sending a boy through the forest on his own, at night, is madness, it's irresponsible.' Father left the room. But I was not to be done out of the adventure. I was already dressed warmly for the night on the ice road and, while others in the room tried to console Mother, I sneaked out and ran to the stables.

I liked riding and this promised to be a really long ride. In the event I learned that, while saddleless riding might be fun, a forty-two kilometre, bareback journey is not a joke, at least not as far as one's nether parts are concerned. By now Dimitri, the stable man, was a friend of mine. 'Do you want Zhemchuzhina?' he asked.

'Oh yes, please.'

He laughed. She was ready and waiting. He liked to give people surprises. 'The office transmitter packed up,' he said. 'It's Saturday and Orlov, son of a bitch, must get the weekly report to those sons of whores in Petrakovo by tomorrow morning. Hence the hurry. Rightly he ought to have sent one of us.' He meant a Russian. More oaths followed. Dimitri was not enamoured of the NKVD, but as swearing went, he was not fit to hold a candle to Andropova. Yet, how did he manage to avoid prison camp? Friends in high places?

'When you hear wolves howling just give her free rein. She is swift, well rested and will get you out of trouble. But mind you, try not to wake up a bear.' He laughed. 'Earlier this week my wife's brother came from Petrakovo and smelled a bear's lair at the river bend near the town.'

He got me worried for a moment, but the prospect of the night's ride soon took my mind off wolves and bears. It seemed so simple. In the winter the river was an excellent road and only an imbecile would lose his way.

I left the stables and rode down to the river. I went off at a trot, so as not to tire the mare, and she kept up the pace for most of the way. The sky was full of stars. The snow-covered forest walls on both sides of the frozen river were bathed in the silvery light of a full moon. Muffled by the thick layer of compacted snow on the river ice, the horse's hooves made barely audible sounds. There was no wind, no rustle of tree branches, no whirring of wings. From time to time a deep throaty hoot of an owl broke the exquisite silence. I was getting bored.

By then I was well into Russian classics. Some weeks before, while roaming at the back of the Kvasha *Krasnyi Ugolok*, Community Hall, Helena and I had found a cardboard box full of books. Unopened and dusty, it must have spent many years there in the dark corner. We appropriated it and, at the time, we were going through volumes of Pushkin's and Lermontov's poetry. I knew dozens of poems by heart. Pushkin's 'Mednyi Vsadnik', ('The Bronze Horseman') seemed to fit the occasion and at the top of my voice I recited:

Na beregoo poostynnykh voln	At the edge of a watery desert
Stoyal on, doom velikikh poln	Stood he, in deep thought,
I v dal gladel.	And gazed into the far horizon.
Pered nim shiroko reka neslas;	At his feet the wide river flowed.

Poems, even some I had not realised I knew by heart, came to me one after another. Time passed quickly, and as my Polish and Russian poetry repertoire ended, I started singing as loudly as I could.

Zhemchuzhina seemed to listen and showed her appreciation – or was it disgust? – by pricking up her ears.

Here the path outlined by compacted snow went up the right-hand shore, crossed a tongue of land made by a bend in the river and returned down on to the river ice. The point marked two-thirds of the way to Petrakovo. I went on singing, but Zhemchuzhina stopped listening, her ears flattened to the side of her head. Was I so badly out of tune? I wondered. But the mare was getting excited or frightened, sniffing and snorting, she kept turning her head sideways, this way and that. Then, unbidden, she was off at a gallop. It was scary.

I held fast to the mare's neck. My bottom was sore from the long ride and I was practically flat on my belly. I heard no barking, no howling. I had never heard wolves before, but I imagined that the sound would be not unlike that made by dogs. And yet, the forest stayed silent. After several minutes at a mad gallop, Zhemchuzhina slowed down to a trot. Still sniffing and snorting, she seemed to have calmed down. Soon lights appeared on the left shore of the river. We were in Petrakovo.

It must have been near midnight and the little town, not really more than a village, seemed fast asleep. The snowy path left the river and went up the bank at the place where we had spent that last night on our way to the settlement last summer. The main street was deserted and dark, only an occasional window was lit. The light was surprisingly bright. Oh, electricity! I had not seen electric lights for over six months.

Most buildings were just log barracks, like ours in Kvasha; there were a few small log cabins. One house was a little different and bigger than the others, but it was in darkness.

Let's try there. Very stiff, weary and aching I dismounted with great difficulty. After the long, intimate contact with the mare's backbone, my legs and bottom were rigid. I had to force myself to walk. Tough. Several steps led up to a little porch with wooden columns. I tied Zhemchuzhina to the iron ring on one of the columns and laboriously mounted the steps, one by one. The board on the door said: *Selskii Soviet*, Rural Council. I tried the door, it was locked. No luck.

I looked around. Further down the street a long low barrack was brightly lit. Canteen? Communal Hall? Murmurs of many voices were coming from the building, indistinct shouts, laughter. Then the noise died down and the sound of an accordion filled the air, a deep male voice intoned a wistful song, others soon joined in.

Nothing could induce me to get up on my mare's back again. We walked down the street side by side, a very tired mare and a very sleepy boy with stiff and numb legs.

It *was* a canteen. Rows of people sat at the long tables. The air was bluish-grey with smoke and heavy with the stink of *makhorka*. As I walked in, the singing stopped. A man in an NKVD uniform in a state of disarray, sitting near the door, barked at me, '*Ty chevo*? What do you want?'

'I brought letters from Kvasha. Our transmitter broke down.' I showed him the packet.

'Aah, come,' he said. I followed him further up the street to the NKVD office, one of the few houses with a light in the window. The man was unsteady on his feet. Climbing up the few steps of the porch both of us had to hold fast on to the banister, but for very different reasons.

In the office my guide stood slightly askew to attention. 'Messenger from Kvasha, Comrade Lieutenant,' he announced. I gave the packet to the man behind the desk.

'Well done,' he said. He had another look at me and turned to my guide. 'Take his horse to the stable,' he said as he got up, 'and you come with me.' I followed him to a room behind the office. He pointed to a corner with a palliasse on the floor. I was asleep before I hit it.

In the morning there was another NKVD officer on duty next door. There were voices in the building; work was in progress; electric lights were on.

'For the canteen,' the duty officer said and gave me a chit for breakfast. 'Be back in half an hour.' I was starving. The breakfast was a feast, the best I'd had in months: a bowl of oatmeal *kasha*, two thick slices of bread with butter and jam, which tasted of real plums, and a white enamel mug of milky coffee. It tasted very much like the grain coffee which children used to get in Poland.

Perhaps I ought to volunteer for the NKVD, they eat well, I smiled to myself.

Time came to return to the office and to start on my way back. It was still dark, at least two hours to daybreak. I did not relish the thought of another bareback ride, even in daytime. The lower half of my body was still aching and stiff. But there, in front of the building, was a sledge with two horses in harness and with my Zhemchuzhina tied to one side. I was to go back in style. That suited me fine. The sledge was comfortable. The seat, which I shared with a young man, Yosif Nikolayevich, was spread with thick rough blankets and we had a bearskin for cover.

Yosif was a man in his twenties, a bachelor. He was a radio technician and was being sent to Kvasha to repair the transmitter.

We talked a lot. His parents lived in Krasnoborsk, the river port at the mouth of the Uftyuga. He had learned his trade in Arkhangelsk and thus had seen some of the 'big, wide world'.

Or at least that's what he thought of Arkhangelsk. He was a
patriot and a candidate member of the Party. He kept asking me
questions about pre-war life in Warsaw and about Poland in
general, but he did not wait for my answers; he answered them
himself. When I said that life was not bad even for the working
classes, he snorted, just like my mare. I had to admit that, as a
doctor's son, I didn't have first-hand knowledge, and I didn't
argue.

'Anyway,' he concluded, 'the capitalist system is bound to
succumb to the inevitable march of the revolution and is
therefore not really worth talking about.'

On the tongue of land where Zhemchuzhina had given me
such a fright the night before, I told Yosif what had happened.
'It could not have been wolves,' he said. 'The area for many
kilometres round Petrakovo has been cleared of them years ago.
The noise of your passing must have woken a bear. It was the
speed of your mare which saved you. A lean and angry bear can
be swift, but a good horse has the advantage.'

Just as well that it had been a bear, as evidently no horse could
get away from a pack of wolves bent on having a meal. I did not
tell Yosif what woke the bear; I did not mention my thespian
efforts; I felt too foolish.

Our journey was uneventful and we arrived in Kvasha about
noon. My father was asleep after the night on the ice road.
Mother was greatly relieved to see me back and none the worse
for wear.

I was glad to be home. Kvasha was home.

CHANGING FORTUNES

✳

By the end of May 1941, the long winter was slowly and erratically staggering towards its end. On some days the midday temperature rose above freezing, but only for an hour or two and only when the sun parted the clouds to peep shyly through. The cushions of snow that weighed down the trees shrivelled, and the tree branches, so much lighter, would slowly rise like the arms of an old man stretching his limbs on waking up. The white bearskins sitting majestically on tops of the spruce and fir trees shrank perceptibly from one day to the next.

The massive accumulations of snow which had stayed all these months on the roofs of our warm barracks, now caressed from above by an occasional tepid breath of the sun, were thawing fast. It was dangerous to stand under the eaves, as masses of wet snow and ice would crush down at unexpected moments. Huge icicles, the size of a man's thigh, were hanging from the roofs, dripping water like so many faulty taps; but, once the sun passed the peak of its low arc or hid behind heavy clouds, all melting and dripping stopped and the world froze once more into white stillness. The spring was coming.

I had my personal and easily reproducible proof of this when, one midday, in the shelter of a tree, the stream of piss, instead of raising a cone of ice, made an orange-yellow hole in the snow.

The snow was now dirty, useless, and water for drinking and washing had to be fetched in buckets from holes in the ice. But the layer of ice on the river, here and there surmounted by puddles of water, was getting thinner. Cracks appeared on the surface and the river, previously as safe as any highway, became dangerous.

One morning in early June we woke up to strange sounds: the *staccato* cracks of a whip against the background of sustained rumbles of distant thunder. Gunfire? Fireworks? 'The ice on the river is breaking up,' said Father.

In the summer the Uftyuga is not a mighty body of water; like other Siberian rivers it is slow and plods ponderously along. In Kvasha it is only about forty or fifty metres wide. Yet its breaking out of the icy embrace of winter was a dramatic event. For most of the following day huge blocks of ice were rushing past the shore. Here a huge floe, still covered with fantastic snow drifts, would suddenly break and the two halves would rise against each other like two enormous polar bears locked in a deadly fight. There, smaller floes heaped up on one another were floating downstream like miniature icebergs, one or two metres high.

In the afternoon of one of our rare free Sundays, Helena and I went for a walk along the river and by then the picture was far less dramatic. With the little icebergs gone, single sheets of ice of varying sizes were making their way to the White Sea. The water level was steadily rising, the opposite shore was flooded and the stacks of timber, so recently reverberating with shouts of men working on them but now deserted, seemed on the point of being washed away.

By the next morning the icy traffic on the river had thinned to just an occasional passing floe, the work of floating the timber from the riverside stacks began in earnest. In order to complete the task in the shortest possible time, almost the entire working population of Kvasha was taken by boats to the other side. But, just as Alyosha had predicted, it took much longer than stipulated in the current five-year plan and the job was not even half finished when the river overflowed its banks. Our bank was a little higher than the opposite one and Kvasha was spared, but on the other side the water spread far into the forest taking the floating logs with it. While some logs stayed in the midstream and were soon out of sight, other ones never reached it and, carried by the flood waters, disappeared in the forest. Still others, entangled in the low-hanging branches of trees on the riverbank, stubbornly refused to leave their birthplace.

It was obvious that a large part of the year's production would never reach the sea and was destined either to rot, provide firewood, or end up as pigsties in some local collective farm.

We, the ice-road maintenance team, were spared the dangerous work on the stacks. But we did not know that until the day came.

In the morning Father and I got up as usual and went to the canteen. By then the days were very long and the nights were almost white; by 6 a.m. the sun was well up. We took our place in the queue. As we were passing the table used by the bosses, to my surprise Orlov, the Kvasha headman, called me to sit next to him.

'Get his *kasha* for him,' he said to my father.

'Listen carefully, Stepan,' said Orlov very quietly as was his custom. 'I am going to give you an important and very special job.' He paused for a while and then, in the usual manner of a Soviet official, he went on and on about the significance of the still-unspecified job for Kvasha, for the Soviet Union and for the Party.

It all sounded very grand yet puzzling. What sort of a job? Perhaps in the settlement, I hoped. Oh, God! Not in the saw-pit again. By now I was getting immune to Party jargon and waited resignedly until he came to the point. When it finally emerged I found myself appointed leader of a new special team. Its job was to clear the fire-protection strip round Kvasha. 'As you see the Party is charging you with a most responsible job,' concluded Orlov.

The composition of my team was rather strange. The only able-bodied workers in it were the two 'children', namely Helena and me; our sixteenth birthdays were still to come, mine in two weeks and Helena's in two months. Of the other members of the team three were old men, *stareek*, and one a breast-feeding woman. The men were my father, Helena's father and Mr Gruszyński, none under fifty.

Mr Gruszyński still had a bulk problem. He had been a high-powered consultant engineer in Warsaw; now he lived with his wife in the other half of our barrack. I remember him mainly for his size in general and for his huge belly in particular. Originally, when we walked from Petrakovo to Kvasha, this awkward protuberance preceded him some distance. Admittedly, by now, after one year of Kvasha's diet, his belly had shrunk considerably and whereas his wide shoulders were still too big to fit easily between trees in the virgin parts of the forest, at least he could pass between them sideways. Several weeks earlier Father and I had met Mr Gruszyński in the *banya*, the Russian sauna. There, in the nude, his imposing physique was a pathetic sight. He was about two metres tall and his shoulders were truly bear-like, but loose folds of skin hung limply from his upper arms and back. A kind of flesh apron hanging down from his belly to his mid-thighs totally covered his genitals. I couldn't take my eyes off the strange sight. Father noticed my astonishment. 'With his fat gone,' he explained in a whisper, 'his skin, no longer elastic, forms this kind of empty sac. In a civilised country he could have had plastic surgery to remove the redundant skin, but in this God-forsaken place . . .' Father sighed deeply.

While Mr Gruszyński was not a good worker, at least he tried. Our young woman, Anna, did not even try. Her baby was two weeks old and she was breastfeeding him. In Kvasha there was no alternative to mother's milk. While she was at work her own mother looked after the little boy. Every few hours either Anna, like Zhemchuzhina before her, ran to the barrack to feed her baby, or the grandmother brought him to be fed. In between the feeds Anna mostly rested and had neither inclination nor energy for work. We were very sympathetic, but she was not much use to the team. Similarly, neither Helena's nor my father could be expected to do heavy work.

'We are not going to earn our keep,' I told Helena in our first lunch-break. 'Mind you,' I hastened to add, 'I am not complaining. It's just a statement of fact.' I would hate Helena to think of me as a grumbler; I wasn't really. But there, at the start of my working life, I liked to have my efforts recognised at the end of the week by at least one *chervonets*, the red ten-rouble banknote.

But Helena, for a change, took an optimistic view. 'Not to worry,' she said. 'My father preferred talking to working as far back as I can remember. At present he has sufficient money to keep us for a while. Your father has enough too, I guess. Mr

Gruszyński has his remaining fat to feed his body and mind, while Anna's husband and father between them earn enough in the forest for the family to survive. Don't worry, Stefan. If the fire-protection zone is never finished, so what? Surely we will be out of here before the next fire season.'

But I did worry. The dry season was coming and Kvasha needed protection from forest fires. Since the bombs in Otwock I was terrified of conflagration, though I would not readily admit it. We had had a minor forest fire in Kvasha in July the previous year, soon after arrival, and that was enough to bring back my fear.

It started one midday. The forest was dry and the flames spread fast. They leapt from one treetop to another, mysteriously bridging the gaps between them. They also spread underground: 'Along the roots,' said the young Russian woman standing next to me in the human chain passing buckets of water from the river.

At the time, the plague of insects made daytime lumbering in the forest impossible and the forest teams were thus available to fight the fire. Within an hour it was brought under control and the settlement was saved. But it might be worse next time.

And yet Helena was right. Nobody in the team was likely to be bothered by our poor earnings.

Yevgenii Ivanovich, or Zhenya for short, the man from the office who came at the end of the day to calculate our pay, was very scornful of our efforts. 'None of you will get even one helping of *shchi* for today's work,' he said. And *shchi*, the cabbage soup, was one of the cheapest items on the menu.

'I am sure we'll do better,' I said. 'It's only a start. You'll see, tomorrow we shall clear more land,' I assured him.

'You'd better.' He laughed and turned away.

I did some thinking on the way home. The fire-protection zone was a strip of land which started at the river above Kvasha, curved along the edge of the forest and ended at the river below it. It was some twenty-five to thirty metres wide. It had been neglected for a long time and was now overgrown with mature trees, clumps of saplings and thick bushes. Our job was to fell all trees, remove the roots, clear the bushes and burn the debris leaving only scorched earth.

This was not really the proclaimed light work for youngsters and old men, and neither elbow-grease nor brute strength were my team's attributes. Tree-root clearing, in particular, brought us all, except Helena's father, out in a sweat – Mr Romer enjoyed the spectacle more than the work. Fortunately, most trees round the settlement were young and relatively easy to shift. In spite of that I had to beg the stableman now and again to lend me a couple of horses to drag the roots out. As once before, my authority as team leader was nil and I had no doubt that most of the hard work would have to be done by Helena and me.

I confided in Helena. 'Let's watch carefully tomorrow the way Zhenya calculates our pay.'

Forest teams were paid by the bulk of timber accepted by the master forester at the end of the day, so much per cubic metre. He checked the diameter of each log, guessed its length – there were only several standard lengths – copied the volume from his printed book of tables and added the figures he had obtained.

We, on the other hand, were paid by the square metre of ground cleared of all vegetation and that figure involved multiplication. Arithmetic was not our Zhenya's strong point, even though he worked in the office. He could correctly measure the length and the width of the area cleared, but multiplication gave him a headache and he lingered a suspiciously long time over it.

Actually, at the end of the first day, he got his sums mixed up to our disadvantage, but I realised it too late to bring it to his attention. I did not suspect him of cheating us on purpose. At the end of the second day I helped him with the calculation and, compared with the first day, our pay doubled. I was honest, I really did not cheat. Cross my heart . . . On the third day I showed him a 'quicker' method of multiplication and our pay doubled again. This time I did cheat, but only a little.

After that it was easy. In truth, we had gained experience and did work better and quicker, but the fact that Zhenya came to rely on my calculations had a magical effect on our end-of-the-day figures. A little cheating went a surprisingly long way. The others knew about my machinations and patted my shoulder approvingly. Helena only smiled.

Father was worried. 'I don't like you being dishonest,' he

said. 'But perhaps these are special circumstances,' he admitted. 'I hope that they won't notice the fiddle in the office. Surely they would know the total area to be cleared. It might all come out in the end and you will be in trouble, Stefanku.'

'It might and it might not,' said Mr Romer. 'And even if it did, they would be afraid to admit that they let Stefan do the calculations. They will just massage the figures. As usual. They will record a fictitious figure for the zone cleared and get a medal for exceeding the five-year plan. The whole system is crazy, it's all one great deception, at all levels.' I had to admit to myself that my thoughts on the subject did not reach as far as that, but I kept my mouth shut and I was grateful for Mr Romer's assistance. Father shook his head disapprovingly.

The discussion took place as we were walking home along the edge of the forest. It was mid-June and a beautiful sunny evening. I was holding Helena's hand. Life is not too bad, I thought. Helena must have thought the same as she started singing in her surprisingly deep voice:

'*Pyatiletka, pyatiletka, pyatileto-o-ochka . . . a . . .*'
(The five-year plan, oh the five-year plan.)
I joined in: '*Posle etoy pyatiletki budet semileto-o-o-chka . . .*'
(After the five-year plan, there comes the seven-year plan.)
The echo came back from the dark wall of the forest: *. . . o . . . o . . . oochkaaaa . . .*

And then Mr Gruszyński added his basso-profundo:
'*Pyatiletkoo vypolnyalim kharasho pitalimsya . . . a . . . a*
Vsyu koninoo pereyelim za sobak imalimsya . . . a . . . a'
(While fulfilling the five-year plan we ate so well,
With no horse meat left we took to eating dogs.)

Hundreds of such two-liners called *chastooshki* were sung in the Russian countryside. Mocking, sometimes risqué, or simply dirty, these ditties often had thinly veiled political meaning and many an author and singer lingered in a prison camp.

But who cared? Helena and I went on with one of our favourites:
'*Khorosho tomoo zhivyotsa oo kovo odna noga . . . a . . . a*
Sapogov yemoo ne noozhno i portyanina odna . . . a . . . a'
(A one-legged man leads a jolly old life,
he needs no boots and only one foot-wrap.)

At the end of the first week our earnings were at the official norm (recorded as a hundred per cent efficiency.)

On Saturday, at the end of the second week, in the canteen queue, Helena shouted, 'Look!' and pointed to the *Pochotnaya Tablitsa*, or the Board of Merit, next to the menu board. Its top half under: *Stakhanovts*, or Stakhanovites, was blank, but the bottom half headed: *Udarniki*, Shock Workers, had my name on it, as the leader of the only *Udarnik* team. My name had been misspelled: Waiden-Feld, but there was no doubt, our team had exceeded the norm.

This was a surprise, but it worried me. Did I push my luck a bit too far? Would they start wondering how this could have happened?

But I need not have worried. In the next minute our Zhenya was slapping me on the shoulder: 'Good lad, Stepan. Pity you'll finish the job in another week or two. It will not be so easy in the forest team. Not just weeds and bushes to clear. Eh? Good, isn't it?' he pointed to the merit board.

We managed to keep our exalted *udarnik* status for the remaining two weeks on the fire-prevention zone. Every week we earned more than the forest teams and never again did my weekly pay-packet in Kvasha reach the height of over thirty roubles. We kept quiet about our little fiddle and everybody was happy, including our Russian masters who boasted of having real *udarniks* in their work force. As far as I knew, our cheating never came to light and nobody was penalised.

About the same time a major change took place in our family's fortunes.

Some time in June the Kvasha nursing post was upgraded to a medical post and, at last, Father was appointed Medical Officer of the Sloboda Forest Station, which combined Kvasha and its outpost, Vasilyevo.

It was not Father's greatest professional achievement, but at last he was taken off the manual work which had given him a hernia and recurring chest pains. He attributed these pains to indigestion. Now I have no doubt that he had angina, that he knew it at the time, but the label of 'indigestion' was meant to spare Mother's anxiety.

His new job was to provide medical care for about 800 Polish and Russian inhabitants of Kvasha and Vasilyevo. With the post came the quarters vacated by Katya, the nurse, who was transferred to Petrakovo. At last we had a room of our own.

Our new quarters occupied half of a small barrack in the Russian section at the far end of the settlement, near the wall of the forest. To enter our residence one had to climb several steps to a small, but our own, roofed-over porch. From there the door opened into a corridor which was furnished with a bench and served as the waiting-room. From the corridor a door on the right led into the surgery and the other, on the left, into our room.

The surgery was quite a large room, about five paces by six. It was furnished with a table, two chairs, a wooden couch and a cupboard. Our room was much smaller than the surgery. It contained an iron bedstead and a wooden washstand with a white enamelled bowl and jug. This was a real luxury. Perhaps some Russian families did own washstands, but I had not seen one in any of the Polish barracks.

Another luxury was a small kitchen range in the corridor, ostensibly there for sterilising instruments, but which we could use to make toast and grill wild mushrooms on. We pushed the iron bedstead against one wall and placed my folding bed along the other. With the two-foot space between the beds leading from the door to the window, the room looked like a train compartment.

Many a time, on my own, I sat by the window with my eyes shut, day-dreaming. I was in a compartment of a fast-moving train. I would conjure up the image of the window-frame in my mind's eye, but with the motionless forest erased. My train crossed miles of picturesque countryside, big towns, rugged mountains and lush valleys, bridges spanning wide rivers. The wheels went ram-tam-tam . . . ram-tam-tam, particularly loudly in the tunnels.

One late evening I was so far away on my imaginary journey that I did not hear my mother opening the door. I only realised she was there when the bed suddenly sagged a little more. She put her arm round my shoulders. 'Do not cry, Stefanku,' she said. She did not ask why I was.

'I am not crying. My eyes are sweating.' This had been our

secret code in my childhood. I opened my eyes. The dark forest wall was still there, motionless, in the window, under the pale sky of another white night.

I turned to Mother. She smiled.

Suddenly I noticed how thin her face was, how angular her usually soft features had become, how her appearance was altered by the wrinkles I had never noticed before. We cried together, Mother and I. Noiselessly.

On the morning of the 'great change' I went to work as usual, my team depleted by Father's absence, while my parents moved us to our new home. It must have been a relief to our room-mates when the number of the room's inhabitants was thus reduced from seven to four.

The first night in the new quarters was a disaster, however. I tossed restlessly for a long time before going to sleep, then I woke up itching and scratching furiously. My parents were also awake, Father sitting on the edge of the bed scratching his legs.

Mother was quick with the diagnosis: 'Bedbugs.'

We got up. Our beds were crawling with insects the size and shape of ladybirds but dark and devoid of spots. Engorged with blood, they were uniformly reddish-black.

In our later travels through the USSR the crushing of bed-bugs on my skin, or of lice between the fingernails, became an automatic action which did not warrant a second thought, but the first time was different. I was furious: how dare they drink my blood?

Lice, fleas and bedbugs were widespread on the Euro-Asian continent. In Poland bedbugs were usually confined to cheap hotels and lodging houses, fleas to dogs – strays mostly – and lice to the very poor and to beggars. I knew what a bedbug, a louse, or a flea looked like from pictures in my biology book, but so far I had never met any of them face to face; or skin to jaw? But the Soviet Union was different. In the months to come we would crawl with lice, but in Kvasha so far, thanks mainly to the efforts of women, the Polish barracks were largely bedbug and louse free. Katya, the nurse, whom we succeeded in our new quarters, was obviously not so particular.

Unlike the louse, the bedbug – *Cimex lectularius* – does not usually carry diseases, but it is, literally, a bloody nuisance. We spent the rest of the night exterminating the pests. I had no idea what experts my parents were in fighting bedbug infestation. The experience gained in the First World War and the Bolshevik Revolution stood them in good stead. Mother took command. First we took the beds outside and stripped them; it was well after midnight, but the white-night sky shed enough light to see by. The iron bedstead presented no problem. We emptied the palliasse, burned the straw and scalded the cover and the bed linen with boiling water. Then Mother passed a candle flame slowly over every nook and cranny of the ironwork.

My folding bed, though, was made of flammable material. We could not risk setting it on fire and had to rely on copious amounts of boiling water alone. That done, Mother and I hung our duvets and blankets on tree branches and beat them with sticks. By the time we finished the job, it was time to go to the canteen for breakfast. Mother, who normally did not bother about breakfast, came with us.

Our plight was discussed at length at the table. Did I detect a *soupçon* of *schadenfreude*?

'Now that you have a room of your own, what do a few bugs matter?' Helena pulled my leg. And then she added under her breath: 'At times, I would not mind sharing my room with bedbugs instead of my family.' I looked at her; she was serious.

Mr Wasserman, as usual, examined the problem from a practical point of view. 'Unless you manage to clear the crevices in the walls and ceiling you will never get rid of them. You have to keep your beds away from the wall and stand their legs in bowls of water. Even then you will have bugs dropping from the ceiling on to you. Anyway, as long as you live next door to Nina or any other Russian you will never get rid of them. They are not bothered. It's their way of life,' he concluded with contempt.

He was right. We never managed to get rid of the bedbugs for good.

The other half of our barrack housed the Kvasha post office and the bed of Nina, the Kvasha postwoman, all in one big room. In truth, I could not imagine Nina fighting bedbugs or, in fact, banishing anything live from her bed. She was said to be exceedingly friendly. I had experienced Nina's *joie de vivre* one morning several weeks previously, when I had gone to the post office to mail a letter for my mother. The post office was open on alternate mornings, before Nina started on her daily and lonely forty-kilometre walk to Petrakovo. She would go there one day and come back the next.

I opened the door. The post office was empty, except for Nina. She was still in bed, but awake. She gave me a sideways look and stretched her arms lasciviously: 'Stepanooshka,' she gurgled, '*A ty menya poyebyosh segodnya*? Will you fuck me this morning?'

It was not that the activity was far from my mind. Actually, like most boys of sixteen, I hardly ever thought of anything else. But somehow the idea of starting my sex life with Nina frightened me. Or was it the suddenness of the proposition? I turned round and ran. I ran all the way to our barrack, the letter still in my hand.

'Has Nina gone to Petrakovo already?' asked Mother who was busy writing another letter. I was not able to answer. I was hot. I was sure that my face was beetroot red. My mouth was dry and no sound came out. With deliberate, slow movements I took off my fur cap, scarf, boots, coat. Undoing my coat buttons one by one took a very long time.

When I regained my composure, I put the unposted letter on the table and said, 'The post office is closed. She must have returned from Petrakovo late last night and is sleeping it off.' Mother looked at me suspiciously, but asked no further questions. For a long time I told nobody about the episode, but many years after the event I have dined out on it repeatedly.

In the morning after our nocturnal battle with bedbugs, Mother was ready to start a long-term campaign. 'Today,' she announced, 'I shall treat the walls with boiling water. An open flame would be too risky, I suppose. I have no idea how to treat the ceiling though.'

The walls were indeed a problem. The wisps of dry moss protruding through the cracked clay in between the logs would catch fire only too easily.

The spaces between the logs gave refuge to, among other creepy-crawlies, swarms of pale brown cockroaches. All wooden buildings in Siberia were full of them. They preferred the warm cracks round the large Siberian stoves, but their preference for warmth did not seem a good-enough reason for setting the barrack on fire. Anyway, they did not suck blood, did us no harm and had to be accepted as inevitable cohabitees. Incidentally, they were excellent swimmers. Should a cockroach fall from the canteen ceiling into one's soup, it would do a beautiful 'crawl' to the rim of the plate and, before you could say *psia krew*, dog's blood, it would get lost in a crack in the table. It would not stop one finishing one's soup, of course.

Yet bedbugs were different, remedies had to be put in hand. When I got home on that first day, my parents were busy fixing blankets as canopies over our beds. The purpose of the contraption suddenly dawned on me: 'So that was the reason for four-poster beds in the old days: to prevent insects parachuting on one.'

'We have to go back to the time-tested methods,' said Father, as we tied long sticks to the legs of my bed and stretched a spare blanket over it.

With fresh straw in the palliasse of my parents' bed and the upholstery of my bed dry once more, with the improvised canopies above us, our beds away from the walls and their legs in water-filled old tins, jars, saucers and suchlike, we were ready to repel another onslaught of bedbugs, including their parachute regiments.

Father's appointment to the new post did not affect my work. We finished clearing the fire-protection zone and then my team was dispersed. Helena and I were separated. She was assigned to a forest team to do the usual woman's job, while I, as was my ambition, became a *zvalshchik*, or tree feller.

I got the job by accident or, more precisely, as a result of Mr Wasserman's repeated mishaps. One night, during the evening meal in the canteen, my friend Mietek was very angry with his father: 'Dad, you must give it up before you get killed or maimed. I want you to be fit to leave when the time comes.'

'What's the problem?' asked Father, joining the discussion.

'I had a close shave in the forest. I just felled a large tree and did not jump out of the way fast enough. Mietek had to pull the end of a broken branch out of my thigh. Nothing to worry about,' said Mr Wasserman.

'Don't fib, Father,' said Mietek. 'You are getting too slow for tree felling, and you know it.' Mietek turned to my father. 'Please tell him. He might listen to you. He has had several mishaps lately. So far minor accidents only, that's true. But one day his luck will run out. This time we worked adjacent strips, so I saw what happened and ran to help. I found him with his leg skewered on a spike of a broken branch. I had to hack the branch off the tree and pull it out of the wound.'

'It's fine now,' said Mr Wasserman. 'It does not hurt. I can walk. I am going to work tomorrow and that's final.'

But Mietek would not give up. 'Okay, but you ought to change to another job, like cutting. It pays the same and is less risky. Act your age, Dad. I want both of us to return home to Płock.'

❊ ❊ ❊

The German attack on the USSR several weeks previously, on 22 June 1941, rekindled our hope of leaving Kvasha. At last the two dictators, Hitler and Stalin, were at each other's throats. But did this change us into Soviet allies? Does one's enemy's enemy automatically become one's friend? As yet this was far from clear.

Anyway, one thing became certain: we would leave Kvasha, and soon. We did not know when, or how, but leave we would.

But leaving the USSR and returning to Poland were two different things. In the event, neither of the two Wassermans ever returned home. I heard many years later that Mietek had joined the Polish infantry division fighting on the Russian front and was killed in the battle of Lenino. His father became a black-market dealer in Moscow, made a fortune, and eventually died there.

❊ ❊ ❊

It was then, in the Kvasha canteen, I grasped the opportunity: 'We are going to finish work on the fire-protection zone in a few days,' I said. 'Perhaps I could become your tree feller. I don't really want to be the team leader, I'd rather not, honestly. You could do the cutting and remain the leader.'

Mietek became agitated: 'Yes, Father. Let's do that. I am going to talk to Volkov. Get my *kasha*, Stefan.' He patted my back and left the table. Volkov was sitting with his chums nearby, at their usual table.

Mr Wasserman continued brooding aloud. 'He thinks I am ancient. I am only fifty-one.'

In the next moment Mietek was back at our table smiling broadly. He winked at me. 'Volkov agreed,' he said. 'He wants you to start in Father's team as their feller as soon as you have finished the fire-prevention zone. Father will be the cutter and remain the team leader. It's all settled.'

So that was the start of my new career. Mother was not happy about it, but I managed to persuade Father not to argue with Orlov again. After all I was now officially an adult, sixteen years and three weeks old.

'Dad, you might jeopardise your new job,' I suggested, 'and that would be a disaster for us all.' This stopped him in his tracks. I liked tree felling and I was becoming wily in getting my own way. I knew that Father would be loath to lose his medical post.

He was a good doctor and he was doing his work in his usual conscientious way. He held daily surgeries, visited the sick, inspected food stores and canteens. He did a lot of walking in Kvasha and twice a week walked several kilometres to Vasilyevo. He was a general practitioner, district health officer, midwife and dentist all rolled into one.

With the nearest hospital about eighty kilometres away in Krasnoborsk, Father, though primarily a paediatrician, had to deal with all the injuries and all the medical conditions during the remainder of our stay in Kvasha.

His take-over of the medical-room equipment and supplies in Kvasha's surgery was completed in about five minutes; all they consisted of were two wooden boxes, one containing two scalpels and a pair of tweezers and the other a set of dental extraction forceps, several packets of cotton-wool, some bandages, a large bottle of surgical spirit, a small bottle of iodine and two jars of powder, one of aspirin and the other bismuth; an apothecary scales with a box of small weights and a roll of brown floral wallpaper – the purpose of which eluded me – completed the inventory.

In view of the fact that the Russian male, and to some degree the female, have a constant and irresistible urge to drink anything even remotely alcoholic, from vodka to eau de Cologne, from antifreeze to methylated spirit, the almost intact bottle of surgical spirit was a surprising find.

As no local or general anaesthetic was available, painful treatments or procedures, such as the lancing of boils or abscesses, the setting of broken bones, extraction of rotten teeth and such like were just . . . well . . . painful.

Not all treatments were the doctor's preserve. As dentistry in Kvasha almost inevitably meant extraction, my old friend Vasya, the blacksmith, with his strong-man reputation and pliers readily available, probably pulled out more teeth than either my father or the nurse who preceded him.

Some time in the spring I did have a toothache but, having seen Vasya's methods in the smithy, I preferred to suffer in silence, eventually taking the offending and rotten tooth out myself, bit by bit, over a period of time.

Fascinated by the apothecary scales, I became Father's 'dispenser' and thus also discovered the purpose of the wallpaper. From time to time Father would ask me to prepare a supply of single dose packets of aspirin, the white powder, and of bismuth, the brownish powder. My job was to weigh the appropriate amounts of either preparation, to wrap them in small squares of the wallpaper and to label the packets. Bismuth was used to control diarrhoea, a very common problem in Kvasha; any other ailment had to be treated with aspirin.

My father's appointment aroused mixed feelings among the inhabitants of the two settlements. No doubt that sick people and mothers and children now received better medical care, but there were also losers. Mietek, for instance, complained to me: 'Life was easier before your Dad took over. About Christmas I had a few days off, and again was signed off a couple of months ago. Do you remember? Perhaps I did not tell you, but I just went to the nurse's room, dropped my trousers and told her that I had a pain in my groin. "Must be a hernia," I said. "Perhaps you ought to have a closer look." Every time I did that she blushed, looked away and gave me a certificate. It would not wash with your father, would it?'

Mietek was not the only man with an imaginary rupture in Kvasha. Apparently there had been an 'epidemic' of ruptures before Father took over.

Not all the problems the nurse had to deal with were fictitious, and she had not always been able to cope with them. She was a shy girl of eighteen, fresh from a two-month nursing course. For instance, in the winter of 1941 she had to deal with an epidemic of scarlet fever in children. Before the advent of antibiotics scarlet fever was a serious and frequently fatal illness. One evening Helena and I went to see Julka, Helena's friend in one of Kvasha's two communal dormitory barracks, which had no internal walls and were divided into family areas by flimsy partitions of old, often torn blankets and sheets. As we sat on Julka's bed, I heard a child's whimper coming from behind the partition.

'Józio has scarlet fever,' said Julka. 'Last night, Nina brought some new injections from Petrakovo and the nurse is coming to give him one, which we hope will cure him.' This was puzzling. I had read popular medical books and had listened to my parents talking about the current epidemic, but I never heard of injections for treating scarlet fever.

The girls went on gossiping and by the time the nurse came, I was bored.

'May I help you?' I asked the nurse. She knew me well, many a time had she come to Father to ask for advice. She gave me a box of ampoules to hold, while she went to the kitchen range to sterilise the syringe and the needle.

I looked at the box in my hand. It was labelled in big letters: *Toksin Skarlatinovyi, For Prophylaxis of Scarlet Fever.* Suddenly I felt anxious. I had heard that small doses of various toxins were being tried to induce immunity in the healthy. I was pretty sure that even a small amount of scarlet fever toxin given to a child who already had scarlet fever could cause serious trouble, perhaps even kill him.

Katya, the nurse, came back. 'Don't you mean to give him the *anti*toxin?' I asked her in a whisper. My anxiety was rising. Meanwhile, at the sight of the needle, the little boy stopped whimpering and started screaming his head off.

The nurse became confused, blushed. 'But I have no antitoxin,' she said. 'Nina brought this box last night. It's supposed to stop the epidemic, there were no instructions with it.'

In the meantime, Helena, who had overheard us, ran back to our barrack and was coming back with my father. He looked at the box and motioned the nurse to follow him out of the barrack. They were out only a couple of minutes. To the little boy's great relief the injection was abandoned and he eventually recovered on aspirin alone.

There was another case of scarlet fever which Father had to attend to. It was the daughter of Borisov.

Borisov was the Kvasha militiaman, a proud owner of the only, if very ancient, rifle in the settlement. He was a benign militiaman as militiamen go, a good soul in fact. One morning, well before Father's appointment to the medical post, when we just got into bed after a night on the ice road, he burst into the room, tears streaming down his cheeks. 'Vladislav Mikhailovich, I beg you, save my daughter. Nadya is dying!' Sobbing loudly, he did not speak for a while and then, the Russian *muzhik* that he was, he dropped down to his knees pleading.

His four-year-old daughter, who had scarlet fever, had become much worse during the night. 'She is as hot as a winter stove. She keeps puking and screaming with pain in her head. *Ryadi Boga*, in God's name, come with me. Katya is there already.'

'But you know,' said Father, 'that I am not allowed to treat people here.'

'God is my witness that nobody will know. Come, please come,' begged Borisov.

'She probably has an ear infection,' said Father in Polish, the language we always used between us, 'if not a brain abscess. I'd better go. Or might this be a trap?' He hesitated for a moment.

'His tears seem genuine,' said Mother.

Father was already out of bed and putting his shoes on. 'Well, let's go.' Father was afraid to treat the sick before his qualifications were officially recognised, but giving advice to Katya was different.

They left. Father returned a little while later.

'The child's eardrum was bulging,' Father reported, 'and we

had to pierce it with a thick needle. I got Katya to do it. She held the needle and I guided her hand. Copious pus came out. She will be all right,' he smiled.

Nadya recovered quickly, but for weeks afterwards, whenever she saw Father, she either ran away or hid in her mother's ample skirt.

Another emergency happened soon after. One morning, just as we entered the drying-room after the night's work, Katya burst in very agitated: 'Hurry up, please doctor, a little boy has a dreadful pain in his head . . . something terrible must have happened . . . haemorrhage? . . . I don't know what to do . . . Trepanation of the skull?'

Only then did I register the ear-piercing screams coming from the barrack across the street. Father doubled his efforts to get his ice-bound coat off and so did I. Trepanation of the skull! Trepanation, the oldest surgical operation in history. The caveman's method for releasing evil spirits. That would be something! Father and Katya ran across the street. I shouted to Helena, 'Let's go.'

But, pale as a sheet, she shook her head. 'You go.'

So I did. I was not going to miss it.

In a hopelessly rumpled bed a boy was wriggling and squirming as if possessed. His movements were so violent that I could not recognise him. He was about ten or eleven. He kept hitting his right ear with one hand and his violent screams were frightening. A pale, terrified elderly woman – his grandmother? – tried to hold his other hand, but he kept pushing her away.

'Oh, doctor, sir,' she exclaimed in Polish, 'thank God you are here, Katya did not know what to do. He has been screaming like this for the last half-hour. The drum in his right ear had to be cut over a year ago and he has had trouble with the ear ever since, but never like this. He isn't going to die, is he?' She sobbed, her hands held together as in prayer, her chin shaking.

Father placed the boy on his left side and, while Katya and the old woman held the patient down to stop him wriggling, he looked in the boy's ear by candlelight. 'Something is moving inside there,' he said. He pulled the ear this way and that. 'I need some warm clean oil on a clean spoon,' said Father.

As the grandmother let him go, the boy started wriggling

again. She came back with a teaspoon full of oil. 'It is pure olive oil. Thank God, we had a food parcel last week.'

Father held the spoon over the flame for a while, tested it with his finger and poured the oil into the boy's ear. At once the boy stopped screaming. Father set him up, leaning the boy's head to the right. The oil came out of the ear and, with it, a small cockroach.

This was amazing. Dramatic. This was pure magic.

I was not really sorry that I had missed a trepanation of the skull.

Ever since, in my medical practice, I have longed to repeat that feat of my father's, but the opportunity never came my way.

ELEVEN

THE BEGINNING OF THE END

✳

In our exile the transition from the end of its beginning to the beginning of its end was very rough indeed.

Kvasha was cut off from the world, except for old newspapers and the radio.

Actually there were two radios in the settlement. One was the office transmitter–receiver, the only link with Petrakovo and the outside world. The other was not a proper radio, just a loudspeaker mounted on a mast. It was connected to the office wireless and its output was controlled by Orlov and his staff.

This was the norm throughout the USSR. Every place of work, be it a collective farm or a factory, every village or settlement, most town squares and street corners, many private dwellings and communal dormitories, had loudspeakers spouting the slanted and mostly boring programmes.

After the initial few days in Kvasha I learned to ignore the loudspeaker. Music – mostly patriotic songs – apart, its output consisted of statistics (e.g. figures for the milk output in various districts of the Tatar Autonomous Republic), announcements (e.g. of increased coal production in the Donbas area), or boring verbatim reports of meetings of various Soviets, or Councils. Heroic milkmaids exceeding the norm by a hundred and fifty per cent were mentioned by name, children denouncing their parents were praised. What was more interesting were the educational broadcasts and, in particular, the corrections of history. Not only had most battles (known to me previously as Russian routs) been won by the Russians even in the pre-

Bolshevik era, but I also learned that most of the seventeenth-and eighteenth-century scientific advances had been wrongly attributed to western scientists, Italian, French, English, German or Polish, but were all really the work of one Mikhail Vasilyevitch Lomonosov, the Russian 'Leonardo da Vinci'.

Often this garbage was interspersed with excerpts from speeches of Lenin, or from collected works of Stalin, or by a harangue from some Party *apparatchik*.

No wonder that Kvasha radio – or the loudspeaker – was largely ignored by all the Kvasha inhabitants, Polish as well as Russian.

One day, it was 3 July, on our way to lunch from the fire-prevention zone, we passed a group of people standing by the loudspeaker mast. They were quiet, they looked serious. They listened without the usual mocking comments. It was a strange sight. Curious, Helena, her father and I joined them. Was it an announcement? Was it a speech?

It was a man talking. His language was not the melodious literary Russian of the usual radio announcers. His voice was hoarse, his delivery dull, monotonous, he spoke with a harsh accent. Due to this and the frequent crackles, I missed a lot. At times the voice faded away altogether.

'Who is it talking?' Mr Romer asked.

'Stalin, the organ-grinder himself,' said a man.

'The head devil,' said a woman; she crossed herself and spat in disgust.

'Our great leader, our sun. The old Georgian, Dzhugashvili himself. Should have been strangled at birth,' opined the first man.

'Quiet . . . let's listen,' muttered some others.

I listened: '. . . They broke the treaty . . . the solemn declarations of friendship . . . they treacherously invaded our sacred soil . . .' The speaker sounded frightened. He complained, as if an injustice had been done to him personally by a close friend. Was it really Stalin? I had never heard him before. Had Hitler, after all, attacked the USSR?

That evening in the canteen, arguments flew from every direction. Opinions differed widely.

'We shall be released any day now. They will need us.'

'Nonsense. Nobody will bother about us. We shall be forgotten.'

'The Germans will take Moscow before Christmas.'

'They will never get past Minsk. Winter will stop them before
long.'

In their excitement people shouted, quarrelled, argued, with
much table-banging. Some almost came to blows. Father
ventured no opinion. 'I have no idea what might happen,' he
said when questioned directly. I thought that he was right not
to speculate, there were too many unknowns.

'We ought to leave this place as soon as we get organised,' said
Mr Wasserman. 'And the sooner we start the better.'

Others disagreed. 'The Germans will never get as far north as
this. This must be the safest place to sit out the war.'

'Hear, hear!'

At this point I didn't know what to think. When we left the
canteen my head was so full of contradictory ideas that I just
went to bed and slept like a log.

The weeks that followed were an anticlimax. Nothing
changed in Kvasha: we went to work as before, had our soup
and *kasha* in the canteen, went to bed in our crowded quarters.
The war was far away and it left Kvasha undisturbed. Or did it?

News on the loudspeaker had never before been listened to as
eagerly as now. Even in working hours there were always people
gathered around the loudspeaker mast. Names of towns taken
by the Germans were passed from person to person. The Red
Army was 'assuming new defensive positions', 'straightening
out the front', or 'shortening its lines of supply'. On other
occasions it was 'regrouping for an offensive in preparation for
the final victory'.

I felt no loyalty whatsoever to the Soviet Union, but I was
terrified of the Germans. As yet we had no inkling of the mass-
murders committed by the Nazis and by the German Army in
the occupied territories, but the little I had seen of the war was
enough to make me feel frightened. At the same time I could
not help the feeling of *schadenfreude* at the defeats suffered by
the Red Army which, in 1939, colluded with Hitler and knifed
Poland in the back. Now it was they who were being routed, as
our Army had been two years before.

One immediate effect of war on Kvasha life was that the mail bag brought by Nina from Petrakovo was getting lighter from one delivery to the next. One evening, as we were walking home from the canteen, Mother broke the silence. 'I suppose now there is no hope of ever getting any news from Jurek.'

I had almost forgotten my older brother. Since 1936 he had been studying abroad and we had had no news from him for nearly two years.

'Now, more than ever, they are bound to intercept all letters from abroad,' confirmed Father putting his hand round Mother's shoulders.

'How does he manage without his allowance?' Mother said wonderingly and added, turning to me, 'thank God you are with us.'

'By now Jurek must have joined the army. I am sure he has. I would have,' I exclaimed, and bit my tongue as I looked at Mother. Her shoulders were shaking, and her handkerchief went up to her eyes.

I felt stupid. A mixture of guilt, tenderness and compassion brought tears to my eyes. She had always loved Jurek, her first born, more than me, I knew that, but she was my mother too. 'My eyes are sweating,' said Mother with a faint smile.

I could not, or would not, take my eyes off her face and an invisible vice squeezed my chest. How thin she was! I must have eaten much more than my own bread ration!

Father was of medium height and there, at his side, she did not even reach his shoulder. Nowadays her head just about reached the top of my arm. Her face was pitifully small. She suddenly looked old, and she was only fifty-one.

As these thoughts flashed through my mind, Father gave me a stern look and changed the subject. 'We've had no letter from Adam for over a year now. I wonder what happened to him? How are the Soviets treating imprisoned Polish officers?'

Adam had been held in a PoW camp somewhere in the Ukraine. His last letter reached us in Pińsk, before our deportation, but we had heard nothing from him since. By now the area of the camp must surely have been overrun by Germans.

❊ ❊ ❊

We never heard from Uncle Adam again. With many thousands of other Polish PoWs, mainly officers, he was murdered by the NKVD in the Katyn forest. The massacre was carried out well before the Germans attacked the USSR.

With barbed wire they tied the prisoners' hands behind their backs and shot them one by one in the back of the neck. I still shiver when I think of the manner of his death.

❀ ❀ ❀

Then, one evening, Nina returned from Petrakovo and her bag was almost empty. It contained only one letter, the last-ever letter Mother received from her sister Rose. I had never met Aunt Rose, but I knew that she had eloped with a tsarist army officer during the First World War, well before I was born, and that he died soon after. She was a dentist and Yuri, her only son, was a fighter pilot in the Soviet Air Force.

Disjointed but meaningful fragments of her letter have stuck in my memory: '. . . the war caught up with us even here . . . I may have to leave Zaporozhe . . . I had no news of Yuri since the start of the war . . . is he alive? . . . God help us all . . .' Poor Aunt Rose. She was probably a refugee on the roads now, with thousands of others, just as we had been in September. Suddenly Kvasha felt safe.

❀ ❀ ❀

At the end of August 1941 Kvasha was thrown into turmoil.

One afternoon three dugout boats came from Petrakovo bringing two NKVD officers and several civilians. Big cardboard boxes filled another boat. The new arrivals with their boxes slipped into the office and left us wondering and guessing.

In the evening, in the canteen, Volkov scribbled on the announcement board: 'Tomorrow – day free from work. Heads of families will report in the morning to the Community Hall.'

Instantly the canteen was abuzz with rumours: This can only mean another deportation further east . . . work in mines . . . in factories . . . on collective farms . . . men will be made to 'volunteer' for the front. The potential scenarios were endless.

Earlier in the day somebody mentioned hearing on the radio the words: 'amnesty for Poles.' Or so he thought. He was not a fluent Russian speaker, however. But if he was right, it was puzzling. We had never been sentenced, or imprisoned. So how could we be 'amnestied'?

The canteen closed. It was a warm August night, not really a white night any more, but a bluish grey one. Arguments continued in the open well past midnight under the sky seeded with millions of stars.

In the morning my parents and I joined the crowd outside the Community Hall. I managed to squeeze through to a window to have a peep inside. The newcomers from Petrakovo and our office staff were arranging chairs around several tables spread about the hall.

I returned to our group consisting of our old room-mates and neighbours, the Romers, Mietek and his father, even the Brzezińskis. Yesterday, Mr Brzeziński, the alleged NKVD informer, had been locked out of the office.

Orlov, the Kvasha headman, came out of the Hall and pinned a notice printed in large letters to the door:

ANNOUNCEMENT
THE SOVIET GOVERNMENT HAS GRANTED AN AMNESTY TO ALL
POLISH PRISONERS AND DEPORTEES. THE AMNESTY DOCUMENT
WILL SERVE AS THE FAMILY PASSPORT AND AS A ONE-WAY TRAVEL
PERMIT TO THE DESTINATION OF YOUR CHOICE.

The crowd broke up into smaller groups and the announcement was analysed. All kinds of possibilities were read into it. Orlov was there, at the door, waiting. Dozens of questions were fired at him. He answered them calmly and softly and managed to throw some light on our immediate situation. Heads of families were to be interviewed in alphabetical order and would be expected to state the destination to be entered on the amnesty/travel document. The document would not be valid without the destination having been clearly stated. With the document we would be free to leave Kvasha.

The first question was thus: Where should one go? When? and How? were of secondary importance for the time being.

Lively discussions followed, friends consulting one another, families putting their heads together. Names of Soviet towns and cities were bounced about like ping-pong balls, some having already been overrun by the German Army. But the USSR was still a very big country, even what remained of it was many times the size of Europe.

We stood in one group, my parents and our friends. The situation was totally unexpected. We had all dreamt of being freed one day, but being asked to choose one's destination was not even the stuff that our dreams were made of.

Disappointed with the indecisiveness of the adults, I touched Helena's arm and led her aside. 'My mother alone is talking sense,' I whispered. 'She says that it does not matter what destination we name. The chaos on the roads and railways will make it impossible to reach it anyway. What about Astrakhan? It is almost due south and over one thousand kilometres from here.'

'Don't be silly,' said Helena. Then she thought for a moment. 'Well, why not? It is as good as anywhere else. Yes, let's go to Astrakhan.'

I returned to our group and tugged at Father's sleeve. 'I think we should try for either Astrakhan or Tashkent,' I said in all seriousness. Puzzled, Father frowned, his head to one side. He glanced at Helena and then back at me.

Suddenly he smiled broadly. 'Is it caviar, or is it bread that you are after? A pity we can't have both together, now,' he laughed. Father knew me well. The very expensive kind of caviar, which I loved and which before the war he sometimes brought from Warsaw, came from Astrakhan.

He also knew that Helena and I had been reading a novel, *Tashkent, the City of Bread* by Aleksey Tolstoy, nephew of the author of *War and Peace*.

He turned to Mother. 'Stefan and Helena want to go either to Astrakhan or to Tashkent. What do you think?'

'It doesn't really matter what the travel paper states,' said my mother. 'It will just be chaos anyway,' she repeated. 'People will board any train going south or east and only then will they try to guess its destination, same as during the revolution.'

A large crowd soon gathered around us. People kept asking:

Why Astrakhan? Why Tashkent? Father tried to answer, but his words were drowned in an avalanche of questions. 'I shall opt for Astrakhan,' he concluded with a smile and we went home.

The magic of '*Pan Doktór*, The Doctor,' worked once more. As a result a large proportion of Kvasha Poles gave Astrakhan as their destination.

At the Community Hall Father's turn came early: in the Cyrillic alphabet letters V and W are one and the same and it comes third after A and B. When he returned, Mother and I looked at our amnesty document. It said in plain Russian: 'Destination: Astrakhan'.

Later in the evening Alyosha knocked on our door. He greeted Father: 'Zdravstvuytye Vladislav Mikhailovich.' His manners had improved perceptibly since Father became Kvasha's doctor. He now addressed Father by his name and patronymic, no more of that '*stareek*, old man,' he had used on the ice road.

Then he turned to me: 'Tomorrow morning you will help me and the stable man to take the horses to their holiday pastures. They need fattening up.'

'All right,' I said, but Father was not happy. Where to? Why him? For how long? We were supposed to be leaving Kvasha any day now.

'Don't worry, Vladislav Mikhailovich, I shall look after Stepanooshka for you. He rides well. We shall be back in three days. It's not that far. When not required, our horses always go on holiday to be looked after by an old couple who live near the summer pasture. They have a lovely house.'

'Why will horses not be required?' asked Mother. 'Does it mean no more forest work in Kvasha?'

'Strictly speaking I don't know what's happening,' answered Alyosha. 'But this is the order I had been given.' Then he turned to me: 'I'll wake you up on my way to the stable, early in the morning. Shall I knock on your window? We must leave very early.' He started on his way and then stopped on the threshold. He could not restrain his curiosity. 'Tell me please, why the hell do all of you, Poles and Jews, want to go to Astrakhan?' he asked, his brows knitted in concentration.

'The caviar,' said Father. 'They make it there.'

Curiosity in Alyosha's eyes was replaced by amazement: 'They make caviar there,' he repeated and smacked his lips. 'That's a snack for the top dogs. To go with vodka, of course,' he laughed. 'I have seen it, but I have never tasted it. Have you?' he asked me.

'Oh yes. And I liked it,' I said. 'Even without vodka.'

He woke me up very early indeed. The canteen was still closed and the settlement was just stirring to life. I helped Dimitri, the stable man, and Alyosha to lead the horses one by one to the paddock. Thinking of the long bareback ride to Petrakovo last winter, I brought a thick blanket in lieu of a saddle.

'Where is Zhemchuzhina?' I asked the stable man.

'She is working for the collective farm now,' he said. 'Take *Dooshenka*, Sweetheart, instead,' he suggested pointing to a chestnut mare snorting impatiently outside.

I patted her face: 'I hope we shall be friends, you and me.' She just snorted again.

Soon the stable was empty, silent. Without further ado, we set off. The stable man led the way, followed by the troop of some thirty horses, with Alyosha and me closing the rear. We forded the river and, for about an hour, followed the track of the old ice road on the other side. Soon we left it for a forest path. The path was narrow and we could progress only in single file. The horses kept to the path, but at every glade or clearing they scattered to feed on the lush grass and we had to round them up again. From time to time, as the path returned to the riverbank, we would stop at the water's edge and have a drink, side by side with the horses and in much the same position.

By the afternoon, in spite of the folded blanket covering Dooshenka's back, I was getting stiff and sore. Whether my bottom was less well padded than those few months earlier, or whether Dooshenka was leaner and bonier than Zhemchuzhina, this ride was much tougher on my legs than the night expedition to Petrakovo. It was also considerably longer. We travelled all day with only short rest breaks, and even those were for the sake of the horses. After a short night's rest at the riverside, we dipped again into the forest. Here the tract was wide, almost a road. It was some six or eight paces wide and originally must have been paved with closely packed parallel logs laid across it. By now, however, most of the logs were broken, rotten, slippery with mould and moss and overgrown. Only a few here and there remained level and in their original side-by-side position. Elsewhere they were scattered randomly, like so many matches clumsily set in a row by a bored and angry child. Its surface was thus a hindrance rather than a help and we made our way on a narrow path between it and the edge of the forest.

'What sort of a road is it? Who had built it?' I asked the stable man when the path widened a bit and I found myself riding at his side.

'*Kulaks*, rich peasants, deportees from Samara,' he said. 'They were not keen on collectivisation. In 1928 they were brought here in their thousands. Men, women, children, old people. On foot. With only few belongings. But they worked hard, they built good houses, they made it almost a small town. They called it Gusino. You will see for yourself. It's not far now, ten kilometres. Then the Bolsheviks made them build this road through the forest and through the bogs. It was hard work, many died. Less than half of them were left when they let them go back south.' He stopped suddenly.

'Shut up, you horse shit,' Alyosha caught up with us. 'Be quiet, you damned horse's arsehole,' he repeated. 'Do you want us to end our lives in prison?'

The conversation stopped. Alyosha never called the stable man by his given name of Dimitri or his patronymic, not even by the diminutive, Dima. He either called him stable lad or used a contemptuous epithet instead, mostly with undisguised scorn.

Was the difference in status between a master forester and a stable man too great to be bridged? Even in the Soviet, so-called classless, society?

A *kulak* was a land-owning peasant, an occasional employer of casual labour, which was enough for the communists to label him an 'exploiter of the masses', or an 'enemy of the people'. In the 1920s millions of *kulaks* were starved, shot or exiled on direct orders from Stalin, who feared their independence and their opposition to the collectivisation of land into *kolkhozes*.

But by now I was too tired and too sleepy to think serious

thoughts. We had only one short rest during the night and that was some six hours ago. My bottom was sore and I was rigid with fatigue. Only my arms wound tightly round my mare's neck kept me from falling under the hoofs of the horses. Nobody would even notice if I did, I thought, feeling sorry for myself.

I have only a vague recollection of the rest of the day's journey. I remember a loud '*Stoy, stoyyy . . . stoyyyyy*,' repeated again and again woke me from my precarious doze.

Alyosha and Dimitri were rounding up the horses. 'Here we are!' shouted Alyosha. But I was not able to help them, I couldn't even get off the horse on my own. I was dead below the belt. I looked round. We were in a wide unpaved street with houses on both sides. They were one-storey log cabins, but they looked quite different from the Kvasha barracks. They betrayed some individuality, even a kind of prosperity. The one by which we had stopped had painted shutters and wild flowers growing in boxes under the open windows. Other houses looked deserted, their shutters tightly closed.

Two people came out of the house. First a woman in a wide skirt – she was enormous, a veritable giantess – followed by a grizzly bear of a man, not much shorter than she. '*Zdravstvuy-tye*, good day, how are you?' lively greetings were exchanged with much hand-shaking and back-slapping all round. Animated chatter went on for a while, all four of them talking simultaneously.

Then the woman noticed me. 'And who is that?' she asked.

'This is our Polack boy, Stefan,' said Alyosha. I did not like this contemptuous 'Polack' epithet, but I let it pass, not able to keep my eyes open. When I opened them a moment later the big woman was by my side.

'Poor boy, he is tired out.' She put her arms round me, lifted me bodily off the horse, carried me into the house, babe in arms, and deposited me like a fragile doll on a heap of brown skins in the corner. The skins stank. Bear skins, I thought, as my eyes closed again.

And then, something hard was pressing against my lips. I looked up. Our hostess was leaning over me with a broad smile on her surprisingly kind face and was pressing a bottle to my mouth. 'Poor lad,' she repeated. 'You are exhausted, have a drink and go to sleep.' The liquid was bitter. It burned my mouth. But it was not vodka, though certainly some kind of alcohol. Was it some industrial or surgical spirit? Sickly, sweet odour. Then I recognised it, it was eau de Cologne!

I woke up to loud voices in the room. The sun was high in the window, it had to be near noon. Had I really slept away the rest of yesterday and the whole night?

Repeated toasts of '*Na zdoróvye*, your good health,' the clinking of glasses, all the smacking and champing sounds, made me feel hungry. All I had to eat or drink since leaving Kvasha was half a loaf of our clay-like bread which Mother had given me, washed down with a lot of Uftyuga water – not counting the gulp of eau de Cologne; I chuckled to myself at the memory.

'Are you awake Stepanooshka? Good day to you. Come and eat with us, my son,' the woman called to me. She did not have to repeat the invitation. I was up and, after a brief visit behind the house, I was ready.

'Wash your hands, lad,' the woman pointed to a bench under the window, where there was a large white enamel bowl, a jug of water, a saucer with a cake of dark-yellow soap and a white towel on a peg above it.

I washed my hands. I would have done anything for a good meal. 'Grigori, give him a drop of vodka,' said our hostess. Her husband put a glass – the usual hundred-millilitre size (over three fluid ounces) – in front of me and half-filled it with vodka. A big white plate in the middle of the table was still half full of *zakooski*, savoury snacks: pickled mushrooms, onions, pieces of dried salt fish and slices of warm, home-baked bread.

'Your good health, Mother,' I said politely, lifting my glass. She smiled and blushed with obvious pleasure.

'And yours . . . and yours . . .' The rest of the company lifted their glasses too and all of us emptied them in one gulp. It was real vodka, not eau de Cologne this time. Hands stretched to the still half-full plate and at last I could do the same.

'How old are you?' she asked.

'I was sixteen last June.'

She smiled, shook her head and clicked her tongue in amazement. 'Our Pashenka would have been the same age now.' She crossed herself in the Russian manner, reaching far out to the tips of her shoulders, first to the right side, then the left.

The old man refilled our glasses, with another half portion for me. 'Once more your health, Anna Mikhailovna,' said Alyosha and clicked glasses with the hostess. We had another 'drop' of vodka, a few more titbits, then Anna Mikhailovna left the table.

While I was helping myself to more bread, the lady of the house returned bearing a plate with a whole big baked fish on it. A pike? Would she give me some? I had not been given a plate.

She said: 'Grigori caught it this morning while you were all asleep.' She left again and returned this time with a bowl of millet porridge and another one full of bread. And with a plate for me! A true feast. I had not eaten so well for over a year. To top it all off we had mock tea with real honey cakes.

What a feast! Pity I couldn't take a cake for Helena. Or could I ask? Better not.

The meal was finished. I was replete and joined the others, as custom required, in a polite belch. We sat for a moment in silence and then Alyosha said: 'We ought to start on our way back.'

We went out into the street. Anna Mikhailovna sat down on a sunny bench outside the house. 'Dimitri, bring your horses,' said Grigori Fedórovitch, 'from the other, western meadow. They are fat after their six weeks' holiday. And you, Stefan, come for a walk with the old man.' We walked up the street in silence for several minutes in the direction of the forest.

Only then did I notice a small hillock among the trees, topped by a big orthodox cross. It seemed unusual in this god-less country.

At the edge of the forest the street ended and Grigori took the path which led gently up the hill. Soon we left the trees behind. The hill was bald, green with fresh grass, speckled with clumps of wild flowers. At the top, in front of the cross, Grigori dropped to his knees and crossed himself. He said softly: '*Góspodi pom luy.* God have mercy.' His lips kept moving, but I could not discern the words.

I waited, motionless and silent.

Grigori got off his knees and we turned round. The hill was small, not more than a hump, but it offered a good view of the village over the top of the trees. It was large, bigger then Kvasha, but not as big as Petrakovo. Its straight streets met at right angles, reminding me of street plans of American towns in geography textbooks.

But there was not a soul to be seen in the streets. The village looked deserted, desolate. The houses were very different from our barracks in Kvasha and even from the standard log dwellings in Petrakovo. They had doors and roofed-over porches with wooden balustrades, window shutters and empty flower-boxes. But most roofs were in need of repair, most shutters and the window-boxes were hanging at peculiar angles.

I looked at Grigori. His face was set hard, his unblinking eyes fixed somewhere high above the horizon. And then he looked at me, smiled and reached for his pipe. He proceeded to fill it with *makhorka* from a rabbit-skin pouch. He took his time over it.

'I suppose you have plenty of questions, but are not going to ask them. People are afraid to even *think* of questions nowadays. But you are a good lad and I will answer them for you all the same.

'With thousands of other families they rounded us up in 1928, in the villages of the Samara province. They called us *kulaks*. First they loaded us into cattle wagons and brought us north. From Kotlas they drove us here like cattle. This was wilderness, a small glade in the forest, but we worked hard, cleared the trees and built our Gusino.'

Pipe firmly in his teeth, he spread both arms sideways in an expansive gesture and then crossed them over his chest, as if to embrace the empty village, or his memory of its people.

'We had no seed grain to grow anything. Anyway, hardly anything would grow in this frozen land.' He stopped for a while to draw vigorously on his dying pipe. 'So, we became lumberjacks,' he continued. 'Used to hard work, we worked hard. Then they made us build the timber road to the riverside. Ten versts of it, across the swamp. Many had drowned.

'The first winter was the worst. Children and old people died like flies. Measles, scarlet fever, typhus. Even simple colds took them away. Hundreds had died. We buried them in common graves. On this hillock. On all its sides,' He stretched out his hand pointing to unidentifiable graves: 'Here, and there, and there . . . We marked the graves with crosses, our true-faith crosses. But the Bolsheviks came, tore the crosses up and burned them. So we put up this big cross at the top and kept watch day and night, for weeks. They came back, but they did not dare. . .

'Now I don't even know exactly where our Pashenka and our Dunichka lie. Our son died that first winter, on Christmas Day. He was three. God took our little girl two weeks later, she was only one. '*Góspodi, pom luy*, God have mercy.' He crossed himself again.

'Some years later, when they let us go back to Samara, which they had renamed Kuybyshev by then, fewer then half of us were left alive. They went home, only Anna Mikhailovna and I stayed behind to tend the graves on the hill. I am older than Anna Mikhailovna and she will bury me when God calls, but who will bury her?' He sighed again, '*Góspodi pom luy.*'

Indistinct shouts reached us from the village. Alyosha and the stable man were waving their arms, but I could not hear their words.

We rejoined them. Dimitri was holding three fresh horses in readiness. The one for me, a chestnut, had, I was glad to observe, a flat back and rounded sides. I was about to mount it when Anna Mikhailovna ran out of the door holding something in her hands. It was a long strip of bearskin folded in two, hair inside. Two leather straps hung from it. 'That's to go under your bum,' she said and showed me how to put it on the horse's back and strap it under its belly.

'Many thanks,' I said and, with my best Polish manners, kissed her hand. She smiled, blushed and kissed me loudly on both cheeks.

Off we went. I looked back, they were both waving to us. I kept looking back and waving until we entered the forest and lost sight of them behind the trees.

In years to come the kind smiling face of the big woman, Anna Mikhailovna, kept coming back to me in dreams. The good dreams.

Our way back to Kvasha was quick and uneventful. Unencumbered by the pack of loose horses we made good progress. We slept the night in a glade and reached Kvasha at noon the following day. I didn't know whether it was the new saddle or my well-padded horse, but I managed to dismount unaided, and I was not too sore.

But something unusual was happening in Kvasha. At noon I would normally expect children to play in the street or at the edge of the forest: hide and seek, cowboys and Indians, soldiers, lumberjacks. I would expect to see old people and women plodding their way to or from the canteen or the shop or, with buckets in their hands, the river. Yet the riverside and the street were quiet, deserted. Not one deportee, not one Russian to be seen.

A sudden fear almost immobilised me. Had all the Poles left? Surely my parents would not have left without me. But could they have been made to do so? What about the Russian inhabitants of Kvasha? I was stricken with terror. Afraid to go home I ran to the canteen. It was closed. I ran home in a panic.

I was almost there when Mother emerged from the forest. I ran to her. Seeing me, she put down her leaf-lined basket full of wild mushrooms. 'Thank God you are back.' She gave me a hug and then held me at an arm's length saying, 'You must be tired, and hungry . . .'

I hugged her again. 'Never mind, Mother, but what's happening here? Where is everyone?'

We turned to go home. 'They are all in the forest, building rafts,' she said. 'Father is there too. They won't be back until very late. Let's sit down.' We did so on the steps of our porch.

'Now, let's start at the beginning. The day you left with the horses all forest work stopped. In the morning Volkov announced in the canteen: No horses, no work. They did it on purpose, sent all the horses away, I mean. Apparently food stores are low and they just want to get rid of us. So we had to get organised. A Polish *Soviet*, Council, was elected and Father is on it. They have been talking all day and well into the night. They decided to build rafts and to lay down food stores. This is the third day that we have all been at it. Older women were sent out to the forest to gather wild mushrooms, berries and other edible plants for the journey, but Volkov told me that you might be back today and I stayed close.' She stopped talking and stroked my hair and cheek.

'What about food in the meantime?' I asked. 'Is the canteen closed?'

'Yes. The authorities refused to sell us food in the usual way,' said Mother. 'They would not listen to reason. Orlov knows only that: He who does not work, does not eat. He kept repeating it again and again. People got angry and forced their way into the canteen. Eventually the Polish catering staff took it over. They took charge of the store and of the bakery. Janek, the head cook, is now in command. Borisov threatened him with the rifle. It was scary, but he took no notice. Brave of him, don't you think? The canteen opens only once now, in the evening, and everybody, Poles and Russians, gets one free meal a day. Janek says that at this rate there will be enough *kasha* for three or four weeks. We also get free bread, half a loaf a day each. There is enough flour for six weeks. We shall have to leave here well before the food runs out.'

Suddenly, Mother got up. 'Here I am talking and you must be starving and thirsty. Wait a moment.' I found a sunny spot and lay down on the grass. Janek, the cook, came to my mind. Would I have been able to stand up to Borisov as he had done? Perhaps his doubling as a barber and his skill with the cut-throat razor had boosted his courage.

I woke with a start and sat up. The sun was down over the forest, for a moment I did not know where I was.

Father was there, sitting on the grass with me. I got my bearings.

'I came home early hoping that you might be back,' he said. 'Mother wanted me to wake you up. She prepared grilled mushrooms on toast for you, but they have gone cold. You have slept most of the afternoon.'

Grilled mushrooms on toast, even when cold, were very good. I didn't waste a crumb.

'You have heard about the Council. Thank God we have got organised. Helena's father chaired the meeting. The first day, the day you left, they argued ceaselessly. As usual, they all knew best. By midnight we were all exhausted and started talking sense. We decided that the only way out of Kvasha was the river and in order to use it we would have to build rafts. We have to provide transport for over four hundred people and all their belongings. We cannot afford to leave behind a stitch, nor a single pot. In Russia, in wartime, anything is good for barter, and barter may be the only way to survive.'

'Does anybody know anything about building rafts?' I asked. 'Quite a job without nails. How would we hold the logs together?'

'We need at least twenty, perhaps twenty-two rafts. Sasha, the saw-setter, showed Mr Wasserman how to tie logs together with plaited birch twigs. Very ingenious, I must say. None of the other Russians would help. They are all afraid of Orlov and he must have his orders from above, I suppose. They want us out of here, but hinder us at every step. Not very logical, is it? Still . . . Do you remember Sasha?'

'Of course I remember Sasha,' I said. 'I worked with him in the saw-pit a year ago. He hates the Bolsheviks. He would be helping us just out of spite,' I added.

To get over four hundred people of all ages out of Kvasha, with their bedding, their suitcases, their bundles and boxes, was a staggering undertaking. The Council's choice of the Uftyuga river as our route and of rafts as the means of transport was dictated by geography and by the sheer realities of the situation. Other than footpaths in the forest, the only way out of Kvasha was the river. Some eighty kilometres downstream, as the Uftyuga flowed into the Northern Dvina river, was the port of Krasnoborsk. So down the Uftyuga we had to go. As the only river transport available in Kvasha were the five or six dugout boats, rafts were the only answer.

Kotlas, our nearest railway station, was also on the Northern Dvina river, but upstream from Krasnoborsk and thus not reachable by rafts. Cargo ships plying the Northern Dvina from Arkhangelsk to Kotlas stopped in Krasnoborsk and we hoped to board one of them.

This information came from the Kvasha Russians, who on the first day or two after the amnesty had still remained friendly. It was their opinion that our best bet was rafts to Krasnoborsk and then the boat to Kotlas.

Our journey to Kvasha had been bad enough, I thought to myself. A week locked up in cattle wagons, then that long walk from Petrakovo to Kvasha. Yet, compared with the problems of

leaving our place of exile, it seemed like the pleasureable walk of
a nursery school crocodile through the town park. Was that the
price of freedom?

The rest of my first day back in Kvasha passed quickly. The
following day we got up at five, as usual, in a hurry to get down
to the forest. We all worked much harder than ever before. Men
felling trees, women removing the branches, children collecting
them in heaps. Every tree-trunk was cut into logs six metres
long. At intervals we had to stop tree felling to get the logs to
the riverside. We had no horses: all Kvasha horses were 'on
holiday' and I had helped to get them there. We had to carry
each piece of timber out of the forest. We either lifted the log on
our shoulders and carried it like a coffin in a funeral procession
or, if it was too heavy, we would push two or three stout sticks
under it and carry it two, three, or four men to a stick. Roughly
speaking, each raft required twenty to thirty logs for the
platform, two thinner pieces for the transverse beams, two more
for the oars and two strong short, Y-shaped timbers for the oar
supports.

By the end of my first day, the third day for the others, we
had less than a quarter of the timber required.

Our work was in fact illegal. We were actually stealing the
State's timber, though without any compunction on our part,
while the settlement's authorities shut their eyes to our deeds
and even our existence. All they wanted was to get rid of us and
we were obligingly doing their job for them. Besides, stealing
timber in Siberia was really like stealing sand in the Sahara.

The evening meal in the canteen was very animated, and after
we finished Mr Wasserman expounded on his newly gained
technical knowledge: 'To make a raft you set your logs side by
side on the ground, as near the river as possible, their thick and
thin ends alternating. Then you place the transverse beam across
the top, about six hand-breadths from the logs' ends. Next you
make a ring of two or three birch twigs twisted or plaited
together and push it round the ends of two adjacent logs, say
log one and log two, until it touches the side of your transverse
beam. The ring must be big enough to go round the two log
ends with a little to spare. You tighten it by driving a sharpened
peg through the extra bit and under the beam like that.'

He drew a picture on the announcement board. 'You do exactly the same with logs two and three, logs three and four, logs four and five, and so on. Another team does the same at the other end of the raft. Properly done, the construction is very strong,' continued Mr Wasserman. 'We will need two stout oars for each raft to keep it in midstream. They are simple enough to make. You fell a sapling about three or four metres long and about ten centimetres' diameter at the base. You hack off the twigs and with the axe you flatten the thick end like that.

'For the oar support you need a stout Y-shaped piece. You flatten the base and drive it vertically between two middle logs, one support on each end of the raft. You secure it with pegs on each side and with birch twigs.'

Mr Gruszyński, our other engineer, agreed: 'Yes, this ought to be strong enough. I suggest that in addition we provide each raft with a clay fireplace. Easily done . . .'

'That's a good idea,' said Father. 'But would we be able to stop and get firewood on the way, or should we take a supply with us?'

'There will hardly be room for firewood,' intervened another Council member. 'We must carry between twenty and twenty-two people on each raft. What with luggage, food and the fireplace, there will be no room for anything else.' Here the meeting became bogged down in details.

We were planning for a journey lasting four or five days. In preparation, the catering staff were excused from forest work in order to bake sufficient bread and hardtack for the voyage. My mother headed the team of women given the task of gathering mushrooms and berries and possibly some edible leaves, all of which were to be distributed on the eve of our departure. For several more days we worked hard from dawn till dusk: felling trees, cutting the trunks, carrying the logs out of the forest. The days were still reasonably long.

Materials gathered, we started building the rafts. Mr Wasserman was in charge and he had become quite an expert. The rest of us were inexperienced apprentices and by the end of the first day of feverish construction not a single raft was completed. We persisted and we learned as we went along. After a week of back-breaking toil we had twenty-two rafts ready, each equipped with oars and with a clay fireplace.

Mr Wasserman proved to be an excellent organiser. On the first day, without any further meetings or vote taking, he took overall charge of all raft construction. 'It's amazing,' said Father. 'Poles have usually more officers than foot-soldiers, more chiefs than Indians, but here we have one top general and nobody demurs.'

The achievement was indeed remarkable. After all, our collective experience of raft-making was nil, we had fewer than a hundred fully able-bodied men and perhaps a dozen women capable of heavy physical work. The only available raw materials were those provided by the forest. For tools we had nothing but saws and axes.

We were lucky with the weather, it was dry and cool. There was hoarfrost in the morning, but it rapidly disappeared under the pallid early-morning sun. Other than denying us the use of horses, Orlov and his minions eventually left us alone, but nobody offered to help. Perhaps Sasha was the only man with real experience of raft-making and rafting on Siberian rivers. One evening in the canteen he joined us and the two Wassermans at the table. He sat down next to me.

'We had worked well together, Stefanooshka,' he said, as Father offered him one of his Kazbek cigarettes. Sasha accepted it with obvious pleasure. 'Thank you very much, it's a real treat,' he said and continued. 'You have a good boy, *Vladislav Mikhailovich*, a good worker. You and your wife will not go short in your old age.'

'I hope so,' said Father, smiling at me and changing the subject. 'It was good of you to help us with the raft-making; we are really grateful. We shall be leaving you any day now; would you be able to give us some practical advice on rafting? Or would it be against the rules? We are not really enemies of the people, you know.'

'Oh, I do know that. And I am not afraid. I am sixty years old. Not that many years left. I don't really care.' He looked round all the same and lowered his voice. 'It's the Bolsheviks who are the true enemies of the people, not you and not us.' He inhaled the fragrant smoke deeply and looked round the room again. 'Now listen carefully,' he said. 'On the way down the river, when you stop for the night, use ropes or your belts to secure both ends of the raft to strong trees or to protruding roots, and always keep watch through the night.'

'Why keep watch?' I asked.

'There are collective farms and forest settlements on the way, especially the other side of Petrakovo, between it and Krasnoborsk, and a few before Petrakovo. They may be a long way from the river, but people know all about you and about the treasures you will carry with you: all that bedding, sheets and towels, clothes, pots and pans. These are worth a fortune in this poor and miserable land of ours. The Bolsheviks have made thieves of us all. You should not leave your belongings out of sight, not for a minute, not even if the shore looks deserted. Not along the river and not in railway stations. Not anywhere. Thieves are always there, waiting. They will pinch your raft with everything on it if you are not careful. People are envious of you and of your possessions.'

This was news to me. The locals envious of us? Was that possible? But then, to think of it, we had lived a better life than the natives. We had more worldly goods, we had worked just as hard, but we still had some of the luxuries of our 'capitalist' past with us. Now we were leaving, while they were stuck here for the rest of their lives. While we had hope, they had none.

'Good cigarette, not like our stinking *makhorka*,' said Sasha. 'I haven't had one like that in years. Now listen carefully,' he repeated. 'This is very important. At all times you must keep to the middle of the river. Always be on your guard. When the current pushes you to either side, run to your oars, two men to each, and work them with all your might to keep in midstream. Or you'll be drawn into a *pleso*.'

'A *pleso*? What's that?' asked Mr Wasserman.

'As the river turns one way or the other in some places, it also becomes very wide, so wide that on one side the bank is almost like a bay. The back current is very strong in the bend. It drags you to the side and, if it gets you into the bay, you will never get out. Once you hit the shore in the bend, no matter how hard you work the oars, you are stuck in a whirlpool. We call it *pleso*. It's not so bad in a boat or a canoe, but on a raft . . . Those bays are often very deep, your feet wouldn't reach the bottom to push the raft. Anyway you would soon freeze in our river.' He turned pensive now. 'Some say that *leshiy*, the forest demon, lives in the *pleso*, but I don't really believe that,' he concluded with more showmanship than conviction.

All this was extremely important knowledge and at the next Council meeting Father passed Sasha's advice on to the others.

The Council met in the canteen every night after the evening meal. The meetings lasted well into the night. The rafts were given numbers and they were painted with whitewash on the oar handles. People formed groups of about twenty per raft, each headed by an elected 'captain'. After much discussion it was decided that once we had left Kvasha, every raft was on its own, every group had to make their own decisions when and where to stop for the night, for how long, how to proceed when stuck and what to do on reaching Krasnoborsk.

Our raft, number eight, was to carry eighteen people. The group, apart from us, consisted of the Romers, Mietek and his father, the Zóltyńskis, the Gruszyńskis and a married couple with a small boy. We chose Mietek's father as our captain.

Sometime in mid-September 1941 we were ready. It was quite a job to manhandle twenty-two rafts, to move them from the shore and launch them on to the river. But we brought the rafts safely downstream from the construction site to Kvasha. Mietek Wasserman, Olek Romer and I manned our raft and soon we got the hang of it. Luckily, on the way to Kvasha the river meandered a little, but there were no dangerous bends and we had to man the oars only to keep the raft straight and to bring it to the shore.

Heeding Sasha's advice we kept guard over our rafts, both at the construction site and in Kvasha, even before they were loaded.

Our last night in Kvasha was very busy. Bread had been baked and divided between the groups, so were the supplies of wild mushrooms and berries picked by my mother's party and the stores of *kasha* set aside by the canteen staff. We appropriated a couple of axes and one saw per raft; Mr Romer, the chairman of the Council, and Father signed the receipt requested by Orlov. After all a journey through the Siberian forest without an axe was unthinkable and he knew that.

At dawn, with all aboard, with our suitcases, boxes and bundles secured and providing seating, we untied our vessels and were off.

In late summer, the Uftyuga, like other Siberian rivers, is exceedingly calm and slow. Without difficulty we reached the midstream.

As we were leaving, the Kvasha shore was deserted. Not a soul came to wish us *bon voyage* or God-speed. All the Russian inhabitants of Kvasha kept to their huts. Orders from above? Envy?

We departed nonetheless. The lack of a send-off committee at the Kvasha riverside did not stop us.

TWELVE

ON THE RAFT

✳

Siberian rivers and rafts made of Siberian timber belong to each other, like lovers, and, like lovers, they have their quarrels.

We were lucky. We learned later that of the twenty-two rafts that had left Kvasha only nine reached Krasnoborsk. The remainder were abandoned along the way for various reasons, though their passengers eventually did reach Krasnoborsk, one way or another. Our trip was also far from straightforward. Instead of the planned five days, it had lasted eight and we arrived in the mouth of the Uftyuga cold and tired. There, we abandoned the raft tied to a tree at the riverbank. Without regrets.

As we were leaving Kvasha the weather was good, the morning air crisp, while the sky, speckled with white clouds, resembled a boy's bedroom after a frantic pillow fight. With no wind the river surface was mirror-smooth but, nonetheless, within hours of leaving Kvasha, our little armada dispersed and we had no choice but to let the river carry us on our solitary way.

'The speed of current changes from one part of the river to another,' explained Mr Wasserman in, for him, an unusually laconic statement of fact.

Mietek, Olek, Helena, her two sisters, Henryk and I manned the oars in two-hour shifts. Not that we had much to do. The river meandered gently through the still, peaceful forest. The oars were heavy, but only an occasional movement was needed to keep the raft in the midstream. As the river curved, on low, flat promontories, the forest receded giving way to meadows, silent and sleepy under a carpet of the last of the summer grass.

Towards the end of our first day on the raft, the summer ended abruptly. Dusk came quickly and with it a cold wind. I had just come off oar duty. I was hungry. We'd had our last meal of bread washed down with ice-cold river water about noon, hours ago. I was also getting chilly. We had a clay fireplace on the raft and a small supply of firewood on board, but on that first day our elders were reluctant to light a fire. 'It might set the raft alight,' they said. What nonsense. In the middle of a river? But now we were all shivering. It was time to stop for the night.

No sooner did we manoeuvre the raft to the riverbank when the first snow, a harbinger of winter, came down. The snowfall was light and short-lived. The flakes were moist, sticky, clamped together and thawed quickly. It was 12 September, an early winter, even for Siberia.

Using several old belts – there was no rope available – we secured the raft to a couple of thick roots protruding bracket-like from the bank of the river. In minutes we had a fire going. The smell of *kasha* with pork fat – the last of somebody's food parcel – and wild mushrooms made my mouth water.

Before allaying our hunger we had yet more work to do. We cut some saplings to build a shelter, keeping the branches to make a roof. There was no lack of suitable trees within ten paces from the riverbank. And, as advised by Sasha, all through the night we kept watch in pairs, in two-hour shifts.

We untied at dawn. Another uneventful day followed. The river looked deserted. Yet the waters were very much alive with fish of many shapes and sizes. Though some reminded us of those in Polish rivers and lakes, we could name but a few. Our only fellow travellers in that enormous emptiness called Siberia were birds. Some big, some small, they skidded the surface of the water diving repeatedly for food. Others, in big formations, crossed our path high overhead, flying south. 'Wouldn't you like to be one of them?' I said across the oar to Helena. She smiled. These were our only companions, we saw no people. None on the river, none on its banks. Nor had we met any four-legged animals coming to the shore to drink.

The days were cold and, from the second day onwards,

having overcome our initial misgivings about setting the raft ablaze, we kept the fire going on the raft all day long; it was the only way to keep ourselves warm and our clothes reasonably dry. Several times a day we had to pull in to the shore to cut some firewood. Every evening, at dusk, we tied the raft up and built a big fire. While our mothers set to cooking *kasha* with mushrooms – pork fat was off the menu after the first night – we would get busy erecting a shelter.

On the fourth morning we passed Petrakovo. The little town was deserted, its inhabitants still asleep. Only several yapping dogs came to the riverbank to see us off. By midday the Uftyuga became much wider and we kept floating in midstream, until another day came to its end.

Then, one afternoon, as the clouds parted and the sun came out, without the slightest warning, the raft turned one hundred and eighty degrees. One minute Helena and I stood by the bow oar, while Mietek and Lala minded the stern one, when suddenly we were astern and they were at the bow. Our attention must have slipped for a moment. The river here was nearly a kilometre wide and the current was pushing us out of midstream and into a wide bay-like recess of the right bank. 'Come on, Helena, push!' I shouted. We started rowing with all our might. So did Mietek and Lala in the bow.

My shouting brought the others out of their afternoon slumbers. A general commotion ensued. Mr Wasserman, our captain, took command: 'All men to the oars,' he shouted. With every second the right bank was closing in on us. Two or three rafts seemed to be tied up there. People on the rafts and on the shore were shouting and waving their arms. Their words were indistinguishable, but their gestures were not: they were waving us away!

'Pleso! Whirlpool! Back current! Step on it!' shouted Mr Wasserman. 'Harder! Harder! In. Out. In. Out.'

With every stroke the oar was getting heavier, I was sweating profusely. The current was still carrying us into the bay. 'It's no good, we are going to be sucked in,' I said resignedly. Helena gave me a nasty look. Then . . . slowly . . . barely perceptibly at first . . . then more definitely, the shore was slipping away. We had won! More shouts came from the shore, as the silhouettes of the people there melted into the reddish-gold of the sunset. We had done it, we were back in the middle of the river, out of danger. Others took over the oars and, exhausted, we flopped down in one big heap, like a litter of new-born mice. I was somewhere at the bottom of it but the cold and wet timbers of the raft were as cosy and soft as never before.

There was a lesson to be learned here. From now on either our captain or his personally selected deputy were to be constantly on the lookout for potentially dangerous changes in the shoreline. With timely warning and hard oar work we managed to keep the raft in midstream avoiding further traps.

In the following two days our careful seamanship paid off and nothing untoward happened. The river was getting steadily wider. The banks, covered by never-ending forest, were still largely deserted. As far as the eye could see the land was flat; not a hill, not a mound to catch the eye. Occasionally, we passed a cluster of log cabins or bigger barracks on the shore – probably Kvasha-like forest settlements. But for our raft, the river was empty and silent.

We were utterly alone. Except for those caught in the whirlpool, we had met no other Kvasha rafts. 'It's strange,' said Mr Wasserman, 'but we ought to meet them in Krasnoborsk. They will all try to board the Arkhangelsk–Kotlas boat.'

'How often does it put in to Krasnoborsk?' asked Father.

'Once a week,' replied Mr Romer. 'Anyway, that's what Volkov thought. But nobody in Kvasha had been really well informed about it. I had a feeling that the usual Russian time-table applied: *Today, or tomorrow, or perhaps the day after . . .*' Mr Romer concluded with disgust.

'So, we might have a long wait,' stated Mr Wasserman.

'Not too long, I hope' said Mother. 'Our stores of bread and *kasha* won't last us more than two days now, and that's at a pinch.'

'But surely, there will be shops in Krasnoborsk,' said Mrs Romer, forever optimistic, 'and there must be a market.'

On the eighth day, several hours after we tied off from our night's mooring, the river widened even more. It was now much more than a kilometre in width. Krasnoborsk could not be far off. Also, suddenly, the Uftyuga ceased to be a simple open waterway. Everywhere, as far as the eye could see, the surface of the water was broken by tips of stout piles driven into the river bottom, most were upright, some had been bent by the current, a few were linked together by long and rusty iron chains, others by rows of thick, floating wooden beams held together with iron clamps. Careful as we were, from time to time the raft bounced off a stake on either one side or the other. The captain took control: 'Gently, gently to the left . . . iiin . . . ouuut . . . iiin . . . ouuut . . . iiin . . . ouuut . . .' And then: 'Steady as she goes,' or, 'Hard to the right!' And suddenly very quickly: 'In . . . out . . . in . . . out . . .' To emphasise the point he would flap his arms like a featherless fledgling, until we floated on to a clear waterway again.

'They are traps for timber,' said Mr Wasserman. 'We had them on the Vistula, near Gdańsk. You need them when . . .' Suddenly the raft jerked, shuddered. He stopped in mid-sentence. He was about to restart when the raft lurched to one side, then it turned a bit and seemed to rise on a gentle wave. It shook, turned some more . . . One minute we were carried by the current and the next the water on both sides of the raft rushed by, leaving us behind. What had happened? Why had we slowed down?

Then, slowly, the raft turned half a circle. We looked at each other with amazement. Our oars were out of the water, useless. What was the matter? With water eddies and larger whirlpools all round us, there was no fixed point of reference. Were we still? Were we moving? If so, which way?

Damn. Damn. We were stuck. Our captain stood there, motionless, with his mouth open, like a fish out of water. He did look rather funny. On the other side of the oar, Helena giggled under her breath.

Women! It was not a laughing matter. I looked round. We were not anywhere near the riverbank, not anywhere near another *pleso* but in the middle of a very wide and straight part of the river. Our captain, his mouth shut now, still stood there statue-like, except for his Adam's apple moving up and down like a yo-yo. Then he swallowed hard: 'I guess I missed a submerged stake just under the surface,' he confessed. 'I am very sorry.' He sighed. And then suddenly, all businesslike, he took command again: 'We are stuck on it. The way the current turned the raft, the stake must be somewhere under there.' He pointed to the part of the raft which a minute ago had been its left-bow corner, but now was its stern. With all our eyes on him, 'To work!' he shouted. Next he tugged at his pullover, as if to take it off.

'What do you think you are doing?' asked my father.

Our captain looked very unhappy again. 'I'm going to dive in to see what happened,' he said. 'It's the only way and it's my responsibility. If I am right, we have to figure out a way of lifting the raft over the stake. I must try.'

'Nonsense,' Father interrupted him. 'If it has to be done, it's hard luck, but it's a job for the youngsters and not for the likes of you or me. Stefan, Mietek, Olek, Henryk get ready.' Mr Wasserman hesitated, then pulled his sweater back over his head. He stood there for a moment in some distress before recovering his composure.

'All of us will have to help,' he said taking command once more. 'The stern has to be made lighter. We shall need some vodka, anyone got a bottle? Out with it. Also towels and blankets and a bigger fire. Let's build it up.'

The raft became a hive of activity. Some set about moving the bags and boxes from the stern to the bow. Others added more firewood to the dying fire and brought it back to life by blowing on it and fanning it. Still others rummaged through their bags for towels and blankets. Triumphantly, Mrs Romer produced a bottle of vodka. The raft was again shaking and shuddering. 'Slowly! Slowly!' shouted Mr Wasserman. 'Gently does it. We won't capsize, but the bundles can easily slide off.'

Mietek was first to strip to his underpants. He dived in and disappeared under the raft. A minute later he scrambled back on board. He was shivering violently. His lips were blue and his teeth chattered. Wrapped in warm towels and a blanket he sat down by the fire. He took a mouthful of vodka from Mrs Romer's bottle, quivered. 'As you thought, Dad,' he said. 'We are stuck on a stake with a rugged end. I tried to push the raft off it, but it's deep. My feet would not reach the bottom and I couldn't get a purchase. Have to give it another try, or we may have to saw through the stake.' Then he started shivering violently again.

Гражданин *Вайденфельд Стефан Владиславович* направляет

к избранному им месту жительства в *Астраханский округ*

гор. Астрахань

Удостоверение действительно на три месяца и, подлежит обмену на паспорт.

Изложенное удостоверяется подписью и печатью.

Начальник *Красноборского* РО УНКВД АО

Госбезопасности

Удостоверил
паспорт. Вайденфельд

Ш. а.

Алф. *Вай*   ЛИЧНОЕ ДЕЛО № *22269*   С сек

Пол. м.

ПЕРСОНАЛЬНАЯ КАРТОЧКА

Стр. уч. книги №

Дата пр

Обл. Архангельская. Район *Краснобор.*

Свой поселок *Слобода*

1. Фамилия *Вайденфельд* после брака или развода

2. Имя *Стефан* Отчество *Владисл*

3. Год и месяц рожд. *1925*

4. Национальность *еврей*

5. Место рожд.: область _____ район

город, деревня *Обводж* 6. Образование *9 кл*

7. Соц. полож. к моменту высылки *пересел*

8. Служба в армии с *нго* должность

9. Специальность _____ 10. Сем. полож.

11. Трудоспособность *нетруд* Группа _____ для инвалид

12. Судимость _____ дата _____ Нарсудом _____ указать как

Приговорен _____

Сведения о выполняемой работе

Место работы	Дата направл.	Выполняемая ра (должность)
Слободской л/п Красноборского л.п.х.	15/VII 40	Разные работы в л/п.

СССР
НАРОДНЫЙ КОМИССАРИАТ
ВНУТРЕННИХ ДЕЛ
УПРАВЛЕНИЕ НКВД
по
АРХАНГЕЛЬСКОЙ ОБЛАСТИ

Красноборское ОО

10 *Сентября* 1941 г.

№ *66/78*

г. Архангельск

УДОСТОВЕРЕНИЕ

Предъявитель сего гр. *Вайденфельд*
(фамилия, и

Стефан Владиславович
имя, отчество,

рожд. *1925 года 18/V родился г. Обводж*
год рождения, место рождения

Варшавской области

На основании Указа Президиума Верховного Совета СССР амнистирован, как польский гражданин, и имеет право свободного проживания на территории СССР за исключением пограничной полосы, запретных зон, местностей объявленных на военном положении и режимных городов первой и второй категорий.

При нём находятся _____ (перечислить членов семьи до 16 лет,

_____ с указанием фамилии, имени, возраста и отношения

Копия

нач. ЭКО УНКВД АО
ст. лейтенанту госбезопасности
т. Тнюкову.

г. Архангельск.

На № 4/6122-4 от 26 ноября 1940 г.

Сообщаем, что ВАЙДЕНФЕЛЬД Вольф Мозесович 1890 г. уроженец г. Плоцк б/польши, по национальности-еврей, врач работал по своей специальности 20 лет; его жена Вайденфельд Чеслава Захаровна 1889 года рождения, уроженка г. Плоцк б/польши, еврейка по профессии врач-бактериолог, работала на этой специальности 18 лет, сын Стефан Владиславович 1925 г. окончил три курса гимназии.

Все выше указанные лица высланы из г. Яхлин Пинска как беженцы подавшие заявления по разрешении выехать на жительство в г. Варшаву.

В настоящее время Вайденфельд работает на с/поселке "Слобода, Красноборского р-на к работе относятся честно, все работают прогулов не имеет. Компрометирующими материалами на Вайденфельдов Красноборское РО не располагает.

Использовать их по специальности в Красноборском р-не не представляется возможности.

Со своей стороны считаем, что Вайденфельдов было бы полезное использовать по своей специальности, а для чего необходимо перевести их из Красноборского района.

Нач. Красноборского РО УНКВД АО
мл. лейтенант госбезопасности (Семихин)

СВЕРЯЛ: Делопроизводитель-машинистка
(Лавронтьева)

A selection of documents relating to the Waydenfelds' release from Kvasha and permitting them to travel to Astrakhan

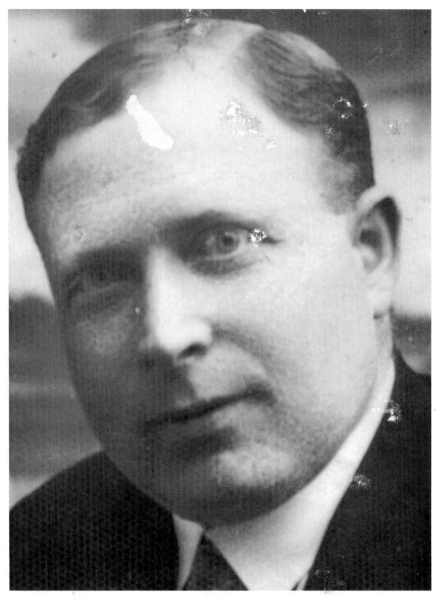

The author's father in 1938

The author's mother in 1938

ABOVE: the author's parents in 1941
BELOW: the author's parents in 1942

Dr and Mrs
Waydenfeld in 1942

Danuta, 1942

The author, 1945

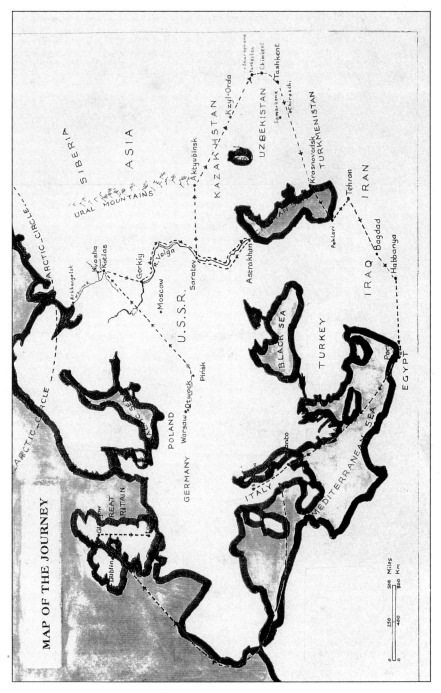

The author's journey

Olek looked at me and I looked at Olek. It was our turn. 'Let's put our backs to it,' said Olek.

I had an idea. 'First, let's wrap our arms and legs round the post,' I said. 'Then let's try to heave with our backs. You are taller, so I'll dive first and get up as high as I can under the raft. Your legs should fit round the stake just below mine.'

'Okay,' nodded Olek.

I dived in. It was freezing. I put my arms and legs round the post, but it was slippery and too thin to hold firmly. Olek joined me. He put his arms round the stake, with my chest also in his grasp. I could see a cloud of air bubbles escaping from my mouth.

I could not bend far enough to get my back against the raft and I tried to push it up with the top of my head. I kept my eyes open and saw Olek doing the same. We heaved, once, twice. The raft did not budge. My chest was about to burst. In a flash, I broke the surface, gulped some air, while Father and Mr Wasserman pulled me aboard. Olek scrambled out next to me. I crawled to the fire. Somebody wrapped warm towels round me. A bottle touched my mouth: vodka: It stung, it burned, but a warm glow spread through my body. I kept my eyes shut for just a minute. Then it was time for another go.

I was scared. We had another try. Henryk, Mietek, Olek and me. All together. No luck. The raft would not budge. This was not the way.

While we were thawing out by the fire, our elders held a council. We would have to saw through that bloody pile, I thought to myself. Underwater, under very cold water. I wished I were fifty and somebody else would dive in my place.

The 'war council' was soon over. 'The stake will have to be sawed through,' Mr Wasserman confirmed my worst expectations. 'We can't do it from the raft. It's too far from the edge. You boys will have to dive in turns. Mietek first.' He passed our string-saw to his son. 'Start the cut and try to get it deep enough to retain the blade. If you can't remain there long enough, come up with the saw – we can't afford to lose it – and Olek will have to deepen the cut.'

I wished that I could shrink, become invisible, or very, very small, to be forgotten, overlooked. Nothing doing. 'After Olek,

Stefan, Henryk, then Mietek again . . .' our captain continued. 'I need a few belts, gentlemen.' He bent down, put his own belt round Mietek's naked waist, then took the belt offered by Mr Gruszyński – it was extraordinarily long – looped it round the one on Mietek, but retained its free end in his hand. 'I shall keep time,' he banged his fist on the raft's timbers. 'Stay under only one minute and as I pull,' he yanked the free end of the belt, 'you come up. Is that clear? If you feel you have to come up sooner, just do it. Do you understand?' he repeated.

Down Mietek went. He came back without the saw. He got a good cut at the first go. Good old Mietek. Olek dived next. 'Oh, bloody hell. No point being frightened.' As Olek surfaced, I dived. The water did not get any warmer. My chest ached.

Isn't it peculiar that something you fear is much less terrifying the second time round? I don't know how many times I moved the saw there-and-back but, as the belt jerked for me to come up, the cut was far from halfway through; yet at least the whole blade had disappeared in it, and the blade was some four or five centimetres wide.

Painfully cold, I was out, breathing deeply. All four of us rested by the fire until it was time for another round: first Mietek, then Olek, then me.

That's how it is. When your turn comes, you dive. You move the saw forwards and back, forwards and back, as many times as you can before your chest bursts. You surface, you sit by the fire with warm towels wrapped round you, you have a sip of vodka and you hope that the saw will be through before your turn comes again.

No such luck. As the shivering calms and as the chatter of teeth stops, as a warm glow begins to spread through the body, it's your turn again. You are about to shout: 'I've had enough! I am not going back there!' But you don't, you clench your teeth and you dive into the ice-cold water. You are not frightened any more, you just hate it.

I have no idea how many turns we had to endure before the saw was through the pole and the raft was free and once more floating down the river. The vodka did not help us to keep an exact count. I woke up lying down by the fire with my head in my mother's lap, Helena holding my hand. Olek was asleep on the other side of the fire with his head in his mother's lap. Mietek and Henryk were already up, each with a chunk of bread in one hand and a mug of tea in the other. I was ravenously hungry. Helena let go of my hand to get me some bread and tea.

It was lovely to be warm again and good to be appreciated. The older men were manning the oars, but they did not have much to do. The raft was in the middle of the mouth of the Uftyuga. It was very wide and there were no more piles or stakes, no traps. It was late afternoon when the raft was slowly swept into a much larger body of water: the Northern Dvina River. A couple of kilometres downstream was the port of Krasnoborsk.

We spent another night on shore under a makeshift roof of freshly cut branches. In the morning, Father and Mr Romer took the riverside path hoping that it would lead them to the port.

They returned about noon. Just in time to join us in our midday meal of the last of our *kasha* and some hardtack. We had no more bread left. 'We might just as well spend another night here,' said Father. 'The ship to Kotlas is not expected before tomorrow afternoon.'

Mr Romer continued with other news: 'There are no hotels, no shops open to the public, nothing of any use. We had to bribe a guard to let us into the port. We bribed the harbour master to tell us about the ship and then again to prepare the ship captain's palm for the same treatment tomorrow. We would not go far without our bribe pool. There is not much left in it, we need more money. What a terrible country!'

'Indeed,' said Mr Wasserman. 'Not that different from the old Russia of the tsars. Everyone took bribes then and everyone expects bribes now; all one needs is ready money.'

Mr Romer nodded. 'Goods or money, they don't mind which.'

'So tomorrow,' suggested Mr Wasserman, 'we'll float further down the river and into the port.'

'No, out of question,' said Father. 'The harbour master wants us to come on foot, in small groups carrying our luggage, like ordinary passengers. He is terrified of the NKVD. We'll have to comply.'

The rest of the day was long and lazy. We split into groups.

We read books, played bridge and chess. Helena was very good at bridge. It must have been hereditary, her father was an inveterate card player. She did not think much of him. 'On their wedding night,' she said when we went for a walk, 'he played poker and gambled away the house which was Mother's dowry. You wouldn't do that? Would you?' She laughed, looking at me sideways.

'Oh, I would be otherwise engaged,' I assured her, feeling myself blush. 'Just you wait and see. But let's get out of here first.'

Next morning we got up very early, repacked our bags and boxes. They made a large heap at the riverside. We abandoned the raft without regrets, together with the Kvasha saw and axes. Having reached civilisation – of a kind – we had no more use for them. The port was more than a kilometre away. We wouldn't be able to carry all our belongings in one go.

'I suggest,' said Mr Wasserman, 'that we take as much as we can to the port now, leaving two ladies to guard the remainder. Then two more ladies will stay in the port with the belongings, while we return for the rest. It shouldn't take us more than an hour.'

This seemed like a good idea. And so my mother stayed behind with Mrs Żółtyńska, as the rest of us, loaded with well over half of our belongings took the footpath along the riverbank and then cut through the forest to the gate of the port. The guard commander recognised my father and Mr Romer and waved us through. The harbour master greeted us like long-lost friends and showed us into a shed. We had a drink of *kipyatok* and, after a short respite, started on the way back. Helena's mother and Mrs Gruszyńska stayed behind in the shed. When we returned with the rest of our belongings, the ship had already entered the harbour. After it unloaded its cargo, our appointed expert bribers went on board to see the captain. The ground having been prepared by the harbour master, he graciously accepted the 'offering' and in no time at all we embarked on the second leg of our journey.

The skipper, his palm well greased, greeted us at the top of the gangway and with an expansive gesture gave us the freedom of the deck. 'Anywhere you like,' he said. 'It's only for one night.

We shall be in Kotlas in the morning and there you'll find trains to take you wherever you want to go.'

This was our first taste of freedom. It was quite a change from Volkov's introduction to Kvasha: 'Here you shall live.'

Mr Wasserman, still comfortable in the role of our captain, took charge: 'Once she starts on her way the bow will be very windy. Let's make our camp at the stern.'

We found enough free deck space at the stern to accommodate our bundles and bags in the middle and all of us in a ring around them. It took us hours to fix a roof of canvas and blankets over our quarters, but at last the job was finished.

Soon the gangway was pulled up and, with several long mournful *oo-oo-oo-ms* of the horn, we were off. It was late September 1941. Snowflakes drifted about, all aglitter in the ship's few lights. The night was murky with no moon and no stars, Helena and I stood at the port side bulwark watching the dim lights of Krasnoborsk rapidly melt into darkness. With my right arm round Helena's shoulders I felt very protective of her. We talked about our uncertain future. The only certainty we had was that we would face it together.

We talked well into the night, until Mrs Romer called: 'Helena, we are getting ready for bed.' Figuratively speaking, of course. Left alone, I stood there for a while longer and finally also turned in.

Since leaving Kvasha we had slept in the open, under roofs of tree-branches and usually in a circle round our belongings. My place was always between my father and Helena. We were both utterly naive and innocent, but even now, fifty-six years later, I am grateful to my own and Helena's parents that, in spite of the mores of the times, they allowed us to share the few crumbs of comfort that our closeness offered.

In the morning I woke up in Kotlas. We breakfasted on one slice of hardtack each and the *kipyatok* from the tap on the deck. That was the end of our food stores.

'I remember Russian railway stations from the time of the Revolution,' said Mr Romer. 'Utter chaos.'

'I am sure the Bolsheviks have improved on them since,' said my father, ever the optimist. 'They have had over twenty years to do so.'

Mr Gruszyński was sceptical about the comforts of a long railway journey in the USSR: 'I went to Moscow in 1932 with a trade mission. Government business, you know. From Moscow we went by train to Gorkiy and to other industrial towns. Huge distances. We travelled first class, of course. Upholstered seats. With Party members: high officials, commissars, you know the type. But most people, ordinary people, not just the riff-raff, had do with hard seats – wooden benches. Or they had to stand in the corridors. Not very comfortable. Though bearable for short journeys,' he mused. 'And now we are the riff-raff,' he concluded.

'At least wooden benches don't harbour lice,' said my mother, practical as always.

'All the stations were chock-a-block with people,' continued Mr Gruszyński. 'They seemed to be living there, in the halls, in the corridors. Masses of them . . .'

When we got to Kotlas station it was crowded, but not as badly as we had expected. It was a large building adorned with a monument of Lenin and Stalin in repose on a bench by the main entrance. The sometime white material of the monument was now dirty with grime, water stains and bird droppings. In the main hall all the wooden benches and the floor between them were packed. Similarly, the corridors were full of people sitting on their luggage. Children noisily played hide-and-seek. Their elders snored away lying on the benches and strewn all over the stone floor, like so many ripe pears in some grotesque autumnal orchard. But the unmistakable smell of unwashed humanity fed on cabbage soup and black bread was overwhelming, not at all reminiscent of an orchard.

Were these people waiting for trains, or did they live here? Some bivouacked in family groups of two or even three generations. They were not all in rags, some wore decent padded jackets and trousers. Many sported *valenki*, which was more than we could boast of. 'Do we have to join this crowd?' I asked my father. 'Do we have to stay here in the station?'

'I don't know,' was his answer. He turned to Mr Wasserman, but our captain's self-assurance had left him, evaporated. Here, on dry land, he seemed to have abdicated his status and looked askance at my father and at Mr Romer, as if awaiting orders instead of issuing them. The impromptu council lasted only a few minutes and its conclusion was that any train going south would do. Father and Mr Romer were once more delegated to spy the land and to grease palms. With difficulty, we found a relatively uncluttered, probably just vacated, recess in the station hall to park our belongings and prepared for a long wait.

'Mind the luggage,' said Mr Romer. 'Don't take your eyes off it for one moment.'

Father added, 'Keep it in one heap and sit or stand all around it. Without goods for barter we are lost.' Then they left.

It would be silly for all of us to stay round our mound of bundles. Hungry, and always hopeful, Mietek and I went in search of the station buffet, a stall, a street market, a black marketeer, anything. We explored the station – thoroughly. Nothing. *Kipyatok* tap? Yes. Anything to eat? Forget it. Even if your belly button stuck to your backbone there was not a crumb to be had. Anyway, not for money, and certainly not for love.

It was midday. A few lucky people were munching bread, or even bread with bacon fat. Continuing our search for food we left the station building.

Hurrah! There was a bakery around the corner. The queue was not too long. Fifty, perhaps sixty. We took our place at the end. Almost immediately, a young woman, head covered with a brightly coloured scarf, stopped next to us. She had a pleasant face, almost beautiful.

'Are you the last?' she asked.

'*Da*, Yes,' Mietek said in Russian. Then he turned to me, 'Isn't she a looker?' he added softly in Polish. Our Mietek had an eye for the girls.

'You are not Russian?' asked the woman.

'No, we are Polish,' we answered in unison.

'I guessed so,' she said in a faltering Polish and a broad smile lit up her pleasant features. 'My grandfather was Polish. An exile from *Polsha*,' she used the Russian word for Poland and reverted to Russian again. 'He had been deported to Siberia in the tsar's time. When I was a little girl, he used to tell me about his home village, but I forget its name.' And then suddenly, all businesslike, 'Have you got your ration cards?' she asked.

Good God. Ration cards? We had none. In Kvasha bread was rationed, but this was a big town. Nobody had warned us. The woman noticed our consternation. 'Never mind,' she said. 'I'll go in first and you wait for me.' In the meantime the head of the queue has been melting rapidly away, but behind us it kept growing. A hundred? A hundred and fifty? Mietek chatted the woman up. Her name was Sofia Antonovna. I was even more shy than usual and kept quiet. Mietek had a way with people. Especially with girls. I envied him. 'My grandfather called me Zosia,' she said. 'My father still calls me by my Polish name. Sometimes.' She was on the verge of saying something further, but we reached the bakery door and she just whispered, 'Wait for me.' We stepped to the side and waited. She re-emerged after what seemed a very long time. 'There is another queue inside,' she said. She had four loaves of bread in her net carrier bag. Four loaves! White bread! A long-forgotten sight.

'Come with me,' she whispered. We followed her down the road. She stopped at one of the staircase halls of a large tenement block. 'Two loaves will do us today,' she said. 'My father is ill and does not eat much. I also have some bread left over. I would give you more, but my children come home from school ravenous.'

'*Jedz na zdrowie*, for your good health,' she said in Polish. 'My grandfather used to say it to me, but that's about all the Polish I remember.' Mietek wanted to pay her. 'I am not in the black-market business,' she chuckled. It was infectious and we all laughed.

She refused money; she did not even want the couple of roubles she laid out for our two loaves. 'My grandfather would turn in his grave and my father would give me hell,' she concluded the discussion.

Momentarily it seemed as if a cloud had darkened her face. She crossed herself the Catholic way and said, 'Petya, my husband, is in the war. May the good Lord protect him.' But then the cloud passed and she smiled again. 'I would ask you home,' she continued, 'but we all live in one room and Father keeps coughing his lungs out. He came back from Kolyma last spring, after eight years of prison camp and with tuberculosis.'

'Anyway,' I said, 'we must run back to the station, or our group will leave without us.'

She waved to us, 'Good luck, lads. So long,' and she disappeared into the dark stairway.

'There are some good people,' said Mietek. 'They have next to nothing yet are still prepared to share it.'

Would I have shared my bread ration with a stranger? I like to think that I would, but I'd rather not be put to the test.

When we returned to the station, Father and Mr Romer had just finished reporting on the results of their bribing expedition. It was successful. The first train going south was expected to arrive later in the evening and its destination was Gorkiy. The station master promised to have two compartments reserved for us. We would thus travel in relative comfort. But what about all those people crowding the station, wouldn't they invade the train? Could the bribed station master really deliver? Difficult to believe. There was no timetable and no maps displayed anywhere. In my school atlas the distance to Gorkiy was about five hundred kilometres. We ought to make it overnight.

Life is full of surprises. Helena and Olek suddenly appeared carrying between them a bucket of soup and a large brown bag full of bread rolls. My father must have noticed the look of utter astonishment on my face and laughed: 'The manager of the staff canteen had also proved bribable.' Fresh rolls would go well with the soup. And, by general consent, Sofia's two loaves were left for breakfast.

'I must go to that good woman,' said Mother, 'and thank her myself. Sofia Antonovna, you say. When you have eaten, Stefanku, lead me to her house and we'll take something for her. Her father is ill in bed, you say. Let me think. Perhaps a bath towel, or a bed sheet.'

Mother started rummaging in one of our bundles, but I had doubts. 'I can easily find the house and the staircase,' I said, 'but it's a large tenement building and I know neither the flat number, nor her surname . . .'

'And,' Father added, 'open contact with foreigners may do her harm. Better not risk it, for her sake.'

Fortunately, our bowls and eating utensils were never far away. The soup was very good, thick with cabbage and with bits of meat and potato.

After the meal I felt my father's hand on my shoulder. 'We

have at least two or three hours before the train is due,' he said. 'In truth one never knows, but let's go for a walk.' Curious, I followed him out of the station building and into the street. 'I want to tell you about Helena's father,' he started hesitantly. 'He is not an honest man and not very clever either. I think you ought to know that.'

'I do,' I said. 'She told me a lot about him. She does not even like him. What has he done now? Did he try to cheat you?'

It was a minute or two before my father answered. 'Don't get me wrong,' he said. 'Helena is a nice girl and both of us, Mother and I, like her. But I think you ought to be aware that her father is not to be trusted.'

'Fair enough. As I said, Helena told me as much herself. But what happened?'

Father waited a short while. 'Keep it to yourself,' he continued. 'I don't want bad blood in the group. I will keep an eye on him myself and now that he knows that I know, he will try to keep his hands clean, I hope.' Father stopped to light a cigarette. 'You remember that we went to bribe the station master. I left him in the station master's office to hand over the money. Perhaps that was unwise, but the fewer people that witness that kind of transaction the better. He rejoined me after a few minutes and said: "The man demanded three hundred roubles, one hundred for himself and the same for each of the two guards." But on the way to the staff canteen Mr Romer visited the gents, and one of the guards came up to me. "Thank you,' he said. "Fifty roubles! Two weeks' wages."'

Father puffed for a minute on his cigarette and then continued: 'At first I thought it was the station master who cheated. That might have been expected. But as we were walking back and I started sharing my suspicion with Mr Romer, he interrupted me and admitted to having been the culprit. And what's worse, he did not seem the least bit upset at having been caught red-handed.'

We walked for a while in silence.

'Perhaps as a lawyer he is used to having his cut,' Father mused. 'Or perhaps he is just a crooked lawyer. Now you know. But do keep it to yourself,' he repeated turning round. 'Yet he is very skilled at bribing people. He is better than me, but on no account must he be left in sole charge of the bribe pool. He must be watched, every time and all the way.'

It was just as well that we did turn back. The train had already arrived and was puffing its way along the platform. It was empty. It probably started here in Kotlas and was about to leave almost two hours' earlier than we had been told. The bribe worked very efficiently. One of the guards let us through a side door on to the platform, well before it was open to the public. He guided us to the car marked 'Reserved' and showed us into two compartments leading from the middle of the corridor. 'Don't leave the slightest bit of the floor empty and fill up all the shelves,' he warned us and left. The warning was unnecessary. The two compartments would have been quite adequate to accommodate all eighteen of us, but there was not nearly enough space on the shelves and under the benches for our luggage. Yet we could not leave our bags and bundles in the outside passage unattended. We had to compromise: some of our belongings with Helena, Mietek and me, had to stay in the corridor.

Then the platform gate was thrown open. The crowd flooded the platform and stormed the train. The rush was unbelievable, the disorder was total. People were pushing, falling, rising again to make their way. The train could not possibly accommodate that multitude! Miraculously, little by little, the platform emptied. The crowd paid no attention to the 'Reserved' board on our car. Like the rest of the train it was soon chock-a-block with people. The corridor on either side of us was packed.

'How did all that crowd from the station manage to get on one train?' I asked nobody in particular.

'Did you not see?' said Mietek sitting next to me on our large plywood suitcase. 'The guards let only so many in and shut the gate in the faces of the rest. They will wait for another train. "*Tomorrow, the day after, or next week,*"' he said in Russian and laughed. Then he returned to Polish. 'Poor, misguided, miserable people. What did they need their revolution for?'

The press of people on either side of us, the stench, the noise, did not bode well for our five-hundred-kilometre journey. The night was bound to be uncomfortable. We sat on our luggage in the corridor. Helena half-lay on a large bag next to me, with her arm and head in my lap; soon she was fast asleep.

A few puffs of the locomotive and we were on our way. With Mietek on my other side, also asleep with his head on my shoulder, I dared not move – and how he snored!

By then the noise in the corridor died down, or was drowned in the rhythmical clatter of the wheels. Even the stench seemed to decrease or one just got used to it. It was my left thigh which went to sleep first under the weight of Helena's head. My right shoulder, which served as Mietek's pillow, followed soon after.

Then, I must assume, the rest of me fell asleep too. I don't remember much more of the night-long journey.

THIRTEEN

JOURNEY SOUTH
DOWN THE VOLGA

✳

The train we boarded in Kotlas was bound for Moscow, but we had no permits to enter Moscow and we disembarked at Gorkiy. In the USSR even a Soviet citizen needed a special permit to set foot in the capital.

The train puffed into Gorkiy station in the morning in a cloud of steam and smoke. The air outside was cool and bracing; it glimmered with rays of early-morning sun. Together with the mass of people pouring out of the carriages we entered the station hall, still a group, the raft contingent.

Gorkiy station was unbelievably crowded and dirty. Its population density must have been in the order of five persons per square metre. Literally. There was no escape from the stench of unwashed bodies. It was much worse here than in Kotlas station. After all Gorkiy was an important railway junction.

The halls, the corridors, the restaurant, some rooms which looked like offices, even the toilets were full of people. They did not seem to be in transit. They had moved in for good, they had taken root here. Finding space for a group of eighteen was out of the question. We had to split into twos or threes and that was the end of the group.

My parents and I stood there helpless, trying to get our bearings, to find a gap somewhere. It was my mother who suddenly shouted, 'There, look, they are going!' She pointed to a pillar and, leaving my father and me by our possessions, she pushed her way through the crowd. I followed her with a couple of bags and, indeed, there was a space, two strides wide, between a pillar and a wall, just vacated by a couple with their children.

Having left the two bags with Mother, I returned for another load to where my father watched over the remainder. I made several round trips with our suitcases and bags until Father and I between us could carry the rest of our luggage. We followed this routine again and again in all our subsequent travels. Sitting on our packs, between the pillar and the wall, we just about filled the available space.

We sat there in silence for a long while. Was this the freedom of movement which the 'amnesty' offered us? What next? Mother sat close to Father, her head on his chest. Her eyes were closed, but she did not seem to be asleep. Just weary?

Father, his back against the wall, his right arm around Mother's shoulders, seemed deep in thought. Or numb? His gaze was fixed somewhere in the distance, his face set in stone, frozen.

It seemed to me that hours had passed. Suddenly, I could stand it no longer. 'What are we going to do now?' I asked loudly to overcome the noise of the crowded station. But there was no answer. Were they asleep? Yet Father's eyes were wide open.

'*Tata*, Dad, are you asleep? What are we going to do now?' I insisted.

I knew that both my questions were silly; it was my impatience and my boredom speaking. I guessed there was no immediate answer.

Father turned his eyes towards me. 'I don't know, son,' he said with a deep sadness in his voice.

Mother then opened her eyes. 'Oh, yes, you do,' she said with unexpected firmness. 'First you get *kipyatok*, Stefanku, and we will have tea with sugar and some bread. It's late afternoon already. An empty stomach is not conducive to clear thinking.'

Kettle in hand I pushed my way through the crowd, looking for the *kipyatok* tap.

I also had to use the toilet. I had to choose the right queue, preferably the toilet queue first, then the *kipyatok* one and then perhaps a food counter . . .? I found the lavatory without difficulty. Luckily the queue was not too long and next to it there was the line to the hot-water tap. But there was no food counter queue anywhere, because there was no food counter.

We had mock tea with real sugar. Wasn't it clever of Mother to have saved it? There was a small hoard of white lumps of sugar. We also had a slice of white bread each, the remainder of Sofia Antonovna's gift. The meal brought Father back to life. 'You are right, *mateczko*,' he said, using the endearment that we both employed. 'No use sitting here and brooding.' He got up. 'I shall have a look round,' he said and then turned to me. 'You may go in search of Helena, if you wish. But don't leave Mother alone for long, rather bring Helena here.'

'Go, go,' Mother said to me. 'I will be all right. The Romers are near the door over there.' She pointed to the other side of the hall. 'I saw them find a place there about the same time as we settled here. Mrs Romer waved to me.'

I found all the three Romer sisters sitting on the floor, with their backs against the wall, in a row, leaning against each other, fast asleep. 'Take her for a walk,' said Mrs Romer. 'She had a headache. Fresh air will do her good.' She shook Helena by the shoulder. But fresh air was not there to be had. The square in front of the station building seemed even more crowded than the station, as were all the streets leading from it. The little green space in the middle of the square was also full of camping people, latter-day nomads.

Some fresh air! On the station side of the green, people were squatting in the bushes. In public, just like that? This was only the beginning. I did not know, as yet, that modesty crumbles away very early on the road to degradation. 'Let's get out of here,' I said, taking Helena by the arm.

That day we did not talk much. Was she as sad and unhappy as I was? The future was not just bleak; there seemed to be no future. We turned aimlessly one way and then the other. The streets were all crowded, dirty, smelly. People camped on the pavements, on parts of the roadway. Luckily there was little traffic; only an occasional van or car, a horse-drawn cart.

We returned to the station and sat with Mother. Mother and Helena chatted. Then Father came back with no news, none at all, not even gossip. Gossip was important, often the only source of information. A good substitute for a newspaper, which in this country meant reading between the lines, and better than listening to the ubiquitous loudspeakers – all those lies. Gossip was more reliable, at least it left you to draw your own conclusions.

'There is no timetable,' said Father. 'Nobody knows about south-bound trains. There are trains expected tonight, some perhaps tomorrow, local trains, trains west to Moscow, east to Kazan, north to Kotlas, even a trans-Siberian train. Should we go all the way to Vladivostok?' joked Father, but he did not smile. 'I asked a couple of railway men about trains to Astrakhan, or at least in that direction. Nothing doing, they said. Later in the week, perhaps? Nobody seems to know.'

We spent several days and nights in the Gorkiy station. I lost count. Our 'home' was the space between the pillar and the wall. We drank mock tea. Every day, with variable luck, we spent hours in the soup queue, in the queue for *kipyatok*, in the toilet queue. One day Father brought a loaf of bread and some butter. Another day I brought a few black-market rolls. One morning Mother came back from a walk bearing a ring of sausage and a loaf of bread. We had a feast. Perhaps life was not quite as bad as all that . . . Amazing what a full stomach does to one's *Weltanschauung*.

One morning, returning from the toilet queue, Mother said, 'Just imagine. I was about to open my handbag, but it was already open. I grasped another hand, a very small hand, inside it. It belonged to one of those urchins. He was no more than six or seven. A little Tatar boy. "Don't get angry, auntie," he said, laughed and ran away. Empty-handed, I am glad to say.'

In search of fresh air Helena and I ventured further and further away from the station. Streets were still crowded with pedestrians, but there were no campers. Uniformed men were everywhere: militiamen, soldiers, NKVD men, some in uniforms which we did not recognise.

We found a pleasant, clean, well-maintained park with a refreshments booth. But the only item on sale were *semyechki*, dried pumpkin seeds. We ate them out of twists of newspaper. We returned to the park again next day. It was not so clean any more, footpaths were strewn with pumpkin-seed husks. There was a queue to the booth, a good sign. We had a glass of *kefir*, a fermented drink made of milk, and a roll each. Things were looking up.

Then, one evening, my father returned from another gossip-gathering trip, but this time with a smile on his face and a spring in his step. These had been absent the last few days. 'I met a couple of men in rags, talking Polish,' he said. 'I shared my cigarettes with them. They are on the way to a place called Tatishchevo near Saratov. Our Army Organisational Centre is supposed to be there. They were not sure who was in command there, Szyszko-Bogusz or Boruta-Spiechowicz.' Father mentioned the names of two Polish generals that even I knew. 'Do you remember Boruta?' he asked Mother.

'Was he the one in Cieszyn?' asked Mother.

'Yes, he was a colonel then, in command of my regiment,' said Father. 'A highly respected full general since the early twenties.'

My father had spent eight years in the army. First in the Russian army during the First World War, until the communist revolution. When Poland regained its freedom he served in the Polish Army. In the Polish–Bolshevik war of 1919–20 he was the medical officer of the 4th Regiment of Highland Fusiliers (*4ty Pułk Strzelów Podhalańskich*).

'He might remember me,' Father was thinking aloud. 'Saratov is nearly a thousand kilometres from here down the Volga River and Astrakhan is another thousand kilometres further south. The two chaps have also told me that the best way to get out of here is by boat. Tomorrow, early morning, I must go to the port to see about it.'

'By the way,' he continued. 'The Wassermans and the Żółtyńskis left this morning on the Moscow train. The Gruszyńskis and the couple with a child just disappeared without a word to anyone. They must have changed their plans. The Romers are still here waiting for the Astrakhan train.' I already knew this from Helena.

In the morning Father went to the Gorkiy port and at noon he was back, beaming. He had booked a passage for us. Not to Saratov, but to Astrakhan, our official destination. 'They say,' he reported, 'that Saratov is chock-a-block with refugees. There is no accommodation to be had at any price. I would have to go to Tatishchevo, to the Army Centre, perhaps for a day or two. I couldn't leave you at the Saratov railway station. It's supposed to be worse than here.' He lifted both arms in desperation. 'So,' he continued, 'I booked two cabins for us on a ship to Astrakhan. Very pricey, but we are due for a little luxury, aren't we?' Then he turned to me. 'I spoke to Mr Romer about you and Helena. I thought that she might come with us on the boat, but he refused, point blank. Actually, I don't blame him, it's too risky for families to get separated. But he promised to get to Astrakhan and to look for us there. The ship leaves tonight. The river port is a long way from here. We shall need transport.'

'And what happens in Astrakhan?' asked Mother.

'We will find a hotel room and I will go to Saratov on my own, and then to Tatishchevo. I am sure I'll be able to rejoin the army, apparently there is much illness and they are short of doctors. They expected many tens of thousands of PoWs released from camps to flock to the army. Thousands have, but mostly other ranks, some non-commissioned officers, but there is a great lack of officers.'

Father grew silent for a while and then continued: 'Rumour has it that our officers who fell into Soviet hands had been sent to the Franz Iosif Land, an island in the Arctic Ocean, and can't return to the mainland until next summer. Adam might be there.'

'Once I get recommissioned in the army I will either come to Astrakhan myself to fetch you, or send for you. By then they are bound to have facilities for officers' families, and you could get a job in the hospital lab, *mateczko*.'

Subsequent events showed that my father, like many others, including many top generals, naively saw events in terms of the First World War: a relatively stable front, officers' families behind the lines, yet within easy reach.

The rest of the day passed quickly. Helena had already heard from her father about our intended departure. With tears in our eyes we solemnly promised to seek each other out in Astrakhan. Ours was a very emotional parting.

Fascinated, as I then was, by the prospect of a more than two-thousand-kilometre-long voyage by ship on one of the biggest rivers of the world, I had not fully taken in the possibility that

I might never see Helena again. It hit me later and that night my pillow was wet with tears before I fell asleep.

In the meantime, Father organised a horse-drawn cart to take us and our luggage to the river port. There she was, a big, white gleaming ship, a proper passenger ship. Her name was *Lomonosov*. It was the end of our miserable stay, not even really in Gorkiy, but in the Gorkiy railway station. Perhaps the town was interesting, full of history and architectural treasures, but we would never know.

❊ ❊ ❊

Gorkiy was the *nom de plume* of a famous Russian writer who died in 1936, probably on Stalin's order. Gorkiy is also an adjective; it means 'bitter'.

As far as I was concerned, it was.

❊ ❊ ❊

Lomonosov was a fabulous ship. Our cabins, on the boat-deck and next to each other, opened on to a corridor. They had large windows giving on to the deck, wall-to-wall deep-pile carpets and were furnished with brown leather couches, writing desks and chairs. Our bags and suitcases had been hoisted aboard and actually delivered to the cabins by porters. What unaccustomed luxury! They even accepted tips gratefully. As if they hadn't been abolished in the 'classless' society. I helped my parents to sort out our luggage. When we finished, 'Go on,' Mother encouraged me, 'explore the ship. Find out about the canteen or restaurant.' She did not have to say it twice.

The corridor ran the entire length of the deck and there were about a dozen cabin doors on each side. Several of them, in the bow, bore brass plates with rank and name: officers' cabins. At the stern end there were two public smoking-rooms. The doors were open. They were comfortably furnished with deep leather armchairs, ashtrays and the obligatory brass spittoons. There was no sign of a canteen or restaurant.

I descended one floor. A similar long corridor with cabins on either side and glass doors at both ends. I went fore: the door opened on to the observation area immediately under the bridge. Still hopeful, I turned back. Hurrah! The glass door aft had '*Restoran*' written on it in small gold Cyrillic letters. I could have kissed the door. I tried it, gently. Locked. No menu and no hopeful notice of any kind on the door.

Suddenly a thought struck me: where were the other passengers? I haven't seen any. The crew were busy everywhere, but I did not meet anyone else. This was suspect.

On the one hand, this was the first means of transport we had come across in the USSR which was not absurdly overcrowded, for which tickets could be bought without queuing and without bribes and which was well maintained. The ship's corridors smelled clean and the toilets did not emanate the usual stench; they did not even reek of disinfectant. But, on the other hand, did we have the right to be on board? Might she be reserved for Party members and high officials? Had we been allowed on board by mistake? Would we be exposed as impostors and put ashore?

I went on deck and stood at the rail, next to the officer who supervised the crew loading boxes and crates of all shapes and sizes. The man had a young, pockmarked face and his slanting eyes betrayed his Tatar origin.

'A very nice ship,' I said.

'So she should be,' he was visibly proud of her. 'She had been built in the best German shipyard, for the Tsar, before the revolution. A pleasure boat for the court.'

'What about passengers?' I asked. 'There are only three of us. Aren't we going to cast off soon?' There were many questions at the tip of my tongue: How many days to Astrakhan? Any stops on the way? What about food on board? But one of the lessons I had learned was not to ask too many questions, they made people suspicious.

But this man didn't need asking. 'We shall sail as soon as we finish loading. Won't be long. Passengers? We probably won't be taking any more here, only cargo. Tickets are expensive and people prefer to go by train. Only officials on expenses-paid trips board her nowadays. There might be some coming aboard in Saratov, to keep you company,' he laughed. His was a pleasant, friendly laugh. 'It's mostly cargo for us,' he continued. 'Shame, isn't it? But many passengers are waiting for us in

Kazan. That's for sure. Hundreds. Men only, worse luck. Passengers without tickets. You'll see,' he laughed again. 'But I must return to my duties. *Izvinite*, excuse me,' he saluted and left me alone by the rail.

A nice chap, I thought. It was a new experience for me to be addressed as *vy*, you, but in second person plural, as a respected adult. But it was time to return to the cabin. Had Mother managed to find anything edible? Her ingenuity in this respect was prodigious. Was the restaurant open now? Had a notice appeared on the door?

The restaurant was closed and there was no notice.

Mother had been busy. She had made enquiries and found the *kipyatok* tap. 'I was just about to go looking for you,' she said. 'The restaurant is not going to open today, but there might be a meal for passengers tomorrow, or the day after. Let's have tea and bread now and then the two of you will have to go and get provisions for the voyage. The man in the restaurant told me there was a market nearby.'

I joined my parents at the writing desk which was doubling as a table. The meal finished, Father and I set out on our foraging expedition. The young officer was still supervising the loading. 'Good day, lieutenant,' said Father. 'Do we have enough time to find some food ashore for now? Or will we be able to eat in the restaurant, later perhaps?' he asked hopefully.

'Plenty of time,' said the officer. 'We won't finish loading for another hour. The market is just around the corner.' He pointed to a turn in the waterfront street, the other side of the port fence. 'Make sure that the guard recognises you and lets you back on board.' And then, 'I don't know about the restaurant, I would not count on it. They are supposed to serve something every day. Boiled ham with lentils usually. That's in theory. But they are not likely to open until Kazan, tomorrow night. Yes, you'd better get some food for a couple of days.'

It was a typical town market, with goods displayed on rickety tables, on stools, on shawls spread directly on the ground. We bought bread, lard, a couple of onions. The prices were ten to twenty times the official ones, but we did not expect anything else. This was a free market: peasants, all of them members of collective farms, were allowed to ask any price for the produce of their own miniature plots. In town it was the same old problem. Shops were either shut, or, if open, they were either empty or had long queues at their doors, and we had no ration cards.

The window display of one of the several shops we passed made my heart go faster. Whole, unnaturally rigid, hams, rings of strikingly pink sausage, hefty sides of pallid pork fat. Father looked at me and laughed. 'Mock-ups made of plaster,' he said.

We returned to the ship. The loading was finished and we cast off within minutes.

Having left the food in our cabin, we went to the observation post at the bow. Even here, in the north, close to its source, the Volga was a mighty river. It was much wider than the Vistula in Warsaw, or the Northern Dvina river at Krasnoborsk, but its shores were dull, monotonous. With the smoke-belching factory chimneys of the city well behind us, the view on both sides was probably unchanged from the one that Ivan the Terrible had encountered on his Kazan expedition. Forests, villages, small towns with an occasional onion dome of a church, fields, meadows with some cattle grazing, a few horses.

Next morning the view was very much the same. At noon the restaurant opened and we were served boiled ham with lentils – exactly as promised by the young Tatar officer. Apart from us and a couple of the ship's officers sitting at the other end of the same long table, the restaurant was empty, but it was a memorable meal. And so was its price: sixteen roubles per portion, or more than a doctor earned in a day. But Father, his usual generous self, treated me to two helpings. In the distant past, when I was a small child, he used to say to me: 'Remember, Stefanku, money is there to be spent.' How right he was! We were soon to have proof of it.

In the afternoon the river became even wider and both shores disappeared from view. We were not to see much of either shore again except in ports or, much later, when the ship navigated the enormous delta of the river.

As to the restaurant, it remained shut for the rest of the voyage. My appetite must have exhausted its supplies.

The following morning I woke up to a great noise, such as made only by a large crowd. Men were talking just outside my cabin window. I understood not a single word. I pulled up the blind. The deck was crowded with men with slanting eyes, Tatars. We must be in Kazan, the capital of the Tatar Republic. So these had to be the passengers the young officer was talking about. I washed and dressed quickly and went to my parents' cabin. Father stood by the open window talking to the men outside. I joined him. They spoke Russian – sort of. 'Conscripts,' said Father. Shabbily dressed men, each with a huge loaf of bread, the size of a cartwheel, under his arm. Turning to Mother, Father said in Polish, 'Time to barter?' and turned back to the men outside.

Suddenly I became aware of other noises coming from the shore. Loud crying, weeping, screams. Sounds of despair, grief, lament. Subdued wailing, like so many hired mourners at a funeral. Mother handed me a chunk of bread, I grabbed it and ran out on deck.

With difficulty I pushed my way through the crowd to the rail. The waterfront was jammed full of people: women, children, old men. Some down on their knees with arms stretched up to the heavens, others maniacally waving their kerchiefs. More shouts. Incomprehensible words. More crying and wailing.

Fascinating, sad and heart-breaking. I had never seen anything like it before.

❈ ❈ ❈

Some time later, when I returned to the cabin, Mother told me that she had witnessed similar scenes during the First World War. Women seeing their menfolk off to the army, as now, keening, crying, wailing in a sing-song voice: ' . . . They are taking my little dove away . . . aaa . . . My beloved, I'll never see him again . . . aaa . . . he will be soaring in the sky, my eagle . . . my hawk . . . aaa . . . far away from home, they will put him in a dark grave . . .'

'They had often been right then, of course, as they might be right now,' she concluded and added: 'War is particularly hard on women and children.' I puzzled over it for a minute or two. Isn't it the men who do all the fighting, aren't they the ones who die?

❈ ❈ ❈

I watched the crowd for a while longer and turned round to go back to the cabin. I was hungry again. Perhaps Mother might conjure up a treat, at least another hunk of bread, sweet mock tea with it or even *kipyatok* would be good, but would we have any sugar left?

In the meantime the crowd had closed around me and once again I had to elbow my way through. In contrast to the noisy multitude on the waterfront, the tightly packed crowd of conscripts on the deck was quiet and almost still, except for some apathetic, curiously resigned, hand-waving.

Wait a minute! Something was happening at my parents' cabin window. Men pushing, shoving each other out of the way. 'Hey! What's going on?' I heard myself shouting. Working hard with my elbows I made some headway. What was happening? I was getting worried. I couldn't move! I changed my tactics and, left shoulder first, I pushed, I wriggled and, worm-like, proceeded little by little through the crowd towards the window. Then, between the shaven heads and Tatar faces, I caught my father's eye. What was that? He winked, smiled, winked again and my anxiety evaporated. I nudged closer and closer. There he was, in the cabin window, with lumps of sugar spread in front of him on the window-sill. Some lively trade was going on. I saw lumps of sugar changing hands for wedges of country bread. Father passed the bread to Mother who was standing behind him. Judging by the queue at the cabin window, we ought to have enough bread for the rest of the journey. Where and how did my father lay his hands on all that sugar? There were at least five or six more lumps left on the window-sill waiting to be bartered for bread.

The lumps of sugar were not the geometrically regular, pleasing to the eye, small pieces we know today. At the time sugar often came in big sugar-loaves, cone-shaped and several kilos in weight. Hit repeatedly with a hammer, or other heavy object, the sugar-loaf split into a multitude of irregular fragments.

How did such a store of sugar escape my notice? Mother must have hidden it for 'a rainy day'. And then a thought struck me: has she been deliberately hiding it from me? Hurt, ashamed, I turned round to go back to the rail.

What was going on there now? The whole crowd was pushing to the rail. Oh, I understood. The deck had been shuddering under my feet for some time. The engines were working. We were off! The sobs and screams from the riverside grew and, echoed by the houses enclosing the harbour, became a deafening, high-pitched, inarticulate wail. The crowd on the deck was also noisy, far from apathetic now. Men pushed to the rail shoving others out of the way. Some were crying, others shouted what sounded like words of encouragement, promises. I didn't understand a word. A few, their features rigid, stood quiet and still.

Judging by their smooth faces, still innocent of the first shave, most of the conscripts were not much older than me, perhaps seventeen or eighteen. Did Mongols shave? I was not sure. Anyway, I did not envy them going to war. The Red Army was now in full retreat. I had done enough retreating, or running away in September 1939, that it should last me for a while. The thought of war frightened me. I was glad that I had at least another year before I could even volunteer, and then it would have to be with the Polish Army.

Among the rising tumult I made my way to the rail again. The gangway was up and the space between us and the riverside was rapidly widening. A few more minutes and the crowd on the deck grew silent, the wailing from the shore faded in the distance. We were reaching the middle of the river, the shore became just a low line on the horizon, then it disappeared altogether.

I returned to the cabin. A lovely aroma, like a baker's shop's, hit my nostrils. A heap of bread was piled on the couch. Mother handed me a steaming mug of tea, a small lump of sugar and a big hunk of bread. It was crusty and fresh – real country bread. I sipped my tea *na prikooskoo*, filtering it through the lump of sugar held in my mouth. What bliss! Had Mother decided that the 'rainy day' has arrived?

The subsequent few days left little trace in my memory. The ship continued mostly in midstream. When we neared either one bank or the other, a thinly populated steppe country came into view and an occasional village with its onion dome slid by in the distance. We stopped in big towns or cities: Saratov,

Kuybyshev, Stalingrad. Somewhere on the way, it might have been in Stalingrad, the Tatar conscripts disembarked and the ship seemed deserted again. Afraid of getting lost, of not being allowed back into the port enclosure, never sure how long the loading or unloading of cargo would last, we could do no sightseeing. Viewed from their harbours, the towns and cities along the Volga River were unremarkable, drab, with sprawling concrete residential blocks and heavy municipal buildings, Stalinist style.

One afternoon Father came out with me for a walk on the deck. The river had become narrower, now and again divided into smaller channels. Most of the time both shores were visible. We must have entered the delta. The area here was more densely populated. But it took another night and most of the following morning before we entered the port of Astrakhan.

What a disappointment! The towers and domes of the city were visible in the distance, but on disembarkation we were allowed into the harbour park and no further.

Large numbers of police were waiting at the bottom of the gangway and along the waterfront. They took a long time going over our travel documents. They could not stop us from disembarking in Astrakhan – after all we had a valid travel document with the destination 'Astrakhan' written on it and crowned with a round rubber stamp, the ultimate sign of authority.

The round stamp was a sacred symbol of Russian officialdom under both past or present systems of government. Without a round stamp on your travel document you could not travel, without the round stamp on your ration book you could not eat, without the round stamp on your identity document you did not exist and, I presume, without the round stamp on your death certificate you could not be buried; officially you were still alive.

So, the police could not prevent us from disembarking in Astrakhan, but they could confine us to their chosen and carefully selected area, and this was what they did. It had once been a nice park with lawns and flower-beds, with benches and a bandstand, but there certainly was no stall selling caviar. Sadly, caviar was not the only item missing in the Astrakhan harbour park.

We had finished the last of our country bread the day before we disembarked and there was no food here whatsoever to be bought, stolen or found. There was no *kipyatok* tap, in fact no drinking water at all; the river water was polluted with oil. In addition we had no roof over our heads; the only available roof, that of the bandstand, had already been taken by other refugees.

There were thousands of them in the Astrakhan harbour park.

FOURTEEN

WRONG TURNINGS,
WRONG STOPS

We took a wrong turning in Gorkiy. My choice of Astrakhan
for our destination had proved to be a bad joke.

The harbour park, with its gates closed and guarded, was some
two hundred metres wide and extended for over half a kilometre
between one of the channels of the Volga River to the east and the
town with its old towers to the west. There was no sea to be seen
in Astrakhan. The area had looked very different in my school
atlas when I studied it in Kvasha. Astrakhan was supposed to be
a port and, at the time, it did not occur to me that it was a river
port and that the sea was some fifty kilometres further south.
Still, the spur of the moment decision was Father's and nobody
blamed me. I blamed myself though, even if not too much.

Looked at from the riverbank, the park appeared crowded. It
was also noisy. It resounded with a variety of languages, a
veritable tower of Babel. I picked up words of Russian, Polish,
Yiddish, even German. The cacophony of sounds included
angry shouts, shrieks and yells of children, loud conversations,
bursts of laughter.

So there we were, my parents and I, in Astrakhan, standing
on the bank of the river with all our worldly goods, uncertain
where to turn, totally lost, bewildered, utterly confused.

Suddenly, I heard a deep and unmistakable voice calling,
'Stefan, Stefan!' Slightly husky, followed by laughter and the
insistent call: 'Stefan, we are here, come and join us.'

Good God! Helena's voice? Impossible! Helena? Here? The last time I saw her was in Gorkiy, over a week ago. We had parted in great sadness. We had promised to look for each other in Astrakhan but, deep in my heart, I knew that we were unlikely to meet again.

Now here she was, in the Astrakhan harbour park, standing on a park bench, waving frantically with both arms extended high above her head, laughing.

By the time I recovered my equanimity, they were with us: Helena and her brother Olek, her sisters Magda and Lala, the two Wassermans, Mietek and his father. They helped us with the luggage and in no time we rejoined our remaining friends. A good part of the 'raft contingent' was here. Crowded as they were on two park benches and an adjacent section of the lawn, they made room for us. Mr Romer related their story.

The Romers, the Wassermans and the Gruszyńskis had arrived in Astrakhan over the previous few days by different trains, but none were allowed to stay in the town. On reaching the ancient city, all refugees, whatever their nationality and whatever documents they held, were herded on to lorries and taken, under guard, to the harbour park, which had thus become a kind of refugee camp. Several young people who had managed to sneak out at night over the park fence were brought back by the militia within hours. The food situation was desperate. It was more than two days since a lorry-load of bread had been distributed in the park and our friends made it last until this morning. The meagre food supplies that people had brought with them had run out by now. As nobody was allowed out of the park, one could not look for food in the town. And, according to those who had enjoyed the few hours of illegal freedom, food was available, quite freely, without queues, without ration cards, in shops, restaurants and markets. Prices were high, but food was there, waiting!

Listening to Mr Romer talking about food I suddenly felt very hungry. I thought that we had finished the remainder of our Kazan bread the previous night. But, as my stomach started rumbling, Mother reached into a bundle and, lo and behold, out came several wedges of the Kazan bread. Trust Mother to secrete 'iron rations'. The bread was stale, hard, but she broke the chunks into smaller pieces and, Jesus-like, fed the 'multitude', or at least all thirteen of us.

'Even water is a problem,' Mr Romer continued his tale of woe. 'The park taps are dry. They turned the water off at the mains and we can't find them. The river water is filthy and stinks of oil. Undrinkable. There are no means to boil it.'

'Has anybody complained to the guards?' asked Father.

'Yes, I did,' said Mr Wasserman. 'The guard took me to their commander, a sergeant. His answer was: "Never mind, it will rain soon, and your bread rations will be here in the evening." That was the day before yesterday,' he sighed and shrugged his shoulders.

'He was right about one thing,' Mietek took over. 'It did rain that night and we had a surfeit of water. We got no sleep, none at all. We were soaked to the skin. We filled what we could with rain water. But that was also the day before yesterday and the supply is running out. We are filthy.'

'I honestly don't know,' Mietek continued, 'whether to wish, or not, for another downpour tonight and pay for it with another soaking and sleepless . . .' Interrupted by a distant rumble of thunder somewhere down the river he stopped in mid-sentence.

I looked up. The sky was blue and clear, except for several innocuous-looking white cloudlets hanging low down in the east, where the opposite bank of the river merged into the horizon. The surface of the water, lightly caressed by a gentle breeze, shimmered with the reflected gold of the sun setting behind the towers of the old town. Big oil stains in all colours of the rainbow extended from the harbour only to be lost in the distance, in the tremulous gold surface of the water.

The evening was short and the night rapidly closed in on us. The noise in the harbour park slowly died down as the crowd settled for the night. We spread our blankets and duvets on the benches and on the lawn. Between us we had only two benches to share. To have one to oneself, virtually a single bed, was a luxury and Mrs Romer was accorded one. The other, which had served as a bed for Mr Wasserman, he, always a gentleman, ceded to my mother. The rest of the group, like the great majority of inmates of the Astrakhan harbour park, slept on the lawns, tightly packed head-to-foot, sardine-like in fashion.

Yet Helena and I found just enough room to fit side-by-side, head-to-head. Though under separate covers. Nobody objected, at least not openly. Our parents and friends were getting used to us being almost 'a couple'. We whispered well into the night.

The night was warm; Astrakhan lies at the same latitude as the south of France. My stomach started rumbling again and my mouth was parched. Talking became difficult. And then Helena said, 'I am hungry. My mouth is dry . . . Good night.'

The sky was pebbled with millions of stars. I thought to myself: 'That's Ursa Major and there is the Polar Star.' My eyes were closing.

I woke up with a start. It was cold. The sky was black; not a single star to be seen. My face and lips were wet. Rain? Still half asleep, automatically, I licked my lips. And then, fully awake, I sat up and collected rain water in my hands. I drank it, I was parched. 'Helena, wake up, it's raining,' I shook her by the arm. She sat up. Her hands cupped, she collected the rain water, drank it. I looked around. Men and women all round us were drinking from their cupped hands.

Water from heaven? Will manna follow?

Then a rumble of thunder. A storm. The rain became a downpour. Each thunder clap was followed by cascades of water. Lightning, one flash after another in quick succession, illuminated the weird spectacle of motionless people sitting with cupped hands stretched to heaven, like some peculiar congregation at prayer.

With the immediate thirst quenched, the mass stupor lifted. Cups and jars came out to be drunk from. Then pots and buckets were filled with the precious stuff. Basins and bowls. Some tried to catch the rain in hats and caps. In seconds our bedding and clothes were soaked, the gravelled path by the benches became a stream. We collected enough water for a few days.

The rain prophesied by the guard sergeant did come, but the bread did not. And we stayed four more days in the Astrakhan harbour park. Frequent showers provided us with enough water, but of manna we had none.

On the second evening Mother gave me two large lumps of sugar, which she had somehow managed to hide all this time, but that was definitely the last of her rations.

I shared it, one lump each, with Helena and we licked them slowly and deliberately. Then we starved, like everybody else.

❋ ❋ ❋

I do not remember much of these four hungry days; not even the feeling of being hungry. I do remember being surprised that the harbour park grew silent, eerily so.

And I do remember a large family of Bessarabian Jews who resided on the lawn across the path from us. Their children of assorted ages cried a lot on the first day, but then only whimpered weakly until consoled on the lap of one of the women. The only visibly happy member of the family was a small baby, who was repeatedly breastfed by a beautiful young woman with very long tar-black hair. I was fascinated by the intimacy of breastfeeding. After each feed the baby burped and went to sleep. I blushed when the woman's eyes caught me staring; she smiled and I looked away. Helena laughed.

But the supply of mother's milk must have failed, perhaps on the third or fourth day, and the baby went on whimpering even after the breast was offered.

I was dozing on and off; I saw others doing the same; we lost all sense of time. One day, when I woke up still dazed, the baby was not there. Worried, I shook Helena from her slumber and pointed to the babyless mother. Without a word Helena got up and made her way between the scattered bodies and across the path. They exchanged a few words and then they both waved to me and smiled.

Helena came back. 'The baby is okay,' she said. 'The grandmother is feeding him over there.' She pointed to a group of people further away. 'Her baby, *our* baby's uncle,' Helena blushed, 'died a few days ago and the grandmother has plenty of milk left.'

❋ ❋ ❋

On the morning of the fifth day, as I woke up, the harbour park was unusually noisy. I sat up and looked around. People were on the move. They converged on to the harbour gate and a crowd collected there. People were talking animatedly, pointing to the park entrance. Had food arrived? Bread? Soup?

I got up. I was dizzy. Sea sickness? Nonsense, we were not at sea. I clenched my teeth and the dizziness went. I joined Father and Mr Romer by the gate. A long wooden table had been placed in the small square just inside the park entrance and two guards, their rifles hanging loose from their shoulders, were placing chairs behind it. Other guards with rifles at the ready, bayonets fixed, kept the crowd at a distance. Mr Romer tried to engage a guard in conversation, but failed. Father tried to talk to another with equal lack of success.

Speculation was rife. They will let us out of the harbour park ... They are going to deport us ... They will transport us back to Siberia ... All men will be drafted into the army ...

Stupid talk. I stopped listening.

But Mr Romer talked sense: 'They have been starving us on purpose. The softening up process, you know. It does not augur anything good. Mark my words. The militia, or NKVD troops, will surround the park before the night is out and one way or another they'll move us from here.'

He was not far wrong. A number of open militia lorries arrived and stopped in an orderly column outside the park gate. Nothing happened for hours. No NKVD materialised. Exhausted as we all were, the crowd dispersed. We returned to our bivouac on the lawn. Father waved his hand dismissively. 'Never mind,' he said. 'We'll find out soon enough,' and dozed off.

'You are right,' said Mr Romer and shut his eyes.

I woke up again some time later to a renewed noise by the gate. As I looked, passenger cars disgorged several officers and a couple of civilians. Another lorry arrived, this one covered with a tarpaulin. A small crowd of refugees had formed again by the gate. Father, Mr Romer and Mr Wasserman, Olek and Mietek were awake and we rejoined the crowd.

The new arrivals sat behind the table, except for one officer who walked slowly in front of it and faced the crowd. He raised his arm and the crowd fell silent. 'As you must have realised,' he started, 'we have neither work nor housing for you in Astrakhan. But out there,' he described a vast circle with his outstretched arms, 'collective farms, workshops and factories are crying out for workers. *Grazhdanye*, citizens!' he shouted. 'There is a war on! We must fight it all together. Under the leadership of the Party and of our great commander, Comrade Stalin, the victory shall be ours!'

'Allah is great and Mohammed is his prophet. Another bloody political meeting,' I whispered to Mietek.

The officer stopped, suddenly short of oratorial inspiration, and passed slowly along the front of the crowd looking into people's eyes. 'Like some bloody general inspecting the guard of honour,' said Mietek under his breath.

'He probably wants volunteers for something,' added Father.

'That's the carrot,' whispered Mr Wasserman. 'Now let's have the stick.'

The officer returned to his previous place facing us, his back to the table. 'You are free citizens.' He reasoned like a teacher trying to explain something to a class of naughty children. 'You may stay here in the harbour park if you wish.' He stopped to allow this information to sink in and then, as another wave of inspiration hit him, he shouted at the top of his voice, 'But he who does not work does not eat!'

We had heard that one before.

After a dramatic pause he continued: 'There,' his arms again described a circle. '*Rodina*, our Motherland, needs your hands and your brains to help in the fight against the fascist invader, against the German dogs and the spit-covered lackeys of capitalism!' He shouted another worn-out slogan for good measure. 'Out there, you will be welcome. Excellent accommodation, suitable work, plenty of food, all that is awaiting you.'

He paused again. His eyes wandered across the faces of the crowd, then he turned away from us, walked slowly round the table and took the last empty chair behind it.

Once seated he gave up the rhetoric and proceeded in a more business-like manner: 'We are here to help you. We shall call heads of families to sign the papers and off you go. The transport,' he pointed to the lorries mustered outside the gates, 'is ready and waiting. Surnames starting with letters A to G, heads of families only. Line up from this side.' He pointed to the end of the table.

'Oh, yes,' he added as an afterthought. 'The papers signed, the head of the family may collect bread, one loaf per person and half a loaf for each child, no matter what age. Even for babies,' he added magnanimously and pointed to the tarpaulin-covered lorry by the gate.

'*Timeo Danaos et dona ferentes*, I fear the Greeks even when they bring gifts,' commented Mr Romer under his breath.

'More of the usual,' said Father. '*Obiecanki cacanki a głupiemu radość*, promises, promises – joy to the fools.' Father quoted a Polish proverb and then turned philosophical: 'Fear of the unknown may be thrilling, but fear of the known impairs judgement. God knows what to do. Stay put? Or take up the offer?'

We walked slowly back to our place on the lawn. The choice was difficult. Since Gorkiy, where Father had heard about the Polish Army camp in Tatishchevo, the idea was that, having secured for Mother and me temporary living-quarters in Astrakhan, Father would rejoin the army, get a posting to an army hospital, find local accommodation and then send for us. But Tatishchevo was near Saratov, almost a thousand kilometres north of Astrakhan, and the choice of leaving us here in the harbour park, or allowing Mother and me to go to an uncertain destination was no choice at all, either would be madness. Families which split up could not count on coming together again.

But Mother settled it quickly. 'No point staying here,' she said. And once again our friends agreed.

'Only we must make sure that we go together, as a group,' said Mr Gruszyński. Once the fattest man in Kvasha and now much more shapely, Mr Gruszyński, who had spent most of the last few days sleeping, suddenly came to life and lifted his still impressive bulk with some difficulty. 'Okay,' he continued, 'leave it to me. I shall try and go first and see what's on offer.'

He joined the line of several men by the table. In ten minutes he returned, a picture of bliss. On the way back he was munching the corner of a white loaf. In his right hand he brandished a piece of paper. 'They gave me little choice,' he said. 'I had to decide on the spot and we are all going to a place called

Kopanovka by cargo ship. I told them that we were one large extended family and I signed for all of us. You can collect your bread now.'

So it came to pass that next morning, replete with white bread, in the polyglot crowd of about two hundred refugees, we boarded a small cargo ship. Some eight hours later, under a sky blackened by heavy clouds, we disembarked in the harbour of Kopanovka. Another thunderstorm was coming our way. This time, at least, we were going to have a roof over our heads, or that was what we thought.

The Kopanovka harbour consisted of a short wooden jetty and a shed. As the boat tied up, a uniformed man – the harbour master? – came out of the shed escorted by a grey-haired guard with a rifle hanging on a string from his shoulder. I jumped onto the cobbled bank. As the ship disgorged its load of men, women and children, the expression of surprise on the harbour master's face turned into one of disbelief and then into that of dismay and anger as he read the paper handed to him by a crewman. As the last refugee stepped on land, the crewman tied off the boat, jumped on deck, the others pulled the gangway up and the boat was on her way.

In Kopanovka nobody had expected us; there was no welcoming committee. 'Work, food, accommodation . . . Here, in Kopanovka?' The harbour master roared with laughter. 'Did they promise you paradise too? Only fools take the promises of the NKVD seriously. You may sleep here in the harbour tonight and tomorrow we shall see.' He turned round as if to go back to his shed but, surrounded by the crowd, he had no choice but to stay put. The harbour, in reality, was just a fenced and cobbled yard, empty except for about a dozen wooden hand-carts.

Faced with the prospect of yet another night out in the open and with no food the crowd became angry. Shouts of frustration were soon replaced by unambiguous threats in Russian.

'Let's take over the harbour office for the night!' shouted one man pointing to the shed by the jetty.

'Fat lot of use,' countered another. 'There are two hundred of us and ten would make a crowd there.'

'Let's get them!' a tall, thin, cadaverous-looking man shouted. He towered over both the harbour master and his guard. In the next instant, before either of them could react, he had them both by the collar, almost lifting them off the ground. The crowd, now amused, voiced suggestions:

'Give them a ducking in the river!'

'Let's drown the sons of bitches.'

'The two shits will float.'

'Let's compromise. Let him send a telegram to *tovarishch* Stalin and ask for instructions,' suggested a female voice.

The crowd laughed.

'First let's break into the nearest food store,' suggested somebody else. The harbour gate was unguarded, but it gave on to a deserted street, not a shop in sight.

'Some hope.'

More suggestions, threats, curses, cries of children, wailing of women came thick and fast from all sides. The crowd became a mob. Ugly. Men and women dragged the harbour master and the guard to the riverbank, threatened to cut off their balls, to duck them in their own harbour, to hang them from the lampposts (in the best revolutionary tradition, but fortunately there was no suitable lamppost in sight), unless the station master conjured up food and a roof over our heads. Frightened out of his wits, and with good reason, the harbour master promised to do so. When the crowd let him wriggle free, with several men close on his heels, he ran into his 'office' and grabbed the phone. Within minutes he yelled for the guard to take us to *Krasnyi Ugolok*, the communal hall, for the night. 'You can sleep there. Plenty of room. And you will get bread, soup and *kipyatok*, as much as you want.' The guard, who having escaped a ducking in the river wisely kept out of sight, now emerged from some hole and placed himself at the head of the crowd.

'*Obiecanki, cacanki*, promises, promises,' said somebody in Polish. But we were tired and hungry, so the prospect of a dry floor to sleep on, a roof over it, with perhaps some food thrown in, sufficed to make us meekly follow our latter day Pied Piper through the empty streets of the little town.

Kopanovka was not some Hamelin conceived in Hollywood; it was a miserable small township, but its communal hall was huge. It was also deserted. There was enough floor space for all two hundred of us to sleep in several parallel rows side by side.

Not even sardine-fashion, but in a more civilised way: head to head.

By the time we got there a van loaded with bread was waiting for us. Half a loaf each, just enough for supper. The promised soup did not materialise, but *kipyatok* was on tap – unrestricted, as promised. The night passed uneventfully.

I woke up in the morning just as Mr Romer ran in from the street very agitated, out of breath. 'They are selling food in the kiosk in the square. Give me a big container. Whatever. Quick, quick,' he urged his wife who was feverishly trying to unpack the bundle of kitchen utensils.

He grabbed the first handle which came to view and pulled hard. In the next moment he had a large white enamel chamber pot, the biggest I had ever seen, in his hand. Mrs Romer held on to its rim. 'It is a chamber pot!' she shouted the obvious and pulled it her way.

'Never mind. Will do!' yelled Mr Romer and ran off clutching the precious container to his chest.

'It's all right really,' said Mrs Romer with an embarrassed smile. 'It's clean. Hasn't been used much. Anyway, I washed it well before packing.'

In the meantime, Mother handed me an enamel bucket and a bundle of roubles. 'Quickly, follow him,' she said. I joined the queue. It was long, but as the only produce on sale was curd cheese, easy to dish out, it moved quickly. The woman in the kiosk used a large ladle. In less than fifteen minutes I was back in the hall with a bucketful of white curds.

In the queue I learned that there was a large milk-processing plant in Kopanovka and while its main product, tinned butter, was reserved for the army, the by-products – buttermilk and curd cheese – were either sold in the kiosk, or fed to pigs in the collective farms surrounding the town. This was fine with me. For five kilos of curd cheese I paid just one rouble, equivalent to the official price of two loaves of the cheapest bread. I also learned that in another kiosk one could buy pork and beef offal – trotters, tripe, livers, lungs – at state prices and without ration cards. But when I reported this discovery to Mother, she shrugged her shoulders. 'We can't eat that kind of stuff raw,' she said, 'and there is no way of cooking it.' She was right, of course. I did not think about the technicalities. Steak tartare was a delicacy in Warsaw restaurants, and I loved it, but I could see that perhaps it did not originate in pork or beef offal. Oh well . . .

The next few days are just a blur in my memory. We spent them in the same communal hall, mostly lying on the floor, living on a diet of buttermilk and boiled water, with curd cheese made palatable by the addition of salt, and with an occasional slice of bread procured on the black market. It was certainly better than Astrakhan.

There was no work for us either in the town cannery, or in the milk-processing plant, or in the surrounding farms. The promises made to us in the Astrakhan harbour had proved a sham. They were meant to get us out of the way, which they did, all for the price of a lorry-load of white bread.

The town, Kopanovka, was a miserable little place. Clean, but devoid of all interest. An overgrown village really. There was a cinema, but we were too apathetic to go there. We did not even attempt to go for walks; the streets looked uninviting, there was no park. I spent most of the time either reading or in a daze.

One evening, our third or fourth in the communal hall, during another meal of curd cheese and hot boiled water, Mother made up her mind. 'I have had enough of Kopanovka,' she said. 'We must leave this place. There is nothing for us here.' She was right, of course.

Mrs Romer leaned over a bundle separating our 'dining-room' on one of our suitcases from theirs and almost shouted with relief, 'I did not dare say it. But we must, we must!' It struck me then how timid Mrs Romer was, how different from my mother. Not an equal partner in their marriage, as my mother was in hers.

Next morning Father and Mr Romer left the hall to explore ways of leaving the town. Suffering from a bad dose of boredom, I followed them. First we went to the railway station. Unlike the Kotlas and Gorkiy stations, the small Kopanovka station building was deserted. Eventually, guided by his loud snoring, we found the station master fast asleep on a wooden bench in a small cubicle behind his office. Woken up by two gents in town suits (I kept some distance behind), he took fright and stood up to attention. Then he tried to smooth his dishevelled hair and attended to his ruffled uniform jacket, fastening his collar. Did he take us for inspectors, or supervisors? Gogol's *Revizor*, Inspector General, came to my mind and I could barely suppress laughter. No, he did not know when the next passenger train would stop in Kopanovka, not today, nor tomorrow, maybe not for a week. Goods trains stopped in Kopanovka almost daily, but passenger trains hardly ever did. The Astrakhan–Stalingrad express stopped only to set down or pick up 'very important personages, not ordinary people,' he added with disdain. And nobody was allowed on to goods trains. 'Definitely not. Under no circumstances,' he concluded.

This sounded too definite. Too unequivocal for a Soviet official. Unbribable? Impossible. Standing there by the wooden bench at attention he looked still a little dazed after his snooze, but otherwise not that different from other station masters. Could he really be an exception: an unbribable Soviet official? Unheard of.

Silence reigned in the little office as Father looked at Mr Romer and Mr Romer looked at Father. Suddenly the station master sighed and came out of his reverie. He realised that, in spite of their town suits, the two gents and the boy facing him were no railway inspectors, but just run-of-the-mill refugees. He relaxed visibly. His self-assurance regained, he motioned us into his office and sat down behind his desk, leaving us standing. As soon as he placed his behind on the padded chair and his elbows on the desk he became the all-important official in charge of the situation. He unhooked his collar, so that a dirty grey vest showed through again.

That's more like it, I thought. Mr Romer's mind must have been tuned to the same wavelength as he carefully placed two *chervontsy* (the red banknotes worth ten roubles each), half hiding them under the blotter on the desk. The station master's demeanour changed miraculously. He became pleasant, affable even. 'Where do you want to go?' he asked. 'How many of you?' He listened to Father's story with much sympathetic lifting of the eyebrows, head-shaking, tongue clicking.

'First let's try the harbour,' he said. 'All the produce of the Kopanovka milk-processing plant and cannery goes by the river and they can sometimes take passengers. They even have cabins.' His hand travelled under the blotter and the red banknotes disappeared in his trouser pocket. 'You will have to come to an arrangement with the harbour master,' he continued. 'Go there now and I'll talk to him presently.' He lifted the receiver. Rapid talk in Russian followed, but I missed a lot. A local dialect? A whiff of the Ukrainian?

After several roubles' worth of hand-shaking and shoulder-clapping we left the station and made our way to the harbour. The harbour master, the man so recently manhandled by our angry fellow travellers, forewarned by the station master, was now amiability itself. Yes, the station master had called him. The prospect of a good bribe worked wonders. He called for the guard to bring a hand-cart into the shed for us to sit on. He offered cigarettes all round.

In the event, leaving Kopanovka proved expensive. In addition to the station master and the harbour master, the skipper and the guards on duty also had to be bribed. But we left the next day.

Bribing the skipper presented a problem. The station master warned us that the man did a lot of business on the side and consequently 'was wallowing in money'. As a bribe, euphemistically called a 'token of appreciation', he preferred goods and was 'hard to please, fussy'.

The problem was further discussed in our corner of the communal hall. We were still carting with us our Pińsk camp-bed on which I had slept in Kvasha. It was not just a simple folding canvas bed, but an upholstered, well-padded and comfortable, fancy, deluxe version, greatly admired by the Russians as a splendid product of capitalist technology. Now it bought us the way out of Kopanovka, another of our wrong stops.

After one more night in the Kopanovka communal hall, we said goodbye to our friends, loaded our belongings on a couple of wooden-hand carts and, in a group reduced to the six Romers and the three of us, made our way to the harbour. Our immediate destination was Saratov and, more particularly, the Polish army camp in the nearby Tatishchevo; the remainder of our group – the Wassermans, the Gruszyńskis – not keen on joining any army at this stage, decided to stay put.

I never met my good friend, Mietek, or his father, again.

Back in the port, the harbour master let us stay in the shed. The boat arrived at noon and as soon as we boarded she was on her way. We were not exactly piped aboard, but the skipper personally welcomed us. 'We were not scheduled to stop in Kopanovka,' he said with a genuine smile, 'but I am glad to be able to help you to get out of this godforsaken hole.' We shook hands all round. 'Oh, and I must see this famous folding bed,' he added. He approved of the 'token' and my bed promptly disappeared to his cabin.

Contrary to the Kopanovka station master's assurance, the boat had no cabins and we spent the entire journey from Kopanovka to Saratov, two days and two nights, on the aft deck trying to find protection from the wind. The days were still reasonably warm, but the nights were chilly.

On the first morning we stopped for several hours in Stalingrad, the city destroyed a year later in one of the bloodiest and most important battles of the Second World War. We wandered round the town, not sightseeing, but in search of food. A restaurant? A food shop? A market? Of the city itself I still remember the town centre, its monumental buildings with imposing entrances and marble columns.

Eventually we found a restaurant. A queue outside, must be open! After queuing for an unconscionably long time we were let in only to join another queue inside. The place was not really designated a restaurant, but, as a large sign announced, 'a mass feeding establishment'. The only item on offer was a potato bake, one portion per person, served in individual white rectangular dishes. I could have gobbled up two or three portions without difficulty. It was good, anything would have been. I looked with envy as Helena passed her dish, half full, to Olek, her brother, saying, 'You have it. I have had enough.' Was she ill?

We hurried back to the harbour. Missing the boat with all our belongings on board would have been a disaster. We walked quickly. The side streets were squalid, dirty, with wooden sidewalks full of holes. The houses on both sides were made of wood, and were in urgent need of paint and attention. Here a plank hung loose, there an outside staircase with steps missing.

Then a shop window with mock-ups of hams, sausages and cheeses caught my eye. A food shop! I pointed it out to Father. 'Should we get food for tomorrow?' The shop was open.

'No queue. Probably empty shelves,' said Father.

'Do let's try,' pleaded Helena. So she was not ill. 'Let's try,' she repeated. So now she was hungry! Women!

The shop was huge, but bare. Even with the nine of us and with the two idle, busily gossiping women assistants behind the counter it still looked empty. Father was right. There was nothing on the shelves. Except for one corner. Cosmetics! I looked in disgust: bottles of eau de Cologne of the ubiquitous *Tezhe* brand, toothpowder, massive cubes of dirty yellow laundry soap. Disappointing! But Mr Romer did not give up easily. He investigated and suddenly called out: 'Look! Tinned crab.'

This was the first time that we encountered crab meat in tins labelled '*Chatka*'. Later in our travels we would come across the same product of the Kamchatka peninsula again and again in otherwise empty Soviet food shops; this had only become available because its export was frustrated by the war. It was very expensive, far too expensive for the *hoi polloi* and therefore often freely available. Fortunately, Father still had money to spend. We left the shop in a hurry and round the corner found a stall with *lepyoshki*, flat bread – made of black-market flour, of course. Expensive, but just what we needed.

We reached the port just as the boat was about to leave. 'We have been worried, but I would not have left without you,' said the captain magnanimously.

We were out of breath, but at least we were not hungry and we had some food for the next day.

The next afternoon we disembarked in Saratov and made our way to the railway station. It was big and, as might have been expected, crowded. People camped in the halls, in the corridors, in the square outside, in the offices.

Our intention was to get on a train to Tatishchevo, only about a thirty-kilometre journey, and to make our way to the Polish Army camp there. It all seemed so straightforward. Father would rejoin the army, Mr Romer and Olek would volunteer. All would be accepted with open arms. The rest of us would find rooms in the nearest town, find work perhaps, settle down for a while. Nothing could be simpler.

In the meantime, in expectation of this happy ending, we found a small empty space in the square, not far from the station entrance and, while we sat on our bundles, Father and Mr Romer left to explore the situation. They were gone a long time.

'Let's go for a walk,' said Helena. Magda joined us. We left the square by a narrow street running along the railway line. The street was empty: no people, no traffic. A short way on we came into another tree-lined square, with several benches on one side. Most were occupied by men talking softly. Some seemed to be asleep. The grass verge behind the benches was littered with bodies of more men. All asleep? Several dozen of them, all in rags, some bearded. Others sported many days of wild growth on their faces. They were filthy. Vagabonds? For footwear, with a few exceptions, they had dirty rags wrapped round their feet. The stench of unwashed bodies and of *makhorka* was even worse here, in the open, than in the crowded station itself.

A tramp-like figure in tatters was nothing unusual in a Soviet town. Footwear fashioned of rags with soles roughly cut out of rubber tyres, all held together with string, was also common. But dozens of tramps in one place? Convicts in transit to a prison camp?

I looked round. No armed NKVD guards. Heads not shaved. Anyway, convicts at rest would be made to squat, easier to guard. We had seen groups of them before. These were no convicts. So who were they? I felt uneasy. 'Should we turn back?' I suggested. 'God knows who they are.'

But Magda, impulsive as ever, ran to the nearest bench. 'They are speaking Polish!' she shouted and waved us on. 'They are our people,' she added. Helena and I came closer.

'*Niech panienka siada*, sit down, Miss,' said a man with grey hair, making room for Magda.

'Better not,' countered his neighbour. 'We are covered with lice.'

'But so are they,' answered the greyhead. 'Don't tell me that you can get that far in this accursed land and not be louse-ridden?'

Actually, we were not really lousy, as yet. An occasional

insect perhaps, a whitish speck. Without another thought, automatically, one crushed it between one's thumb nails. But 'being covered with lice' was another matter. I said nothing. They made more room on the bench and we joined them.

'Who are you? What are you doing here?' asked Helena.

'We came here from prison camps all over Siberia,' said the greyhead. 'This lot,' and he gestured with his right arm to encompass the benches and the body-strewn lawn behind them, 'have gathered here over the last few days. We were on our way to the army in Tatishchevo, but it's difficult to get there. Trains are packed. People hang like bunches of grapes out of windows and doors, they sit on buffers. We reported to the Polish Army station officer and he,' he sniggered, 'sent us here to wait. So we are waiting. Patiently. We can hardly do anything else, can we?' He looked round and his rhetorical question was answered by a murmur of assenting voices, with much nodding. In his rags he looked just as unkempt and dirty as his companions, but he was clean-shaven. It was difficult to guess his age. He wore well-worn black leather high boots, the only such footwear in sight, and his Polish was that of an educated man. An officer, I thought with respect. 'But several men,' he continued after a pause, 'got on a passenger train yesterday, a few more on a goods train this morning.'

I had another look round. They were all grey-faced, emaciated. The man sitting on the other side of the officer appeared even older. His straw-coloured tousled hair and rumpled beard with strands of silver in it made him look wild, even frightening, but his infinitely sad eyes, their gaze fixed somewhere in the distance, belied the first impression. With their bodies wrapped tightly into torn and dirty navy blue *foofaiki*, padded jackets, and their hands drawn up their sleeves, they were visibly cold in spite of the miserly, stepmotherly warmth of the autumn sun. Many had their heads covered with soiled, ragged caps with earflaps. The flaps were hanging down, untied, which made them look like so many mangy hunting dogs with floppy ears.

'When did you last have anything to eat?' asked Helena.

'We had soup last night,' said the greyhead. 'And good it was too,' he added with a smile. 'A couple of Polish women in uniform brought a cart with a cauldron on it here. Didn't they look funny in khaki trousers? Women in trousers . . .' he repeated with wonder. 'And this morning one of them brought bread and *kipyatok*. Fresh, white bread,' he repeated, shaking his head, his tongue clicking. 'Wonders will never cease . . .'

But it was time for us to rejoin our families. I nudged Helena gently in the side. 'We are going to Tatishchevo too,' she said. 'Perhaps we shall see you there.' And we made our way back to the station square.

When we got there, Father and Mr Romer had been back for some time. The latter had just finished talking. 'All we could get were two places on the Moscow train for tomorrow morning. It stops at Tatishchevo. We shall take it and we ought to be back in the evening.'

'God willing,' added Mrs Romer.

'Let's go,' said Olek grabbing two suitcases.

'Where to?' I asked. 'Have we missed anything important?'

'We've got a hotel room for the night,' laughed Mr Romer and Father showed me a key. Loaded with our luggage, we followed Father into the station building and then made our way through the crowd densely packing the hall and the corridors. At the end of a dark narrow corridor, Father unlocked a door to a small room. The sign on the door said 'Number six'. 'We had to bribe the minor official who presides in this office,' he said. 'This key has cost us fifty roubles. Let's hope it is worth it.'

It was. The night was getting chilly and the dark starless sky spelled rain for the night. Here at least, except for a layer of dust easily dealt with, the floor was clean, the stench not so oppressive and the chance of us becoming louse fodder was less than in the crowded hall and corridors.

We moved the empty desk and chairs, all dusty, to the side and spent another night on yet another floor. But having the entire room for just nine of us was a luxury. In the morning Father and Mr Romer caught the Moscow train.

'In times of war women and children are left on their own,' was Helena's philosophical comment.

Tatishchevo, a thirty-minute train journey away, proved to be another wrong turning. The two men returned in the late afternoon with a bag of black-market bread, which was very welcome, and news which was not. Conditions in the Polish Army camp in Tatishchevo were bad. Men lived in over-crowded tents. Everything – tents, blankets, uniforms – was in very short supply. Hundreds of men were arriving every day, adding to the thousands already in the camp.

'They look like a rabble,' said Father. 'Can they ever again become an army? Or will they just serve as cannon fodder in the best Russian tradition?'

He paused for a moment as if waiting for an answer and then continued: 'It looked as if we would have to queue for hours just to get into the recruitment tent. We wouldn't have been back until tomorrow. We were on the point of giving up, when I heard somebody mentioning General Boruta-Spiechowicz as the man in charge. I had known him well in 1919–20. I scribbled a few words on a scrap of paper, an officer walking past agreed to take the note to the general and we decided to wait. Anyway, we would have had to wait six hours for the train back to Saratov. I wondered whether he would recall my name. After all, more than twenty years has passed since that other war. But it was not long before his adjutant came for us. The general did remember me and invited us to the officers' mess for lunch. Just *kasha* and bread, but washed down with ample vodka.' The memory brought a momentary blissful smile to Father's face and he continued: 'They do need doctors, badly. They need officers of any kind and they can't understand why the rank and file are coming in droves, but so very few officers are returning. There must have been tens of thousands of regular and reserve officers among the PoWs taken by the Red Army in September 1939. Hundreds of army doctors, Adam among them.' Having mentioned his brother, Father stopped and looked at Mother.

Mr Romer took over: 'Conditions in the camp are indes-cribable. Only a few people wander about, many are too sick to move, and all look emaciated and are in rags. Walking corpses.' He stopped talking. A lawyer short of words?

Silence reigned for a few minutes and then my father took up the tale again: 'They suffer from all the present-day plagues: tuberculosis, dysentery, typhus, typhoid fever. Food rations are below survival level. Overall mortality is very high. They dread the winter coming. Night blindness, scurvy, pellagra, beri-beri are common and they can't get any vitamins. They have no medicines. They are still waiting for the promised delousing station.

'After the meal the general took me to his own tent for a private talk. The gist of it was that the entire Polish Army, at present scattered through several camps, is shortly to be moved to Soviet Central Asia, probably to Uzbekistan. He strongly advised us not to stop in Tatishchevo, but to try to get to the Tashkent area. Tashkent, the City of Bread, your second choice,' said Father, looking at me with a smile.

❊ ❊ ❊

Even then, in late 1941, under the German onslaught, with the Red Army falling back all along the front, the Soviet authorities treated the Poles not as allies prepared to fight together against the common enemy, but as a thorn in their side. This official attitude was an important factor in the eventual decision made by the Polish Government in exile in London, and supported by Churchill in his talks with Stalin later in the year, to evacuate the Polish Army from the USSR to the Middle East, where the men would be first given a chance to recover their health, then to train and, subsequently, to prove their worth in battles on the Italian front.

The shortage of officers and non-commissioned officers among the thousands of men flocking to the army camps in the USSR, such as Tatishchevo, remained a problem.

In September 1939, working in collusion with the Nazis, the Red Army took hundreds of thousands of Polish prisoners. Some other ranks were released. But most of them, with their officers and non-commissioned officers, were imprisoned in various camps. Many were now flocking back to the colours, but thousands – officers in particular – were missing.

Enquiries by the Polish Government in London and by the British Government met with Soviet refusal to discuss the question, except for repeated statements to the effect that all Polish PoWs and deportees have been set free and that any delay in their reporting must be due either to the problems of transportation or to their unwillingness to enlist.

The uncertainty as to their whereabouts gave rise to endless rumours. The terrible truth came to light later during the war, but was denied by the Soviet authorities until several decades later. Katyn, the name of one of the sites of extermination of Polish officers, prisoners of war, by the NKVD on the explicit order signed by Stalin and other Soviet leaders, briefly echoed round the world and was soon forgotten. Just another atrocity. The victims of Katyn, who with their hands tied with barbed wire were shot in the back of the neck, included my Uncle Adam.

FIFTEEN

THE LONG HAUL

✳

As the crow flies the distance from Saratov to Samarkand is some 2,300 kilometres, about four hours by passenger jet. By rail the distance becomes about 4,000 kilometres. In a goods train it took us six weeks to cover it.

We boarded the wooden box of a cattle wagon in Saratov. It was mid-October 1941. It was the usual situation in Saratov: each train, as it entered the crowded Saratov station, was stormed all along its length by a mass of travellers trying to force their way in. Like a vast ocean wave the throngs surged forward, people jostling for places. The train usually stopped for only a few minutes. As soon as the coal bunker had been topped up and the locomotive had drunk its fill from the overhead pipe, the train would set off, leaving most of the would-be passengers behind. As it was gathering speed some of the people left on the platform would make the last attempt to hoist themselves in, grabbing the helpful hands of friends or relatives on board. Others would give up in despair and step back from the moving train. Still others would jump out of it, to rejoin their families left behind. We had seen it all before.

So, the arrival and the departure of every train going south or east, whether a passenger or a goods one, was accompanied by shouts, cries, yells and screams, by loud swearing and by merciless pushing and elbowing. The commotion continued even after the train's departure, as people jostled for position at the edge of the platform in expectation of the next train. The billows of steam and smoke, their acrid suffocating smell, the soot, the malodorous emanations of a crowd, added to this Dante-esque scene from hell. As Saratov was a busy railway junction, the pandemonium was repeated several times every hour.

The dismally grey, polyglot crowd consisted of Poles, Belorussians, Russians, Ukrainians, Romanians, Lithuanians – refugees all. Many of them were Jews fleeing from the advancing Nazi armies and the, as yet unconfirmed, rumours of persecution. The full extent of German bestiality was still unsuspected and the word 'holocaust' was not to be used in this context until many years later. The majority of the non-Jewish population of the Soviet lands overrun by German armies – Ukraine in particular – had mistaken the invaders for liberators and had stayed behind.

We spent all day on that platform. Little by little we nudged nearer its edge. Mr Romer and my father agreed to wait until such time when both our families could get on the train together.

Then suddenly, almost without warning, the night was upon us, dark and menacing. The crowd was a little thinner, perhaps. Some had managed to get away, others, tired and resigned, returned to the station building for the night. Slowly the platform grew quiet. I was exhausted. Helena, half-asleep, was leaning against me.

I was praying, *in petto*. I didn't even know how and to whom . . . Please let the next train stop with a wagon door just here. Incredibly, my 'prayer' was answered. I could hardly believe our luck. A goods train rolled in and a car came to a standstill right in front of us, its sliding door wide open.

For once we were in the right place. With our arms locked together we barricaded the entrance to the wagon. A group of people wanted to get out, we made way for them. As soon as they got out, we threw our bundles in and helped each other inside. The crowd pushed us further in and more people managed to squeeze in behind us. Father held Mother's arm and I hung on to his sleeve. I lost hold of Helena's hand but Mr Romer clutched his wife's shoulder and kept calling out the names of his brood. No one went missing.

The wagon was an exact replica of the one which took us to

Siberia, though the doors remained unlocked. Also, we thought that this time we knew our destination: Tashkent, the capital of Uzbekistan, in Soviet Central Asia, and after that a Polish Army camp somewhere nearby.

The corollary of our status as free citizens, as opposed to that of deportees, or of valuable cattle, was that nobody bothered either to feed or to water the train's live cargo. Another item on the debit side was that, whereas so far, on our journey to Siberia, in Kvasha itself and in our peregrinations since leaving Kvasha, we had managed to keep reasonably clean, here, within minutes of boarding the train, almost as soon as we made our beds on the shelves, we were scratching furiously, set upon by innumerable hosts of lice.

We spent most of October and November in the wretched train. The journey was mainly dull, but sometimes unpredictable. One day the train would keep going steadily without a break. On another day it stopped frequently, sometimes for a few minutes, sometimes for hours. We were on a single-track line and the stops were usually on a siding, where we would wait to let another goods or passenger train pass by in either direction. Though that was not always the case. At times the train would stop at a signal in the middle of the steppe; the signal arm would stay down for hours, while the steppe remained empty, with not a man nor a beast, not a herdsman's shack, not even a tree in sight. Sometimes it would just stop without even the excuse of a signal.

Our coal-fired steam engine was operated by a driver and his mate. The crew kept changing and we never managed to establish contact with them – they knew better than to talk to strangers. Now and then, the crew would leave the train without a word of explanation and walk away. In due course they would be replaced by another couple of men who would just walk in from the steppe.

We whizzed through large towns at night, probably by design, stopping only in deserted stations long enough to fill the boiler with water from the overhead pipe, to refill the coal bunker, or to change the locomotive or its crew. The names of the stations confirmed our direction, we were going east. On the second day after leaving Saratov we passed the town of

Uralsk, crossed the bridge on the River Ural and turned south-east. We were in Asia!

My memory of the long journey is sketchy; some events remain vivid in my mind, but individual days, even chains of monotonous days, have been irretrievably erased.

The wagon that had been our home for six weeks was one of many thousands which plied the length and breadth of the USSR. Such goods trains often carried freight, occasionally cattle or horses, but mostly they conveyed people. Like the Pińsk–Kotlas Siberia train, this mobile home of ours had sliding doors, a shelf on each side of the central area and the same 'hygenic facility' in the form of a wooden gutter by one of the sliding doors.

There were forty of us in the wagon, including several small children. My parents and I shared the shelf with the six Romers.

One of my lasting impressions of the journey was the unbelievably filthy state of the track and the stations. The Soviet equivalent of popcorn was *semyechki*, either pumpkin or sunflower seeds; the husks, spat out by all, covered the floors, the ground and the platforms and whirled about in the wind. The toilets were disgustingly dirty and even the tracks themselves and the long strips of land on either side of the railway line were covered with excrement – in the siding areas one had to step very, very gingerly. There must have been tons of 'night soil' deposited parallel to the railway tracks in vast stretches of the country.

The reason was simple. People spent weeks travelling in cattle wagons and in-train facilities were primitive. We got used to passing water in our built-in wagon 'toilet' screened with a blanket, but more serious business had to wait for the train to stop. In the beginning, people would wait for a station and rush to join the enormous toilet queues, others would search for a bush or a tree to hide behind. Later, as the train stopped in an empty steppe, covered at this time of the year with meagre grass, searching for cover was useless. Some sought 'privacy' between the wheels, but the train was liable to move off without warning. You had to be quick on your feet to jump out from under it in good time. Soon all the vestiges of modesty were lost.

In time an epidemic of diarrhoea compounded the general misery. Yet, of the Four Horsemen of the Apocalypse only two accompanied us: Hunger – intermittently – and War – at a distance. To the best of my recollection neither Pestilence nor Death caught up with us in earnest, though both were possibly waiting just round the corner. Other than the minor intestinal infections, there were no major outbreaks of disease and no deaths that I recall during the journey. Father's services were not called for, but he could not have been the only doctor on the train.

'Being constantly on the move,' said Father, 'we have no chance to develop resistance to the local germs.' With no cooking facilities, we had to rely on locally purchased food. Even the hot boiled water obtained from taps at the stations was rumoured not to be reliably safe.

Once again food became a problem. The flat bread and tins of crab meat procured in Saratov kept us going for a couple of days, but the day came when Mother's 'larder' was empty. In the morning, at a small station, we filled a bucket with *kipyatok* so that we had enough to drink, but we didn't have any food – not a crumb all day. There was nothing else for it, but go to sleep. Lying there with my stomach rumbling, I could not even read and, with the Astrakhan experience in mind, I kept telling myself that only the first day or two were likely to be really bad. My daydreams were modest, requiring little imagination: a hunk of bread and butter, a slice of ham or salami. A plate of scrambled eggs and a roll. One couldn't call that extravagant.

On that hungry day, the October darkness came swiftly and mercifully early, and I went to sleep in my usual place between my father and the wooden wall of the wagon. In a speeding railway wagon it is often a change in the rhythm of its movement which wakes you up. The train was slowing down. I looked through the rectangular hole in the wall, which acted as a window. As we were going almost due south and my window was facing east, I expected to see a rectangle of the golden morning sky over a featureless steppe. But no, the window was filled with roofs of houses and wooden telegraph poles.

I half sat up. The window was too small for me to lean out, but I could see a little more of the outside world. The train was going very slowly, then, with a long hiss of steam, it stopped.

Odd! We had stopped along a platform next to the station building, not in a siding, nor in the middle of nowhere as before. The big black letters above the entrance said Aktyubinsk. Then the station door opened and a cart loaded with bread rolled out, pulled by two uniformed men. I had not seen so much bread in one place for a long time. I could not take my eyes off it. Loaves and loaves of white bread! Such a beautiful sight. Who was it for? What lucky people!

There was something puzzling about the cart's escort. With my mouth watering, my eyes dashed from the cart's load to its escort and back again. What were their uniforms? Not railway-men, not Red Army. Who were these men? Not NKVD, not militia, not railway police. It was an ill-assorted dress. But . . . wait a minute . . . was that the white eagle of Poland on their hats?

Then another man emerged from the station building. He was very smart. A four-cornered cap, *rogatywka*, a definite white eagle, two stars: a Polish lieutenant!

'Start distributing to everybody. A loaf per head.' The order, in unmistakable Polish, was music to my ears; the sound no less than the contents.

'Wake up, wake up, bread is here! And Polish soldiers!' I shouted and shook my father by his arm. He was instantly awake and so were the remaining passengers. The next minute Olek was pulling the sliding door wide open. The cart was just outside. 'How many?'

'Forty.' Olek was passing the loaves of bread into out-stretched hands, counting aloud. Two more soldiers came out pushing another cart bearing a gleaming urn inscribed *Kofe* in big Cyrillic letters. It was grain coffee, of course, but it was hot and sweet and my happiness was complete.

Our wagon was predominantly Polish, but the nationality of the passengers did not seem to matter. The soldiers were distributing bread to people in the wagon next to ours, mainly Ukrainians and Romanians. In the meantime, more bread and coffee trolleys appeared along the trains with non-Polish escorts.

Aktyubinsk was our city of bread, I thought. Let's hope that Tashkent will also live up to the name.

The train remained stationary for an hour or more. Having finished their task, the officer and the soldiers walked up and down the platform chatting to people. The elegant lieutenant stopped by our wagon. We crowded round him, all talking at once. Then Olek raised his arm. 'Shut up all of you!' he shouted. 'Is there a Polish Army camp here? Can we enlist now?'

'No, not here,' answered the lieutenant. 'There is no Polish Army camp anywhere near Aktyubinsk. We have only a small station unit here. Our job is to feed you and to make sure that you continue on your way south. The whole Polish Army in the USSR is on the move. We shall reorganise in Central Asia. Your train is going to Tashkent and you will get further information there.' He saluted with two fingers – the Polish way – and proceeded to the next wagon.

Then, as usual, without warning, we were on our way. With our stomachs full and in a good mood, we sat on the floor in the open wagon doorway, with our legs dangling, with the wind in our faces and we started singing. As soon as we finished one popular Polish song, Helena intoned another and another. Polish passengers in other cars picked up the songs as the train continued on its journey south.

The Aktyubinsk bread and coffee were our last taste of that luxury for a long time. There were no more Polish units on the way; no stations with either restaurants, bars or food trolleys. More often than not the train stopped in the middle of the empty steppe, so that hunger and thirst were our constant fellow travellers.

The station names became increasingly exotic, with overtones straight from history book, or half-forgotten novels: Cherkal, Aralsk, Kzyl-Orda, Yany-Kurgan. Occasionally the train would come to a halt in a small station or a siding within sight of a village or hamlet. Women and children would run to the train with baskets of local produce: pumpkins and dried pumpkin or sunflower seeds, *lepyoshki*, the local bread, which came in round cakes about a foot in diameter and two fingers in thickness, *katik*, an excellent local yoghurt, red and white onions (very mild and a welcome dressing for the dry flat bread); and, further south, fresh sweet melons, water melons, dried apricots, strips of dried fruit (those of sweet melon were particularly good). One local 'delicacy', however, *kurdyúk*, or the thick fatty dock of the local breed of sheep, was of no use to us: it could not be eaten raw and we had no cooking facilities.

As we went deeper into Central Asia the facial features of the natives became increasingly Mongolian and their tongue incomprehensible. They spoke little Russian, barely enough to name the price of their wares and to haggle. Trainloads of hungry people were commonplace to them and they knew how to fleece us.

Again food and drink became our main preoccupation. Whenever the train slowed down as if about to stop we, the youngsters, grabbed our buckets, pots and jugs, ready to jump to refill them. Stops at signals or in sidings out of sight of human habitation were no good to us. Stops at an overhead pipe for topping up the boiler were better; if the engine driver was well disposed he would allow us to fill a few buckets.

Stopping at a station was an entirely different proposition. There was, however, no way of telling in advance how long any particular stop would last: one minute, one hour, half a day? Not infrequently the train would just slow down almost to a stop, only to gather speed again, as if eager to shake off those a little too swift of foot. There was much shouting and swearing as those who had jumped out were trying to get on board again. But should the train stop, within seconds we would be searching for the *kipyatok* tap. Almost instantly the tap queue snaked its way along the platform. While waiting one's turn, one had to keep one's ears constantly attuned to the first sounds of the train stirring, the hiss of steam, the first tug of the engine, the clatter of wheels, so one could rush back in time, whether one's bucket was full or not. Missing one's wagon was not a disaster, friendly hands would help the straggler into another, but missing the train often was: couples were separated, many a family lost a son or a daughter this way. Their chances of catching up with the train, or otherwise rejoining their family at a later date were slim. The country was vast and none of us had a forwarding address.

This almost happened to me in one God-forsaken station the name of which I do not recall. It was my turn to get *kipyatok*.

The station building came into view. The train slowed down. One hiss of steam, another, and I was at the door ready to jump, bucket in hand. I jumped even before the train stopped. All along the train people were leaping on to the platform. I ran to the building; our wagon was in the middle of the train; the only *kipyatok* tap was level with its end; about a dozen people were already standing in the queue.

Will the train move off soon? Have I got enough time? I kept looking anxiously over my shoulder. The train was standing still, the buckets were filling rapidly, then the flow began to slow down and became a trickle. People behind me were leaving the queue, hurrying back to the train. But why? Had I missed something?

Now there were only two people in front of me. Only two buckets to be filled. I looked at the train again, no hint of movement, no tell-tale hiss of steam. At the wagon door Father was waving me back frantically. Only one girl was in front of me now, only one bucket, she half-filled it and ran. Had she noticed something I had missed? My turn, I was alone, the queue had disappeared.

The tap was painfully slow. I shifted from foot to foot. My legs were on the move even if I wasn't. The tap was slow . . . slow . . . It dripped like an old man's nose. I heard the hiss of steam, the clatter of buffers, they were off, they had left me behind. Panic gripped me. I chanced another second . . . another . . . 'We need *kipyatok*,' I said loudly to myself. 'I can run fast, I really can – even with a bucketful of hot water.' I kept my eyes on the train. Jerks, one after another, spread from the locomotive to the last wagon, the train gained speed. My bucket was almost full, I turned off the tap and ran.

Our wagon was too far away, no hope of reaching it, any wagon would do. I was out of breath, I tripped, I recovered my balance. Precious water splashed all over the place. I slipped on the wet platform stones and almost fell, not quite. I grabbed a hand stretched out from the last wagon door. It broke my fall. Another violent tug of the locomotive deprived me of my support, but I stayed upright.

Without thinking, with the half-full bucket in my right hand, I grabbed an iron bar projecting from the back of the last wagon with my left hand and half-jumped, half-lifted myself to sit on the buffer. The train gathered speed and all I could do was to hold on tight and not let myself be shaken off. The buffer was slippery and my left wrist hurt. I am safe, I thought, but not very comfortable. There were more horizontal bars above my head, all the way up to the roof of the wagon like a kind of ladder. There was an iron hook to the side of my bar; I grabbed the bar, with my right hand still holding the bucket while my left hand transferred the bucket on to the hook. No good. The water, not too hot now, splashed all over me. I took the bucket off the hook and hung it on the thumb of my right hand, fingers clinging tightly to the bar. With my left hand I grabbed the hook.

'I am here! I am on the train!' I shouted in Russian and Polish, again and again, but I could hardly hear myself above the clatter of the wheels. I had to let my parents know that I had not been left behind, Helena, too. I let go of the hook and tried to bang on the wagon wall with my fist, with my elbow, with my head, but it was no use.

Was the next stop ten miles away, or a hundred? I had no idea what to do next. I did not fancy a long journey on the buffer. But what was the choice? I could try to get up on to the roof and hop from wagon to wagon. Was it Gary Cooper who I had seen do that in a Western? Probably too risky outside Hollywood as the sheet-metal roofs were very slippery, and the bucket, very light now, was too precious to lose.

Suddenly I was very tired. I mustn't go to sleep. To free one hand, I returned the almost-empty bucket back to the hook. I undid the buckle of my belt, passed the end of it around the nearest bar and fastened it. I felt safer.

❊ ❊ ❊

I woke up with a start. I must have dozed off. Suddenly I remembered where I was and was panicky again. I managed to calm down by reciting poems learned long ago. In the incessant din I had to shout to hear myself.

As I learned later, my efforts at signalling my presence had passed unnoticed. Nobody had heard me. My head banging on the wall had been heard but dismissed as something loose in the wall of the wagon.

I do not know how long I lasted on this perch of mine. I longed for the comfort of our wooden box, where I could have sat on the edge of the shelf, or stretched out on it, or sat on the floor in the open doorway next to Helena. It must have been several hours before the train stopped at a siding. My adventure had started about midday and finished in darkness. I was tired and stiff, and, though the wind had dried my clothes, I was shivering with cold.

I wanted to run to our wagon, some twenty cars away, but I could not. I hobbled to it, painfully stiff and aching – worse than after the bareback riding in Kvasha.

My mother was in tears, so was Helena. Father was visibly upset. 'You had missed the short whistle,' he said. I could not understand why I had.

A woman was sitting on our shelf with Mother, one hand around my mother's shoulders, the other hand holding a rosary, praying. It might have helped, I was not sure of anything any more.

They all crowded round me, touching me, as if to reassure themselves that I was back among them. They all kissed me on one cheek, then on the other. Mother pressed my head to her breast and Helena held my hand. The greetings over, Mother gave me a piece of flat bread with *katik* to eat and Helena presented me with a strip of delicious dried melon for pudding. Covered with several blankets, I was soon fast asleep and did not wake until morning.

There were other incidents during the journey. One morning, when the train stopped in a siding in the middle of the steppe, both the driver and his mate walked away southwards along the track. As the crew's absence extended past midday, more and more people took walks in the open but, just in case, kept near the train. There was still no sign of a replacement crew. Far away to the east, the flat steppe merged into hills rising against low clouds, beyond which high mountains glittered golden brown in the midday sun. Children were running, shouting, playing games, frolicking, happy to be out of the stifling car. Helena, Magda, Olek and I went to explore the area. It was lovely to wander about without constantly having to watch the train.

There was a line of bushes and low trees about half a mile away. 'Do you think there is a stream over there?' ventured Helena. 'I'll race you!' and off she went. She was right. Clumps of tall grasses, bushes and dwarf trees marked the banks of a river. It was about ten metres wide, the banks were steep and the water reddish and dark.

'It's quite a big river, and it looks deep,' said Olek. 'I wonder what it's called.'

'Stefan will know,' said Helena with conviction. 'He has his head in the atlas often enough.'

Was she teasing? What the hell, I didn't mind showing off. I stuck my tongue out at her and said, 'Let's try and work it out. Yes, I have been looking at the maps. As far as I remember, from about the level of the Aral Sea the Tashkent railway line follows the right, or the north-east, bank of the Syr-Darya River. These mountains,' I pointed to the rugged line of peaks on the eastern horizon, 'must be the Karatau chain, the northernmost of the mountain chains which branch out of Pamir, the Roof of the World, at the western end of the Himalayas. Many tributaries of the Syr-Darya start there . . .' Oh, hell, here I was lecturing again. I blushed and shut up.

'Go on, Stefan,' said Olek, of all people, and he was over twenty. 'It's not a bad idea to know where we are, even approximately.'

Perhaps they were not teasing me after all? So I continued, 'I don't know for certain, but this river is probably a tributary of the Syr-Darya, one of the great rivers of Central Asia. In Turkish the name means North River; the ancient Greeks called it Jaxartes. This was the northernmost point reached by Alexander the Great in his conquests, somewhere here he turned around and went south-east to India.' I finished my *exposé* and blushed again.

We walked up and down the river, but we were not alone any more. By now the riverbank was crowded with people from the train washing their dirty bodies and clothes. Naked children shrieked as they splashed in the shallow water of the river bend. Several women were busy filling jugs and bottles with the precious stuff. 'You'd better fill your bottles further upstream,' somebody shouted. The women laughed and moved obediently away from the washers.

'I am going to have a dip,' said Olek. 'I can't smell it myself, but we must all be high by now. Let's get away from the crowd.' We ran upstream, past the washers and well past the water collectors, until we came to another bend in the river where the line of dwarf trees cut across a tongue of land covered with grass. Here we were alone. Out of everybody's sight we stripped, all shyness gone. The water was too cold for a long swim, but we dippped in and splashed about like children. We had no towels with us and there was a chill in the November air.

'Olek, have you got matches on you? Let's build a fire,' exclaimed Magda. Olek was the only smoker among us – when there was anything to smoke – and he did indeed have two matches in his trouser pocket. The matches, a very precious commodity, and a piece of match box to strike them against were wrapped in a rouble banknote.

We collected handfuls of dry grass and a few dry sticks, while Olek tried to break off a branch of a dwarf tree, but it would not be severed. 'Let me try,' said I, opening my penknife. It proved useless, the wood was exceedingly hard. The knife pierced the bark, more like a thick skin, but it wouldn't even scratch the wood.

'Strange tree!' I shouted in disgust. 'My knife is sharp, but it's like scratching iron.'

Using both hands Olek attempted to break off another branch, it hardly even bent. 'This must be *saksaoul*,' he said. 'At the beginning of real frosts in Kvasha, as I was starting to fell a tree, my axe just bounced off the trunk. Volkov was passing by. When I complained that the axe was useless, he said: "It's not the axe, the wood is frozen through and through. You must try again and again – it's not nearly as hard as *saksaoul*." So this must be *saksaoul*.'

The fire built of grass and twigs did not give off much warmth. We were wet and we were cold. It was getting dark and we ran back to the train. The riverbank was already deserted. And our locomotive was cold, dark and unmanned.

A chilly night came. Under the moonless, star-studded sky the steppe lay black and silent. The train lay in darkness, except for several wagons lit with precious candles. People gathered by the candle-lit cars talking, singing: discordant sounds, the usual Babel of tongues. Little by little the singing stopped except for a choir in the car next to ours. More and more people gathered to listen. Sad, plaintive, Ukrainian songs succeeded one another: a man would lead in a sonorous deep baritone, followed by male and female choruses in turns, as in a question-and-answer session. We listened long into the night.

In the morning there was still no sign of a replacement crew. Another day ended. Had we been forgotten? Were we that dispensable?

Several weeks earlier in Saratov, there was talk of the thousands of missing Polish PoWs. Gossip had it that they were left to starve in holed barges pulled far out into the Arctic Ocean. Was our plight just another way of getting rid of unwanted people – '*Lishniye lyudi*, superfluous people', in Party jargon. The break in our journey, welcome at first, became worrying. We were running out of food and, here, out of sight of even the most modest hamlet, there was no chance of buying anything. People were feeling gloomy and resigned. We, the youngsters, splashed about again in the river, but it was less and less fun. We tried fishing, but without success – bare hands and old caps were not the best fishing implements. Another night passed.

In the morning a committee was formed. Men ran up and down the train calling for one delegate from each wagon. We appointed Mr Romer.

We waited outside for him. He came back accompanied by a man representing another Polish wagon. 'It was a down-to-earth meeting,' said Mr Romer. 'The committee, mostly Ukrainians and Russians, know the system better than we do and I had no argument with their proposal. One of them is a Party member and a professor of Marxism and Leninism at Kharkov University. God knows how he found himself here, a simple refugee. The long and the short of it is that six men, including you, Doc,' here he looked at my father, 'are to jump on to the next passenger train going south, get out at Chernak, the nearest town, and send a telegram to *tovarishch* Stalin. The professor read the proposed text to us and it sounded fine. The usual Party jargon.'

'In all honesty, I thought it was silly,' the man who returned with Mr Romer said hesitantly. 'But they were all so sure that this was the right way, I had no guts to oppose them. And then again, I don't know, it's a strange country. Perhaps they know what they are doing.' He looked at the faces of the people around him. 'Another funny thing is,' he continued, 'that *tovarishch* professor himself is not going. Being a good communist, he is sending others.'

'That figures,' said Mother, 'but why should Władek [meaning my father] go? He is not even on the committee. Would you be able to jump on to a moving train?' she asked Father anxiously.

As it transpired later, that was the easiest part. The goods or passenger trains slowed down considerably in a siding while passing another train, so that leaping on to the steps required no special agility.

The elected men, Father among them, kept in readiness. For their leader, the committee nominated a burly Ukrainian called Pasha. He was a teacher, a bull of a man, who with his bulging muscles, flat nose and short, thick neck looked more like a boxer. It was a long wait. Several hours passed and then slowly, ponderously, a packed passenger train going south rolled by. The waiting men jumped on to the steps.

We spent the rest of the day waiting for their return. We walked along the river, talked, read, played bridge and chess. Several trains passed us on the way north, but there was no sign of our men. The sunny day was coming to its end in another golden-red sunset, when somebody shouted, 'Look, look there is another train coming! It's very short.'

'It's a locomotive.'

'Must be for us.'

'They are coming back.'

The news spread up and down the line. 'They've got another locomotive!'

Daylight was slowly receding from the cloudless sky, but in the motionless steppe a moving object easily caught the eye. Far towards the south horizon, where the railway line veered to the west, a black smoke-belching squat caterpillar was lazily negotiating the bend. For a few moments it would stand out clearly against the pinkish golden sky, only to disappear in a cloud of steam and smoke. In the next minute the caterpillar became a locomotive pulling a coal bunker. Then silhouettes of people sitting on the coals came into view against the darkening sky.

Father's report was simple and, in places, verbatim. 'To begin with the Chernak station master refused to talk to us, but we were determined, desperate and we had a plan – an effective combination. Pasha sent three men to find the telegraph room, while I and another man followed Pasha to the station master's office.

'Our train had been conveniently "forgotten". Apparently, we had not been assigned the priority normally granted to goods trains with human cargo and, "convinced" that ours was an empty goods train for which he had no immediate use, the station master stopped it in the siding, but he could not explain why the crew left us there. He mumbled that perhaps they lived near there and went home.

'He was about to walk out on us,' Father continued, 'when Pasha locked the office door and said calmly: "Three of my men are now in your telegraph office sending a cable to *tovarishch* Stalin. He might be interested in what sort of outfit you are running here. Perhaps we ought to enlighten him as to the details: an empty goods train kept for over two days in a siding, when it should be moving men, tanks and ammunition to the front. Is this your contribution to the war effort?"

'We were standing some distance from the station master's desk when, suddenly, Pasha lept forward, banged the desk with his fist and bent down over it with his nose only inches from the other man's face. 'Saboteur!" he shouted. The usual torrent of curses, oaths and choice swearwords followed. 'They will know in Moscow what to do with you!" he roared hitting the desk again. "It's not the way we do things in the Party. You won't wake up in your own bed tomorrow. Moscow won't be moved by your tears."

'This was an excellent example,' continued Father, 'of how effective a simple threat of denunciation can be. That's part of the system.' He paused for a while. 'It was enough to get things going. You should have seen the station master's expression – utter terror. Pasha had played the part of a fierce Party member beautifully.

'And we got away with it. The station master panicked. "Stop the others, no telegrams please," he was pleading in a most humble manner. "Stop them now! Leave it all to me." He grabbed the phone.

'Pasha calmed down. He sent Oleg, the third of our trio, to the telegraph room to stop the others proceeding, relocked the door after him, pocketed the key, sat down on the edge of the desk, winked at me and motioned me to the only empty chair in the sparsely furnished office. We did not have to wait long. The station master replaced the receiver. "I have another crew and a special additional locomotive for you," he shouted with obvious relief." It will be here within an hour."

'Pasha accepted the peace offering. "Okay," he said, "but you will stay here with us until it comes and I shall be the last man to leave on it. We have been waiting in the siding for two days, so another hour won't matter, and you don't seem to be all that busy."'

As Father finished his vivid report of the Chernak encounter a sudden jerk transmitted from wagon to wagon confirmed that, at last, we had a crew. A long whistle followed and all along the train people were climbing into their wagons.

The remainder of the journey is hazy in my memory. Soon after leaving the siding, we steamed through Chernak, a miserable little town, and then Turkestan, a much bigger place. Next morning we puffed our way through a place with the evocative name of Timur; wasn't he a successor of Genghis Khan? It was November 1941, the nights were chilly, but as we continued further south, the days seemed to be getting warmer. The landscape too was changing. The steppe petered out and we entered a densely populated agricultural country, criss-crossed by irrigation ditches, with lush vegetation: fields of vegetables, orchards, cotton plantations. Food was much easier to obtain now. At every stop local people were keen to sell us their produce, barter was no longer necessary, they were happy to accept roubles.

One morning the train sped through the outskirts of a big city without stopping; it was Tashkent, *The City of Bread*, our would-be destination. Soon afterwards, it slowed down to its usual leisurely pace as the track climbed steadily up and up. We crossed peaceful lush valleys surrounded by hills with orchards covering their slopes and high mountains in the background on both sides. Then the train veered almost due west and next day we passed Samarkand. The railway line skirted the town, outside derelict city walls and gates framed by peeling blue towers, not much to show for the famous city of Genghis Khan.

Another day came to its end, but we were approaching the end of our journey at last, I could feel it in my bones. Anyway, we could not go much further. I kept looking up my atlas. We were not far from the southern frontier of the USSR; only some two hundred kilometres to Afghanistan. The train slowed down to a snail's pace, as if it were looking for a convenient place to stop. It stopped and this time, surprisingly, not in a deserted siding, but at the end of a side line, in a meadow and within sight of a town. Several militiamen and civilians who were sitting on the grass got up and came towards the train. We were actually expected. The men walked up and down along the train shouting, '*Zdravstvuytye* – greetings. Disembark here, this is the end of your journey. Everybody out.' The unloading took the rest of the day. In the evening field kitchens arrived and distributed unlimited soup and bread. The night was warm and spending it outdoors was not a hardship.

Was this really the end of our journey? Had we arrived in a land at peace, a land of plenty?

SIXTEEN

CHIRAKCHI — A RESPITE

✵

The soft meadow by the railway station where we had disembarked provided a very different bed from the hard shelf of the cattle wagon; it did not jerk, quake, or shudder.

When I woke up the meadow was quiet and peaceful. I was lying on my side, uncovered. I must have kicked off my duvet during the warm night. My 'bed', a rough old blanket folded in two, was luxuriously comfortable; or was it the grass underneath? The unaccustomed morning fragrance of a dew-covered meadow hit my nostrils and I breathed in deeply. How blissfully different this morning was from every single morning of the last six weeks: no stench of the crowded wagon, no rattle of the train wheels . . .

The sky was greyish-blue, the greyness slowly receding before the pale gold of the rising sun. The few remaining stars twinkled to nothing one by one, as if extinguished by a night watchman putting out street lights in a town of old. To the east the sun was half up over the edge of a distant mountain chain, unleashing a fountain of brittle gold into the valley. 'Do I have to wake up?' I thought to myself and shut my eyes, but as the sunrise became a red afterglow under my lightly shut eyelids, I opened them again.

Helena was awake. She sat up.

'Look,' I said softly. 'Dawn.'

She said nothing, but stretched her hand out to me over her mother's sleeping body and, holding hands, we marvelled in silence as the break of the day changed from one minute to the next. Soon, too soon, the sun cleared the mountains' edge and the magic of the dawn dissolved in a riot of colour.

The camp was coming to life. A field kitchen had arrived with hot mock coffee and fresh bread. With the remains of the dry fruit bought somewhere on the way, they made an excellent breakfast.

In the meantime, several official cars and a dozen trucks arrived. Their drivers and passengers left their vehicles and shared our breakfast of bread and coffee. Then for a long time nothing happened. We repacked our bedding and just sat there ready for a further journey. Did we have to leave this beautiful meadow?

Father was sitting on the grass next to me. 'Let's have a look at your map,' he said. 'The town is, I gather, called Chirakchi,' he pointed to the railway station about a kilometre away, where our side line branched off, and the cluster of houses next to it. 'Let's see where we are exactly.'

All through the journey I had kept my atlas handy. I found the map of Uzbekistan, one of the Soviet republics in Central Asia. Samarkand, which we had passed yesterday, was on it, but Chirakchi was not.

Father continued: 'You were already asleep when Mr Romer and I talked to one of the militiamen, the one in command, last night – a captain, half-Russian. He was friendly and talkative. He told us that we would be staying here for good. He was sure that all of us would find suitable employment. Most able-bodied men and many women have been called up, there is a great shortage of manpower.' Father paused for a moment. 'Now let's see,' he repeated leaning over my atlas. 'No, you hold it, Stefan. I can see from here. We are about seventy-five kilometres south-west of Samarkand . . . yes . . . and about 600 kilometres from the Chinese border, but that's Sinkiang, the wildest part of China,' Father mused aloud. 'Foreign devils would not get very far. Persia, about the same distance, but less than half that to Afghanistan . . .' The exotic names remained there hanging in the air. Father kept looking at the map. Suddenly I got the message. I looked up from the atlas. 'Are we going to try and escape?' I whispered. This was exciting. 'We could hire guides with camels.'

I could already see us crossing the deserts and mountains with a caravan of pack animals: camels, donkeys, perhaps yaks. My imagination was running wild.

'It's not that simple,' intervened Mr Romer. I had not noticed that he sat down on the grass next to Father. 'I could not sleep last night,' he continued, 'and after all of you went to bed, I joined the Russian group by the fire, along with the Kharkov professor – you know, the one who headed the committee the other day. They were talking about *basmachi*. The wilderness here and all along the Afghan border is rife with them, they said.'

Father looked askance at Mr Romer. '*Basmachi*, who are they?' he asked.

'Uzbek freedom fighters,' said Mr Romer. 'Until quite recently this was a troubled area and in the late thirties, they said, a real war was going on here between the Soviets and the natives. *Basmachi* are therefore either patriots or brigands depending on which way you look at it. Uzbeks have always been reluctant to submit to Russian power, whether imperial or Soviet. The area has now been kind of pacified, but there are many individual bands still about. A lot of smuggling goes on: of goods, of people.

'One of the Russians really seemed to know what he was talking about. A lecturer at some institute or other, he had spent a couple of years in Bukhara. "Unless you have nothing to lose you cannot trust the *basmachi*," he said. "You might just as well entrust your life to a pack of hungry wolves," were his exact words. He'd heard of people who had paid handsomely to be taken across the border, only to be found later minus their belongings and with their throats cut.'

'Are these facts or official propaganda?' wondered Father.

'Who knows?' replied Mr Romer. 'But after last night I wouldn't dare trust them. Especially with the family and with those massive belongings of ours. It would be too much of a temptation, if you ask me. Were I alone and empty-handed, it might be different. Even then my boots and trousers would tempt them, if what I heard is true.'

'So that's another hope gone,' said Father. 'Pity, I was daydreaming. All the same, I would give a lot to get out of here.'

'Wouldn't we all,' said Mr Romer, 'but we'd have to be mad to attempt it. With families . . .' he repeated.

The conversation was stopped by a sudden commotion. Another column of cars and lorries drove up the meadow track and stopped. It disgorged more civilians and militiamen, some carrying tables and chairs. The newcomers placed themselves behind the tables in twos or threes. An officer called through a loudhailer: 'Attention, please. Heads of families will line up for interviews. First, those whose names begin with A to E here,' he pointed to the first table, 'Zh to K there,' and he proceeded to plan out the whole alphabet.

My father took his place near the head of the line at the first table, I stood by his side. We did not wait long. There were three men at the table, two Uzbeks and one Russian. They recorded the usual data: first name, patronymic, place and date of birth, occupation. On hearing that my father was a doctor and my mother a bacteriologist, the Russian who presided at the table perked up and said, 'We really need you here. We have a new modern hospital in Chirakchi, but our two male doctors have been called up and now my wife is the only medic left. You've arrived just in time, she can hardly cope.' He got up. 'Come with me Vladislav Mikhailovich,' he said to Father, as he motioned us to follow him. He led us to another table. A young Russian woman was sitting there alone, interviewing a couple.

Our man shook hands with her. First he introduced us and then continued, 'Galina Fedorovna is the hospital administrative director and I am sure that she will be keen to have you on the team.' I looked at Father. His face beamed with a broad smile I hadn't seen for a long time.

'Miracles do happen after all,' I thought to myself.

Once more I had to say goodbye to Helena. The Romer family had been assigned to a collective farm some twenty kilometres away. Not for long, I consoled myself; I will go to see her, or she will come to us from time to time. There will be a bus, or some other way of getting there. But a coldness had crept between us on that last day together. I didn't know why. Did I imagine it? Did both of us have other problems on our minds?

About midday, in the company of the other families recruited for work in the hospital in various capacities, we boarded one of the waiting lorries. The road crossed the railway line and after a short drive through Chirakchi, a small, unremarkable town, the vehicle deposited us at the hospital.

The hospital entrance was monumental in the true Stalinist style and out of keeping with the rest of the modest white-stuccoed two-storey building. But even the entrance with its columns and portico was dwarfed by a huge statue of Stalin. The statue was new and still snow-white. 'Our Great Leader' stood with his back to the hospital, slightly to the right of the entrance. This Stalin was different from the many others we had seen on our travels. He was definitely bigger, he was standing, arm raised, as if addressing a multitude. There was one thing wrong though with the Chirakchi Stalin: a large part of the left side of his midriff was missing, leaving a gaping hole. As we discovered later, this huge statue was mass-produced and, because of its size, came in sections. So far the missing section had not been delivered; perhaps it was adorning another city on its own?

The Chirakchi hospital building was modern and it looked better than many a hospital I had seen in Poland. As we unloaded our chattels, several staff came out to greet us. These men and women, Russian and Uzbek, seemed a nice and friendly group. Galina, the administrator who had recruited us and who had travelled with us in the driver's cabin, disappeared inside the building and returned with another woman, this one in a white coat, with a stethoscope round her neck. She looked too young to be a doctor. 'This is Vera Nikolayevna,' said Galina, 'our medical director.' Then she thought for a while. 'But you, Vladislav Mikhailovich, are more experienced,' Galina spoke directly to my father, 'and, by right, you ought to take over. I'll talk to the hospital authorities,' she added.

'Oh no,' said Father hastily. 'I'd rather keep to the clinical side. I am no good at paperwork, but I will gladly help you whenever you wish me to,' he continued, extending his hand to Vera. The doctor's stern expression dissolved in a broad smile. She was obviously not happy at the prospect of giving up her status and the salary which went with it.

Vera shook hands with Mother and with me. 'This is your

son, I take it,' she said. 'Follow me. I'll show you to your quarters.'

We loaded our possessions on to a hospital goods trolley standing by the entrance. I grabbed the handle and we followed Vera through the hospital entrance and along a corridor with several half-glazed doors on either side. The wards were large and clean but devoid of furniture. A hospital without beds.

I stopped by one ward door for a better look. Palliasses and straw mats were scattered untidily all over the cement floor, though only half a dozen or so were occupied. Some had proper bedding, white pillows, white blankets, white sheets; other ones were covered with grey blankets with no sheets, thus showing the bare edges of the palliasses or mats. Perhaps they didn't use beds in Uzbekistan? So far all we had seen of the country were railway stations. Hadn't I read somewhere that the Chinese, or was it Japanese, didn't use beds? Perhaps the Uzbeks followed the same custom. But before I could voice my query, Vera volunteered the answer. 'We are still waiting for furniture,' she said. 'The hospital was opened two years ago, but we have had no delivery of beds as yet. We only have them in the children's ward and in the reserved ward.'

I wondered who the reserved ward was reserved for. I was about to ask, but my father must have sensed my intention; he raised his hand, winked at me and I bit my tongue.

At the end of the corridor Vera opened a door on the right. 'This is your room,' she said. Pulling the trolley behind me, I followed my parents through the door. The contrast with Kvasha could not have been greater. The room was large and it was ours, not for three families, just us.

In Kvasha, however, we had iron bedsteads, a table and several chairs. This room was bare, straw mats on the floor comprised all its contents.

Vera discussed something briefly with Mother, then said, 'I'll send them straight away,' and disappeared.

I looked round. The window in the wall opposite the corridor door was largely obscured by a tree. It looked like an almond tree. The wall on the right was windowless, with a wide vertical hump in the middle, perhaps a chimneybreast, but there was no stove and no cooking range. Most of the left wall was taken up by a double door which gave on to . . . a lawn? A garden? Our own garden? I left the trolley in the middle of the room and rushed to the door; it was not locked and I stepped out.

It was a warm November afternoon. More doors and French windows in the hospital wall opened on to the garden. So it was not just for us, never mind. The garden was lush but disorderly, overgrown with weeds, with tall uncut grass. Here and there a few surviving wild flowers gave it a spattering of colour. Outside most of the doors stood small brick structures; were they cooking fires? Barbecues?

'Stefan!' Mother called to me and I returned to the room. 'First things first,' she said. 'And the foremost one is to get rid of lice. Let's hope it will be for good this time. There are shower-rooms just two doors down.'

So that's what she had discussed with Vera. Mother opened one suitcase, got out clean pyjamas. 'You two go first,' she continued and presented Father with a small, folded, brown canvas bag. 'Everything you take off goes into the bag.' There were several large canvas bags already full and tied up on the floor. 'That's our bedding for delousing,' said Mother. 'We got it ready while you were exploring the garden.'

'I am sorry,' I said, 'but I had to . . .' I started.

'All right, all right,' Mother cut me short, but smiled. 'There will be lots of time for the garden. I'll wait for my shower until you two are back. Remember, one of us must always stay in the room, we don't know how much we can trust these people, better to be careful.'

The shower-rooms were empty, clean and smelled of carbolic. The water was hot. Our first shower in months. I kept scrubbing my skin, soaping and rubbing. What bliss! Father was doing the same, he was scarlet all over. Oh! To stop itching, that would be lovely. We had become used to lice on the train; we must have killed thousands of them in the last six weeks of travelling, but millions more had taken their place. Squashed between fingernails they burst with a satisfying pop. We did not talk about it, but I had not lost hope of one day returning to a world without lice, without constant shameless scratching, without a sore groin, sore armpits and itchy head.

Radiating cleanliness, in crisp pyjamas we returned to our room. Mother gave us a complete change of clothing each. She had kept them unused, and therefore louse-free, since Kvasha, for just such an occasion, when, at the end of the journey, we would be clean once again.

Was it the first time in my life that I was conscious of enjoying a scrubbed skin and fresh underwear? Like most boys, I had to be reminded about taking a bath or a shower. Swimming was different, a pleasure, but washing was something that grown-ups kept nagging about. Now I changed into my old greenish-grey plus-fours, which had somehow survived Kvasha and our travels, unused. They still fitted me well as I had not grown much. I put on my white Russian *rubashka*, a side-fastening shirt, bought in Pińsk, with red embroidery on the collar and down the front edge.

'You are a handsome young man, Stefanku,' said Mother. 'Be sure you wear this outfit when you visit Helena,' and she smiled as she left to have her shower. I blushed and ran into the garden.

On Mother's return, I pulled the trolley piled high with canvas bags and followed Father to the delousing station at the other end of the hospital. 'This again means greasing some palms,' said Father. 'Let's first find the attendant. That should do it,' he added getting two red ones out of the wallet, 'twenty roubles . . . more than enough.'

A delousing station was an establishment of importance in the USSR. Every town boasted at least one and in Chirakchi it was part of the hospital. People were processed in batches, often of many dozens. The procedure was standardised: first you stripped in the communal ante-room, you handed your clothes, underwear, bedding if you had any, to the attendant and received in exchange some disgusting thick liquid for the hairy places and, if you were lucky, also a small piece of disinfectant soap. Then you proceeded to the communal showers and had a wash. You recovered your supposedly deloused clothing and other items on your way to the exit.

This was the theory, but in the USSR theory and practice were often miles apart. The station boilers were coal-fired, but most of the coal never reached its official destination and found more lucrative outlets on the black market. Consequently, the pressure and the temperature in the disinfecting chamber were usually too low to kill either the hardy insects or their even hardier eggs, or nits. A person trusting the system would often leave a delousing station not so much disinfested, as boasting a new collection of fauna.

And so, after about two months' travelling, we settled in our room in the Chirakchi hospital. We did not really unpack; as we did not have a single stick of furniture there was no point. We lived 'out of suitcases' as we came to call it. 'Perhaps,' Mother said, 'we could buy some shelves, a table and a few chairs. There has to be a market somewhere near; perhaps even shops.'

'Oh yes,' laughed Father. 'A Chirakchi branch of Jabłkowscy Brothers' or Herse's,' he said, naming the two well-known Warsaw department stores. 'Why not Harrods or Galeries La Fayette?' I hadn't seen him so merry for a long time. Was he at last happy, being able to work in his profession?

'And why not?' Mother asked with a smile. 'After all this is the regional capital. There must be some shops in town. Anyway,' she continued, 'we have absolutely no food left. You'd better go and look for a market or a shop. A La Fourchette will do.' She laughed loudly as she mentioned the well-known Warsaw bar-restaurant. A La Fourchette was near the Central Railway Station, so that before boarding the Otwock train we used to drop in there for a snack. They also had a take-away service. The thought of their open sandwiches made my mouth water. Resonating with Mother's laughter the room seemed brighter and warmer. In the last few months we had had little enough reason for merriment. 'But seriously,' said my mother. 'Vera told me that I could use the hospital staff kitchen, but apparently it is very crowded and she suggested that it might be better to build a cooking fire in the garden. She offered to lend us her spare iron grate until we could get one.'

She paused and then continued, 'Anyway, in the communal kitchen the other women keep looking into your pots. Every little scrap of meat is a source of envy.' I thus volunteered to stay behind to build the cooking fire outside our garden door, while Father and Mother went in search of provisions.

First I looked at the contraptions built by our neighbours. They were all much the same; each consisted of three walls, about half a metre high, made of stones and broken bricks held together with clay. Within them, about half-way up, was a cast-iron grate resting on several unbroken bricks placed upright. Heaped next to our next-door neighbour's cooking fire was a number of round brownish-yellowish objects resembling thick pancakes, the like of which I had never seen before. Some building material? I stood there looking at them and wondering when I heard a noise. I looked up. A nearby door opened and a little girl came out. 'Are you Stepan Vladislavovich?' she asked.

She couldn't have been more than five or six years old. Her light golden hair was gathered in two long braids tied with bright blue ribbons, the colour of her eyes.

She could pass for a Polish peasant lass, I thought to myself. Such a funny girl, so serious. Children don't use patronymics addressing each other. '*Da*, yes,' I said aloud. 'But in Polish it's Stefan not Stepan. And who are you?'

'My mother is the medical director of the hospital,' she answered frowning a little haughtily, but then she smiled and extended her hand to me. 'My name is Zina.' And she added self-importantly, 'Zinayda Vladimirovna. But you can call me Zina.'

She reached inside the door and produced a packet wrapped in newspaper. 'Mother told me to give you this,' she said undoing the wrapping. It was the iron grate for my cooking fire. 'But it's not for good, mind you,' she added. 'It's only on loan.'

I took the grate and thanked her. 'I'd better start putting up the cooking fire then,' I said and returned to our door. 'Somewhere here, I suppose.'

'Oh, Stefan, please, please! May I help you? May I help you build it? Please, please!' Excited, she was jumping up and down. 'I would love to do it with you. I did it with my father. Please, let me,' she repeated.

That was the beginning of my friendship with Zina. It was a pity it did not last very long.

'If you are so knowledgeable,' I asked Zina, 'tell me what are those *blini*?' and I pointed to the mysterious heap of pancakes by the neighbour's cooking fire.

'They are not *blini*,' she laughed. 'Silly billy! Pancakes are made with flour, this is *kizyak*. *Kizyak* is made with poo, camel poo. You know. Don't try to eat them.' And she laughed uncontrollably. 'So what did you use in Poland for a fire? Haven't you seen *kizyak* before?'

As it happened I had not. *Kizyak*, or camel dung mixed with straw, shaped into flat cakes and dried was the main domestic fuel in Central Asia, where firewood was rare and coal very expensive. Come to think of it, I must have seen it before, as these round shapes could be seen everywhere, stuck to walls and clay fences, drying in the sun. But I did not make the connection.

Zina was a great little helpmate. She took me by the hand to an overgrown corner of the garden which must have been used as a builders' dump. There I found clay, stones and broken bricks. She brought a bucket of water and mixed the clay to just the right consistency. By the time my parents returned from their shopping expedition the job was finished, though the clay was still soft.

They brought two net-bags full of shopping. With pride Mother displayed half-a-dozen flat cakes of local bread, several kinds of dried fruit, red and white onions and a whole *kurdyúk*, the tail of a special breed of sheep which we had first come across on our southward trek. This delicacy was a U-shaped bag of fur-covered skin, which when cut open displayed its contents: a big lump of hard yellowish fat. The other net-bag contained an iron grate for our cooking fire and some *kizyak*; strangely, my parents knew what it was.

Our first meal in Chirakchi consisted of onions fried in mutton fat and heaped on top of the flat bread. The onions were mild and could also be eaten raw on bread; that was to become our usual lunch. We would breakfast on flat bread and dried fruit. Sometimes, when Mother managed to get it in the local market, we had *katik*, a kind of yellowish baked yoghurt with a brown skin on top. It was a local speciality and I loved it.

Father was enjoying his work. His patients, mostly Uzbek mothers and children, spoke only rudimentary Russian, but were friendly, very grateful for whatever he did for them and showed their appreciation by bringing gifts: a couple of eggs, a jar of honey, small, flat, seed cakes sweetened with honey, sometimes a lump of cheese, a nugget of butter, occasionally a cut of mutton, a chicken. We never went hungry in Chirakchi. Life began to look up.

'It's school for you, Stefan,' said Father one day. 'There is a ten-year school in town. You could start in the new year.' Predictably Christmas was taboo in the USSR, but schools had a short winter break around the New Year, transformed into the festival of *Dyed Moroz*, Grandfather Frost.

I had been thinking along these lines myself. I was bored, I looked forward to going back to school. In the last year my Russian had become quite fluent. I had problems finding the correct stress in some words, but I was sure I knew more Russian poetry and classics than my average Russian contemporary.

In the meantime I adopted Zina as my teacher. We talked a lot. She corrected my Russian pronunciation while I read to her from her book of Russian fairy-tales, as well as Lafontaine's fables in Russian translation. I knew some of them in French and, delighted, she tried to repeat the foreign words after me. She asked me again and again to read to her from my volume of Pushkin: 'The Tale of the Fisherman and the Fish', 'Ruslan and Ludmila', 'The Story of Stenka Razin', when we would sing together the Volga river song, and of 'Lermontov': Mtsiri, Demon . . . We also played draughts and chess – sort of.

Mother was the only member of the family who was not happy in Chirakchi. She was utterly frustrated through her inability to get a suitable job. Soon after our arrival I discovered a door marked 'Laboratory' on the first floor of the hospital. It was unlocked and I looked in. The room was empty. There was a sluice in one corner and that was all. No microscope, no bottles of reagents, no test-tubes, not even a table disturbed its total bareness.

I returned to our room with this information. 'I know,' said Mother. 'Vera told me. She has to recruit an entire laboratory team before her request for equipment can be considered. An odd way of going about it, but still, *autres peuples, autres moeurs*,' Mother paraphrased the proverb. 'Perhaps one day . . .' she continued. But it was not to be.

The first disaster struck two or three weeks after our arrival.

One day, in the early afternoon, I was poking in our cooking fire which was producing more smoke than heat, when Mother opened the door. 'Don't come in,' she said. 'Stay outside until I call you.' What had happened? I put my face close to the glass of the French window. Father was back early, he looked gloomy, he was changing into his dressing-gown.

I knew this look on his face. In Otwock, during school holidays, I would sometimes accompany him on his rounds in our *britzka*. If, on a home visit, the diagnosis was scarlet fever, he would frown in the same way and this look, combined with his hand raised, palm facing me, meant: 'Serious infection, you are to walk home by yourself, my boy.'

Now, as Father left the room to have a shower, Mother opened the garden door. 'Scarlet fever,' she said. 'There are three children down with it in the ward.' She paused and then continued, 'I am sorry, Stefanku, one of them is Zina. She is in a bad way.'

Zina died three days later. I was very upset. I had not cried much in the last year, but I did on that day, and again, at the time of the funeral I hid in the garden, in the thicket, and sat there, tears running down my face for a long time. All I wanted was to bury my face in Mother's lap. Not a thing to be done at my age.

Zina's funeral was followed by a wake. It lasted three days and many litres of alcohol were thrown down Russian throats. My parents were invited, but Father alone went against his better judgement. But he did not last the course. Vodka, surgical spirit and *samogón*, or moonshine, flowed freely. 'Ridiculously so,' he said. He returned on the second evening feeling ill. He slept well into the next day, then he took a whole day to recover.

Life returned to normal, but I missed my little friend. She was a bright, precocious little girl. Her death left me bereaved and lonely.

I kept thinking vaguely about visiting Helena on her collective farm. But there was no transport and I did not fancy the long walk, twenty kilometres each way. There, in the Chirakchi station meadow, a kind of awkwardness and uncertainty had come between us. I had written Helena a letter since, but received no reply. Now perhaps I was trying to deny the truth. A month earlier I would not have hesitated. I would have covered the twenty kilometres between us on a run. So what was happening now? Were we growing apart? In Gorkiy, as we were grieving about the separation, Father dropped hints about us getting married. He would provide for us until we could stand on our own feet. 'Yes, I know,' he said. 'It may mean years, but I will see you both through university.' Mother, though, was sceptical. Helena's father was not keen at all. Helena got cold feet, did I too? Perhaps, at sixteen, neither of us was ready.

The second disaster struck soon after Zina's death, about the fourth or fifth week of our stay in Chirakchi. One day, as we sat down to our evening meal, there was a knock on the door. I opened it. It was a militiaman, one we knew by sight from his frequent visits to the hospital. He handed me a piece of paper.

'I am very sorry, Vladislav Mikhailovich,' he said looking at my father. The paper in my hand was a *prikáz*, an official order with a round rubber stamp. I passed it to Father. The militiaman stood in the doorway for a moment and before leaving apologised several more times: 'I am very sorry, very sorry indeed.'

I watched Father, he went pale and without a word handed the paper to Mother. Mother read audibly but softly under her breath. I caught most of the words: 'the border zone . . . extended . . . unreliable people . . . to be removed . . .' With a look of infinite sadness Mother passed the paper to me. 'What are we going to do now? No sooner have we settled than they are moving us again.' Then she was angry. 'Damn . . . damn . . . damn. And where to next?'

The gist of the order was that the Afghanistan border zone had been widened, so that it now included Chirakchi, which thus had to be cleared of 'the unreliable human element'. Thus we had to present ourselves the following day at 8 a.m., with our belongings, at the Chirakchi railway station to board a special train . . . to be transported to a safer location . . . blah . . . blah . . . blah.

We were all stunned. Father was first to recover his composure. 'I am hungry,' he said. 'Let's have something to eat and then I will have a word with Vera.'

'Do go and see her by all means,' said Mother, 'but it won't do any good. Damn the Bolsheviks . . . damn them all the way from Minsk to Vladivostok. We'd better start repacking.'

I couldn't remember having ever seen my mother quite so angry. She was livid. She slapped the plates of fried onions fiercely in front of us. There goes our supper, I thought. Luckily the plates did not break and we were not splattered with grease. 'Damn . . . damn . . . damn . . .' she kept repeating.

As Father went to see the medical director, Mother and I packed all our chattels. It was done in half an hour. 'Just as well we have been living out of suitcases,' I said to Mother, but she did not reply. She did not hear me; she was calm now, but miles away.

'Vera can't do a thing,' she said after a long while. 'Even if she could, she wouldn't. She would be afraid even to try. I can't blame her. In this accursed country she has to think first of herself and of her family. She might even be glad to see the back of us, Father's presence here is a constant threat to her position. I wouldn't be surprised if she had denounced us under some pretext just to get rid of us.' She thought for a moment. 'But this must be a general order, I am doing her an injustice.'

Mother paused again. 'The station will be full of people,' she continued. 'The Romers will be there, and Helena,' she added as she smiled at me. 'You are no longer so keen on her, are you? It happens. There will be other girls . . .' I blushed, but Father's return put an end to my embarrassment.

'You were right,' he said. 'They were both there, Vera and her husband. I told them about the deportation, they pretended that it was news to them – perhaps it was to her, but he knew all about it, I was sure of that. He recited many good reasons for the order, he spouted on about the mortal struggle . . . fatherland . . . the unreliable human elements . . . You can't argue with slogans. I just left. Before he finished . . .'

A timid knock on the door interrupted my father in mid-sentence. Vera was on the doorstep. 'May I come in?' she asked in a small voice.

Mother motioned her in. 'Sit down, have tea with us. I got it yesterday on the black market. Real Georgian tea.'

'I want to apologise for my husband,' Vera said shyly. 'He is on the hospital Party committee and he has to toe the Party line. We have to live here, you do understand. My brother is our consul in Kabul and we cannot put him at risk. A foreign posting is a great thing. You do understand. Don't you?' she repeated anxiously. 'I am very close to my brother and when he comes home on leave he tells me about life there, so different from ours. But not in my husband's presence. He wouldn't talk about those things even in front of our parents, Father is also a Party member. But there you are, our life here . . .' She stopped in mid-sentence, looking lost for words. But a moment later she turned to my father and continued, 'I am sorry you have to leave, Vladislav Mikhailovich. I felt so much safer with you here. You have no idea what a comfort your presence is, was,' she corrected herself. 'And yours, Cheslava Zakharevna. Between us we could have made it a great place, this Chirakchi hospital, I mean. The Hospital Authority promised to equip the pathology lab. Honestly, just yesterday, as I phoned them again. It will all be wasted now, I am really sorry, these are terrible times. And you, Stefanooshka, have been such a good friend to my poor little Zina. She loved you, you were like a big brother to her,' and she covered my hand with hers. She sounded genuine. She did not have to come and bid us farewell, under the circumstances we would not have expected it. The instant we were labelled 'unreliable' and marked for deportation we became pariahs, lepers, the untouchables.

'Let's have an early night,' said Mother as Vera left. 'We have to get up at dawn.' But sleep was a long time coming. I did not fancy another journey, another cattle wagon, another excursion into the unknown.

Where will they take us now? I wondered. Back to Siberia, to the Urals, to the Far East? The possibilities were infinite in this vast country.

At least it had not been another midnight knock. We were 'free' now. Unreliable, but 'free'. We were not being arrested, we were not being taken to the station under escort, but the effect would be much the same.

In the event we left in great style in the hospital lorry, with the compliments of Vera Nikolayevna, the medical director.

SEVENTEEN

THE SHORT HAUL

✴

We were among the first to arrive at the Chirakchi station, a lorry having conveyed us to the same meadow on which we had spent the night of our arrival six weeks earlier. From outlying localities others were coming in dribs and drabs well into the afternoon. By the evening the meadow was full of people. We knew some of them from the preceding journey, the Long Haul. Was it really only six weeks ago? Some were old friends and some we knew by sight, but the great majority were strangers: the usual mixture of nationalities.

Rumour had it that our train was scheduled for the morning: 8 a.m.? 12 noon? Nobody bothered to inform us, nobody seemed to know.

The winter night was fast descending on the valley when Helena arrived with her family as part of their collective farm contingent. With the Romers, several old friends from the Long Haul and a few new friends from Helena's collective farm, we made a sort of Wild West camp for the night: a central pile of luggage and our makeshift beds taking the place of covered wagons, arranged in a circle round it. Helena and I were head-to-head. As usual, we talked long into the night. I wanted to ask her many questions, but I didn't, I wasn't sure how.

Life on the collective farm had not been too bad, Helena said. They had a room of their own and, after a good harvest, enough to eat. Helena's father had an office job, Mrs Romer helped in the stores, Helena and her brother and sisters laboured in the fields; the work was very different from that in the forest in

Kvasha, but it was also heavy-going, often in ankle-deep mud. They were just about getting the hang of it when the deportation order arrived.

Eventually I went to sleep, without having asked the question which was permanently on the tip of my tongue. Almost immediately, or so it seemed, somebody was shaking me by the shoulder. A man was bending over. 'It's 2 a.m. You and Olek are on guard duty now,' he said. We kept guard over our little group's possessions in two-hour shifts. The night was silver bright with a full moon and innumerable stars. The camp was still, except for groans, snores, a baby crying in the distance. Our two hours' watch dragged on for ever.

At 4 a.m. Olek and I roused our respective fathers and went to bed. Bliss! But again, as soon as I had shut my eyes, I was woken up. It was my father going to bed; our beds were foot-to-foot. It had to be 6 a.m., the end of the night and I was cold. I pulled up my blanket and, half asleep, stretched out my foot to feel for my boots, which I had left next to the bed; my foot searched in vain. Wide awake, I sat up. My heart missed a beat. Where were my boots? Through the night, I had kept feeling for them with my foot and now they were not there! My high boots had disappeared. I felt like crying. My beautiful high boots.

To tell the truth, they were not exactly beautiful and not even that warm. In Kvasha they still needed layers of newspaper over the woollen socks and foot wraps. But I had been awarded them, which was the euphemism for being given the special privilege to buy them, in the Kvasha shop, as a prize for 'outstanding productivity'. They had black waterproof canvas leggings, dull leather uppers and thick rubber soles – a far cry from the elegant high leather boots worn by Polish cavalry officers, but they were the only such pair of boots in the whole of Kvasha and I was proud to own them.

I wore them the day before because it was cold and the ground was muddy. Anyway, they were easier to wear than to pack. Now they were gone; a thief must have snatched them at the time when my father was on guard. He must have dozed off for a moment. I couldn't believe it. Father would be so upset when he heard of his dereliction of duty. I wouldn't be able to forgive him, not ever.

I did not go to sleep again. The train, a long row of cattle wagons, approached like a ghost, in the morning twilight. The sun was still hidden behind the mountains to the east, but the eastern sky, resting on the craggy dark outline of the peaks, became brighter by the minute. The moon had disappeared behind a low cloud and the stars were fading rapidly. As the train slowly rolled into the siding, the meadow came to life. Soon people were gathering their bedding, marshalling their children and feverishly packing, arguing, re-packing.

'What's the hurry? The train won't leave without us,' I remarked to Helena.

She answered with another rhetorical question: 'Why is a crowd always made up of idiots?'

The seasoned travellers, which we were by now, settled down in the wooden box promptly. Accompanied by the Romers, we occupied the upper rear shelf: the shelf with a view. I claimed my customary place by what passed for a window. Half lying and half sitting, with my head against the timbers of the wagon wall, I liked to look in the direction of the journey. Disregarding the soot and the dust in my eyes, I liked to feel the wind on my face. For hours, however, the train remained stationary. I shut my eyes.

I was despondent. Was all my life destined to be like that? Coming and going; without choice and without sense; God knows where and God knows why. Nothing seemed to matter any more. I did not have much of a past, my present was not worth speaking of and as for the future: there was none.

I didn't even feel like reading. No point in reading the same books over again and again. I stopped listening to the idle talk of people round me, the same old rubbish, all sheer speculation. They knew nothing, they had learned nothing. Or they talked endlessly about food. 'Do you remember *rybka po żydowsku*, fish Jewish-style . . . but for *bigos* the cabbage must be sliced really thin and you must use three kinds of sausage . . . The best steak tartare in Warsaw was served in the Bristol Hotel. The meat was always fresh, safe. Thursday was the day they always served tripe . . . mouthwatering.'

I clapped my hands over my ears, but the stupid talk did not go away. There was no sense in anything any more. Helena sat by the other window, at the other end of the shelf. Silent, in a world of her own, no doubt different from mine.

I had to do something, I decided. I was about to get out one of my textbooks, but thought better of it. I was fed up with physics, maths, chemistry and biology. Covering the same ground again and again, problems solved a dozen times ceased to be problems. Anyway, there was no point. They were all daydreams: my high school certificate, university, medical studies. It was all so unreal. I was old, over sixteen, really old. I would only grow older and remain an ignoramus at that.

What did I have to offer Helena? Nothing. Home, children, a secure life? It was laughable, but I did not feel like laughing. Just as well that we were not talking about a life together any more. Not that we had agreed to avoid the subject, it just never came up. Was I losing my grip by feeling sorry for myself?

A series of jolts brought me out of the black reverie. I opened my eyes. The train was on the move. The line of trees at the edge of the meadow glimmered in the rays of the setting sun. We had spent all day in that bloody siding. The peaks of the distant mountain chains, superimposed one upon the other, stood golden against the darkening blue of the cloudless sky. We were going north, towards Samarkand. We passed it early in the night and turned east, perhaps towards Tashkent. Again, we were retracing our steps.

I made a new friend on the journey: his name was Józek. His place was opposite mine, on the front upper shelf. He was almost eighteen and he was travelling with his mother and a younger brother. They had lived in Baranowicze. His father, a civil engineer, was arrested within weeks of the Bolshevik invasion of Poland in September 1939, whereas Józek was deported with his mother and brother in April 1940 to a place very much like Kvasha and not far from it. They had no idea where his father was, or even whether he was alive. Like me, Józek had worked in the forest, but he had never heard of an ice road. He was hoping to join the army.

The journey was mercifully short. On the afternoon of the third day after leaving Chirakchi, the train stopped in a siding. Several militiamen, in pairs, rifles hanging loose from their shoulders, ran along the train banging on wagon walls and shouting: 'Out, all out, get out.' There was no 'please' this time, I noticed. Were we not 'free citizens' any more? The afternoon was cold and wet, a fine drizzle hung in the air and the mountains in the east, much nearer now, were covered with snow from half way up. Helena, Olek, Józek and I, in that order, were sitting in the open door of our wagon. A couple of militiamen passed our car.

'What's this place called?' asked Olek. 'Where are we?'

'You will learn all in good time,' snapped one.

'They are not convicts, Zheniya,' said the other, a sergeant. 'They are *grazhdanye*, citizens,' he smiled at us, 'and deserve a polite answer. You are in the Soviet Republic of Kazakhstan,' he said solemnly. 'The town over there,' he pointed to something invisible in the distance, 'is called Kentau.' Then his right arm traced a vast semi-circle. '*Zdes zhit budete*, here you shall live.'

'We've heard that one before,' I said in Polish. 'Do they repeat it in their sleep?'

'Live here? Surely not in these hovels,' said Olek. 'Even at a distance they reek of cattle. Look at them, they are falling to pieces; there are holes in the walls and the roofs are leaking too, I bet.'

There was no alternative. We had to get all our stuff off the train. The place was crawling with people unloading their bundles, running to and fro, shouting, swearing, quarrelling and almost coming to blows over one ramshackle building or other. Somehow we managed to secure a small barrack that was just big enough for our group.

It was not much of a dwelling. The flimsy walls, lattice-like in places, consisted of a single layer of planks, many of them partly detached, and they were not likely to provide adequate shelter from the keen wind. The window panes were broken. Olek was right: chinks of light showed through the roof and patches of grey sky appeared through holes which were big enough to put one's fist or even one's head through. The dirt floor was littered with torn mats, dirty straw and sheep droppings. A small iron stove lay overturned in a corner, still attached to a length of pipe; another piece of pipe was hanging loose from the roof.

'First we must clean the floor,' said Mr Romer. 'We'll be stuck here until our transport comes; so the sergeant said. Tomorrow, the day after . . . The usual.'

'It's lucky,' said Mother, 'that the last occupants were sheep and not people, no lice, at least.'

We spent the rest of the day preparing for the night. The women cleaned the floor and the path leading to the cabin. Somebody produced a packet of nails and the men went about repairing the walls, fixing the stove, securing the windows with pieces of timber and broken planks or larger fragments of the broken glass which was scattered over the ground.

Olek, Józek and I got up on the roof and tried our best to patch it up with torn-up shrubs, dry leaves, branches and pieces of wood handed up to us by Helena and her sisters.

The work finished, the stove repaired and the fire started, the cabin became almost cosy. Tired and chilled we had sat down by the stove to rest when Helena came up with a bright idea: 'We have to unpack our bedding for the night. Why don't we do it now and stick the empty bags in the holes in the roof? What you did may not be weatherproof.'

Perhaps she was right, after all the bedding was packed in tough canvas bags offering good protection. That meant starting all over again, once more climbing on the slippery roof in the cold drizzle.

Olek and I tried to object: 'Somebody will pinch the bags and then what?' But we were overruled. Without enthusiasm, Olek, Józek and I climbed up on the roof again to do another hour's work.

'I am not going up there any more,' I declared firmly on our return. It was time for a quick bite to eat and for bed. The barrack was roomy and I made my bed in a corner, away from the rest, away from Helena and from my parents. I was angry and needed to be on my own.

The night was cold, but dry. The canvas bags on the roof proved unnecessary, a precaution too many, but they survived the night unstolen. In the morning a clutch of militiamen and civilians arrived. With their writing pads and their indelible pencils they scattered in pairs between the huts. While waiting our turn, we passed the time reading books and talking. About midday we were called out. A couple of Kazakhs stood outside:

a militiaman and a civilian. They were swarthy with typically wide Mongol faces and slanted eyes. In very good Russian the civilian introduced himself as the chairman of the *kolkhoz* Kzyl Dykhan, or the collective farm, the Red Cockerel. 'We have proper housing and work for you,' he promised with a broad smile.

Yes, he needed manpower badly and yes, he was absolutely sure that *stareeki*, the old people, could be employed in the office or in the store, while jobs in the fields and workshops were there in plenty for all the other adults and children. He was sorry about wasting Father's skills: 'No, I regret,' he said, 'but you will not be able to work as a doctor. My *kolkhoz* does not qualify for its own medical officer. We have a nurse on the payroll, but we may apply for an upgrading,' he said frowning. 'That's a thought. We shall see,' he concluded. That was honest enough.

All this time the militiaman kept quiet. He was scribbling laboriously on his writing pad, noting our replies to the chairman's questions: name, place of birth, date of birth, the maiden name of the mother, grandmother, etc. Bureaucracy in action. Every few words the business end of his purple indelible pencil – the usual 'weapon' of Soviet officialdom – wandered into his mouth, in one corner, then in the other. The dye was staining his lips and chin and purple dribble was running from the corners of his mouth and over his chin.

Our entire group of about thirty signed up for work on the Red Cockerel farm. 'Stay here until I send for you.' He pointed to the dwelling next to ours. 'Twelve people from that hut are also coming to us. Two lorries will pick you up tomorrow.' He pointed to the east. 'Kzyl Dykhan is just on the other side of the mountains. A couple of hours' drive.' He left and Mr Purple Chin followed without a word, still scribbling.

I looked at the mountains in the east. They towered over the valley, some of their snow-clad peaks merging into the clouds; the snow extended down towards the foothills. 'Are those the mountains we have to cross?' asked Helena anxiously.

'Hope not,' I said. 'They seem quite near, not more than two to three kilometres away. Judging from my atlas they must be the Karatou chain – they were the only ones in this area I could find on my map. There ought to be a road, or at least a dirt track, around them, somewhere to the north, or north-west from here.' I did not fancy crossing the forbidding-looking mountains by lorry and it didn't even occur to me that some of us would have to climb them on foot.

By now the sky began to show bits of blue between the heavy, grey clouds. The sun was trying to peep through and suddenly, it became warm. My parents, Helena's parents and most of the people from the two adjacent barracks gathered outside. They stood there talking, discussing the 'happy future' awaiting us on the other side of the mountains. I just listened. Kzyl Dykhan began to sound like some promised land, a safe haven for the rest of the war. I did not know what to make of it all. What a flock of sheep, I thought. 'One can only hope for the best,' I said to Helena. 'But I don't believe in promises any more.'

'Neither do I,' she replied. It was strange that we, the youngsters, were becoming cynical as the adults became gullible. She took me by the hand. 'Let's go for a walk,' she suggested.

A wide stony path, broad enough for us to walk abreast, took us away from the reeking hovels, away from the crowd and towards the mountains. We climbed up steadily and soon found ourselves in the foothills, among small patches of snow. The midday sun was warm overhead. The path narrowed, but we still walked side by side, our arms entwined; some of the old closeness came back. We talked in simple phrases, in half sentences, understanding each other even without words. We talked about the past, not venturing into the future; pressing questions were left unasked.

We found a secluded sunny spot and sat down on a big, smooth weather-polished stone, like a solid bench, placed between two man-size boulders, our backs towards the snow-covered mountains, the valley with its barracks at our feet. We could clearly see people milling around, lazing in the sun, gesticulating, still, no doubt, deceiving themselves and each other about the rosy future. Here, mercifully, silence reigned. Their voices failed to carry up the mountainside. The cold wind from the mountains kept the stench of the hovels at bay. Here the air was fresh, balmy even, with that late autumnal fragrance made up of rotting vegetation, withered mountain flowers and herbs. As the last carload of officials was leaving and as the sun was swallowed by the bank of clouds on the distant horizon, we started on our way back. Little did we know that this was the last time that we were to be alone and close together.

In the morning lorries started arriving and continued coming singly or in small convoys throughout the day. The population of the camp rapidly dwindled. The day ended and the two lorries promised by the chairman of our collective farm failed to materialise. The exodus continued the next day and by the afternoon the camp was empty except for our Red Cockerel contingent. Our food supply was shrinking fast. Luckily, the water pump was in good working order and we boiled water on the hut stove, but we ran out of firewood before the night.

'There is plenty of firewood there,' said a Russian from the barrack next to ours when we were waiting at the pump. He pointed to the steppe which we had crossed in the train. At the time I had noticed large balls of vegetation being blown about by the wind, it had not occurred to me that they might be of any use. 'Be careful when you collect them,' he added, 'we call them *kolyutchki*, pricklies.'

The third morning came and there was no sign of our lorries. We needed firewood and we went into the steppe to collect the pricklies. They consisted of dry stems and branches of some shrub with thousands of spiky thorns. The stems were hard and difficult to break while the thorns were two to three centimetres long and sharp as needles. Forewarned, we wore our thickest gloves, hats and covered our backs with blankets. The balls increased in size in front of our eyes. A single branch torn off its parent stem and blown about in the wind would get entangled with another and another, and thus start a ball. In minutes the ball grew to a metre or more in diameter. It was a windy day and whichever way one looked the peculiar, ethereal, abstract, spherical sculptures raced in all – and mostly changeable – directions, propelled by gusts of wind. They were an eerie sight in the empty steppe. They were difficult to catch, so we helped each other to hold them down, to load them on each other's back – where they held to the blanket and to each other by their thorns. They were light, yet one had to carry them bent in half, not because of the weight of the load, but because of its size – we carried two or three balls on top of one another. As one tried to straighten up, they dragged behind one on the ground, like the tail of some prehistoric monster. When Józek and Olek piled the first load on to my back, a gust of wind threw me over. Reloaded, I lost half the load to the side wind on my return journey.

Later, I removed dozens of thorns from my blanket, coat, gloves, hat, as well as some from my face and neck. *Kolyuchki* burned quickly, like dry tissue paper, and we had to keep going back to the steppe for another load and another. In the evening, the almost-empty camp was dark and quiet. 'This place gives me the creeps,' said Helena. 'What will happen if they don't come in the morning to pick us up?'

What indeed? But I said nothing.

The barrack was cold. Again we ran out of firewood, so it was an early night for everybody.

In the morning, as we breakfasted on cold water, too despondent to talk, the unusual silence was broken by distant shouts. Olek and I went to the door. A pack of donkeys driven by three men was entering the camp. They were followed by a lorry and a car. They were all Kazakhs: the donkey drovers, the lorry driver and the two militiamen in the car. They stopped by our hut and engaged us in a long conversation in an incomprehensible tongue.

Then a donkey started braying. It was a horrid sound: it combined the neighing of a horse, the laugh of a hyena and the squeal of a butchered pig. It came in explosive short bursts until stopped by a sharp, harsh in-drawing of breath followed by more braying. The other animals joined in. This ear-splitting chorus continued for a minute or two, until the sonorous muzzles found another occupation in patches of half-rotten winter grass and shrubs on the sides of the path.

One of the militiamen was the Russian-speaking sergeant who had welcomed us to Kazakhstan several days before. 'This is your transport,' he said, 'to the Red Cockerel. The donkeys for your bags and packs and the lorry for the old people and small children. You three lads,' he pointed to Olek, Józek and me, 'will help with the donkeys across the mountains.'

That was that. I looked at the three Kazakh drovers, they were big men and each had his dagger in his belt. Perhaps the sheepskins and the massive fur caps were making them look even bigger than they were. Olek was about six foot and was the tallest of the three of us, but the Kazakhs towered above him. I was the widest at the shoulder, but puny compared to them. Józek was slender and short, smaller than me. I did some quick thinking and shivers ran down my back.

Father won't allow it, no chance. Just the three of us guarding all our precious belongings against those three . . . *bandits*? We had not come all this way to have our throats slit. There was no earthly reason why they should not do just that – after all they were the descendants of Genghis Khan. In that instant, I clearly saw our bodies on a mountain pass left to jackals, or vultures, or whatever the local scavengers were, while the caravan with our packs and bundles continued on its way. Our possessions would be a great prize for the bandits, as I was sure they were, or could be – given a chance. They could live on the proceeds happily ever after. I was feeling very sorry for myself, for Olek, and for my new friend, Józek.

I looked at Father. He won't allow it, he mustn't. He looked worried and turned to the sergeant and said, 'Let's go inside and discuss it.' Two red ones should do it, I thought. But no.

The man cut him short: 'Nothing to discuss, citizen. These are the orders and so be ready to move as soon as the animals have rested. You have two hours.' Visibly angry, he got back to the car and then turned and added more kindly: 'You should be grateful that I took pity on you and found a lorry, or all of you would be going on foot. Anyway, it won't be long before your lads and your bags will rejoin you in Sharapkhana, on the other side of the mountains. Let's go,' he shouted to his driver.

Repacking and then loading the suitcases, boxes and bundles of all shapes and sizes on thirty donkeys took the best part of the morning. Then the time came to say goodbye to my parents, to Helena and to the others. Sure that I would never see them again, I even kissed Mrs Romer.

We left the camp following the same rocky path which Helena and I had taken the other day. Two animals abreast, the caravan spread out and slowly climbed up and up. Half-a-dozen animals were left unladen. A little way up the mountains our guides mounted them and motioned to us to do the same. It was bareback riding again, but these animals were well covered compared with the Kvasha horses.

In the winter the night comes early, especially in the mountains and especially when it is moonless and cloudy. A bitterly cold wind came with it, driving first light flurries and then heavy curtains of snow erratically before it.

Numb with cold, I got off my mount and walked. After a few minutes, as my feet started warming up, my behind – missing the donkey's warm back – got painfully cold. I climbed on to the animal's back again, only to dismount a couple of minutes later as my feet began to freeze.

In the meantime the wind grew stronger and imprisoned in deep gorges it howled its way up and down the mountain. In more exposed portions of the path it tried to shove me and my donkey off the rocky shelf into the precipice, then it would steal up from behind and try to throw me to my knees. A moment later, with a wail and a roar, it would toss a cloud of fat snow-flakes in my face. I walked close to the animal, holding on tight to its warm neck. It didn't seem to mind.

The path climbed up among drifts of snow driven against the rocky sides of the path. The wind made the cold worse than in Kvasha. I was hungry and thirsty, so I picked up a handful of snow and lapped it up from my glove.

As we were leaving, Mother had put a crust of flat bread wrapped up in a handkerchief in my coat pocket. Now I could not take my gloves off as my fingers were frozen stiff, and it was with difficulty that I got the handkerchief out. I tried to undo the knot, but I couldn't, so, like a rat, I gnawed my way through it and bit off fragments of the crust to chew.

❄ ❄ ❄

This episode came vividly to mind some thirty years later.

We were on holiday in Ohrid, in Macedonia, then part of Yugoslavia. One evening I rescued a big grasshopper, at least seven or eight centimetres long, which landed on our restaurant table and stood there, as if hypnotised.

I pushed the immobilised creature on to my handkerchief and gathered the corners of the cloth above it. I shook it out – or so I thought – through the open window on to the flower-bed below. Satisfied with the good deed for the day, I repocketed my handkerchief. On reaching for it in the morning I found the grasshopper still wrapped in my handkerchief. It was dead. The handkerchief had holes in it, the insect had tried to gnaw its way out. For years that dead grasshopper returned to me in my dreams.

❋ ❋ ❋

I was dead tired. All three of us, Olek, Józek and I, tried hard to keep up with the caravan, but we failed and one by one found ourselves straggling at its tail. The snow was coming down thick and fast as we were walking into the howling wind, but the path was now flat; we must have reached the top of the pass.

We walked close together. 'I've had enough,' complained Józek. 'We must find a shelter and rest. How do we let them know?'

'We have just passed a suitable place,' said Olek. 'Looked like a cave entrance. I tried to talk to the big one. What's his name? Isatáy? I heard the others call him that. But he just shrugged his shoulders. They don't seem to understand Russian at all,' he sniggered.

'One of the others,' said Józek, 'pretended not to understand when I tried to show him by gesture that we needed to rest, to sit, to lie down, or whatever. I am sure that he got it all right, but did not want to know.'

Then it dawned on me: 'They hate Russians and that's what they think we are.'

Olek brightened up. 'You are right,' he said with some animation. 'But how the hell do we explain to them that we are not Russians? There must be a way. Let's catch up with them.' Easier said than done, as by then we were far behind. We managed to catch up with the caravan, only to be met with unfriendly grunts.

The daggers in their belts now looked even more menacing and sharper than before.

Olek put his index finger on the leader's chest. 'Isatáy,' he said. Then he pointed to himself. 'Alexander.' He repeated the manoeuvre.

I watched the man's face, suddenly he smiled and said, 'Iskander, Sasha?' He smiled! He understood! Sasha was the Russian diminutive for Alexander, as Olek was the equivalent in Polish. Good beginning.

Olek again put his finger on his own chest. 'Iskander no Russki,' he said. Then he pointed to me, to Józek and again to himself repeating: 'No Russki, no Russki, no Russki.' I kept watching the man's face for a glimmer of comprehension.

Another moment passed and the wide Mongolian face of Isatáy broadened further with a smile. The caravan stopped and the two other Kazakhs joined him. A long conversation followed. They turned to us and asked question upon question, all equally incomprehensible, but each with an unmistakable question mark at the end. But what were they asking?

Anyway, they laughed merrily. From that moment on they could not have been more friendly. Even their daggers began to lose their sharpness. Then I had another brain-wave: 'They want to know who we are.'

How could we tell them? We tried, repeatedly: *Polsha, polskiy*, Russian words for Poland and Polish were met with bland incomprehension. Between us we managed Pologne, Poland, Polen, Polonia – all of which proved meaningless. Words for France, England, Britain, America, in all our languages, drew similarly puzzled expressions. We were stuck.

Then Olek had a bright idea. '*Lekhistan*,' he said. Pointing in turn to himself, Józek and me, he repeated: '*Lekhistani, Lekhistani, Lekhistani.*'

Isatáy seemed to savour the words. '*Lekh, Lekhistan, Lekhistani.*' He seemed to turn them round and round in his mouth, taste them. Then, like a football, he passed them to the others. Then he scored a goal. Something clicked. It was one of the others who got it first. An animated discussion followed and the effect was amazing. They smiled broadly and a one-sided 'conversation' ensued with much hand-pumping, head-nodding, back-slapping, shoulder-squeezing. Not any the wiser, totally baffled in fact, I was suddenly a much happier man.

Lekhistan is the old Turkish and Tatar name for Poland. It goes back to the medieval invasions of Europe by Tatars, the ancestors of Kazakhs. The word comes from the name of the legendary Slav prince, Lech (pronounced *Lekh*), the supposed founder of the Polish nation. He had two brothers: Czech (pronounced *Chekh*) and Rus – with obvious implications.

Our ordeal was over. Within minutes we were in a large wooden shelter under a rocky overhang, with a covered enclosure nearby for the animals. The shelter continued into a large cave. Whether this was a stop intended anyway, or the result of the newly forged amity between people who at last half-understood each other, I knew not and did not care. There was a supply of firewood and *kizyak* in the cave. In no time we were all sitting round a lively *kizyak* fire, munching flat Kazakh bread and chasing it down with soured milk. Noodle soup served from a big cauldron hanging on a chain over the fire was next on the menu. Conversation, hesitant at first, became easier with each gulp of *koumiss*, or highly alcoholic fermented mare's milk. Our Kazakhs did speak a kind of rudimentary, broken Russian. Warm and satiated, more than slightly tipsy, buried in foul-smelling furs, I was soon fast asleep. I did not even dream of long daggers and slit throats, of my body left to decay on a mountain pass.

I woke up to a breakfast of hot milk with an odd taste (sheep's? donkey's? – I did not ask) and flat bread. The day was grey but it was not snowing and the wind had died down. The path soon descended into the valley. At one point Isatáy stopped the caravan. 'Sharapkhana.' He pointed to a cluster of barracks and mud huts at a crossroads. It took us another hour to get there.

We made straight for a long, low building of stone and clay. Isatáy called it *chaykhana*, a teahouse. Helena and her sisters were outside waiting for us; they had seen us descending the mountain and they had called the others. I was hugged in turns by my parents, by Helena and by Mrs Romer, who seemed to have developed a liking for me – I wondered why.

EIGHTEEN

UNPREDICTABLE CONSEQUENCES

✳

To call Sharapkhana a town, or even a village, was to pay it an undeserved compliment. The valley might have been beautiful in the spring but now, in December, it looked anything but inviting. It was muddy and grey, enlivened by sheets of dirty snow and patches of greyish-green shrubs. The valley stretched long and wide between snow-capped mountains. A rough-surface road ran its whole length, in a roughly north–south direction. At both ends of the valley the road snaked its way up over the hills and disappeared into the mountains. In the middle of the valley, the main road was crossed by an east–west dirt track.

I never found out whether the name Sharapkhana applied to the valley, or to the crossroads, or to the hamlet at the crossroads. The hamlet was a cluster of about a dozen mud huts, most of them close to the teahouse. It was inhabited by Kazakhs who spoke not a word of Russian, so that the several days that we stayed there we spent incommunicado, except for an occasional chat with a Russian lorry driver who might have stopped for a rest. The heart of Sharapkhana, its *raison d'être*, was the teahouse, a long barrack-like structure parallel to the road.

The emotional reunion over, the three of us, shepherded by our mothers, went inside the teahouse. It was good to sit on real chairs, at a proper table again. From a counter at the end of the hall they brought us drinking bowls full of green tea and a plate of flat bread and cheese. 'Sheep's cheese,' my mother said. 'It's good.' The drinking bowls were quite beautiful. They were made of fine china, the kind of china I had not seen since home, and were white with a delicate blue line along the edge and a blue and red design inside and out.

I let Olek and Józek answer questions about our adventures while I concentrated on eating. At the same time I looked around. The hall was large and rectangular, about thirty by ten paces and filled the entire barrack-like structure. It had only one door, in the middle of a long wall, flanked by two windows. The most striking feature of the room was a raised podium which ran the entire length of the long wall opposite the entrance and was covered with grey and brown blankets.

'Is it a stage?' I softly asked Mother. 'An odd place for a theatre, in the middle of nowhere.'

She laughed. 'These are sleeping quarters. Last night we slept on the dais, all thirty of us, side by side.

'This is a kind of roadside inn. We paid five roubles per night per head. Lorry drivers apparently stop sometimes for the night, but thank God so far there were no strangers here. Yesterday, when we arrived, the podium was covered with pretty rugs, but they did not look clean and were probably crawling with lice. We asked the owner to remove them and scrubbed the surface with soap before we spread our bedding on it. I was glad not to have to share our communal bed with total strangers. This morning, before you arrived, a few lory drivers stopped for breakfast. This is the dining area,' she concluded pointing to several tables and chairs between our table and the counter at the end of the hall.

The counter was a long table placed across the hall, with drinking bowls and plates stacked neatly in the middle. Behind it sat a Kazakh with a long, wispy, pointed beard. He seemed oblivious of our arrival, or of the company in general, engrossed as he was in a newspaper. He wore a long kaftan and a black skullcap, which was very austere compared with the colourfully embroidered *tubeteykas* worn by the Uzbeks in Chirakchi. Behind his chair there was a door-shaped opening in the wall, where rows of leather strips formed a curtain. 'That's his kitchen,' said Mother. 'Just a cooking fire, very much like the one you and Zina built in Chirakchi. He seems to have an unlimited supply of this green tea as, I suppose, befits a tea-house. It's not bad, even without sugar.'

Life was very primitive in Sharapkhana. All the water came from one hand-operated pump behind the *chaykhana*. In the morning there was a queue of Kazakh children with buckets, waiting their turn. Toilet facilities consisted of a privy, also behind the teahouse, though this appeared to be reserved for the residents of the teahouse, while the natives, no doubt, had their own facilities.

By this time we were all tired of our nomadic lifestyle and longed to settle down somewhere, even if it were a collective farm in Kazakhstan. But days came and went and there was no sign of life from the Red Cockerel. According to the few Russian lorry drivers who broke their journey in Sharapkhana, our *kolkhoz* was only about twenty kilometres down the dirt road in the easterly direction, but the road was narrow, the last part apparently not more than a stony track accessible only to a horse or donkey-drawn *arba*, a small vehicle on two very big wheels.

On the second night in Sharapkhana we had to share our sleeping quarters with a Russian couple, a lorry driver and his female companion. They arrived late in the evening and we had to push our bedding closer together to make room for them. We wouldn't have minded very much, had they not left us a legacy: lice and fleas in abundance.

From then on we were tormented by the insects day and night. In the circumstances there was absolutely nothing we could do about it. We became irritable and apathetic at the same time. Disturbed sleep combined with the diet of green tea, flat bread and an occasional piece of cheese, were not conducive either to physical or to psychological well-being.

Helena and I, sometimes accompanied by other members of the group, would try to go for an occasional walk in the foothills. The weather, however, was unpleasant: both the days and the nights were cold, it frequently rained, or, if it didn't pour or drizzle, the fog, like talcum powder thinly blown in the air, would make us turn back. We were itchy, subdued and touchy. I tried to make it up with Helena and I had a feeling that she was trying too, but it didn't work.

We languished in Sharapkhana for a week or more. Then, one morning I woke up with a headache and a pain in my right ear.

The pain became more severe by the minute and by midday I had a high fever and was delirious. Mother and Helena were sponging me down with tepid water. At times I was vaguely aware of what was going on round me, but most of the time I was unconscious.

My recollection of what happened next is far from clear. It was only later that the gaps in my memory were filled in by my parents.

In the afternoon the fever must have dropped a little and I came round, but I couldn't be bothered to open my eyes. Somebody was holding my hand and I heard my father's voice: 'There is no doubt . . . I ought to try your darning needle . . .' he said. His voice seemed to tremble a bit, or perhaps my perception of it was imperfect.

'We can easily boil it,' said Mother, 'but my big needle isn't very sharp. The other ones are too small, I think.'

Then Father again, 'A blunt needle . . . very painful. Perhaps I could sharpen it on a stone. This drum must be incised and the middle ear drained without much delay. *Cholera, psia krew!*' Father swore in Polish. 'Not even a bloody aspirin.'

They had to be talking about me. Suddenly it was all clear: I had a middle ear infection. On his home visits in Otwock my father always carried a set of instruments which included a special sharp thin knife for incising the ear drum. He used to tell me about those things; show them to me; explain their purpose. A collection of pus in the middle ear could cause the drum to rupture, or else it might find its way into the skull and produce a brain abscess. That's why the drum had to be cut and the pus let out. It was standard treatment. I suddenly visualised Mother's blunt darning needle being thrust into my ear. I drew my hand out of my mother's grasp, sat up and covered my painful ear with both hands. 'No, no!' I cried. Father ran out of the hall.

When I regained consciousness, I was being carried, my head on Father's chest, his hands in my armpits, my legs supported by Olek on one side and by Helena on the other. A small lorry stood by the door. Mother spread a blanket on its floor and Father laid me down on it, under the canvas roof. Mother kissed me: 'Daddy is taking you to hospital,' she said. 'It will be all right; you will both be back tomorrow.' Helena kissed me. Then Father got into the lorry and sat next to me on the floor. A strange man raised the tailgate and we were off. The others stood by the teahouse waving.

When I woke up again the floor was moving up and down, up and down. 'We are going somewhere in a lorry,' flashed through my mind. Then I remembered Mother saying 'to hospital'. There was something on the side of my face, I touched it with my hand, it was wet and had an odd smell. The roof must be leaking, it must be rotting leaves on it causing the smell,' I thought to myself. There was no pain in my ear. I sat up. Ouch! My head hurt.

Father must have dozed off with his back against the driver's cab. He woke up with a start: 'What is it Stefanku? What's happened?'

'The earache has gone,' I said. 'But my cheek and neck are wet. The roof is leaking.'

Father moved closer and looked at me searchingly. He put his hand on my forehead. 'No fever,' he said as he turned my head to the side and looked at my ear. '*Dzięki Bogu*, thank God,' he said. 'The drum has burst. Everything will be all right now. Thank God,' he repeated and smiled his gentle smile.

The lorry was still hopping up and down on the rough road. 'It must have been these potholes, all those jumps and jerks, which helped it to burst,' said Father. 'It will heal now, *syneczku*, my son.' He produced a clean handkerchief and with great care dried my face, ear and hand.

Except for a headache, I felt well. I moved to the back of the lorry and looked out. It was raining and getting dark. We were in an urban street, dimly lit, with one-storey houses on both sides. There were lights in the windows – electric lights!

'Where are we?' I asked. 'What's happening? I have a bit of a headache now.'

'Lie down. Put your head here,' said Father and I lay down with my head in his lap. He gave me another clean handkerchief to hold to my ear. 'I decided to take you to hospital in Chimkent. We were in luck: I waved down the first lorry going south and it stopped. It was empty and when I told the driver about you, he got out, just opened the back and said, "Bring him in." He did not even ask for money. He is a Russian, a good man. That was three hours ago. I must talk to him.' Father banged three times on the driver's cab wall.

The lorry slowed down and stopped. The driver's head appeared at the side of his cab. 'Has he died, the lad?' asked the Russian.

'*Slava bohu*, thank God,' said Father, 'He is all right. The drum burst, no need to go to the hospital now,' Father said.

The driver dropped the tailgate, climbed in and sat down next to my father. A long conversation followed. He was going to the railway depot on the other side of Chimkent, but he would leave us at his sister's place. 'Her husband is in the army,' he said. 'She is lame and can't work. For a couple of red ones, she will gladly let you use her bedroom. She only gets a small allowance, not nearly enough to live on. She will move to the kitchen and I can sleep in the depot. She will have soup and bread for you. That way everybody will be happy,' he concluded.

Father gave the driver – Mikhail, or Misha for short – several red ones. 'Not necessary,' he said, but took the money. He stayed with us in the back of the lorry for a few more minutes and smoked one of Father's cigarettes. He was young and was also waiting for his army papers. 'Might come any day now,' he said, 'though this job is classed as essential . . . for the time being,' he added as he jumped out and returned to his cab.

For a change everything went as planned. After a further ten minutes' drive through potholed streets, we stopped. Misha knocked on the door and exchanged a few words with the woman who opened it. Soon after, we were all sitting in the kitchen, drinking mock tea and eating flat bread. I fell on them like a hungry bear. Then Katya, Misha's sister, went, limping badly, to prepare our room. 'I will have soup for you later,' she assured us as she returned. She showed us to her room. 'Don't worry about bringing lice,' she said. 'I know how it is. You can't help it on the road. After you've left, I'll take the bedding to the delousing station, it's not far. Don't worry, I'll manage.'

Compared with the places we had stayed at in the last eighteen months, except for the bare but cosy room in the Chirakchi hospital, Katya's room was amazing – almost palatial. There was an electric light in the middle of the ceiling, complete with a lampshade, an iron double bed covered with a patchwork quilt, a small table, a couple of chairs and two wicker armchairs, a real wooden wardrobe and, luxury of luxuries, a washstand with a basin and a large enamel jug filled with hot water on top of it and a bucket of cold water underneath. There was even a clean towel on the chair and a piece of brown soap in the dish on the washstand. The most welcome sight, however, was the lively coal fire in the fireplace that made the room cosy and warm. 'Quite unusual,' mused Father. 'One person living in a flat like this, not sharing, even her own kitchen. She must know the right people.'

Left to ourselves, we undressed in front of the fire and, first of all, proceeded to pick off lice and let them roast in flames. We spent the next half-hour delousing our clothes and underwear, going through each fold and seam with care. We luxuriated in the hot water, we took turns at washing in the basin placed on the floor. We dressed again and our happiness was made complete by the large helpings of steaming soup and bread. Relaxed for once, we went to bed. My ear didn't hurt any more and the headache was gone.

In the morning we followed Katya's directions and found the hospital only ten minutes' walk away, in a wide, tree-lined street. The hospital building was big, white and modern, resembling the Chirakchi hospital, but devoid of Stalin's monument. A friendly young woman doctor cleaned up my ear. 'It should heal well now, but just in case,' she said, handing me some aspirin cachets wrapped in a piece of old wallpaper, the usual Soviet packing material.

Chimkent, a town of about 80,000 people, was the capital of the south Kazakhstan *oblast*, or province. As we left the hospital, the *Bolnichnaya Ulitsa*, or Hospital Street, took us to a small park crowded with people. It was now midday and all the benches were taken by people busily chewing. 'Like lunchtime in any city park,' I thought, 'anywhere in the world.' Watching them made me hungry.

We crossed the park and emerged into another wide tree-lined street, busy with traffic. 'Look, Father!' I exclaimed. 'There is a café over there, on the corner. Can you see?'

'Yes, I noticed,' said Father. 'Let's have a look. Mind you, we have no coupons, no ration books, or God knows what they might want here, but there's no harm in trying.'

The café comprised two big rooms, both packed. I could not believe my eyes. People were sitting in comfortable chairs, at well-laid clean tables and drinking tea from glasses. 'Look, look, Father,' I kept repeating. The glasses stood on glass saucers and buns were served on china plates. There was also soup, served in white bowls, with a choice of bread or roll.

After a wait of no more than fifteen minutes we sat down at a table shared with several people. A waitress came to take our order. It was a set lunch menu. 'Only one per person,' she said. Fair enough. She didn't ask for any coupons or ration books, you did not even have to bring your own spoon! This was civilisation.

The soup was excellent and thick. It was packed with vegetables, meat and potatoes. I also had a thick slice of white bread. The tea, mock tea, was sweet – with real sugar? Perhaps. The bun was mouthwatering; it was topped with raisins and large crystals of sugar. I devoured mine and half of Father's – he assured me that he had eaten enough.

Warm, full and relaxed I had a look round. There were people reading newspapers fastened, Central European fashion, to long carved wooden handles. With its burgundy flock wallpaper, it could have been a Warsaw café. Lunch-time was evidently at an end and the place was rapidly emptying; the clock showed that it was 2 p.m.

Suddenly, as my eyes swept the room once more, a familiar face caught my attention. I knew that young woman in the corner, I was sure that I had seen the face before, but I couldn't put a name to it. She must have noticed me too, as her uncertain gaze kept returning to our table. Father, sitting with his back to her, could not see her. Who was she? Where had I seen her before? Could it have been in Otwock? Then it dawned on me: it was Halina Kachan who was two years ahead of me in the Otwock *gimnazjum*. Her father owned a drugstore and perfumery in Ulica Kościelna. We used to buy soap, toothpaste and suchlike there.

'It's down there,' said Father pointing to the 'Toilet' sign in the corner of the room, as I got up suddenly.

'Halina Kachan,' I said; he looked at me with amazement as I ran to her table. She must have recognised me too, as she got up, opened her arms and kissed me on both cheeks. You don't meet your school-mates every day in Central Asia, and from a school thousands of kilometres away, at that.

Together we rejoined Father. As he got up to greet the stranger, the look on his face turned from amazement to disbelief, then to recognition.

Halina's story was similar to ours, except that she was on her own. She had left Otwock in September 1939, while her parents stayed behind. She had not heard from them since. She had been deported to Siberia and had worked in the forest. Amnestied, as we were, in September 1941 she had travelled south. Soon after her arrival in Chimkent she had found work as a secretary.

The next bit of information was rich in consequences for our own fortunes.

'I work now in the Polish *Delegatura*,' said Halina.

Father sat up. 'What do you mean?' he asked.

'It's the local branch of the Embassy,' said Halina. 'I mean the Polish Embassy in Moscow, which has now been evacuated out of harm's way to Kuybyshev, on the Volga, you know. There are so many Polish refugees in need of help, even here in Kazakhstan, that they opened a branch, a kind of consular office, in Chimkent. We cover the whole of southern Kazakhstan. Nobody knows how many of our people there are in the area and we are trying to find out. Many are sick, under-nourished, many found their way here from those awful labour camps and mines in Kolyma, in the far east. They were so much worse than our re-education settlements. We were lucky.'

'Indeed,' said Father. 'I suppose you have a medical department. Do you know the doctors? Perhaps they need another pair of hands?'

'I was coming to that,' said Halina. 'We do need doctors and nurses. So far we have no medical staff at all. Not a single nurse has reported to us. Most Polish doctors have joined the army, up north. Not one could be found in south Kazakhstan. Would you . . .?' The question hung in the air.

Though not for long. Indeed, it all sounded too good to be

true. Within the hour my father was interviewed by Professor Kościałkowski, the Delegate, and instantly appointed medical officer to the Polish *Delagatura* in Chimkent, with a salary of 1,000 roubles per month, which was two and a half times the usual doctor's salary in the USSR. Father's entry ticket, so to speak, was his Polish Army Officer's book which, at the time of our deportation, had been saved by our landlady in Pińsk. This stroke of luck changed our plans. Father was to start work next morning and I had to travel to Sharapkhana on my own.

We returned to Katya's. She had no objection to Father renting her room for another night or two. She could do with the money, she said. She also gave me a tip where best to hitch a lift to Sharapkhana, and, before long, I was on my way. I travelled in comfort this time, in the driver's cab. The driver of this big, heavily laden lorry was a friendly Russian girl called Nastya, a chain-smoker of *makhorka* cigarettes. Two hours after leaving Chimkent we stopped at the door of the Sharapkhana teahouse; Nastya was a bit of a speed fiend.

It was still light. The teahouse was quiet. The door was open and, except for the old Kazakh in his wicker armchair, his nose in a newspaper, the teahouse was empty. People and luggage, all gone. He didn't even take his eyes off the paper. I ran back into the road. Nastya was revving up the engine, about to leave. I ran to the front of the lorry waving frantically. She wound down the window: 'What's the matter, Stepan?'

'Mother is gone. They've all gone. I don't know what to do. There is nobody here who speaks Russian.' During the drive we had chattered about ourselves, our families. She told me that she grew up in Kazakhstan and spoke the language.

She killed the engine and jumped out of the cab.

'They left about noon,' she reported, 'in a caravan of *arbas* and, according to him, they must by now be near Kzyl Dykhan. It's only some twenty kilometres away.'

It was a blow. The afternoon was coming to an end and I did not fancy a long walk in the dark. I spent the night in the teahouse, on a rug and under blankets provided by the owner. I was soon itching all over, but that was nothing new.

I set out early next morning. The road to the Red Cockerel was just a narrow dirt track. I kept to the main track, ignoring footpaths branching off. This way, I thought, I shouldn't get lost. I met not another soul on my way.

I walked for hours towards the mountains, but they obstinately kept their distance. The rain had stopped the previous day and the ground was dry and dusty. This part of the valley, rising towards the foothills, looked almost like a desert, rocky and inhospitable. Later, the track climbed up more steeply, snaking between rocky outcrops, around boulders the size of a house, across the tops of low hills covered with bushes and shrubs, between clumps of dwarf trees.

After five hours' walking I reached the Red Cockerel at midday and I found Mother in the Romers' one-room hut. Her first words were: 'What happened to Father?' Reassured that he was all right she hugged me and would not let me out of her embrace for a good while. Then Helena hugged me warmly, followed by all the Romers, who held me and patted me in turns. We had become one large family and now we would have to part; but the prospect of moving to a big town was so exciting that I could not think about anything else. I had no regrets.

Less then forty-eight hours had passed since Father and I left the Sharapkhana teahouse for the hospital, but there was much to report and I was not allowed to miss out a single detail. Many questions were asked about the political situation, about the Polish *Delegatura*, but I had few answers. Mr Romer was green with envy. 'I had a choice of law or medicine. Why on earth did I pick law?' he mused aloud. Mr Romer as a doctor? It was difficult to see him in a caring role, he did not have an ounce of the necessary qualities.

Mother, her anxiety gone and practical as usual, once again started packing. We needed transport for our luggage. Armed with several red ones in my pocket I went in search of the *kolkhoz* office. The chairman seemed genuinely pleased that Father had found a medical post. Being the kind of man he was, he said, unbidden and unbribed, 'You will need an *arba*. I'll send Dzhudzhayev for you. Be ready at dawn and he'll take you to the Sharapkhana teahouse.' Then, putting on a serious expression, 'You pay him two red ones, mind,' he added and winked.

I spent the night sleeping on straw mats in the Romers' room. Our conveyance arrived as promised. We loaded our belongings, bid our farewells and set out on foot following the *arba*. I saw Helena waving to us until the Red Cockerel was lost in the hills.

I did not see Helena again until 1970, when I was forty-five years old.

NINETEEN

CHIMKENT – A RESTRICTED CITY

✳

In Chimkent we encountered a new problem: it was a 'Restricted City Grade Two'.

Mother and I arrived in Chimkent a full day later than my father had expected and he had been worried. We spent another night at Katya's, my parents in the sumptuous bed, while I slept on the floor. In the morning, Father went to work while Mother and I set out in search of accommodation. On Katya's advice we decided to look for a room in Uyúk, the area between the town and the railway station.

In the USSR, towns had a peculiar relationship with their railway stations: they were at a distance from each other. 'It's simple,' said Father. 'In Tsarist Russia railways were built by entrepreneurs. It was a lucrative business, especially if the station "happened" to be two, three or even more *versts* from the town; then passengers could be charged not only for the railway ticket, but also for the omnibus, or *droshky* to the centre of the town.' In time, the area between the town and the railway station would see a mushrooming of workshops, warehouses and cheap housing.

Following Katya's directions we headed towards the station. The street became a wide footpath across a wasteland and it wound its way among low hillocks, ditches half-filled with stagnant water. We went over a rickety wooden bridge that crossed a lazy, filthy stream and then the path merged into a wider dirt track which ended in a maze of unpaved streets criss-crossing a district of brown mud huts. Most of the huts stood in their own small yards, hugged by the brown mud fence.

So this was Uyúk. It looked exactly as Katya had described it to us. 'You are sure to find a room there,' she said. 'Just ask the first Russian woman you meet.'

There was nobody in sight. For a while we stood there at an unnamed street corner uncertain where to turn. Then the door of one of the huts opened. A typical Russian *babushka* came out, with a basket in one hand, a stick in the other and a floral scarf on her head. Mother accosted her. 'Go that way,' the woman said pointing down the street. 'To the corner. Turn right and . . .' She stopped. 'You'll get lost. I'll take you there.' Mother joined her and I followed.

'A friend of mine lives there,' I heard the woman saying, 'with her two sons. Yevdokya Nikolayevna, they call her. Her husband was killed in the war, or perhaps taken prisoner. Anyway, she has a spare room. How long will you be staying?'

'I don't know exactly,' said Mother. 'Several months, perhaps, if the price is right.'

'Good, good,' said the woman. 'I am glad to be of service to you and to Yevdokya, poor soul. She has lost her husband, whether he has been killed or not. Now they are taking away Grisha, her younger boy – he is only sixteen, only a lad, really – to FZO, some kind of a school, they say. But can you believe them? I ask you. As sure as day is day and night is night they'll send him to war, to be killed. It's always the same for us poor people. First Tsar *bátyushka* (little father) sent our lads to war, then they died in the revolution. Now more of the same.' She continued in the same pessimistic vein for another minute or two before changing her tune. 'Oh, but Volodya, her older son. He is educated, an electrician, a scientist. He works in the power station. Surely they won't take him and leave Yevdokya all alone, with her *ishak*.'

The woman kept going on without a break. We learned that Volodya was twenty-five years old, a bachelor, a foreman in charge of the night shift at the Chimkent power station. That he was a good son; that *ishak* was a Kazakh word for donkey; that Yevdokya needed money because so far she had not received any pension for her husband. 'Perhaps he is not dead,' she said, 'and then she won't see a kopeck, poor soul.'

She stopped by a wooden gate and, still shaking her head in pity over her friend's misfortune, banged on the door. The donkey responded with an ear-splitting bray. A Russian woman, who might have been our guide's twin, opened the gate and, looking back over her shoulder, said, 'Quiet, quiet my little pigeon.' The braying abruptly ceased.

'These people would like to rent your room,' said our guide.

'Come in, come in,' said Yevdokya. The small yard was surrounded by a mud fence. In the far left-hand corner of the yard, huddled next to the fence, was the hut itself, its door open. A lean-to, to the right of the hut, clearly housed the donkey whose impatient stamping stopped when its owner repeated soothingly, 'Quiet, quiet, my little one.'

We followed the two Russian women through the door. We passed a small porch and entered the kitchen which was long and narrow, with one window in the far wall and a small range on the left. 'That's the room you can have,' said Yevdokya opening the door on the right. 'I shall move to the kitchen with Volodya. Grisha is going to Dzhambul tomorrow,' she said in the way of explanation to our guide. 'You may move in tomorrow,' she concluded turning back to my mother.

The room was quite large with two small windows giving on to the street. The walls were whitewashed. Along the right wall stood a double bed covered with a patchwork quilt. Snuggled next to the kitchen wall was a narrow single bed covered with a blanket. It was exactly what we needed. Apart from the beds, there was a square table, two chairs and a washstand with a white enamel bowl and pitcher. Another item was a big black vessel on a low wooden stand next to the table. It had two handles and looked like a squat ancient Greek amphora. Puzzled, I kept looking at it. 'It is a *choogoon*,' Mother explained. 'A cast-iron cauldron to store water.' As my mother and the landlady started discussing details, I wandered back into the yard.

I liked the place. Next to the stables was the wooden privy. I let myself in, it was smelly, but I had known worse. Good ventilation was provided by finger-wide gaps between planks in the walls. The seat was smooth, with no evident splinters, and there was even a nail in the wall with a wad of neatly cut newspaper squares on a piece of string.

Next I went to visit the donkey. He was friendly and let me stroke his neck and nose without trying to bite my hand, as other donkeys of my acquaintance had tried to do. In the corner of the yard, by the gate, grew a dwarf tree with several leaves remaining. Next to the hut, partly hidden by its open door, was a long-handled pump, with two shiny buckets hanging on hooks in the wall. A tidy household, I thought.

After another night spent in Katya's room, and with the help of a hired driver, an acquaintance of our landlady, we loaded our worldly goods on to his *arba* drawn by a handsome, well-fed mule, and followed it on foot to our new abode. The footpath through the wasteland was just wide enough for the *arba* to pass and even the footbridge across the stream took its weight without mishaps. 'There is a proper road to the station but it would take much longer,' said our driver.

Having accomplished the move, Father went to work, while Mother and I set about making our room more habitable. We made the beds with our own bedding. In one corner of the room we stretched a length of string from a nail in the window-frame to a wooden peg in the wall; this was to be our wardrobe. Driving the peg into the wall was a problem, though. The wall was too soft to hold it but, eventually, I managed to fix it using pebbles mixed with clay. Both were freely available in a ditch in the yard. 'We always keep clay handy,' said our landlady. 'Sometimes the ground shakes. Walls and fences have to be repaired.'

Earthquakes. I had never witnessed one except in the cinema, how exciting! On second thoughts, though, perhaps we could do without it. We had enough problems as it was.

Actually, I did not have to wait long for the excitement of my first earthquake and, when it did come, it was not much of a thrill. Two or three days after our move, I developed a cold and I had a fever and a sore throat. Mother decided that I should stay in bed and left on her usual food-hunting expedition. I was reading in bed when I felt my bed shaking a little. It stopped, then shook again. I sat up. The naked bulb hanging from the ceiling on a short flex was swaying gently, like a child on a swing, still shy, uncertain of the new skill, and the water in the cauldron was rocking slowly. Curious, I got up and went to the window. It was raining, but there was nothing to be seen. Was that an earthquake? Was that all there was to it? How disappointing.

As I was turning to go back to bed and to my book, I noticed a zigzag crack in the wall between the two windows; it had not been there before. It extended from the ceiling almost to the floor. As I was looking at it, it got wider and as rainwater seeped through it, other cracks appeared alongside it. The electric bulb was still now, but the water in the cauldron was still rocking. No more quakes.

I went back to bed. That was the end of my first earthquake. The next day I helped Volodya to fill in the cracks in the wall and in the fence with twigs and clay from the ditch in the yard.

The next problem was legalising our stay in Chimkent. In the USSR every Soviet citizen had an internal passport and could live anywhere, provided that anywhere was the place specified in the document. Changing one's residence, or moving away from one's place of birth, was difficult. Getting a permit to live in Moscow, Leningrad, or Kiev, the three restricted cities grade one, was well-nigh impossible. Settling in a provincial capital, classed a restricted city grade two, such as Chimkent, was not easy, even for a Soviet citizen. Foreigners, of course, needed special residence permits.

One afternoon Mother and I met Father in town and together we went to the co-operative photographic *atelier* near the *Delegatura* to have passport photographs taken. The forms we filled in at home. Four pages each, a hundred questions or so per person. The job took most of the evening. Next morning, I took the forms and the packet of photographs, the required sixteen photos per person, to the militia station.

I don't like police stations. To this day my heart accelerates whenever I enter the building for whatever reason. Does an NKVD spectre walk by my side?

The receptionist in the Chimkent militia station was polite. He asked my business, checked the forms and counted the photographs. He put my name in a book. 'Sign here,' he barked. I signed. 'Wait there,' he pointed to a bench. I sat down.

He addressed me as *vy*, the second person plural, civil enough, and he treated me as an adult, but I did not feel happy all the same. Most of the time I looked at my feet and I twiddled my thumbs. I waited a long time, until another militiaman took me through a long dark corridor to an office.

The man behind the desk was scribbling something. He wore the blue militia uniform, with three red triangles on the collar. Senior lieutenant. I stood there for a minute or two before he raised his head. 'Sit down,' he pointed to the chair by the desk.

Without another word, he went on scribbling. I looked around. This was my first visit to a Soviet militia station and it was not a small town affair. I was in the militia headquarters for south Kazakhstan. The room was large, the walls were dark brown, and the lino on the floor was also brown and shiny. The office smelled of floor polish and stale tobacco. No wonder: even now, so early in the day, the ashtray on the desk was overflowing with cigarette ends; not twists of *makhorka* in half-burned squares of newspaper but real cigarettes. Near the door there was the inevitable spittoon. Not the cheap white enamel type but brass. Another shiny spittoon stood at the side of the officer's desk, for his personal use, no doubt.

Filing cabinets and a low table in the corner of the room, with two brown leather armchairs next to it, completed the furniture.

Then the man stopped scribbling and got down to business. He knew my quest before I had a chance to state it. He silenced me with a raised arm and started looking through our application forms. Next, he opened the packet of photographs. 'So, as your father works in the Polish *Delegatura*,' he said, 'it's just a formality.' But, formality or not, he scrutinised the application forms and looked carefully at each one of the sixteen identical photographs of me. With every photograph he looked up, as if comparing each photo separately with the face in front of him. This took several minutes. Would Mother and Father have to come in person? But no, he did not even bother to look at their photographs. 'Your mother and father,' he said. It was a statement of fact, not a question.

Then he looked at me again. 'Just a formality,' he repeated as he waved his hand dismissively at the documents on his desk. 'My secretary can deal with all that while we have coffee.' He got up. '*Pozhaluysta*, please, *gospodín* Vaydyenfyeld.' He called me 'mister' and pronounced my name punctiliously, motioning me to one of the armchairs by the low table. He took the other.

I couldn't believe my ears. It was the first time ever that anybody called me *gospodín*. The word itself had been abolished, thrown out, had ceased to exist at the time of the revolution. And now, here, in the Chimkent militia headquarters, I was being addressed as *gospodín*. It was incredible. An inhabitant of the USSR was either a *grazhdanin*, citizen, or a *tovarishch*, comrade, the latter epithet being reserved – strictly speaking – for members of the Party. Now I was an officially recognised foreigner, *gospodín*, no less!

He offered me a cigarette, a Kazbek – an excellent brand. Should I take one for Father? But I thought better of it. *Noblesse oblige*. 'Mister' had to keep up appearances. 'Thank you,' I said, 'I don't smoke.'

A grey-haired woman walked in. 'Please, take these.' The officer pointed to our papers and the packet of photographs on the desk. 'Have the permits prepared, while *gospodín Vaydyenyfeld* waits here with me. Send us some coffee, please, will you?'

After that we talked, or rather he talked. He was used to dealing with foreigners, he admitted. He liked them. 'Well-mannered people,' he said. '*Kulturnyye*,' he added.

He had been on the staff of the Soviet consulate in Teheran – his only posting abroad. 'What a city,' he said. 'Amazing. Shops open until late at night, one could get anything, no need to stock up on food, cigarettes, soap. There were no queues, no shortages. Even toilet paper was freely available in ordinary shops. The restaurants . . . steaks, *shashliks* [kebabs], foreign wines, anything.'

He grew silent and went on puffing on his cigarette. For a minute or two he was far away, dreaming of Teheran. Then he looked straight in my eyes. 'Tell me: Warsaw, before the war, was it also like that? Did ordinary people live well?'

I did not know what to say. I had known Warsaw before the war, but I had only a vague idea about the circumstances of working-class people. Confronted by any other Russian, I would have painted the life in pre-war Poland in rosy colours. That's what every refugee did. I would only be telling my own partial truth, of course. But I knew nothing about my inter-locutor, except that he was a militiaman and had to be a Party member. Why was he asking me a leading question?

The arrival of coffee, real aromatic coffee, with milk and sugar, and with a plateful of biscuits, gave me time to think of an answer. I had to play safe. I was busy drinking and eating. Slowly . . . rolling every mouthful about in my mouth. Real coffee!

'It was all right,' I said. 'We belonged to the class of working *intelligentsia*.' That much he knew anyway. 'And I was at school. I liked school.' In quest for time I was trying to change the subject.

He appeared to be satisfied with my answer, or he had given up. 'Have another biscuit,' he said. 'She won't be long with your permits.' He went back to his desk and picked up another bundle of papers and forgot about me. Thank God. He might have been perfectly genuine in his interest in pre-war Warsaw, but could you trust a Soviet policeman? Better to be on the safe side.

I waited for a few more minutes until the secretary returned. The officer checked the documents, handed them to me, nodded, and his eyes returned to the papers on his desk. I thanked him. Without looking up, he returned my 'Goodbye'. No more of the *gospodín* nonsense, no hand-shaking. Did I imagine that ten minutes earlier the same man was taking coffee with me, dreaming of Teheran?

We lived in Uyúk, with Yevdokya and Volodya for about four months. Grisha, her younger son, had left the day we moved in. At the time of parting Yevdokya constantly dabbed at her eyes and went on hugging the boy and wouldn't let him go. '*Ryadi boha*, good God!' exclaimed Volodya. 'He is only going to Dzhambul, a hundred kilometres away, to the FZO.'

'What is an FZO?' I asked.

'An Industrial Training School,' explained Volodya. Eventually, his mother let Grisha go. Short and slender, with a small plywood suitcase in his hand, wearing a coat he had long outgrown, Grisha cut a pathetic figure as he kept turning his head and waving . . . waving . . . until he vanished round the corner.

Having let us the room, Yevdokya and Volodya moved into

the kitchen. Volodya was permanently on night shift in the power station and returned home about 7 a.m. The two of them shared one palliasse on the hard earth floor, the mother slept on it at night and the son in the daytime. I worried about his nights off, but I needn't have done. Volodya worked seven nights a week and on Sundays he had to 'volunteer' for work, whether he wanted to or not.

'You should not worry about them,' said Mother. 'They can do with the money. Volodya has his wages, but they need more. Yevdokya told me that she gave Grisha a few roubles to take with him and had promised to send him a few more each week. "Volodya is a very good brother and a very good son," Yevdokya said, "but he does not earn a lot." She has no pension. You needn't worry, Stefanku,' she repeated.

Then she added, 'Nobody seems to know whether her husband is alive or dead. We are not hurting them. It was their own choice.'

That was not the end of our landlady's and her son's hardship. Several weeks after our arrival in Chimkent, a new secretary, a Mrs Kempińska, joined the staff of the *Delegatura*. Like so many other Polish women in the USSR, she knew nothing of the whereabouts of her husband, arrested as soon as the Red Army invaded Poland. At present, she and her ten-year-old daughter were sharing one room with an elderly couple. She was desperately looking for a room of their own. One day Mrs Kempińska asked Father whether our landlady might know of a room to let. The next day she moved into our kitchen, Yevdokya and Volodya moved into the stables and the donkey moved into the yard, tied to the tree.

Life in Chimkent developed its own rhythm. Every morning Father would embark on his thirty minutes' walk through the wasteland to the *Delegatura* in the centre of the town. I helped my mother with the chores at home and then would accompany her in the daily search for food and other essentials. We had to collect our rations in shops in town, but all extras had to be bought in our small local market by the railway station. Our diet was much the same as in Chirakchi: regular bread – rationed of course – flat bread, onions, mutton fat, yogurt, dried fruit, occasionally eggs, rarely a chicken or a piece of mutton.

Sometimes Mother bought a sugar beet, which – boiled and cut into pieces – we could pretend were sweets.

Father's pay at the *Delegatura* was good, but he did not enjoy his work. Most of it was administrative: dealing with matters of public health, trying to get hold of medicines which were not generally available, trying to make sure that the diet of Polish refugees was adequate – an altogether impossible task. His work included trips to branch offices in various regions of south Kazakhstan. In addition he had to look after the health of staff and to treat sick Polish refugees in towns, villages and collective farms. There was little he could do for them, other than use his good bedside manner and give reassurance. More often than not he travelled by car, which was safe, yet sometimes he had to use the train, which involved a serious risk of contracting typhus.

Food in the market was expensive and shopping expeditions to town were soul destroying; hours were spent standing in queues. One afternoon rumour had it that a particular bakery had received extra supplies of flour, so that the following day bread would be sold there in addition to rations. The opportunity was too good to miss. The rumour reached us through our landlady, Yevdokya. 'One of you'd better get there in the evening,' she advised Mother. 'The queue will be starting then.'

I left Uyúk after the evening meal. Father looked at me sadly and Mother tried to object. 'You don't have to go, really. We can manage.'

'I shall be all right,' I assured her.

Our landlady had been right. By the time I got to the bakery the queue already stretched round the corner. There were two hundred people, perhaps more. It was getting cold, but I was wearing my winter coat, which had served me well enough in Kvasha. It was February and nights were frosty. Groups of strangers, Russians, Kazakhs, women, youngsters and old people, sat on the pavement in groups huddling together for warmth.

Within a minute of my arrival somebody asked me the ritual question, 'Are you the last one in the queue? I'll be next to you, then.' The queue kept growing.

'They'll never bake that much bread,' remarked someone behind me. 'Half of that extra flour has already gone under the counter. No use waiting.' But we waited just the same. Stories and jokes were exchanged freely at first, then people started nodding off. I spent most of the night squeezed between two Russian *babushkas*, soft and warm – perhaps they only looked like *babushkas*, wrapped as they were in their big shawls; they were talking quietly about their menfolk in the army.

I woke up in the morning to people stirring, stretching, straightening their coats and hats. One by one they went into bushes, behind trees, into side streets. Men one way, women the other. Always making sure that they would be recognised in the queue by the person in front and the person behind; one couldn't afford to lose one's precious place.

The queue started moving. It was proceeding quite quickly. By 8 a.m. I was only some twenty paces from the bakery's door. A woman customer came out and announced loudly, 'They allow one loaf per head and there are only fifty loaves left.' Happily clutching the big brown loaf to her bosom she hurried away. I counted the heads in front of me, I couldn't be sure, about fifty. I ought to wait, I decided.

I got inside at last. There were only six people in front of me and I counted the loaves on the shelves: seven. Just enough for me, what luck.

Then a woman walked in. I had not seen her in the queue. She carried her belly before her like a badge of office. Was she pregnant? More likely she had she padded herself out with a cushion. Armed with her priority, she swept past me and claimed the last loaf. My loaf! I left the shop empty-handed. I was livid and swore under my breath.

One afternoon Father returned to Uyúk with a Polish boy who was almost exactly my age. His name was Szymek. He had arrived in Chimkent several days earlier and found his way to the *Delegatura*. Intelligent and enterprising, he had taken to doing little jobs for the staff. He had been allowed to sleep in one of the offices and soon managed to make himself indispensable. Within a week he was appointed office junior, found lodgings and became the youngest member of the *Delegatura*. Szymek had a remarkable gift: he was an expert briber. Whether the required item was a railway ticket, a pack of carbon paper, a typewriter ribbon, a bottle of ink, that desirable round stamp on a document, the use of an official car and driver, goods from a shop reserved for NKVD staff or for members of the Party, Szymek would be given a sum of money, a pair of socks, a tie, or any other goods from the store, and would invariably succeed where his elders had failed.

The day Father brought Szymek to see us, he shared our evening meal and spent the night on our floor. After the meal the two of us went for a walk. He told me about himself. He could not be sure, but he thought he was an orphan. He was born in Poland of a Russian mother and a Polish–Jewish father. His mother left the family when Szymek was a toddler and went back to Leningrad; he could not remember her. His father brought him up single-handedly.

His war-time story was similar to ours. He and his father were deported to Siberia. Letters sent to his mother in Leningrad remained unanswered. One day, while working in the forest, Szymek's father was killed by a falling tree. Left on his own, after the amnesty, like so many of us, he travelled south and by chance found himself in Chimkent.

Szymek and I became friends. Another boy, Witek Winnicki, joined us soon after. Witek was also sixteen. His father had been a surgeon in Wilno, a Polish city, which in 1939 Stalin generously presented to Lithuania as its capital, before incorporating the whole country into the USSR several months later. After arriving in Chimkent Dr Winnicki came to my father pleading for any job in the *Delegatura*, however menial. On Father's intervention Dr Winnicki was appointed his deputy.

We spent a lot of time together, Szymek, Witek and me. We explored the streets of Chimkent. In the centre they were wide, tree lined, busy and clean. Soviet people, complete strangers, had a habit of checking and admonishing each other: 'Eh, you litterbug, pick it up. *Nye kulturno*, it's uncivilised.'

'When you take your dog for walk you ought to run with it.'

'Don't spit in the street, *Nye kulturno*.'

'Why are you wearing your felt boots in this weather?'

Butts of cigarettes, even squashed ends of *makhorka* twists, were never wasted, they were invariably picked up by tramps of either sex, by young lads, small boys even – not to be sold, but to be smoked. Every scrap of paper found some use. They were recycling, before even the word was invented.

Streets and parks were thus pleasantly clean. In the town centre, houses were in a fairly good state of repair, parks were well maintained, but the outskirts presented a very different picture. Here streets were narrow and neglected, pavements were broken up, houses dilapidated, paint peeling, and the general gloom was unrelieved by any trees or shrubs. Clean though the town centre was, it took time to get used to dead bodies that lay in the streets. It was not an unusual sight. Some bodies stayed where they dropped for the rest of the day: in the gutter, on the edge of the pavement, propped up against a tree. People died of hunger, of disease: most often typhus. Not that they were the only sign of misery. There were no beggars in the USSR, that was the theory, and no prostitutes of course. In practice, life was very different. There were many destitute people, tramps, drinkers who were not choosy: they imbibed meths, antifreeze and turpentine – with eau de Cologne being a luxury. One saw Soviet citizens dirty, in rags, dishevelled, infested and obviously homeless.

January and most of February 1942 passed uneventfully. I helped Mother and read a lot. For some reason there was no more talk about school. Perhaps my parents believed that our nomadic lifestyle and school were incompatible; or that we would be leaving the USSR before long. So I studied, mostly on my own, from my old books of physics, maths, chemistry. There was no problem left which I had not solved before in many different ways, there was no page in my history or literature books which I hadn't already read a hundred times. I read poems by Pushkin and Lermontov, novels by Tolstoy and Dostoyevski. Much of the poetry I learned by heart, some I translated into Polish. I learnt Latin with Father, French with Mother.

Towards the end of February, Father came home with plenty of gossip and a bit of firm news. The news was that American charities had discovered the existence of Polish refugees in the USSR and that American gifts would be arriving any day. The most important bit of gossip was that the Polish Army was preparing for evacuation from the USSR to Persia, with their families.

The tale of American gifts would require a chapter of its own. The gifts consisted of clothes, second-hand but some as good as new, footwear, non-perishable foodstuffs. They arrived in large wooden crates. What surprised us at first was the discrepancy between the size of the crates and their scanty contents. The reason became clear later: the Polish store-keeper and his few selected cronies hit on a clever idea for lining their pockets. This mafia took delivery of the crates, which they then turned upside down, carefully prised open and removed the more desirable items. The list of contents was invariably but conveniently lost and the loss blamed on the Soviets. The next day the boxes, now the right way up, would be officially opened under the watchful eyes of a committee and their contents officially listed. The mystery of the half-empty crates was not solved for several weeks. We only learned about it after we left Chimkent and I don't know what punishment was meted out to the thieves. I hoped they would be sent back to Siberia to work on the ice road.

The rank and file of needy Poles saw little of these American gifts. Those who were close to the source benefited most. Father, though employed by the *Delegatura*, claimed nothing for himself. My less-than-five-foot-tall mother was given a summer dress designed for a giant, while I became the proud owner of a bluish-grey gabardine trenchcoat. This coat, with epaulettes, fitted me well. In one of its pockets I found a bright new coin, one American cent. I liked to think that someone put it there for luck, and it worked – in several ways.

One evening, when Szymek, Witek and I were going to the cinema, for a prank I fastened the gold coin to a piece of red ribbon and pinned it to my lapel, just like one of those miniature decorations soldiers wear. The cashier took one look at it and allowed me in without a ticket. I was surprised but didn't object. 'She took you for an allied airman,' said Witek. 'An *ordenonosyets*, a medal bearer at that. I read in *Pravda* the other day that Australian fliers had arrived in Baku to help to defend the Caucasian oil fields. It might be true, even though it was published in *Pravda*.'

The film, one of the many we saw in Chimkent during the winter, was American, with subtitles. Its Russian title was *Sto*

Muzhchin i Odna Devochka (*A Hundred Men and a Girl*) with Deanna Durbin.

Generally speaking, foreign films were a rarity in the USSR. But this particular one and Charlie Chaplin's *The Modern Times*, depicting unemployment and the rapacious industrial practices in the USA, were being shown again and again. They were thought to be good propaganda, *kosher*, though the propaganda sometimes misfired.

The cinema was packed. At one point in the film, a poor, unemployed musician, played by Edward G. Robinson, returns home and takes a piece of chicken out of the fridge for his lunch. A loud whisper rose in the cinema: '*Smotri, kuritsu yest*, Look, he is eating chicken!' The voices rose, the excited audience almost shouting, 'Chicken! Chicken!' Chicken, their most festive food . . . an unemployed man eating chicken, that was not what the Party had been telling them.

On the way out I saw my reflection in a large mirror in the cinema corridor. Under my new coat I wore my old Polish school uniform: navy-blue jacket, navy-blue trousers with thin, light-blue stripes down the sides, and my navy-blue peaked school cap with light-blue trim, on which I had replaced the school badge with a silver Polish eagle. My one-cent decoration shone in my lapel. It all looked genuine. I had discovered the magic of a uniform.

In weeks to come my friends and I found we were on to a good thing. Using my new 'identity' we managed to trick our way into shops without queuing and get butter, cheese, sugar, rings of sausage, all the rare and sought-after items. We could get into cinemas without payment and without waiting. Bravado, insolence, *chutzpah*, call it what you will, but in a communist society one learned the tricks or one went under.

One day I discovered an interesting bookshop, but the discovery was to put me on a path of conflict with Volodya.

Readable books were difficult to get in Chimkent. Again and again I read the Russian classics I had appropriated in Kvasha. In the Chimkent library they had more of them, as well as numerous translations of Dickens (which, according to their forewords, depicted life in contemporary England), Jack London and other strictly selected western authors. I liked browsing through bookshops. This particular one, near the *Delegatura*, was large and its shelves were well stocked, but the choice was disappointing: *Collected Works of Stalin*, volumes of Lenin, *Das Kapital* by Marx. Pamphlets, brochures and booklets: *Questions of Leninism, Questions of Stalinism, Short History of the Communist Party of USSR* – all required reading for candidate members of the Party.

On this particular day I could not find anything of interest, so for want of anything better to do I leafed through a political booklet with drawings and photographs; page one held a full-size photo of Stalin. I was fingering the pages and was about to replace the pamphlet on the shelf, when a thought struck me: the paper was unusually soft, the size was just right, it cost less than a newspaper, so I bought it. Tearing the pages out and hanging a fresh wad in our privy was the most natural act, with only a *soupçon* of mischief to it.

It was bad luck that it was Volodya who found himself with the photograph of Stalin in his hand. He stormed into our room. 'Do you want to see us all arrested?' he shouted. 'Deported to Siberia, or put against the wall and shot like dogs? Do you? Do you?' This usually quiet and composed man was livid, trembling with rage. He did not know whom to blame, but it had to be one of us.

He looked at my mother, then at me. Father had just returned from work and we were about to have our evening meal. 'Calm down, Volodya,' said Father, 'and tell me what this is all about.'

I confessed my guilt and was told off. The gravity of the deed was spelled out to me. Perhaps I had been childish, silly, or simply naive. I never revenged myself on Stalin this way again, however tempting and however soft the paper. We reverted to using newspapers, saving a page every day for Volodya's *makhorka* twists. His fear gone, he forgave me.

Weeks followed weeks. Some time in March, Mr Kościał-kowski, the Chimkent delegate, returned from one of his trips to the Polish Embassy in Kuybyshev and brought with him brand-new Polish passports, such as those that used to be issued before the war for Polish citizens to travel abroad. They were elegant booklets, bound in navy-blue cloth with the Polish eagle stamped on the cover. Mother's passport was number 007,

Father's was 008 and mine was 009. Having an official identity raised our morale.

Soon after, Father was called to the Polish Army Head-quarters in Yangi-Yul, a small town near Tashkent, about a hundred kilometres south of Chimkent. He returned the same evening. He had agreed to serve on the Army Recruiting Board, a job which involved a lot of travel. Mother was not happy. The unusually severe winter epidemic of typhus was still raging and rail travel greatly increased the risk of contracting the disease. In 1942, before the advent of antibiotics, the mortality rate for typhus was between fifty and sixty per cent.

Father returned from his first trip well but upset. On the train, in Dzhambul, he met, quite by chance, Jurek Makowski, one of my mother's nephews. He had asked him to come and live with us in Chimkent, but the boy would not hear of it. Jurek was about eighteen. Before the war he had lived with his parents and sister in Łódź and I did not really know him, having met him only once in my life. His fate had also taken him to Siberia and after the amnesty he too found himself in Central Asia. He was now keeping his body and soul together by the profitable but dangerous occupation of trading. When Father came across him, Jurek was on his way north to central Russia with a sack of pepper, a commodity that was scarce there. He was a *spekulant*, a persecuted species. The 'speculators', the illegal though courageous entrepreneurs, were hunted down and severely punished in the USSR. Yet they fulfilled an important function: they bought specific goods where they were available and transported them to where they were wanted but unobtainable. In the USSR, a country with a practically non-existent distribution system, the speculators filled a gap and thus made good profits. The danger of the job lay not only in a prison sentence, if caught, but in the travellers' inevitable infestation and the high risk of contracting louse-borne typhus. I don't know what happened to my cousin, Jurek; we never heard of him again.

Father returned in a gloomy mood after the second expedition; he disliked the way the Board worked. Before the war some thirty per cent of Poland's population belonged to either religious or ethnic minorities; in the eastern part of

Poland, by now incorporated into the USSR, the proportion was even higher. The Soviet representative, invariably present at the Board's sittings, refused to recognise Polish Jews, Ukrainians and Belorussians – all citizens of Poland – as Poles. The Russian's job was to veto the recruitment of any man or woman who, because of their name, look or accent, might be suspected of belonging to one of the minorities. The Polish members of the Board fought tooth and nail over any Ukrainian or Belorussian born in the territories annexed by the USSR, but raised no objections to rejecting people with Jewish-sounding names, even those born in central and western Poland. 'I only had the medical regulations to go by,' Father told us. 'I could not get my hands on any relevant written instructions. What they were doing was probably illegal and the result of an inborn, instinctive anti-Semitism. On the other hand it could have been officially sanctioned. This, to my mind, would have made it even worse.'

We never found out.

Disaster struck in early March, after Father's third trip with the Board. He returned home more tired than usual. Several days later he developed a high fever and headache. Was it typhus?

My world turned upside down. Father's deputy, Dr Winnicki, had no doubt as to the diagnosis and Father was admitted to the Railway Hospital, which was supposed to be the best hospital in Chimkent. The clinician in charge was a Romanian–Jewish refugee, Dr Goldring, whom Father had met before. The hospital was reasonably well appointed; it had a pathological laboratory and an X-ray department. Yet two patients per bed was the rule; my mother, however, bribed the sister in charge and Father had a bed for himself in a separate cubicle – almost a private room.

Nursing was a problem: it was virtually non-existent. There were very few nurses, while those present did not show any interest in a patient until several roubles had been placed in their apron pocket. Even finding a nurse to bribe was a problem. They were also, in Mother's opinion, poorly trained. Mother decided that she herself would nurse Father. She took to sleeping curled up at the foot of his bed. Nobody objected.

Food was another problem. *Kipyatok* was available on tap in the corridor, but there was no provision for regular meals, and this was reputedly the best hospital in the province. I helped Mother at Father's bedside as much as I could, but it fell to me to supply all the food. Even the constant round of markets and shops, the hours of queuing, did nothing to assuage my growing anxiety and did not keep the black thoughts away.

It was the waiting which was hard: the days were long and the nights even longer. Father was not getting any better; every day he was weaker, his face thinner, his features more and more drawn. He was shrinking, literally. On my way to the hospital I fervently hoped, almost prayed, to find him alive. On the way back to Uyúk this hope was replaced by a nagging feeling that this might have been the last time I would see him alive.

Whenever Mother was out of the cubicle, Father would look into my eyes, squeeze my hand and say softly. 'Look after your mother, Stefanku, look after your mother.' Then, exhausted, he would shut his eyes and let go of my hand.

One day – it was the end of the first or the start of the second week – he did not recognise me any more, though he looked at me with his eyes wide open. Mother's lower lip trembled as she said 'He has been drifting in and out of consciousness like that since last night.' I sat at the edge of the bed. I sat there for an unconscionably long time, as Father's eyes opened and closed, opened and closed unseeingly. His breaths came in short gasps.

Mother picked up the jug from the stool at the bedside, it was full. 'I will be back in a few minutes,' she said. 'I'll get fresh *kipyatok*.' She left the room.

As soon as the door shut behind her, my father opened his eyes. I sat on the edge of the bed. He grasped my hand: 'I won't make it . . . my lungs . . .' he said. He squeezed my hand a little harder. 'When . . . over . . . mother . . . unable . . . Kościałkowski . . . will help . . . both . . . go to Yangi-Yul . . . find General . . . Boruta . . . go . . . Persia . . .' He stopped as Mother returned with the jug of boiled water. Her eyes were red.

'Doctor Goldring,' she whispered to me, 'wants to see you in his office. He wouldn't tell me why.'

'Your father has double pneumonia,' said Dr Goldring. 'He may still have a chance, a small chance, mind you, if we give him a course of sulphonamide. It is a new chemical antibacterial drug. I can't get it. You must try the black market.' He got up, walked quietly to the door. He opened it in one quick movement. There was no one listening. He closed it softly and returned to his chair behind the desk. 'Do all you can. I need fifty-six tablets, one week's course. It will cost you a lot of money, but your mother said that you could manage. Try this man,' and he passed me a slip of paper with a name and address on it, 'don't mention my name.' Mayakovsky Street. I wasn't quite sure where it was. 'It's near the railway station. Get it as soon as possible,' he continued. 'Go there right now. Get some camphor too, to sustain the heart.' A forced smile, like a flash of lightning, crossed his face and he waved me off impatiently.

I found the street and the house. It was a tailor's workshop. A small shop front in a street of workshops and warehouses, not far from our hut. I looked in through the window and saw a silver-haired woman sitting behind a table, stitching a piece of cloth, her nose practically touching it. In the middle of the room, at another table, an old man was ironing. I had not expected a pharmacy, but a tailor's shop? The name on my paper sounded Armenian. The man did not look Russian, nor Kazakh; he could be an Armenian.

I pushed the door open. 'Come in, come in,' he said in good Russian. 'Do you want some repairs done? If you want new trousers you have to bring your own material.'

'Are you citizen Arkanadyan?' I asked.

He nodded, stopped pressing and replaced his solid iron on the kitchen range in the corner of the room. 'Yes,' he said. 'What of it?'

'I have come about some supplies, medicines,' I said. 'Can you help?' I stopped and looked at the woman, who did not take her eyes off the cloth in her hands.

'Maybe, depends. Never mind her, she is my wife,' he said as he ran his eyes over me slowly from top to bottom and up again, as if taking my measurements for a suit.

I decided to tell the truth. 'My father is in hospital. He has double pneumonia . . .'

'That's not my business,' interrupted the man, silencing me with a gesture. 'Tell me what you want. That's all I need to know. Simple? No?'

I looked at the woman. She stopped stitching and her eyes met mine. She smiled a kind smile and nodded gently, as if to say, 'It's all right, boy. Tell him what you need.'

I took a deep breath: 'I need fifty-six tablets of sulphonamide and a box of camphor in ampoules for injection. I can pay well . . .'

'Of course, you'll have to pay well, no use coming to me without money. You'll need a lot of it, sulphas cost 500 roubles per tablet, so fifty-six tablets will come to 28,000 roubles. You can have them tonight. I don't know about the other stuff. Write it down for me, maybe we can throw it in.'

My heart was sinking fast. I had only 2,000 roubles in my pocket. I had no idea what to expect; but . . . twenty-eight thousand roubles! Over the last six months Father's reserve of money had shrunk considerably. It was hidden in the recess behind the table drawer and it came to just over 20,000; though this was a great deal of money, it was not enough and we had no more.

The man read what was on my mind. 'People recover with a five-day course, forty tablets, 20,000 roubles. Give me 1,000 on account now.' He stretched out his hand. I turned my back to him, reached for the wad of bank-notes fixed with a safety pin to my inside coat pocket, and counted out one hundred red ones.

He said: 'Come back at 9 p.m. with the money.'

I left and walked home in a daze. I had seven hours to raise the money, but how? Where? What to do next? I was asking myself the same questions again and again. My eyes were damp and I dried them with the back of my hand. When I got home Yevdokya opened her mouth to say something, but I just nodded to her, rushed to our room, closed the door behind me and fell on my bed. Suddenly I felt very hungry. I had had nothing to eat since the morning. I found a chunk of flat bread and got a glass of water from the *choogoon*. I wiped my face with a wet towel. I must think . . . think . . . think. We had no friends, no acquaintances with even a thousand roubles to spare, nobody had that kind of money. Should I go to the Delegate? I was prepared to beg . . . Then something stirred in my mind.

Several weeks earlier Mr Talarek, the deputy chief of the

Delegatura and a former trade union leader, had fallen ill. Was it typhus? I didn't know. Perhaps some other infection. Father had been trying to get some new antibacterial tablets for him, perhaps sulphonamides. He had failed and the man had died. 'What a pity,' said Father. 'They expected the consignment to arrive any day, but it was too late for the poor man.' Who were 'they'?

That was some weeks ago. Perhaps 'they' had the stuff now. But what was the stuff? And who were 'they'? It must have been some Soviet authority, but which one?

Suddenly it dawned on me: *Glavaptekoupravlyenye*, Central Administration of Pharmacies. I knew the building, it was on the way to the *Delegatura*.

In an instant I knew what I had to do: I had to get to somebody at the top. The problem was how to pass the doorman. I changed into my old school uniform, I put on my American coat and my peaked school cap, I grabbed my residence permit and the rest of the money from its hiding place and rushed out of the hut like a madman. I ran most of the way through the wasteland. Thoughts kept flashing through my mind like racing cars in a film seen long ago.

The doorman was an old, officious man. 'I represent the Polish *Delegatura* in Chimkent,' I said. 'Our medical officer is ill and there are matters I must discuss with your director.' The doorman was suspicious and asked to see my papers. I showed him my residence permit. I was a foreigner but the round rubber stamp confirmed the legality of my existence. He kept looking at the document this way and that and, eventually, he disappeared with it behind a door.

Several minutes later he was back, without my document. I followed him to another room and he showed me to a chair by a desk. A short bald man entered the room through another door and sat down behind the desk. He took off his gold pince-nez and wiped the lenses with a cloth, then he put his pince-nez on again and looked at my residence permit deposited on his desk. '*Gospodín* Vaydyenfyeld,' he read. 'What can I do for you? Do I know the name?'

Was it a warning? Once more I decided to speak the truth. I told him about my father: 'He was here several weeks ago.

Looking for sulphonamides' – I could only assume that this was the medicine my father had wanted – 'for the Polish Deputy Delegate. Now it is my father's turn; he has typhus and double pneumonia.' Tears were welling in my eyes. I did my best not to blink, not to let them spill over. He looked at me sympathetically. 'Father told me at the time that you were expecting a consignment of the drug, but it was too late for Mr Talarek . . . he died.'

'I'll see what I can do,' he said, got up and left the room. I was left alone for several minutes. A telephone conversation was taking place behind the closed door. I listened carefully but in vain.

A woman walked in. She brought a tray with two glasses of tea, slices of lemon and square lumps of sugar. The telephone conversation stopped and the man returned: 'I am really sorry about your father, such a nice man. We do need doctors. *Pozhaluysta*, please.' He put a cube of sugar in his mouth and started sipping his tea noisily, as he pushed the other glass towards me.

Will I get the medicine? I wondered. Have I got enough money? Surely it is less expensive here than on the black market.

Another woman, in a white coat, walked in and placed a small packet in brown paper on the desk. 'Here it is, *tovarishch direktor*,' she said.

'Good. Thank you,' said the man behind the desk. 'Did you remember to put in a box of camphor?' he asked.

'Naturally. One box, twelve ampoules.'

'Wish your father a rapid recovery,' said the man pushing the parcel towards me. 'Oh, but finish your tea, you look all in.'

I could have jumped for joy.

I looked at the parcel again. I could not believe my own eyes. There, on top of it, was the invoice: 6.40r – six roubles and forty kopecks. I put ten roubles on the box. The woman picked it up and returned with the change.

I thanked *tovarishch direktor*, I thanked the lady. Then I ran all the way to the hospital. There and then I decided to forget the thousand roubles I had given to the Armenian. 'Just in time,' said Dr Goldring. He was a man of few words.

The next morning Father was better. He was fully conscious and his breathing was easier. By the evening he even smiled at me, and he was asking for food. Over the next few days I doubled and trebled my efforts to find the things he liked. I found a contact in a bakery and organised a supply of fresh rolls and bread. I discovered that Yevdokya's brother was a storeman in a *kolkhoz* and walked twenty kilometres to see him. This resulted in twice weekly access to butter and curd cheese. It all cost the earth and the moon – and most other celestial bodies – but I did not mind. Having dispensed with the good offices of the Armenian, I had plenty of money left. Father was fond of fresh fruit, but finding fruit in the early spring in Chimkent seemed a total impossibility. Yevdokya, however, pointed me to a market, which was new to me, at the other end of town. I wandered about and then suddenly I spied two red apples on a peasant woman's stall. A miracle! I asked no questions. I grabbed both and paid thirty roubles, almost a tenth of a Soviet doctor's monthly pay. Extravagant? I didn't think so.

People helped: Mrs Kempińska knew somebody in a state pharmacy and wangled some vitamin tablets for Father; Dr Goldring found a black-market source of an iron tonic. Did he get a cut? Even if he did, it did not matter. Father improved by leaps and bounds and at the end of March he was able to come home. Soon he was up and about, going for walks and dealing with the paperwork brought from the *Delegatura*.

Then my turn came. About a week after Father's return I developed a fever and headache. Father examined me. 'I don't know,' he said, 'I really don't know. I am not up to it, I don't trust myself, I wish I could.' Mother went to the railway station and phoned the *Delegatura*.

In the afternoon Dr Winnicki came. He half opened the door and, never entering our room, took one look at me from the threshold. 'Typhus,' he pronounced. 'No doubt. Off to the hospital.'

In the late afternoon an *arba* arrived and took me to the Railway Hospital, first to their delousing station and then to the paediatric typhus ward. The ward was painted white, the twenty beds were white too and surprisingly clean. Smaller children lay two or three to a bed but several youngsters had their own beds. I was one of the lucky ones. The sister was a motherly Kazakh woman and of the two young nurses, one was Russian and the other Kazakh. There was never a dull moment on this ward. Bodies were carried out, new patients were brought in. A young woman doctor in a white coat, a stethoscope in her pocket, kept wandering on to the ward, examining a child here, shaking her head over another one there. No visitors were allowed.

I was not hungry on the day of my admission which was just as well, as there was nothing to eat. On the second day I woke up with a good appetite. I sat up and there, on the stool by my bed, were two white rolls with butter and a glass of mock tea. The rolls were fresh and crusty, the tea was sweet. My breakfast was over in one minute; I could have done with more. I perched on the edge of the bed and looked around. There were rolls and glasses of tea by every bed – double lots by the beds with two patients. The nurses were helping some children to drink their tea, but most of the rolls were left untouched.

The sister walked in, she came to my bed and put her hand on my forehead. She took a long thermometer out of its metal cover, shook it, looked at it, shook it again and put it in my armpit. 'Hold it tight for ten minutes,' she said. Of course I knew the procedure. I lay down again. She was back ten minutes later. 'Thirty-six and six. Nothing wrong with you, but you can't go home.' This did not worry me, I had other things on my mind: I was looking at the breakfast by the bed of my neighbour who quite obviously was not going to eat it. 'You can have his rolls now,' she said and pulled the sheet over the boy's face.

That was the routine: twice a day, an hour after they were brought in, the rolls were shared by those able to eat them. In effect the three, four, or five of us, well enough to profit, had all the buttered rolls between us and as much sweet tea as we could drink.

Later in the morning the doctor came on her rounds. Whatever I had suffered from, it was certainly not typhus. 'But you will have to stay here two weeks all the same,' she said. 'Quarantine regulations, you understand, don't you? I shall talk to your mother.'

So I stayed for two weeks in a typhus ward with its rapid turnover. I did quite well on the buttered rolls with sweet tea twice a day, an occasional bowl of *shchi*, cabbage soup, and whatever else Mother brought for me. She came every day, but was not allowed on the ward. So she would come to the ward window and we would wave to one another. One day both my parents walked into the yard. Father still looked gaunt; he had taken to using a stick and was leaning heavily on it.

Time dragged and lost its meaning. I slept a lot. I got used to the cries, whimpers, moans and coughs. This background noise of the ward was disturbed from time to time by the arrival of new patients, or by the clanking trolley with rolls and tea. Sometimes, on waking up, I would witness a child being dressed to be discharged. Usually too weak to walk, the convalescent would be carried out of the ward by one of the nurses and passed into the arms of a parent waiting in the corridor. On occasions the body carried out by the nurse was rigid and covered with a sheet. Sometimes there wasn't anybody waiting.

I kept sleeping out of sheer boredom until one afternoon our Kazakh sister brought me a book. 'It will keep you awake,' she said. 'I have more books, if you want them.' It was the Russian translation of Jack London's *Call of the Wild*. The sister kept a small library in her cubicle, just right for such non-sick patients as me. There was nowhere to sit in the ward, so I spent most of the quarantine in bed reading and munching buttered rolls. I even put on weight.

On my return home life rapidly reverted to normal and in late April Father went back to work in the *Delegatura*.

We had no inkling that the branch on which we were so cosily established was being surreptitiously undercut by a man who owed so much to Father.

TWENTY

OVER AND OUT

❋

I like to think that providence had been looking after us. Providence is a kind of computerised fate, even if one does not believe in the programmer.

It all started one Wednesday evening at the end of April 1942. Father returned home from the *Delegatura* in a state of agitation – his recent illness had left him irritable and his usual self-control had been slow to recover. 'We have to leave Chimkent,' he said. 'A branch of the *Delegatura* is being opened in Kzyl-Orda. I am to organise and run the medical service for the region. It was all decided while I was ill. Winnicki is taking over here. Kościałkowski is nice enough, though weak, and he presented it to me as a challenge. "You will have a free hand," he said. "The post is independent of Winnicki. No cut in pay."'

Having delivered the shocking news, Father calmed down. He looked at Mother and at me, smiled and continued: 'There is other, better, news. Several weeks ago part of our army left for Persia. It's not a rumour this time. Kościałkowski spoke to Professor Kot, the ambassador, in Kuybyshev and Kot confirmed the news. The rest of the army is supposed to follow. Apparently, the British want the Poles in the Middle East to help protect the oilfields. There have been problems in Iraq; an insurrection of some kind.

'This presents us with an alternative. I thought it out on my way home. Obviously, we must go to Kzyl-Orda now, but not for long, I trust. The army will have me back, they said so, just as soon as I feel up to it, and I do now, really.' Then he turned to Mother. 'I hope that you have no strong objections. We'd better start packing tonight; we may have to leave at short notice, any day now. Szymek is getting the tickets; for the end of the week, if he can.'

'This is Winnicki's doing,' said Mother. 'It's so obvious: he was after your job. He has coveted it since he came here. I never liked the man. From the very beginning he has given himself airs, throwing his weight about, the great surgeon from Wilno. You were too kind to him when he arrived, as usual. You could have easily had him packed off to some provincial post.'

Father's new posting was a demotion. The Kzyl-Orda branch was only one of several outposts of the Chimkent *Delegatura*, though most had no medical officers. Yet the town was about the same size as Chimkent. There was even a Kzyl-Ordinskaya province. We had passed the town on our way south from Siberia. It lay on the Syr-Darya river about eight hundred kilometres north-west of Chimkent and could probably be reached after an overnight train journey – not another cattle wagon, I hoped.

In the evening we packed our belongings, except for the essentials. Next day, Thursday, was our cinema evening. I went to the cinema as usual, but neither Szymek nor Witek came. Pity. The film, *Posledniy Tabor*, The Last Camp, was quite good. It was about the resettlement of gypsies and how the Party, in their wisdom, put an end to their nomadic way of life – not that the gypsies had been given any choice, of course.

On Saturday morning Szymek came to Uyúk with our train tickets. I happened to be in the yard. 'Sorry,' he said handing me the envelope. 'I couldn't get sleepers. The tickets are for tonight. Sleepers are booked only for the entire train journey from Alma-Ata to Moscow. Say goodbye to your parents from me.' He turned on his heels to leave and then turned back to me saying, 'It's Witek's old man's doing. He's a nasty character. *Chort s nim*, to hell with him,' he swore in Russian. 'He is in cahoots with the store-room gang, too, I think.' Then he was gone. Naturally, now he would have to keep on the right side of Witek.

❈ ❈ ❈

I met Szymek again some twenty-five years later. By then he was well established in the USA, a successful businessman, a millionaire, a high flyer with a slightly crooked flight path, or at least that was my impression.

❀ ❀ ❀

So, on a beautiful, warm Saturday evening, we said goodbye to Yevdokya and Volodya, to Mrs Kempińska and Zosia, and embarked on another journey. Mrs Kempińska and her daughter could move, at last, from the kitchen into our room, but they seemed sorry to see us go.

How different this train journey was from all the previous ones. In fact, only the trek to the station was more of the same: the same *arba* with the same well-fed, handsome mule, the same driver. But we didn't spend hours or days waiting. There was a crowd at the station, of course, but we had tickets for soft seats, the equivalent of first class, on the Alma-Ata–Moscow passenger train. It ran on schedule and we didn't have to wait with the crowd, only people with reserved seats for this particular train were allowed onto the platform. I counted a dozen of us, mainly officers and officials. They were men in the main; well dressed, with leather attaché cases or small suitcases in their hands. No refugee families, no tramps in rags. No lice on the soft seats either, I hoped. There were no classes in the Soviet trains – a true classless society. The hard seats – wooden benches – were cheaper, for the plebs; but not for us! We had gone up in the world: from cattle wagons to soft seats. It was quite a leap.

A whistle, a series of puffs, a few jolts and we were on our way. This time we knew our destination and the time of arrival: tomorrow, early afternoon.

'A room has been rented for us,' said Father. 'We are supposed to be met at the station and transport is to be provided.' That sounded good. There were to be some compensations after all. The overnight journey was uneventful.

In Kzyl-Orda a man from the office was indeed waiting for us, with a peasant cart, its Russian driver and a well-kept horse. He took us straight to our room in Aralskaya Street. The street was just an ordinary, small-town street, planted with trees, each adorned with the usual canine visiting cards. The room was part of a three-room flat on the upper storey of a small two-storey house. We shared the kitchen, bathroom and toilet with the inhabitants of the other two rooms. The ground-floor flat had its own separate kitchen, bathroom and toilet; a luxury by Soviet standards. Our room was large, with two windows giving on to the street, and it was furnished with a double bed, a big wooden wardrobe, a table and several chairs. I slept on a palliasse on the floor.

On the day of our arrival, when we were about to have our evening meal of bread and butter with real tea, all brought from Chimkent, there was a knock on the door. It was our new neighbour, a tall slim woman with silver hair gathered in a bun.

Father and I got up. 'My name is Tatyana Alexandrovna Preobrazhenskaya,' the newcomer introduced herself and shook hands all round. 'Your cart driver told me,' she said, 'that you have come from Chimkent today. You must be tired. Please, don't bother to make tea. Come to our room and have it with us. I have made a lot of savoury rice and some rice cakes, enough for all of us. We are just across the corridor. My son, Nikolay Grigoryevich, will be so pleased to meet you.'

There was something particularly likeable about Tatyana Alexandrovna. 'It's her aristocratic bearing,' Mother said after she was gone.

That was the beginning of our friendship with the neighbours. At first they treated us with reserve – in the USSR people did not trust one another, personal questions were out, your true political views and your past were taboo. So, our first evening at the Preobrazhenskis was not very informative. We learned one thing, though: rice was abundant in Kzyl-Orda and in the surrounding area. It was being grown by the Koreans, resettled (i.e. deported) several years ago from the Korean border zone to the Kzyl-Ordinskaya province, about half a million of them. At least there was one positive result of mass deportations, I thought: we had an excellent meal. The rice cakes with honey were delicious. There were compensations to Kzyl-Orda.

The other room on our floor, down the corridor, was occupied by an eminently forgettable couple who kept themselves to themselves.

My parents spent many evenings in the company of Tatyana and her son. In time they began to trust us. One evening Mrs Preobrazhenskaya admitted as much. 'I only live for the sake of my son,' she said. 'He needs me, but I prefer not to think of how many times I had been on the verge of jumping off some church tower.'

She was a widow, widow of a *knyaz*, a prince, no less. Mother had been right: the Preobrazhenskiys were an old Russian aristocratic family. The prince had been murdered at the time of the revolution and Tatyana fled the estate, their house on fire, with Nicky, her ten-year-old only son. They had lived in Moscow for many years, but in the late 1930s Nicholas had been posted to the Kzyl-Orda Teacher-Training College to teach mathematics.

Our everyday life in Kzyl-Orda was utterly unmemorable, even food hunting was boring. There were queues, of course, but it was all so predictable. Bread, butter, and most other basic foodstuffs were rationed and one just had to queue for the rations. I didn't use my magic uniform in Kzyl-Orda; it was no fun on my own. Vegetables, fruit and eggs had to be bought on the market. They were very expensive but were at least available. 'It does not matter,' Father said, 'we still have money and we may just as well spend it.' I did my best, but Mother was rather more careful. Only rice was cheap and freely available in shops, with practically no queuing. So it was rice for breakfast, for dinner and for supper. After the first few weeks in Kzyl-Orda rice was coming out of our ears.

In June 1942 I went to school, to the ninth form of the local *desyatiletka*, ten-year school. But I attended it only for several weeks, until the summer holidays, and I don't remember much about it, except for one sad incident.

As with all Soviet schools, it was co-educational and I made friends with Stan and his twin sister, Irina. They were about my age, seventeen. Their mother taught us history, while their father taught physics in the Kzyl-Orda Teacher-Training College. Their first names, Stanisław and Irina, sounded Polish and, in fact, their grandfather was one of the thousands of Poles exiled to Siberia in the nineteenth century.* Stan was a member of *Komsomol*, the communist youth organisation.

In history classes we had been dealing with the aftermath of the October Revolution, the Civil War and the revolutionary tendencies throughout the industrialised world. Towards the end of the term, at the end of her last class, as she finished lecturing, our history teacher turned towards the blackboard and started chalking in big letters:

THE SUBSTITUTION OF THE PROLETARIAN FOR THE BOURGEOIS STATE IS IMPOSSIBLE

Then the bell went: end of the lesson and instant pandemonium. That was unusual. I was not familiar with Soviet schools but, so far, in the Kzyl-Orda school we had always stayed in our seats waiting for the teacher to leave first. Now most boys and girls were up, talking, shouting. Was it end-of-term fever? The teacher stopped writing, collected her notes from the desk and left without another word.

Stan, with whom I shared the bench, was quiet and still, his eyes fixed on the blackboard. Something was wrong. I followed his gaze. He seemed to have been hypnotised by the sentence written by his mother. I read it slowly again: 'The substitution of the proletarian for the bourgeois state is impossible.' The sentence was incomplete. Was it part of a slogan or of somebody's statement? No one paid any attention, except Stan. He sat there immobile and pale.

Someone wiped the blackboard clean and nobody said a word about the incomplete sentence. I thought about it on my way home. What did she mean? Impossible . . . The statement seemed wrong when you thought about it. The orthodox view was that the disappearance of the bourgeois, imperialist state was inevitable, not impossible. I was not well versed in communist theories, but I knew enough to guess that something was not

---

* Over the centuries, deporting Poles and unreliable elements had become the habit of the tsars and, later, of their Soviet successors. As the expansion of the empire proceeded at the rate of some fifty-five square miles per day, the number of deportees reached millions (as quoted by Norman Davies in *Europe – A History*, Oxford University Press, 1996, p.869).

right; the sentence, as it stood, was counter-revolutionary.

I was worried and puzzled. I spoke about it at home. Father knew the quotation. In his student days in Moscow and later in the Russian Army in the First World War he had been a member of the Social-Revolutionary Party. 'Yes,' he said. 'Lenin said that "Substitution of the proletarian for the bourgeois state is impossible without a violent revolution," or words to that effect. She had missed out the last few words, but if nobody had paid attention to it and it had been rubbed off in time, it shouldn't matter,' Father concluded. More in hope than in expectation, I thought.

Stan and Irina usually came to school with their mother. Next morning I met them on the way, but they were alone. Irina's eyes were red, she was sobbing. 'What's happened?' I asked.

Irina burst out crying. '*Podlets*, scoundrel!' she shouted.

Stan didn't say a word. I put my arm round Irina's shoulders. 'Easy, easy, Irinochka,' I said. 'Tell me what happened.'

She calmed down a little. 'Mother has been arrested,' she said. 'They came in the middle of the night. It's Stan's doing. It was his *duty*,' she spat the word out. 'Scoundrel!' she repeated. 'He went to his *Komsomol* secretary and denounced our mother for her lack of communist vigilance.' She started sobbing again. 'He is sorry now,' she said. 'Fat lot of good it will do. Idiot!'

I tried to think clearly. Stan was a *Komsomolets*, a member of the school branch of young communists, aspiring Party members. He had denounced his teacher, his own mother, and she had been arrested. I could not understand it.

I couldn't bring myself talk to Stan again. 'You'd better keep it to yourself, Irinochka,' I said when we were nearing the school. 'Dry your eyes now. Here,' I gave her my handkerchief, 'you can't help her by talking, you can only make it worse. Your father has friends in high places and he will find a way to get her released.' I didn't quite believe it, but what else could I have said?

I never saw Stan or Irina again. 'They went to stay with their grandparents in Kazalinsk,' said Nicky, who knew their father at the Teacher-Training College. But Nicky had no idea what had happened to their mother. It was too dangerous to inquire.

Generally speaking, Nicky was our main source of Kzyl-

Orda gossip. Most evenings, he and his mother played bridge with my parents, while I occasionally substituted for one of them. Sometimes he played chess with me. On one such occasion, soon after the start of the summer holidays, Nicky came to our room earlier than usual, with a warning. 'For the next few weeks, you'd better stay indoors, Stefan,' he said. 'Haymaking is going to start any day now. They will be picking up young people in the streets to pack them off to collective farms to help. Unless you want to go, of course,' he said and winked at me. 'It might be fun, or so they tell me, but rough.'

Mother was terrified: 'You are not going out. You will stay here at home. Do you hear me?'

'But Mother,' I said, 'I have no intention of going. We will be leaving Kzyl-Orda soon, won't we? And how would you find me in some *kolkhoz* when the time came? I have no intention of being left behind.'

Father's plan was to rejoin the army in Yangi-Yul, to find accommodation there and then to send for us. 'We mustn't miss the next transport to Persia,' he kept saying.

Nicky knew about Father's plans. 'I wish I could join your army,' said Nicky with a smile. 'But, seriously, do you think they might have me?' It wasn't the first time that he had tentatively asked the question. 'To be able to go abroad,' he would fantasise aloud. 'To travel . . . it's my dream. Paris, London, Nice . . . Mother used to tell me about all those places. But even before the war an application for a foreign passport would have put us in Siberia. You know, wrong social origin,' he smiled wistfully. 'But honestly, Stefan, you mustn't go out at all, the risk is too great. Should your parents have to leave without you, you could be stuck here forever. They will be on the lookout for chaps like you. Too young for the army and just right for haymaking. Stay in tomorrow and I shall make enquiries,' he concluded on a mysterious note.

The following evening Nicky gave me a piece of paper with an address and said: 'Tomorrow, go and enrol in the Technical Institute summer course for motor mechanics. Go there first thing in the morning. You'll get a student card and you will be safe, and you might learn something into the bargain – driving, perhaps.'

The following morning I joined a queue of dozens of boys and girls, mostly my age, and enrolled in the motor mechanics course. The student card in my pocket made me feel better, once more I was free to roam the streets of Kzyl-Orda; not that there was much to roam. In any event, nobody stopped me and I never had to show my card; perhaps the masquerade was unnecessary. On the other hand, I did hear of people who were sent to collective farms.

The course started on Monday at 8 a.m. The room was only half full. Did some others, like me, enrol only to get the student card? The morning lecture was interesting: the basics of the internal combustion engine. I knew the theory, but not in such detail. In the afternoon we left the classroom for the backyard of the Institute and divided into groups of four or five. Each group was given an old carburettor to take apart. Next afternoon we had to put it together again.

Several days passed like that: some theory in the morning – very repetitive – practical class in the afternoon. One afternoon we took the carburettor apart, next afternoon we put it together again. It was always the same carburettor. There was no point exchanging your piece of old iron with another group as they were all the same. 'Old Ford-type carburettor,' said Fyodor, a lad who had worked in an MTS – machine and tractor repair station – in the previous summer holiday and joined us to get the car-mechanic diploma and thus a chance of a job in town.

By the end of the first week every one of us could take apart and put together the carburettor with our eyes shut. So we played a kind of blind man's buff with the bits of iron junk spread out on a piece of tarpaulin. Fyodor, an old hand at the game and the only possessor of a watch, would time us as, in turns, blindfolded, we would put the carburettor together, while others kept moving the parts about.

Fyodor, Fyedya for short, was about eighteen or nineteen years old and as strong as a horse. He had a club foot and had thus avoided the draft. He was a bright lad and already a knowledgeable mechanic. And so, when halfway through the second week he suggested that we skipped the boring lesson and went swimming instead, two of us decided to join him. It was much too hot for work anyway.

We met on the bank of the Syr-Darya. It was a swampy area, part wasteland, part meadow with clumps of trees. It smelt of rotting vegetation. It stretched for a good quarter of a mile along the north bank of the river. The bank was steep, but not more than a metre high. Here and there the soil had been washed away, so that the shore was held together by roots of trees and bushes and it was easy to get one's foot trapped in the overhang. This was the only bathing place in Kzyl-Orda. Though it was referred to as the beach, it did not really deserve that lofty name and on weekdays it was practically deserted.

Here in Kzyl-Orda, some six hundred kilometres from its mouth in the Aral Sea, the Syr-Darya River was about two hundred metres wide. It was a hot summer: the sun burned, the water was warm, the current sluggish and the swimming very good. So, on weekday afternoons a group of two, three or more of us would play truant and repair to the beach. There were no repercussions at the Institute. I didn't mention it at home, Mother would only worry.

Swimming was not a popular pastime among the Kzyl-Ordians and definitely not a strong suit of my new companions. As long as you floated and managed to propel yourself along, you were 'swimming'. The only 'style' they practised was what we, the 'connoiseurs', would call the 'Cossack-style' and looked at with disdain. It was ornamental in its exaggerated arm movements, but a poor imitation of real crawl. As my fellow swimmers discovered that in true crawl and in breast-stroke I could outdistance every one of them without apparent effort, I became a 'consultant'. Within days my pupils picked up my skills and from then on competition was fierce and I had a job to keep up with them, especially with Fyedya.

Our favourite spot was a patch of grass by a clump of trees. The only other bathers were a small group of Russian men, in their thirties or forties, whose habitual place was another clump of trees, a shouting distance away from ours. We met them there every time we managed to play truant. When we arrived in the early afternoon, two, or three, or four of them would already be there and on most days they would stay behind after we had left. Soon we were exchanging greetings. Then they would come nearer to watch us training at crawl or breast-stroke, or to

spur us on in our races across the river: '*Davay, davay!*
Nazhimay! Davay! Faster! Faster! Go on! Faster, Styopa!' or
'Fyedya!' or 'Pyetya!' or whomever they fancied at the
moment. Thus I became 'Styopa', which was a rough kind of
diminutive for my Russified name, Stepan.

Before long I was teaching our new friends the crawl and
breast-stroke. In time, one of them, Boris, became particularly
chummy. In my mind I christened him *Boris Godunov*. He was
the oldest and he seemed to be in charge of the group. He was
forever asking questions, especially of me: Who was I? Where
from? What did my parents do? What was life in pre-war
Poland like? Did we ever go abroad? What work had I done in
Siberia? Yes, he was very curious about Siberia. Oh, just
another inquisitive Russian, I thought, so at first I answered his
questions truthfully.

But Fyedya was more experienced. 'Be careful,' he
whispered. 'They are militiamen. From the province militia
headquarters.'

'How do you know that?' I asked. Fyedya said nothing, but
looked at the clump of trees where the men were spread out. I
followed his gaze, but didn't see anything in particular. Oh, yes,
they all sported identical blue swimming trunks. Ours were
black, the only kind available in Kzyl-Orda. Did theirs come
from a restricted shop? Perhaps that was what Fyedya had in
mind. But what did it mean? I shrugged my shoulders.

'Look in the trees,' Fyodor whispered again. Indeed, there
were greyish-blue militia tunics and trousers hanging from the
branches. I shrugged my shoulders again. I had nothing to hide,
or did I? We were playing truant. Suddenly, the threat of
haymaking loomed large for a few seconds. So what? Anyway,
life was boring. I got up and jumped in the river again.

Weeks passed. At the end of July my mechanics' course came
to an end. I passed the theoretical exam with good marks. In the
practical I had to take apart and put together . . . yes, you
guessed it, the same old carburettor. I got my diploma. During
the whole course we didn't have a single driving lesson. My
student card expired, but both haymaking and the harvest were
over and the streets of Kzyl-Orda were safe again.

At about the same time, Father at last made up his mind and

went to Yangi-Yul, to rejoin the Polish Army. He managed to get the travel permit and the ticket without difficulty and so he left.

Then one morning, in early August, I was returning from queuing for our food rations, when I saw Father waving to me from the window. I ran upstairs three steps at a time. He had come on the overnight train. He looked so different in the khaki uniform. Made of a stiff and rough drill fabric, the uniform did not fit him, but it had the captain's insignia, three silver stars, on the epaulettes, and the Cross of Valour ribbon high on the left breast. Forgetting my age and weight I jumped into my father's embrace and we just about finished on the floor. Mother laughed. 'Careful!' she shouted. 'He is still fragile.'

The next thing I noticed was our big suitcase open on the bed; Mother had been packing. 'Are we going to Persia?' I asked. And, without waiting for the answer, I grabbed Mother and we danced a polka across the room. Father burst out laughing.

'Steady, steady,' Mother tried to calm me down.

'Seriously,' said Father, 'I don't quite know when and how, but there are rumours in circulation. One train is supposed to leave Yangi-Yul for Krasnovodsk on either the tenth or the eleventh. There may be more transport at a later date, but nobody seems to know; it might, however, be the only one. The Soviets might change their mind at any time about letting us go. I have to leave tonight, my pass ends tomorrow and I have a reservation on tonight's Moscow–Tashkent train. We have to get you on it too. I was just telling Mother, I tried to get tickets to Yangi-Yul for you at the station, but they wouldn't sell them to me without permits.' He looked at his watch. It was after 2 p.m. 'We don't have much time to get the permits, only about five hours.' He brought out his wallet and counted his red ones: 'Ought to be enough,' he concluded.

We had a quick meal. 'You go with your father and I'll continue packing,' said Mother, then sceptical as usual: 'I'll leave the bedding out,' she added, 'in case we have to spend another night here.'

We started on our quest. The afternoon merged into evening while we wasted hours in waiting-rooms, in corridors outside offices of the *Gorsoviet*, the town council, the *Voyenkomat*, the

District Military Command, the Party Secretariat. Officials, Party bosses, army officers, listened politely to Father's request, but the answer was invariably *nyet*, no. Father's uniform cut no ice. 'A brick wall,' said Father as we were leaving the last office. 'This must be coming from above. Poles are on the move everywhere, trying to reach army camps in time for the evacuation. The Russians seem to be deliberately sabotaging it in any way they can.'

All hope gone, we sat down on a street bench by the Party office, our last port of call, its door closed behind us for the night. Father was worried and agitated, his power of clear thinking and his determination still affected by his long illness. 'What's the next move? What can we do now?' He kept going round in circles. 'Mother and you might have to stay here until a solution is found. Look after your mother, Stefanku.' He used the same words as on that awful day in Chimkent, in the hospital. But that time he was dying.

I looked at Father's watch; it was 6.30 p.m. All offices would be closed now. Suddenly, I had a ghost of a thought. The NKVD and the militia were bound to be open at night, that's when they did most of their work. We could not possibly try the former, put our heads in the noose, but how about the militia? Why not? 'Let's try the militia headquarters,' I said. 'They ought to be open.' Father accepted my suggestion with alacrity. He smiled. The Kzyl-Orda militia headquarters were just a short walk away and they were not only open, they were busy. People were coming in and out, in uniforms and in civvies.

Here, my father's uniform did take us as far as the duty officer. He was polite, he listened with professional attention, but the answer was still *nyet*. I was paying no attention. Sitting in the office, next to my father, I stopped listening. Something was telling me that we were in the wrong office. This was not the building I had in mind and this was not the man I wanted to see. But who was that man? Where would I find him? Suddenly I knew: the man I needed was *Boris Godunov*, my pupil from the beach. I had not seen him since the mechanics course finished over a week before, but I was sure that he would remember me. Fyedya had told me that Boris worked in the militia headquarters for the Kzyl-Orda province. Judging by the goings-on here, in the town headquarters, the province headquarters should be a hive of activity.

As we were leaving the building Father, not being privy to the turmoil inside my head, was crestfallen. I pulled at his sleeve. 'Come on, Father. Let's go. I have something else in mind.' There was no reaction. Father was miles away. I pulled his arm hard. 'Come on, I'll tell you what I mean, but let's get away from here.' I didn't want to talk with the crowd round us. The Provincial Militia Building was only several blocks away; although a provincial capital, Kzyl-Orda was not a big town. On the way I told my father about Boris.

'Probably no use,' he said, 'but we have nothing to lose. We're just clutching at straws . . .'

It was getting dark, I looked at Father's watch: 8 p.m. It was a warm evening and we had two hours before the departure time. I felt elated. I had a premonition that Boris was going to help us. It was totally irrational. He might want to help, but would it be within his power? Would he be there at all?

The building was small, two-storey and unexpectedly tranquil, silent and almost deserted. Several men were standing on the porch, talking quietly and smoking cigarettes. Their faces were in the dark, but they could see us approaching in the light of the street-lamp. '*Zdrastvuy*, greetings, Styopa,' said one. The words were music to my ears. It was Boris. I started telling him about our quest but he raised his arm: 'Not here. This must be your father.' He stretched out his hand. 'Let's talk inside,' he said. 'Follow me.' He took us to an office at the end of a corridor. He is taking us to his boss, I thought. He opened the door to a room where a big desk was strewn with piles of paper.

As Boris, my *Boris Godunov*, sat down behind the desk my heart started beating fast and loud. I looked at his collar – it was the first time I had seen him in anything other than in his swimming trunks – three red rectangles, a full colonel. My *Boris Godunov* was a militia colonel! In the meantime, Father recovered his composure and Boris asked him endless questions; he seemed to have forgotten me altogether. I didn't mind, as long as we got the permits. I pulled Father's sleeve up; it was 8.30 p.m. I looked at Boris. He must have noticed my expression and laughed, 'Don't worry, Styopa. There is time enough.'

He took a book of forms from his desk drawer. 'Your pass and ticket, please,' he stretched out his hand and examined my father's documents. He asked our full names, scribbled something, signed two forms, stamped them with the big round rubber stamp, handed back my father's pass and lifted the telephone receiver.

A sergeant came in and stood to attention. Boris said something quickly. I picked up separate words: two men . . . a lorry . . . railway station . . . on the double. I could not believe it. The sergeant did a quick about-turn and vanished. Boris stood up, shook Father's hand, my hand, '*Vsevo khoroshevo*, I wish you all the best,' he said with a smile. 'Now you'd better hurry. My men will be outside the street entrance in a minute.'

From then on events unfolded very quickly, but I was in a daze; it was as if a slow-motion film was unwinding in my head. The sergeant, two men and a lorry were at the door and within minutes we were back home. The militiamen stood their rifles in the corner of the room and finished our packing in an instant. Nicky and his mother came to say goodbye. Next we were proceeding, with armed escort, through the usual multitude crowding the Kzyl-Orda railway station. The sergeant went first and cleared us a passage. One militiaman followed with our belongings on a trolley. The three of us and the other militiaman closed the rear. A four-berth sleeper compartment had been reserved for us. The attendant brought us a tray piled high with meat and cheese sandwiches. Tea came from a *samovar* placed in the corridor and was accompanied by strawberry preserve served on little glass plates. It was real *dolce vita*. We slept in comfort between fresh, white sheets. In the morning the attendant reappeared with a proper breakfast on a tray: real coffee, rolls, butter, soft-boiled eggs and honey. It was not until many years later, when I was in the West, that I travelled again in such luxury.

We disembarked in Tashkent and there our VIP status ended as abruptly as it had begun. The Tashkent railway station, like all such places, was crowded, but Father knew his way about and, with the help of two Polish soldiers from the transport office, we made our way to another train. Half an hour later we were in Yangi-Yul.

We piled our belongings on an *arba* and embarked on the

long trek to the Krakowski's rented flat. Father had met Mr Krakowski earlier in Yangi-Yul and had been befriended by the family. In readiness for the expected evacuation, the Krakowskis had arrived in Yangi-Yul some weeks previously and they had agreed to put up Mother and me in their flat; Father was returning to the camp.

The road from the station took us through a district of mud cottages not unlike the Uyúk in Chimkent, with Russian and Uzbek children playing in the road. The centre of Yangi-Yul was different, very Russian, typical of small southern towns; it could easily have been the setting for a Chekhov play. The tree-lined streets were bordered with white, or whatever passed for white, one- or two-storey houses. There was also something unusual about this town; it was unusually crowded, bursting with a great number of men. Most of them were in uniform, but it was an unfamiliar one. Father noticed my bewilderment: 'They are our soldiers,' he said. 'British uniforms had arrived just before I left for Kzyl-Orda. They call it battledress.'

The Krakowski family lived in the centre of town, in a proper white-stucco house. When we arrived the flat was full of people. According to my father Mr Krakowski had been a wealthy industrialist. 'They have been selling their jewellery,' said Father. 'They keep an open house and people go there for a meal and the latest gossip.'

Judging by the size of the flat – three rooms and a small kitchen – and by the lavish hospitality, the Krakowskis were real plutocrats. The table was covered with a starched white cloth, the kind I had not seen for a long time. At one end of the table stood a big brass *samovar* with a brown, earthen teapot on top. Sugar was served not just in one bowl, but in two, one at each end of the table. Plates were piled high with slices of white bread and butter.

Following the example of other guests, I needed no encouragement to fill my glass with sweet tea and my plate with a good helping of bread and butter. Not for the first time, I watched with fascination how tea was served from a *samovar*. The small teapot held the *essence*, a very strong brew of tea, while the *samovar* held the boiling water. Tea was served in glasses on glass saucers. To prevent the glass cracking, a teaspoon would be put in first, followed by a little bit of essence, then the glass would be topped up with water from the *samovar* tap. From time to time a plump young girl would use bellows to rekindle the charcoal fire in the central tube of the contraption.

Busy eating, I watched and listened. Some people had obviously come just for the food and, having eaten their fill, they left; others stayed to talk and to pick up the latest news. The main topic was the expected evacuation to Persia, but it was all rumours: the next transport out of the USSR would leave tomorrow. No, it would not leave for another week . . . or two . . . or three . . . There would be no more transports . . . The Soviet Government would put a stop to the evacuation . . . Polish units will be split up and attached to various Red Army units.

One of the men, a captain, was 'as sure as one could be' that the next transport would be leaving in a couple of days, but that it would not be the last one. Another, a private, addressed by others as *Panie mecenasie*, as due to a lawyer, maintained that the next transport was going to be the last one, at least for a long while.

Our host, a short, grey-haired man with pince-nez, was worried, as he was too old to join the army. Not being an army family was a great handicap, it was virtually a prison sentence to remain in the USSR. 'I am ready,' he kept saying, 'to bribe anybody, whatever the price. But who is in charge? The Soviets? The Poles? Does one bribe both lots?' Somebody volunteered the name of a man likely to be of use. Many Polish families in Yangi-Yul must have been in a similar situation, but few had Mr Krakowski's resources.

After having eaten my fill, I suggested to my father that he and I went for a walk, as the centre of town was only two minutes' walk away. 'A veritable Polish garrison town,' said Father. And, true enough, everywhere we looked there were men in uniform, in the battledress with which I was soon to become so familiar. They all had the Polish silver eagle badges on their forage caps and berets. The dominant language of the streets in Yangi-Yul was Polish, even the majority of civilians, women and children, seemed to be speaking no other tongue.

'The black berets denote the Armoured Brigade,' said Father.

'In the Headquarters we expected to be issued with those funny wide-brimmed Australian hats. My new gear is probably waiting for me in my tent. You may be surprised when you see me next.'

As we turned the corner I spied two girls talking animatedly to one another. One of them, the taller one, looked familiar. Had I met her somewhere before? Probably in some railway station. Vaguely I remembered that her father was a doctor. If it was in fact the same girl, then her name was Zuza and by repute she was a great talker and a gossip. She must have recognised me, as I saw her pointing in our direction and whispering something in the other girl's ear; they giggled. The stranger looked at me; she had dark hair cut like a boy's and laughter in her eyes.

The next few days in Yangi-Yul were frantic. In the atmosphere of tension and of contradictory rumours each hour dragged into eternity. Fed up with the incessant gossip and the hysteria of the adults I spent most of my waking hours reading, or just walking the streets of Yangi-Yul on my own. In the afternoon of our second day in the town, I met Father on my way home. He was sporting his new uniform and the wide-brimmed hat. I ran to him. A big smile lit up his face, a smile so radiant that it could mean only one thing: we were about to leave this accursed land.

Since he had rejoined the army some two weeks before, Father's appearance had improved greatly, though he still looked like a man who could do with a long rest and some more flesh on his body. His limbs, ridiculously wasted after his illness, had remained pathetically thin for a long time; but his back was straight again, his face, so recently pinched and drawn, had lost its haggard look and now, in his battledress, he cut a respectable figure of a military man.

'We are all leaving, starting tomorrow morning,' said Father. 'In separate trains, but that cannot be helped. More goods wagons, I expect. Army families are to travel early in the morning. There will be a long queue, but you are on the Headquarters Company list and you will be in the first group to board. I shall leave in the army train soon after you.'

Father finished relating his news as we were reaching the

Krakowskis' flat. It was full of people as usual, but the crowd
was even more excited and noisy – the news had evidently
spread. Mr Krakowski was out, trying his luck at the last
minute. 'He won't be able to swing it,' said a lieutenant of
military police whom I had not seen there before. 'We have very
strict instructions and not only our men but also NKVD
personnel will be on duty checking people's credentials. No
fooling about, I am afraid, and it is much too late for bribes.'

In the event, the Polish MP officer was proved wrong. True
enough, the evacuation had left about a million Polish citizens
behind. Indeed, some, including Helena and her family, were to
remain in the Soviet Union until 1947, well after the end of the
Second World War, when they were repatriated to Poland, by
then just another Soviet satellite. The Krakowski family,
however, must have eventually found the right person to bribe
and, as I heard later, they had made their way to Persia and,
finally, to Palestine.

The following morning Mother and I joined the thousands of
people thronging the Yangi-Yul railway station. Our transport
was, as Father predicted, another goods train; another long
snake of cattle wagons, but this time the cars had no horizontal
shelves. We were at least forty to a wagon; mainly women, a few
old men and children from babies to teenagers.

In box-cars without shelves the journey was even less
comfortable than our previous ones, as there was no room to
stretch one's legs. The only comfortable place to sit was in the
open doorways, so we used those in rotation. Older people and
women with small children sat on their packs and bundles along
the wagon's walls, which offered a back-rest of sorts. Mother
sat on our bedding bag by the wall while I, nearby, shared our
large, stout, plywood suitcase with an old man. He was tall, thin
as a rake, gaunt and drawn. I was sitting on his left and I noticed
his withered right hand.

Well before noon the train pulled out of the station and soon
the excitement, the animated talk, died down. Our immediate
destination was Krasnovodsk, a Soviet port on the Caspian Sea,
and then a Persian port of uncertain name on its southern shore.
But what was to come after that?

Muddled, disjointed thoughts kept going round and round in

my head. Joining the army was my immediate aim, but what about school? What about my dream of becoming a doctor? 'Forget it! Forget it!' I kept saying to myself. Then I made my decision: I was going to join the Polish Air Force in England. I had read in the Polish soldiers' newspaper that they wanted volunteers. Would Father be able to pull some strings and how about my eyesight? I was short-sighted; I had never worn glasses, but I probably needed them for distance. I could always learn the chart by heart at the medical. By that time Mother should have found work in a hospital, be independent and have no need of me. So, having sorted out my life for the next year or two – the war surely wouldn't last much longer than that – I banished all doubts and relaxed.

I don't remember many details of the two-thousand-kilometre journey. It took a day, a night and most of the following day. Once more we crossed the valleys of Uzbekistan, glimpsed the blue towers of Samarkand, skirted Bukhara and in the early morning stopped for a while on a siding in Ashkhabad, the capital of Turkmenistan, another Soviet Republic. From there on, for hours and hours the railway line ran between mountains on our left and a sandy desert on the right. I checked in my atlas: the mountains were called Kopet Dag and the desert's name was Kara Kum. The desert stretched to the north as far as the horizon. Seen from the wagon door, its wavy, wrinkled surface was uncommonly dark, black almost, and its bleak monotony was broken only by an occasional dusty green patch of an oasis. 'Kara Kum means Black Sands,' said the old man with whom I shared my seat, as he pointed to the name on the map.

'Do you know Turkish, sir?' I asked.

'Yes, a little,' he smiled. 'I learned it when I was posted to our embassy in Ankara. That was a lifetime away.'

There was one event, though, which has stuck vividly in my memory. Somewhere between Ashkhabad and the sea the train stopped on a siding for longer than usual. In spite of the breeze, the wagon became unbearably hot. Polish soldiers were running along the train. 'Don't get out. Everybody stay in their assigned wagon.' Something was happening.

A young officer, one star – a second lieutenant – scrambled

into our wagon. He stood at the door and, pointing with one finger, counted the heads. Aloud: 'Forty-two.' He looked at the papers in his hand, 'Correct.'

And then he proceeded to check the names against the list in his hand. Fair enough. X . . . ski, Y . . . cki, Z . . . icz. All tidy, correct Polish names, his head kept nodding. But then he reached ours. He did not like it: 'W-a-j-d-e-n-f-e-l-d,' he spelled it once, twice, with a sneer. 'What kind of a name is that? It's not Polish. German? Jewish?' With an inquisitor's expression he kept looking at Mother and me. 'You are not Polish. I cannot allow you to continue the journey. Should the NKVD find you here . . .' The sentence remained open-ended, menacing. He looked at me. 'You and the old woman will have to get out at the next station.' He turned to the NCO, who remained outside the wagon. 'See to it.'

My mother did not utter a word. She sat there dumbfounded. She shrank to half her size. Had she heard him? I was not sure. Usually resourceful, capable of putting up a fight, of getting her way, suddenly she seemed to have given up; otherwise she would have dealt with this insolent puppy in no uncertain terms.

So it was up to me. I got up. 'You are wrong, *Panie Poruczniku*, Lieutenant, sir,' I said politely. 'This is not any old woman but my mother, and my father is the medical officer of the Headquarters Company in Yangi-Yul. Our presence here is perfectly legitimate.'

'Is it now?' he said, his face distorted by a sneer even uglier than before. 'We will see about that. I do not intend to argue with you here.' There was a prolonged whistle and we were about to move off. 'At the next stop bring your documents, if you have any, to the command car. We will sort you out there in no time.' Then the arrogant bastard jumped out of the wagon.

When was the next stop? I had no way of knowing. I sat down on our suitcase and tried to think straight but it was not easy. By now Father would be on his way in another train, and Mother and I would be left on our own in the middle of nowhere. We would never get out of this accursed country. Yes, accursed, loathsome, wretched, despicable country, indeed. I ran out of epithets.

'Calm down, son.' The voice of the old man was soothing. 'Cheer up.' He nudged me with his right shoulder. 'Get together all the papers you can find. Documents, letters even. There can be no doubt that you are Polish; one can hear Warsaw in your speech.'

He was right; and we did have documents nobody could argue with: our Polish foreign passports.

Mother sat there clutching the handbag to her chest. She was miles away. Gently, I managed to disengage it. I took out our passports number 007 and number 009. 'Brand-new,' said my neighbour, who looked at them with reverence. 'How did you come by them?'

I explained that before rejoining the army my father had been the medical officer of the Chimkent *Delegatura*. 'We got them from the Embassy. Want to have a look?' I passed my mother's passport to him. Maiden name: Makowska, it said in black and white. 'Here's a name ending with a "ska", you bloody bastard,' I thought to myself. A photograph fell out of it and I picked it up. It was a picture of my brother, Jurek, in tropical uniform, a Sam Browne belt and peaked cap. The picture had come in his last letter in August 1939. 'I will not be coming home this summer,' he wrote. 'The war will start on 1 September.'

Reading that, Father had laughed, 'A wise old man, a prophet.' Jurek had been proved right; the war did start on 1 September, 1939. I had no idea what kind of uniform he was wearing in the photograph, but it would do, I decided, replacing the picture in my mother's passport. Other documents I found in Mother's handbag were our Soviet travel documents which clearly stated that we were Polish citizens. Even the NKVD could not argue with documents bearing their own stamps.

I sat there waiting with the bundle of papers in my hand. The train gathered speed. I was furious, bitter and frightened. Could *they* really throw us off the train? Of one thing I was certain: nobody would lift a finger in our defence. Then with shame I realised that I had been thinking of Polish officers as 'they'. Suddenly, I felt among strangers.

I had encountered the problem before. Our foreign-sounding name had often been questioned. In the 1920s, soon after Poland regained its independence and when both Father and his brother Adam were in the Polish Army, they Polonised the spelling of the family name from the original Weidenfeld to Wajdenfeld, which left the pronunciation intact. I was born a Wajdenfeld.

An hour passed before the train stopped again in a siding. 'Go alone, Stefanku,' said Mother. 'I can't face it any more.' With tears in her eyes, she squeezed my hand.

I turned to my neighbour. 'Will you look after my mother? Please. Until I come back.'

'You will be back soon, son,' he said. 'Don't worry, Stefanku.' He smiled as he used the diminutive of my name. 'That stupid lieutenant is too big for his boots. The train commander is a reserve officer, a captain, an older man. I saw him in Yangi-Yul and he seemed like a reasonable human being.'

'Thank you for the encouragement,' I said. 'Please look after my mother,' I repeated.

He nodded and put his good hand on Mother's.

I jumped out and ran to the command wagon. It was a *soft*, or first-class passenger car. There was no guard, but the young lieutenant was at the entrance. 'Ah, you,' he nodded and motioned me to follow. 'This is the lad with the dubious name I told you about, sir. He is travelling with an old woman, whom he says is his mother.'

The captain was not sympathetic. 'Perhaps she is and perhaps she isn't, one can never know with them, can one?'

My blood boiled. I trembled with rage and fear. Keep calm, I said to myself. '*Można, można*, one can, one can,' I tried not to shout as I dropped the two passports on the small table by the window. They made an instant impression.

'How did you come by these?' asked the captain. 'Have you seen these?' He turned to the lieutenant.

'No, sir,' the lieutenant replied. 'The woman did not show them to me.'

'You did not give her a chance, did you?' I said. I could have killed him.

The lieutenant's face turned the colour of beetroot. His eyes were fixed on our passports.

'How did you come by these?' the captain repeated.

I explained. Name-dropping wouldn't go amiss, I decided. 'Our

Ambassador, Professor Kot, sent them to us at the Chimkent *Delagatura*. At present, my father is the MO of General Anders' Headquarters Company.' I looked at the unadorned tunic of the train *komendant* and added, 'He is also a captain and has *Krzyż Walecznych*, the Cross of Valour, from the Polish–Bolshevik war.'

The captain stood up and, while leafing through my mother's passport, came upon Jurek's photograph. 'And who is that?' he asked.

By now I had calmed down and I began to enjoy myself. 'Jurek,' I said, 'my older brother, Jerzy Wajdenfeld. A captain of the British Army, on a special mission in the Middle East.' This was my fantasy. I was inventing it as I went along, but what the hell? Anyway, he looked like an officer and he wouldn't be wearing shorts in England, would he?

There were no more questions. 'Wait for me here.' The older officer barked an order to the lieutenant. 'I want a word with you on my return.' Next he turned to me. 'Take me to your mother, boy. I want to apologise to her personally.' I looked at the lieutenant. He was standing at attention, pale and taut. I felt like sticking my tongue out at him, but thought better of it.

I showed the *komendant* to our wagon. My mother's eyes were still red, but dry. By now she had recovered her composure and was chatting with the old man. The *komendant* clicked his heels, saluted and apologised profusely. He sounded sincere as he tried to explain: 'In Yangi-Yul we had a briefing session with NKVD officers. They warned us that there would be spot-checks on the way and threatened that should even one Soviet citizen be discovered on any of the Polish trains, the evacuation of families would be stopped. They consider our Jews, Ukrainians and Belorussians as Soviet citizens. The effrontery of it! But what can we do?'

Mother accepted the apology with good grace. 'Your young man's manners could have been better,' she said. 'There was no need for rudeness.'

'Yes,' said the captain. 'I shall have a word with him. Perhaps you would like to join us in the command wagon, madam? There is plenty of room. Several empty compartments.'

'Thank you,' said Mother, 'but we are almost there, I believe. We'd better stay where we are.'

The captain could not have been more gallant. He apologised again, bent over to kiss Mother's hand, clicked his heels and left.

We were on our way again. The atmosphere in the wagon changed dramatically. As I took my place on the plywood case, the old man put his good arm round my shoulders. 'Good lad,' he said. 'Good work. Never give up, especially when the going gets tough. That's the only way.'

'The sea! Look! There! The sea!' shouted one of the boys who was sitting in the open doorway of the wagon and pointing to the steely blue expanse of water to the north-west. 'Mama,' he shouted. 'The sea! I have never seen the sea before. It's so flat!'

I sat down next to the boy. The sea came into view for a little while, far away on the horizon, then disappeared again. I had noticed the boy before. His name was Włodek and he was about ten. His mother was sitting next to mine, with a teenage girl, her arm round the girl's shoulders. The girl wore a ridiculously big scarf around her head. Every so often she would bring her hands to her head, burst out crying and then go on sobbing pitifully. She must have a bad headache, I thought. Most of the time her sobs had been drowned by the clatter of the wheels and I took no notice of them before.

'Why is your sister crying? Is she ill?' I asked Włodek. 'Has she got a headache or an ear infection? I had one not too long ago. It was very painful.'

'Oh, no,' he answered, shrugging his shoulders. 'It's about her hair. They shaved her head in the Yangi-Yul station. You know . . . nits. Mother had cut her own hair short and they let her keep what was left of it, but Janka did not want her plaits cut off, so they shaved her head. Now she is crying.'

I remembered now. They were checking people in the station building before we boarded the train. Hundreds of women had had their heads shaved, some men, too, because they had lice and nits. My hair had always been short, Mother had made sure of that. She kept her own hair short, too, so they let us through.

Half an hour later the train slowed down, skirted a small town, Dzhanga was the name on the little station building, then stopped a good way past it. By now we were used to such stops in wastelands away from human habitation.

Polish soldiers ran along the train. 'All out, all out.' I jumped out of the wagon and looked around. Where was the port? Where was the ship? Where was the sea for that matter? As I stood there trying to use my head, Włodek used his legs to a much better advantage. He ran up a hillock and shouted, 'Over there. Look! Look, Stefan. Come here. Look! The sea!' I joined him. There, in the distance, several kilometres away, was the shimmering surface of a large bay with a town stretching along the shore, several ships at anchor and cranes on the sea front. So this was Krasnovodsk.

The soldiers helped us to unload. Just as well, as most of the passengers were women, children and old people. We ran back to our wagon, climbed in and started passing bags, boxes and suitcases into the hands of the people outside. It didn't take long. Nobody needed encouragement to leave the wagons. There was a whistle, several loud puffs in quick succession and the train moved off in the direction of the port.

We were left with our belongings in a field which had sparse grass, some bushes and clumps of trees. A group of Polish officers and NCOs approached on the track from the direction of the town. They dispersed among the crowd and groups formed around them. In our group, an old sergeant explained the situation. 'A ship is waiting for you in the port. It's not far, about three kilometres. I am sorry, but we have no transport for you; you have to carry your own stuff. This field must be cleared quickly, another train is due in half an hour and yet another after that. Once out of here, you will not be able to come back; it would create chaos and we could not allow that. Just take what you can carry and no more. That's NKVD instructions. Is that clear?' He stopped. We were flabbergasted. All our belongings, the precious luggage, all our worldly possessions, carried, protected, guarded over thousands of miles. 'Listen carefully,' he continued. 'You will be searched on embarkation. You are not allowed to take money out of the country, nor any documents. The NKVD will do the searching. Anybody trying to smuggle money or papers on board will be arrested and the family will be turned back and stopped from leaving. Is that clear? They may even stop the entire transport.

Our soldiers will be presently coming round with bags and you must put all the money and all your documents in them. Search your pockets. Don't miss a single scrap of paper. Remember, contraband found on anybody may stop all from leaving.'

The crowd started rumbling, but the sergeant didn't wait for the outburst, he turned on his heels and left. The crowd fell on their own bags and bundles like a flight of vultures. Packs and wrappings were torn open, suitcases were turned out. What to leave? What to take? The choice was difficult. One could carry only so much. Elegant pigskin suitcases, a reminder of better times, were heavy even when empty, as were the primitive ones made of plywood. Our big brown plywood case, its lacquered surface lost under a thousand scratches, weighed a ton. On top of that we had other cases, bags of bedding, boxes with pots and pans, my books, the atlas – the stuff of our nomadic life.

'We won't need any of that stuff over there,' said Mother, practical as always. 'We will manage. The main thing is to get out of here.'

Soldiers went around with large canvas bags. Mother opened her handbag, got all her money out – hundreds of red ones – and dropped it in. Our documents followed: the amnesty certificate, the foreign-residence permits. The new foreign passports met the same end, but not before Mother took out the photograph of Jurek and pushed it under the partly torn lining inside her handbag. 'As long as we get out of here,' she repeated. 'Whatever the price.' She searched her pockets. I found a few roubles in mine and dropped them in the bag too. The people around us were all doing the same.

Then we returned to our luggage. We emptied our four suitcases and packed as much of their contents as we could into two bundles made of duvet covers. I joined the two packs together with a scarf. In the meantime Mother took charge of the two smaller cases, by now only half full, a weight she was able to carry. She added her handbag, now empty except for Jurek's photograph, the remainder of our bread and a bottle of boiled water to one of them. Thus, Mother with the two suitcases and me with the two bundles, one hanging in front of me and the other round my back, the tie resting on my shoulder, and with an empty suitcase in each hand, joined the crowd on the dirt track.

As far as the eye could see, the field along the railway line was strewn with abandoned luggage. Containers of all kinds and shapes, some empty, others almost full, scattered helter-skelter, made our progress difficult. Here and there heaps of luggage were smouldering, set on fire by people who felt they had been robbed and didn't want others to profit. But many had overestimated their strength and even now more pieces of luggage were being shed and were littering the path almost all the way to the port. The caravan of pack humans looked odd indeed. Some, like me, with big packs front and back looked like pregnant hunchbacks, or backpacking kangaroos. It took us a long time to cover the three kilometres and we arrived exhausted.

We boarded the ship, it was an ancient and rusty freighter. I hoped it was seaworthy. It was empty and clean enough – at least at the start of the journey. People helped each other up the gangway. The crowd was deathly quiet. There was not a single NKVD man in sight. And there was no search. We had been cheated out of our money, documents and belongings. But what the hell . . . as long as we got out of here . . . even naked.

❋ ❋ ❋

Many years later it became common knowledge that, at the time, the commanding officer of the Polish base in Krasnovodsk, one Colonel Berling, had been involved in a split in the Polish Establishment, had quarrelled with General Anders and had tried to sabotage our evacuation. It was on his orders that we were made to leave the train short of its destination and were stripped of our money and our possessions. He was eventually put in charge of another Polish Army which remained in the USSR and fought under Soviet command all the way to Berlin.

❋ ❋ ❋

The voyage was a nightmare. The small cargo ship was not built to carry passengers and was grossly overloaded. It carried – or so we were told – over two thousand people. The three-hundred-kilometre voyage lasted the rest of the first day, the night and part of the next day. Every square inch was occupied: the hold, the deck, the staircases, the gangways, even the lifeboats. There was no room to lie down, only the dying had that privilege; by the time we reached Persia, eleven bodies had been thrown into the sea. Diarrhoea was prevalent. The two lavatories, designed for use of the crew only, could by no means cater for a crowd of over two thousand: they were permanently under siege. Most business was done over the ship's rail; there was no solid bulwark, thank God.

We were lucky, Mother and I. With some others we were allowed onto the central gangway running the length of the ship and we found a place to sit, close together, our backs to the rail, with our remaining belongings nearby. We could stretch our legs across the narrow gangway and the sailors had to step over them; they swore as they did so. They spoke an incomprehensible language, but, for our benefit no doubt, swore in Russian. They didn't look like Mongols as they had swarthy, Indo-European faces. Perhaps they were Turkmenians. I was too tired, hungry and thirsty to give it much thought, or to care.

The afternoon was impossibly hot; thankfully we had with us the bread and boiled water that my mother had saved and we survived the journey in good shape.

Obsessively, I kept checking the ship's course. I didn't trust anybody, I wanted no more surprises. In the afternoon the sun was on the starboard side, a little to the bow. In the evening, it was still on the same side as it sank rapidly into the sea. One could almost hear it sizzle as it touched the water. In the morning it rose gloriously from the blue water to port, halfway to stern. Our course was steady, south-west, no deception this time. The crowd was quiet. About noon the heat became intense, made bearable only by a gentle breeze which blew from time to time. The sea was calm, unruffled and, in spite of the heavy load it carried, the boat seemed to glide effortlessly; a phantom ship carrying a throng of ghosts. As I sat there with my back and head against the rails of the gangway and looked at the intense blue of the sky, the peace was disturbed only by the tremor of the engines under my head and by the nagging questions in my mind. What next? Where to? Would we ever have a place to call home? Would we ever return to Otwock?

Really and truly Otwock had disappeared into the mist of time, even Kvasha was slowly disappearing, and so was Helena. I found it difficult to picture her face against the orange-red of my closed eyelids. I did not have a single photograph of her, nor of Kvasha, nor of my friends. Was it the multitude of events which obscured so recent a past?

I must have fallen asleep. Mother was nudging my shoulder. 'We are coming into harbour,' she said. The sun was halfway down. Was it on the correct side? It didn't matter anymore. We were out of the USSR and in Pahlavi, in Persia.

Compared to the leisurely crossing of the Caspian Sea, the pace of events suddenly increased; the ship of ghosts came to life. People were busy getting their things together. They were talking again, shouting to each other, looking for friends. The noise of the harbour added to the cacophony and I couldn't hear myself thinking any more.

Seasoned nomads that we were, we thought nothing of carrying our bundles the few hundred yards along the shore to the beach which became another of our temporary homes. Rows of empty shelters with no walls, just roofs of straw mats supported by posts, awaited us. Another layer of straw mats was laid directly on the golden sand to make a floor. I followed Mother to one such shelter, which rapidly filled with strangers. Soon the other shelters were occupied too – there were dozens and dozens of these flimsy structures, stretching as far as the eye could see along the beach.

Each shelter was meant to house roughly fifty to sixty people. We slept on our blankets spread on the ground, side-by-side, in two parallel rows of some thirty people each, heads meeting in the middle. The roof of the shelter was long enough and wide enough to protect the two rows of people from the sun. But, as we discovered later, not from the rain.

We lived on the Pahlavi beach for nearly two months. The camp was fenced off and was run along the lines of a Polish Army camp. The British were in command, but kept out of sight and the day-to-day running of the camp was left to the inmates. Each shelter elected its *komendant*. Most of the clothes we brought with us were burned for reasons of hygiene. Men were issued with striped pyjamas, women with orphanage-type cotton print dresses, blue flannel knickers and headscarves. We looked like a mixed crowd of Sing-Sing escapees and orphans.

Life on the Pahlavi beach was leisurely. We brought our meals in buckets from the field kitchen. We could eat as much as we wanted and it was wonderful not to be hungry any more. We swam, we talked, we discussed politics and books. Occasionally, you could get hold of one of the very few books in circulation. All my books, even my atlas, had been left on that distant field.

Our shelter housed fifty-six people, mostly women and children, as the men were in the army. Nearly-men, like me, had to wait a few more months to join. My sleeping place for the night was between my mother and Mrs Gombińska, the *komendant* of our shelter. The mat on the other side of her was taken by her daughter, Danuta. She was the girl with the boy's haircut and the twinkle in her eyes, whom I had seen in Yangi-Yul, giggling with Zuza.

Almost exactly six years later Danuta and I were married. Should our luck hold, in another year's time we shall celebrate our fiftieth anniversary. But that is an entirely different story.

EPILOGUE

BY DANUTA

We were standing on the street corner in Yangi-Yul, when Zuza nudged me and said: 'Do you see that boy on the other side of the road? How old do think he is?'

'Oh, he is quite ancient, must be at least eighteen.'

Zuza laughed, 'You are wrong, he is only sixteen. His name is Stefan.'

We looked at him and giggled. There was something likeable about the boy, the energy in his step, the kindness in his face.

I forgot about him in the turmoil of our departure. There was the train, then the long trek to the port and the overcrowded boat. Fate does play tricks with our lives and it decreed it so that Zuza and her mother were next to my mother and me on that tightly packed deck. Zuza prattled incessantly virtually all the way to Pahlavi. As we were disembarking, she noticed someone in the crowd, gripped her mother's arm and pushing the latter in her chosen direction, whispered, 'Look, there is Mrs Wajdenfeld and her son. Let's go after them.' Holding what was left of our luggage, my mother and I followed in their footsteps.

So we found ourselves in a shelter on the Pahlavi beach sharing our straw mats with Stefan, Zuza, another friend of Zuza's, Irka, our respective mothers – the fathers were all in the army – and fifty-odd strangers. Zuza and Irka laid siege to Stefan, and I became their messenger, taking little notes from each of them, but receiving no reply, just a shrug of his shoulders.

We spent weeks on that beach, carefree at last, eating our fill, happy to be out of captivity. We were still facing an uncertain future, but we felt young again, we swam in the sea, threw sand at each other, fooled around and laughed as we had not done for ages. Then transports to our next stop began. Each week British Army lorries took groups of people over the tortuous mountain roads to the Persian capital. Irka, Zuza and I – along with our mothers – were scheduled to go at the same time; Stefan was destined to stay in Pahlavi longer. But when he got up at dawn with the rest of us, and when it was my luggage that he chose to carry, I knew for sure that he cared for me.

We met again in Teheran and became inseparable, vowing to each other that we would spend the rest of our lives together. The adults smiled knowingly with the we-have-seen-it-all-before look on their faces. Then Stefan reached the age when he could join the army. Although a raw recruit, he looked gorgeous in his uniform.

That was the beginning of our story fifty-five years ago.

One had little choice over one's fate in those wartime years. Stefan's unit was sent to Iraq, which was also the destination of his father's hospital and my stepfather's regiment, while Mother and I, with thousands of other army families, were sent to Palestine, where life took on a semblance of temporary stability. We found a room in a residential hotel, and I enrolled in the Polish school which had been organised for the many Polish youngsters displaced by the war and deprived of their education.

Stefan and I wrote letters to each other virtually every day. We had so much to say, so many new experiences to share. Stefan was a gunner in an anti-aircraft unit, he was training in Habbaniya in the incredible heat of the desert, while I was back in the world of algebra problems, Virgil, essays and playing truant when it came to team games. When he was posted to Gedera to the Officer School, we saw a lot of each other again. Gedera was only a bus ride away from Tel-Aviv and passes were given out every week to hard-working cadet officers. He waited for my schoolday to end, carried my satchel, and smirked on the occasions when he saw me pretending to play volleyball; I may have been good at other subjects, but sport was definitely not my *métier*.

A la guerre comme à la guerre – Stefan graduated from the Officer School and, adorned with new silver braid, was posted to Italy to rejoin his battery. We resumed our daily correspondence. Stefan was now part of a fighting unit. They participated in the battle of Monte Cassino, they defended the headquarters of the Polish Army and they kept moving north along the boot of Italy as the war progressed and the Germans slowly retreated. It is a source of great regret that none of our letters survived the war, but neither of us had any place of permanence, nothing one could call a home for many years yet to come. We were now free, but we were still nomads, our suitcases were still our only storage. The letters, the chronicle of our lives, the description of changing events mirroring history, the vehicles for so much emotion, were lost on our journeys, never to be found.

Mother and I spent two and a half years in Tel-Aviv, going about our daily lives, worrying about our men in the army. Then, as I came to the end of my schooling, an opportunity arose for both of us to join the Polish Red Cross and be posted to Italy. We too donned uniforms and made our way on a troop-ship to the port of Brindisi. We landed on 8 May 1945, the day that the war ended.

We had been given the task of organising canteens and entertainment for the troops and were sent to Capua, near Naples, to a big camp, the centre of sapper training. Now that the war was over and the rigours of army life had lessened, Stefan and I were able to wangle passes from time to time to see each other; he was also given leave from his unit to go on a special course organised by the army to allow young people whose education was disrupted to gain their school matriculation. Following that, selected soldiers were given leave to enrol in Italian universities, and both Stefan and I decided to study medicine, although I gained a place at the University of Rome, while he went to the University of Bologna.

Meanwhile, history played us another dirty trick. All through the war years we thought of our homes in Poland and dreamed of the time when the war would end and we would return, find our roots, reclaim our friends and restart our interrupted lives. Little did we know that few homes in Warsaw were left standing, that so many of our friends were dead. But after the Treaty of Yalta, when Poland became a Soviet satellite, we knew that this road was closed. Having so recently survived a communist régime, we were absolutely certain that no hammer and sickle would tempt us again. We preferred the choice of remaining homeless.

In 1946 the allied forces began to leave Italy. The Polish Corps, part of the British Eighth Army, was shipped to Great Britain, a country alien to us, a country none of us knew, the language of which we had only recently started learning at school. And, as members of the Red Cross unit attached to the sapper training unit, Mother and I found ourselves in an army camp on the bleak moorlands of Staffordshire, where the wind howled day and night and the rain drove us back to the corrugated iron huts. It was quite a shock after the sunshine of Italy.

I kept applying for admission to medical schools only to be refused by one after another, until a kind professor in Manchester advised me to abandon my quest. 'What do you expect?' he said. 'Our boys are coming back from the war, you are a woman, a foreigner, you have zero chance of gaining a place.' Stefan was a man, a serviceman at that, but the mark of foreigner was also upon him; he too failed to get into medical school. Just as peace had given us new hope, another separation was in store for us. I went to London to study physiotherapy, a subject deemed appropriate for a woman, while he, having been demobilised and determined to fulfil his lifelong ambition, went to Paris to continue his medical studies. Paris proved to be a mistake; the promised grant did not materialise, the French medical qualification would not give a non-citizen the right to practice in France and, after a year, Stefan was back, having secured an ex-serviceman's grant and a place at the Royal College of Surgeons in Dublin. For six long years we had been apart, and we had now had enough of waiting, enough letter writing. We decided to get married and put an end to the constant separations.

We married on 12 August 1948 in the Paddington Register Office. There were seven of us at the wedding: my mother and stepfather, my cousin and her new husband and one friend.

With great difficulty, in those times of rationing, Mother procured a chicken, and a wedding feast was held for all present in the furnished flat we then rented in Maida Vale. Soon after, Stefan and I moved to Dublin.

Stefan's parents could not share our happy day with us. His father had served in a Polish military hospital in Iraq but, following a heart attack, was invalided from the army and had joined his wife in Palestine. He ran a civilian TB clinic for Polish children and she worked in a laboratory until the end of the war. Then Jurek, their older son, joined them, back from the British Army. He had rediscovered his old girlfriend in Otwock and, not having experienced life under communism, decided to go back and join her. They were married several months later. Jurek was a very forceful man, determined and persuasive. Under his pressure and against their better judgement, his parents also opted to return to their pre-war home; however, it was not to be. The journey was long and tiring, the anxiety of going back under the red yoke was overwhelming and Stefan's did not make it. He died of a heart attack halfway through the journey, in the military hospital in Venice. Mother and Jurek, broken-hearted, continued to Otwock on their own.

Stefan and I spent five good years in Dublin; I completed my physiotherapy course and thirteen months after our wedding, our daughter, Alice, was born. Stefan became notorious at his college for walking away with every prize for every subject in the curriculum; fellow students laughed and clapped in the assembly, when again and again he marched to the podium to receive another medal.

After he qualified we returned to London. After two years' work in hospitals, Stefan established himself in general practice in Kentish Town, where he became a greatly respected and much-loved family doctor. Even now, five years after his retirement, his former patients remember him warmly and many wish he would come back.

At last our nomadic life was over, as were our student days which were spent in a series of furnished rooms. We were settled, we bought a house, we had a roof over our heads, the suitcases went to the attic; at long last we had a place to call home, a permanence, we had a future. We even had a country, not the one we had been born in, but one which proved a generous host. We did not pine for Poland. It was now a very different country to the one we had known as children; the new rulers with their phoney slogans and their ideological stranglehold had taken over.

We have made a number of trips to Poland since, as visitors, as tourists, to meet old friends and relatives. We speak the language and yet we feel like strangers. Our routes had diverged.

I have had a chequered career. I worked for some years in re-habilitation, in my unchosen profession, wrote feature articles for the *Polish Daily*, became a serious amateur photographer, a marriage guidance counsellor, until eventually I took a degree in psychology and trained as an analytic psychotherapist. That was a profession of my choice, in which I am engaged to this day.

At the time of writing, Stefan and I have known each other for fifty-five years and have been married for forty-nine. All I can say is that, given the chance, we would make the same choice all over again. Alice is now forty-eight and lives outside Washington in Virginia, where she works as a freelance editor and brings up her two sons, Ian and Alexander, aged twelve and fifteen.

What about the other *dramatis personae*?

Jurek, after some years under the communist régime in Poland, wished to put it behind him and to get to the 'decadent West'; with our help, he came to England with Mother, with Wanda, his wife, their daughter, Joanna, and his stepson. Mother lived out her days in London, while Jurek and his family emigrated to South Africa, where in his early fifties he died of cancer. Wanda and Joanna now live in Ealing; Wanda has remarried. Joanna has married a journalist and practises as a dentist.

Helena and her wealthy lawyer husband live in Frankfurt, have two children and a number of grandchildren. Helena, a *grande dame*, no longer thinks of the six hard years she spent in her youth in the Soviet Union.

Szymek became a successful businessman in the USA and Witek, when we last heard from him, was a technical publisher in Washington.

Friends made through the long journey are scattered all over the world, while the Russians, the good and the bad, the kind and unkind, presumably stayed where they were, living their lives out in the grey misery of their country. We were the lucky ones who got away.